Alastair Sawday's

Special Places to Stay

Fifth edition
Copyright © 2008 Alastair Sawday
Publishing Co. Ltd

Published in 2008

Alastair Sawday Publishing Co. Ltd,
The Old Farmyard, Yanley Lane,
Long Ashton, Bristol BS41 9LR, UK
Tel: +44 (0)1275 395430
Fax: +44 (0)1275 393388
Email: info@sawdays.co.uk
Web: www.sawdays.co.uk

The Globe Pequot Press,
P. O. Box 480, Guilford,
Connecticut 06437, USA
Tel: +1 203 458 4500
Fax: +1 203 458 4601
Email: info@globepequot.com
Web: www.globepequot.com

Design concept: Company X, Bristol
Maps: Maidenhead Cartographic Services
Printing: Butler & Tanner, Frome
UK distribution: Penguin UK, London

ISBN-13: 978-1-901970-98-2

All rights reserved. No part of this
publication may be used other than for the
purpose for which it is intended nor may
any part be reproduced, or transmitted, in
any form or by any means, electronically or
mechanically, including photocopying,
recording or any information storage or
retrieval system, without prior written
permission from the publisher. Requests
for permission should be addressed to:
Alastair Sawday Publishing in the UK; or
The Globe Pequot Press in North America.

A catalogue record for this book is
available from the British Library. This
publication is not included under licences
issued by the Copyright Agency. No part of
this publication may be used in any form of
advertising, sales promotion or publicity.

Alastair Sawday has asserted his right to
be identified as the author of this work.

*We have made every effort to ensure the
accuracy of the information in this book at the
time of going to press. However, we cannot
accept any responsibility for any loss, injury or
inconvenience resulting from the use of
information contained therein.*

Responsible business: we are committed to being a green and socially responsible
business. Here are a few things we already do: our pool cars run on recycled cooking oil
and low-emission LPG; our award-winning eco-offices are equipped with solar-heated
water, wood-pellet heating, and rainwater-fed loos and showers; and we were the world's
first carbon-neutral publishing company. Find out more at www.sawdays.co.uk

Paper and print: we have sought the lowest possible ecological 'footprint' from the
production of this book. Whenever possible, we use paper that is either recycled (with
a high proportion of post-consumer waste) or FSC-certified, and give preference to
local companies in order to foster our local economy and reduce our carbon footprint.
Our printer is ISO 14001-registered.

Alastair

Sawday's

Special Places
to Stay

Italy

4　Contents

We are a small company, born in 1994 and growing slowly but surely every year – in 2007 we sold our millionth book. We have always published beautiful and immensely useful guide books, and we now also have a very successful website.

There are about 35 of us in the Company, producing the website, about 20 guide books and a growing series of environmental books under the Fragile Earth imprint. We think a lot about how we do it, how we behave, what our 'culture' is, and we are trying to be a little more than 'just a publishing company'.

Environmental & ethical policies

We have always had strong environmental policies. Our books are printed by a British company that is ISO14001 accredited, on recycled and/or FSC-certified paper, and we have been offsetting our carbon emissions since 2001. We now do so through an Indian NGO, which means that our money goes a long way. However, we are under no illusions about carbon-offsetting: it is part of a strong package of green measures including running company cars on gas or recycled cooking oil; composting or recycling waste; encouraging cycling and car-sharing; only buying organic or local food; not accepting web links with companies we consider unethical; and banking with the ethical Triodos Bank.

In 2005 we won a Business Commitment to the Environment Award and in 2006 a Queen's Award for Enterprise in the Sustainable Development category. All this has boosted our resolve to promote our green policies.

Eco offices

In January 2006 we moved into our new eco offices. With super-insulation, under-floor heating, a wood-pellet boiler, solar panels and a rainwater tank, we have a working environment kind to ourselves and to the environment. Lighting is low-energy, dark corners are lit by sun-pipes, materials are natural and one building is of green oak. Carpet tiles are from Herdwick sheep in the Lake District. The building is a delight to work in.

Ethics

We think that our role as a company is not much different from our role as the individuals within it: to play our part in the community, to reduce our ecological footprint, to be a benign influence, to foster good human relationships and to make a positive difference to the world around us.

Another phrase for the simple intentions above is Corporate Responsibility. It is a much-used buzz-phrase, but many of those adopting it as a policy are getting serious. A world-wide report by the think-tank Tomorrow's Company has revealed quite how convinced the world's major companies are that if they do not take on full responsibility for their impact, social and environmental, they will not survive.

The books – and a dilemma

So, we have created popular books and a handsome website that do good work. They promote authenticity, individuality and good local and organic food – a far cry from corporate culture. Rural economies, pubs, small farms, villages and hamlets all benefit. However, people use fossil fuel to get there. Should we aim to get our readers to offset their own carbon emissions, and the B&B and hotel owners too?

We are gradually introducing green ideas into the books: the Fine Breakfast Scheme that highlights British and Irish B&B owners who use local and organic food; celebrating those who make an extra environmental effort; gently encouraging the use of public transport, cycling and walking. We now give green and 'social' awards to pubs in our pub guide.

In 2006 we published the very successful *Green Places to Stay*, focusing on responsible travel and eco-properties around the globe. Bit by bit we will do more, and welcome ideas from all quarters. Our aim is to be a pioneering green publisher, and to be known as one. We hope one day to offer energy audits to our owners, to provide real help to those who want to 'go green'. And we will continue to champion the small-scale. We will also continue to oppose policies that encourage the growth of air traffic – however contradictory that might seem.

Our Fragile Earth series

The 'hard' side of our environmental publishing is the Fragile Earth series: *The Little Earth Book*, *The Little Food Book* and *The Little Money Book*. They consist of bite-sized essays, polemical, hard-hitting and well researched. They are a 'must have' for anyone who seeks clarity about some of the key issues of our time. We have also published *One Planet Living* with WWF.

A flagship project is the *The Big Earth Book*; it is packed with information and a stimulating and provocative read. It is being promoted, with remarkable generosity, by Yeo Valley Organic.

Lastly – what is special?

The notion of 'special' is at the heart of what we do, and highly subjective. We discuss this in the introduction to every book. We take huge pleasure in finding people and places that do their own thing – brilliantly; places that are unusual and follow no trends; places of peace and beauty; people who are kind and interesting – and genuine.

We seem to have touched a nerve with hundreds of thousands of readers; they obviously long for the independence that our books provide, for the warm human contact of Special Places, and to be able to avoid the banality and ugliness of so many other places.

A night in a Special Place can be a transforming experience.

Alastair Sawday

Each editor adds to the work of the previous editor, with touches of his or her own personality and enthusiasms. Kate helped Emma on the last book and came to this one with a passion born of long periods in Puglia, studies at university and then every possible moment seized to enjoy Italy. She has brought a very real love of Italy to a job that brings one in touch with some of the nicest possible Italians. Her sparkle and determination have breathed new life into an already lively book and she has made dozens of friends among the Italian owners. Of all editorial jobs within this office, this one has given the greatest pleasure to its editors. Kate has brought zest and freshness to the job and the book is a tribute to her energy and efficiency.

With Kate has been Florence Oldfield in daily support, a calm, comforting and effective advisor, helper and friend. Florence has made the whole job so much easier and we owe her much. And in the deeper background lies Emma Carey, away on maternity leave throughout but whose previous work created such a solid structure for further building.

Alastair Sawday

Series Editor Alastair Sawday

Editor Kate Shepherd

Assistant to Editor Florence Oldfield

Editorial Director Annie Shillito

Writing Jo Boissevain, Viv Cripps, Nicola Crosse, Matthew Hilton-Dennis, Florence Oldfield, Helen Pickles, Kate Shepherd

Inspections Richard & Linda Armspach, Norma Barrett Ottavianelli, Lois Ferguson, Jill Greetham, Sue Learner, Florence Oldfield, Kate Shepherd
Thanks to those people who did a few inspections or had a go at a write-up!

Accounts Bridget Bishop, Rebecca Bebbington, Christine Buxton, Amy Lancastle, Sally Ranahan

Editorial Sue Bourner, Kate Ball, Jo Boissevain, Emma Carey, Nicola Crosse, Roxy Dumble, Jackie King, Wendy Ogden, Rebecca Thomas, Danielle Williams

Production Julia Richardson, Tom Germain, Anny Mortada

Sales & Marketing & PR Rob Richardson, Thomas Caldwell, Sarah Bolton

Web & IT Joe Green, Russell Wilkinson, Chris Banks, Brian Kimberling

Previous Editor Emma Carey

With special thanks to Rosaria Marraffino for her linguistic prowess and to Florence Oldfield for her friendship, hard work and good humour throughout the project.

We cannot eat pizza or pasta outside Italy with the same pleasure that they give inside the country. The vitality, freshness and sheer authenticity of the stuff is just better in Italy. And so it should be. If you have been there you will know what I mean.

Well, the same can be said, of course, of the phenomenon of Italian-ness. Try as we might to conjure up Italy in our singing, our cooking, our coffee-drinking, and our Parma ham-eating, we just cannot get near the real thing. If you enjoy your cappuccino and your pesto, you should be planning to experience them in Italy. As the New Yorker said to the confused Englishman who stopped him in the street to say "Excuse me, I am so sorry for bothering you but I am very keen to go to Times Square and I am wondering…" "So, go!"

Here are hundreds of irresistible excuses for going to Italy as quickly as possible. You will meet Italians who lead interesting lives, who have thought clearly about their priorities – and have sorted them. You will be comfortable, welcomed, stimulated and utterly seduced. Italy has a particular charm in having only come together as a modern state in 1870, so Italians still see themselves as being from a region, a town or even a village before being 'from Italy'. This gives the country an engaging variety, a depth of belonging. 'Campanilismo', from campanile (bell-tower), is that devotion to the place whose particular bells you grew up with (rather like Cockneys being born within the sound of Bow bells in London). It affects the food, the architecture, the customs – just as it does in many other countries, but with added vitality and intensity in Italy.

Go to Italy while they are still able to be cavalier with EU rules and regulations, while they are still enthusiastic about life, while they greet you like an old friend when you return to buy tomatoes, while they are still so different from everyone else. We provide you with ready-made friends and contacts, with beautiful and interesting houses to spend time in, with an irreplaceable key to an Italy peopled with wonderful characters.

This edition has more 'green' places, more self-catering in big country houses and city apartments, more style and more passion than ever. So – go. And do try going by train; it is a delightful journey.

Alastair Sawday

Photo: Tom Germain

Italians have left an enduring impression upon many of us. The post-war recession scattered Italians across the world, so, joyfully, we have encountered their bonhomie, their vivacity, their cooking, the admirable closeness of their families and their open affection for one another. It's difficult not to be bowled over by the Italian 'stile di vita'.

This book, too, celebrates the Italian family. The majority of our places to stay, including our hotels, are family-run and you may expect to be welcomed with open arms. You'll return full of stories of prolonged feasts around big family tables, of magical culinary creations that live long in the memory (just taste Mama's homemade pasta), of children who stay up late to relish every moment of family life, of teenagers who take pride in their family and their town. Be prepared for enthusiasm on a grand scale: the Italians have a passion for everything and it won't seem out of keeping if you kiss your host on both cheeks when you leave – in gratitude for their love of the freshness and quality of food, for the daily discussions of the drama of Italian politics and for the intricate stories told of local folklore and history.

Many visitors to Italy have never before encountered so many architectural feats and galleried masterpieces, or such beauty in man-made sights and landscapes redolent with history. Italy has the capacity to make you feel like Aladdin in his cave. From north to south, from village to city, there are riches to be found. At every turn is a cultural jewel.

This book may be used as a cultural and historical guide, if you allow it. Our selection of special places to stay includes some of the finest treasures Italy has to offer. You could be staying in a medieval mountaintop hamlet; discovering Etruscan or Roman remains in a private garden; meeting the descendants of Italy's historic figures in their castles and villas; gazing on frescos from your bed. Wherever you stay, you are likely to be no more than a few paces from some priceless artefact, exquisite church or village untouched by time.

To experience such warm, gregarious people, such wonderful food and such breathtaking culture and history, is one of life's biggest treats. These pages are full of these places and these people. They, and their country, await your exploration.

Buon Viaggio!

Kate Shepherd

Photo left: Relais Guado al Sole Agriturismo, entry 128
Photo right: Il Convento Mincione, entry 232

We look for owners, homes and hotels that we like – and are fiercely subjective in our choices. 'Special' for us is not about the number of comforts but of the elements that make a place 'work'. Certainly the way guests are treated comes as high on our list as the setting, the architecture, the atmosphere and the food.

We have selected the widest range of places, and prices, for you to choose from – castles, villas, city apartments, farmhouses, country inns, even a monastery or two.

It might be breakfast under the frescoed ceiling of a Renaissance villa that is special, or a large and boisterous dinner in a farmhouse kitchen, or a life-enhancing view. We have not necessarily

Photo: La Chiusa delle More, entry 324

chosen the most opulent places to stay, but the most interesting and satisfying. But because Italy has, to quote Lord Byron, "the fatal gift of beauty" it is easy to forget that it hasn't all been built with aesthetics in mind. Don't be put off when you discover that there are swathes of industrial plant (yes, even in Tuscany). These things can't be airbrushed out, but acknowledge that they exist and they won't spoil your fun.

Inspections

We visit every place in the guide to get a feel for how both house and owner tick. We don't take a clipboard and we don't have a list of what is acceptable and what is not. Instead, we chat for an hour or so with the owner or manager and then look round. It's all very informal, but it gives us an excellent idea of who would enjoy staying there. If the visit happens to be the last of the day, we sometimes stay the night. Once in the book, properties are re-inspected every three to four years so that we can keep things fresh and accurate.

Feedback

In between inspections we rely on feedback from our army of readers, as well as from staff members who are encouraged to visit properties across the series. This feedback is invaluable to us and we always follow up on comments. A lot of the new entries in each edition are recommended by our readers too, so keep telling us about new places you've discovered. Please use the forms on our website at www.sawdays.co.uk, or later in this book (p. 420).

Occasionally misunderstandings occur, even with the best of intentions. So if your bedroom is cold or the bedside light is broken, please don't seethe silently and write to us a week later. Say something to the owners at the time. They will be keen to put things right if they can, and it can dissolve tension.

Subscriptions

Owners pay to appear in this guide. Their fee goes towards the cost of inspections (every entry has been inspected by a member of our team before being selected), of producing an all-colour book and of maintaining a sophisticated website. We only include places and owners that we find positively special. It is not possible for anyone to buy their way into our guides.

Disclaimer

We make no claims to pure objectivity in choosing our Special Places to Stay. They are here because we like them. Our opinions and tastes are ours alone and this book is a statement of them; we hope that you will share them.

We have done our utmost to get our facts right but apologise unreservedly for any mistakes that may have crept in. Feedback from you is invaluable and we act upon your comments. With your help and our own inspections we can maintain our reputation for dependability.

You should know that we do not check such things as fire alarms, swimming pool security or any other regulation with which owners of properties receiving paying guests should comply. This is the responsibility of the owners.

Photo: Palazzo San Teodoro – Riviera 281, entry 305

Finding the right place for you

It's our job to help you find a place you like. We aim to give honest descriptions so you can glean from the write-ups what the owners or staff are like, and how formal or casual the place is. Older properties may seem more immediately appealing, but please don't overlook the more modern ones – they too have personality. It's always the owners and their staff who have the greatest influence on the atmosphere you experience.

We try to say when a place is a popular wedding or conference venue, or offers courses such as cookery or painting. If in doubt, pick up the phone to check or you may find your peaceful haven does not turn out to be quite as peaceful as you'd expected.

Maps

Look at the map at the front of the book to find your area, then the detailed maps to find the places. The numbers correspond to the page numbers of the book. Our maps are for guidance only; take a proper road map to find your way around. Self-catering places are marked in blue on the maps; others are marked in red.

Symbols

Below each entry you will see some little symbols, which are explained in a short table at the very back of the book. They are based on the information given to us by the owners and are intended as a guide rather than as an unequivocal statement of fact; should an owner not have the symbol that you're looking for, it's worth discussing your needs.

Quick reference indices

Also at the back of the book you'll find a number of quick-reference indices showing those places that offer a particular service, perhaps a room for under €100 a night, or suitable for wheelchair users.

Green entries

We have chosen, very subjectively, six places which are making a particular effort to be eco-friendly and have given them a double-page spread and extra photos to illustrate what they're up to. This doesn't mean other places in the guide are not taking green initiatives – many are – but we have highlighted just a few examples.

Photo left: Dimora Storica Villa Il Poggiale, entry 151
Photo right: La Sosta di Ottone III, entry 108

Type of places

Each entry is simply labelled (B&B, hotel, self-catering) to guide you, but the write-ups reveal several descriptive terms. This list serves as a rough guide to what you might expect to find.

Agriturismo: farm or estate with B&B rooms or apartments; *Albergo*: Italian word for an inn, more personal than a hotel; *Azienda agrituristica*: literally, 'agricultural business'; *Casa* (*Cà* in Venetian dialect): house; *Cascina*: farmhouse; *Castello*: castle; *Corte*: courtyard; *Country house*: a new concept in Italian hospitality, usually family-run and akin to a villa; *Dimora*: dwelling; *Fattoria*: farm; *Locanda*: means 'inn', but sometimes used to describe a restaurant only; *Podere*: farm or smallholding; *Palazzo*: literally a 'palace' but more usually a mansion; *Relais*: an imported French term meaning 'inn'; *Residenza*: an apartment or house with rooms for guests; *Tenuta*: farm holding, or 'tenancy'; *Villa*: country residence.

Rooms

Bedrooms – We tell you about the range of accommodation in singles, doubles, twins, family rooms and suites as well as apartments and whole houses. A 'family' room is a loose term because in Italy triples and quadruples often sleep more than the heading suggests; extra beds can often be added for children, usually with a charge. Check when booking. Where an entry reads '4 + 2' this means 4 B&B rooms plus 2 self-catering apartments/villas/cottages.

Bathrooms – Assume that bathrooms are en suite unless we say otherwise. Italian bathrooms often have a shower only.

Meals

Eating in Italy is one of life's great pleasures. There is plenty of variety, and each region has its own specialities and its surprises. Many owners use organic, home-grown or locally grown ingredients, and more often than not will have produced some part of your meal themselves.

Vegetarians – Although fresh, seasonal vegetables are readily available in Italy, most Italian dishes contain meat and some Italians still find the concept of vegetarianism quite bizarre. All of our owners who offer a good range of vegetarian options have a special symbol – but don't be surprised if those without it struggle to understand a meal without meat.

Breakfast – What constitutes breakfast varies hugely from place to place. Many hotels don't offer it at all, especially in towns, where it is normal to walk to the nearest bar for your first espresso. (Prices double or triple as soon as you sit down, so if you want to save money, join the locals at the bar.) If you are confronted with a vacuum-packed breakfast it's because B&Bs are only allowed to serve fresh ingredients if they meet certain strict regulations. On farms, however, you should find homemade jams and cakes as well as home-produced cheeses and fruit.

Dinner – Hotels and other places with restaurants usually offer the widest à la carte choice. Smaller places may offer a set dinner (at a set time) and you will need to book in advance. Many of our owners are excellent cooks so, if you fancy an evening sitting two steps from your bedroom on your host's terrace overlooking Tuscan hills or Umbrian valleys, be sure to ask your hosts – on booking or on arrival – if they are able to share their culinary skills and serve up a sumptuous dinner on site. Sometimes you will eat with the family; sometimes you will be eating in a separate dining room, served by a member of the family. Small farms and inns often offer dinners which are excellent value and delicious, so keep an open mind. But be aware that laws in some regions of Italy do not allow bed & breakfasts to serve dinner to their guests.

Prices

The prices we quote are the prices per night per room unless otherwise stated, breakfast included. For self-catering, we specify if the price is per week. For half-board, it may be per person (p.p.). Meal prices are always given per person; we try to give you an approximate price and say if wine is included. Prices quoted are those given to us for 2008. We publish every two years so they cannot be current throughout the book's life. Treat them as a guideline rather than as infallible. We try to list any extra hidden costs – eg linen, towels, heating – but always check on booking.

Booking and cancellations

Hotels will usually ask you for a credit card number at the time of booking, for confirmation. Remember to let smaller places know if you are likely to be arriving late, and if you want dinner. Some of the major cities get very full (and often double in price) around the time of trade fairs (eg fashion fairs in Milan, the Biennale in Venice). And book well ahead if you plan to visit Italy during school holidays.

If you have to cancel please give as much notice as possible. Cancellation charges will vary, so do ask owners to explain their cancellation policy clearly before booking so you understand exactly where you stand; it may well avoid a nasty surprise.

Payment

The most commonly accepted credit cards are Visa, Eurocard, MasterCard and Amex. Many places in this book don't take plastic because of high bank charges. Check the symbols at the bottom of each entry before you arrive, in case you are a long way from a cash dispenser!

Tipping

In bars you are given your change on a small saucer, and it is usual to leave a couple of small coins there. A cover charge on restaurant meals is standard. A small tip ('mancia') in family-run establishments is also welcome, so leave one if you wish.

©Maidenhead Cartographic, 2008

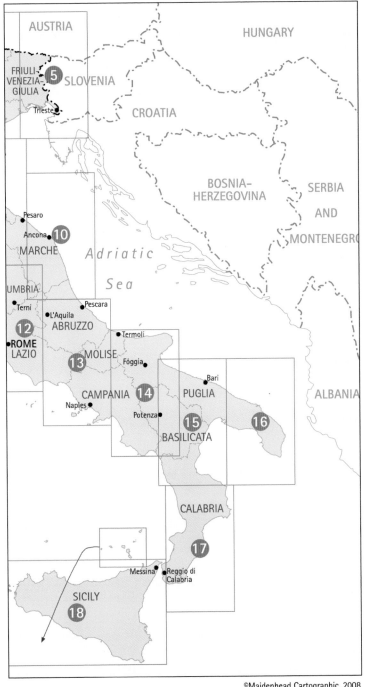

©Maidenhead Cartographic, 2008

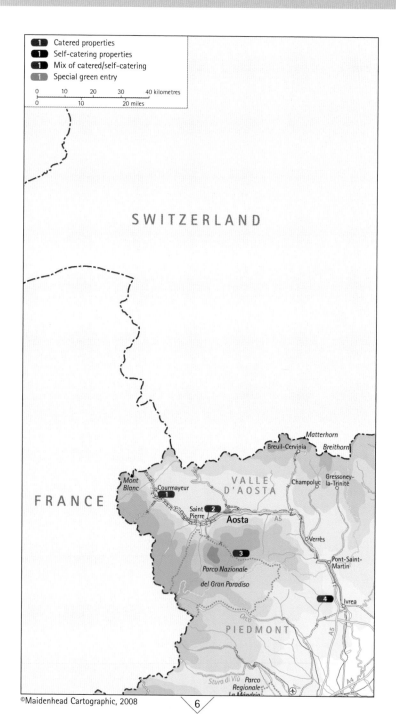

Catered properties
Self-catering properties
Mix of catered/self-catering
Special green entry

SWITZERLAND

FRANCE

Matterhorn
Breuil-Cervinia   Breithorn

Mont
Blanc   Courmayeur   VALLE   Champoluc   Gressoney-
1   D'AOSTA   la-Trinité

Saint   2
Pierre   Aosta   A5

Verrès

3   Pont-Saint-
Martin

Parco Nazionale
del Gran Paradiso

4   Ivrea

PIEDMONT

Stura di Viù   Parco
Regionale
La Mándria

©Maidenhead Cartographic, 2008

Map 2   21

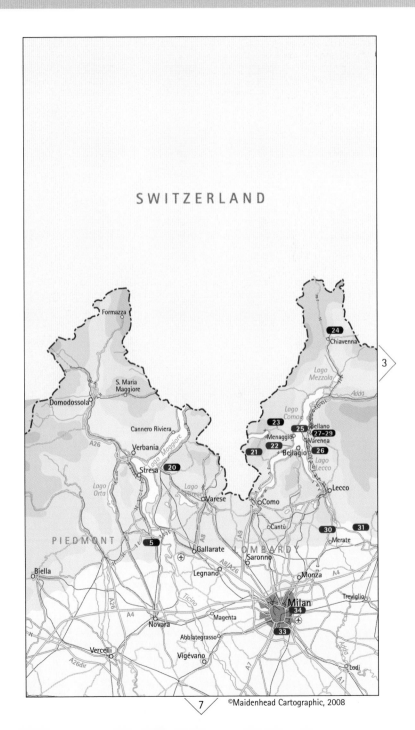

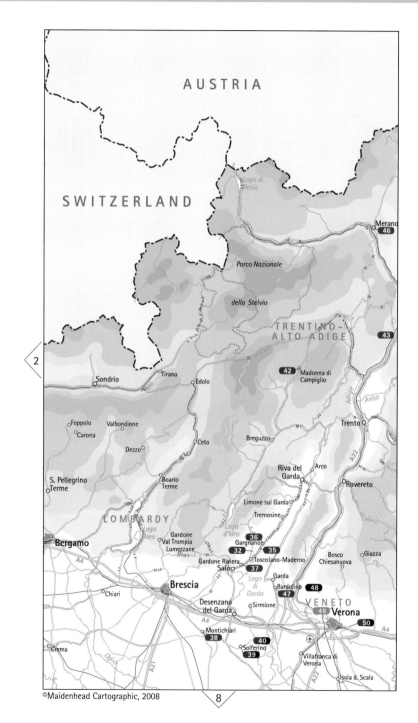

Map 4

23

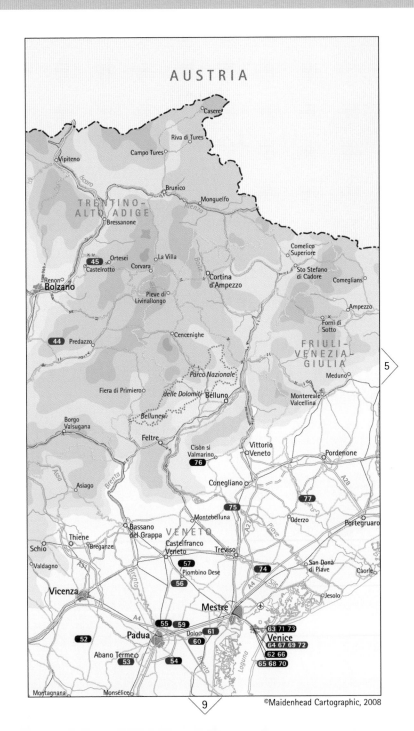

AUSTRIA

Casere

Riva di Tures

Campo Tures

Vipiteno

Brunico

Monguelfo

TRENTINO-
ALTO ADIGE
Bressanone

Comelico
Superiore

Ortesei
45 Castelrotto
Corvara

La Villa

Sto Stefano
di Cadore

Comeglians

Renon
Bolzano

Cortina
d'Ampezzo

Pieve di
Livinallongo

Ampezzo

Forni di
Sotto

44 Predazzo

Cencenighe

FRIULI-
VENEZIA-
GIULIA

5

Meduno

Fiera di Primiero

Parco Nazionale
delle Dolomiti Belluno

Montereale
Valcellina

Borgo
Valsugana

Bellunesi

Feltre

Cisòn si
Valmarino
76

Vittorio
Veneto

Pordenone

Asiago

Coneenghe

Coneegliano

77

75

Montebelluna

Oderzo

Portegruaro

Thiene
Schio
Breganze

Bassano
del Grappa

Castelfranco
Veneto

VENETO

Treviso

San Donà
di Piave

Caorle

Valdagno

57
Piombino Dese

74

56

Vicenza

Jesolo

Mestre

55 59

52

Padua

Dolo 61

63 71 73
64 67 69 72

60

Venice

Abano Terme
53

54

62 66

65 68 70

Montagnana

Monsélice

©Maidenhead Cartographic, 2008

AUSTRIA

Tarvisio

A23

Tolmezzo

Gemona di Friuli

FRIULI–
VENEZIA–
GIULTA

4

Faedis
80

Povoletto
79

Udine

SLOVENIA

Codroipo

A23

Gorizia
81

Palmanova

A4
A4

Monfalcone

78

Lignano
Sabbiadoro
Grado

Lignano Riviera
Bibione

Trieste

CROATIA

©Maidenhead Cartographic, 2008

London–Rome (by train)

When asked by Sawday's to swap my mode of travel from plane to train, I thought about what I would be giving up – stagnant fluorescent airports, humourless staff and cramped seating. These are things that my Italian experience could do without. My job is to find special places and put them in to this guide. We don't usually mention the journey because, let's face it, budget flying is not exactly a special experience – rather something we have to endure before delving into the wonders awaiting us at the other end. Perhaps the journey by train would be different, a journey we could actually call 'special'.

Throughout our books we celebrate owners who are making an effort to be green and encourage readers to consider their carbon footprint. So we're very aware that it is important we keep our 'compilation carbon' to a minimum, too. When I considered the train journey I felt excited. Not only would I be avoiding those tedious queues and robotic frowns, I would be saving carbon emissions and going a little way to lessen the global contribution to climate change.

My fourteen-hour overnight journey from London to Rome was, as I had imagined it to be, special indeed. After a pan-European dinner in the restaurant car with its crisp white tablecloths, I returned to my shared cabin where water was offered at no extra charge; blankets were duly delivered. I imagined the countryside outside my window: the French and Swiss towns we would pass (why, I asked myself, had I not chosen the cheaper option and travelled by day?). I fell into a deep sleep with the train droning peacefully beneath me and awoke just in time for breakfast. Twenty minutes later I was rested, relaxed and pulling in to the station in Rome. My Italian experience had been extended by fourteen enjoyable hours and, as the back of my train ticket told me, I had saved a mass of carbon.

A special experience that helps the environment deserves a page in this book and I urge you to try the experience for yourself – you'll be surprised to find the difference it can make.

Kate Shepherd

• www.seat61.com offers fantastic advice on fares and bookings for all European sea and land travel, and has a special section on Italy.

• www.ferroviedellostato.it is the Italian rail website for train timetables and fares. Remember to type in Italian names for places (eg Firenze not Florence).

• www.raileurope.co.uk is the place to book tickets. If you prefer to speak to a human being, call +44 (0)870 5848 848 and book over the phone.

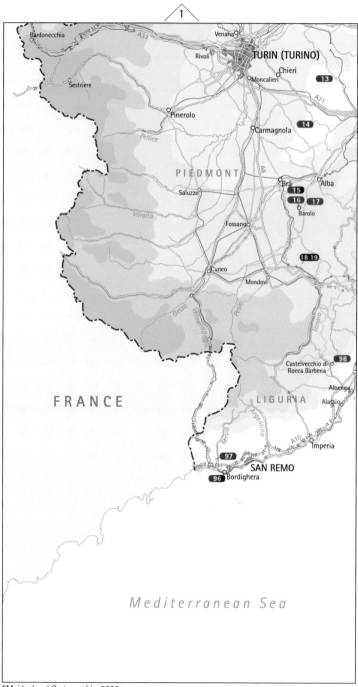

©Maidenhead Cartographic, 2008

Map 7

27

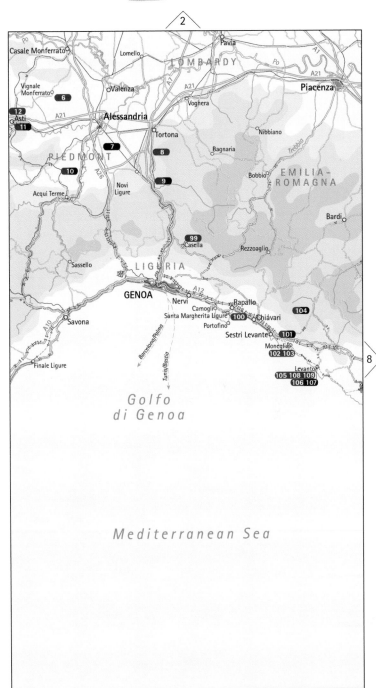

©Maidenhead Cartographic, 2008

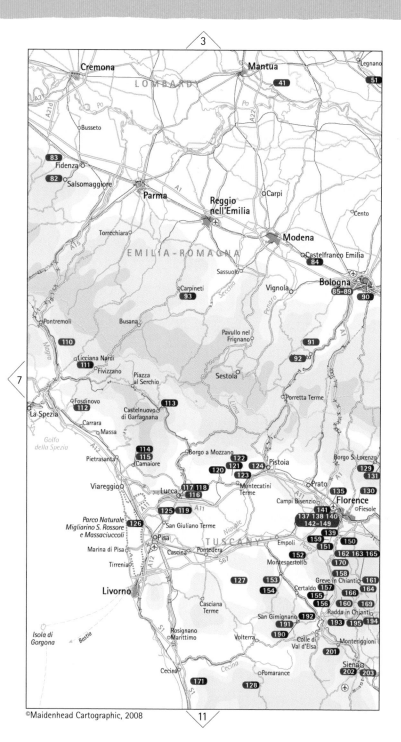

©Maidenhead Cartographic, 2008

Map 9   29

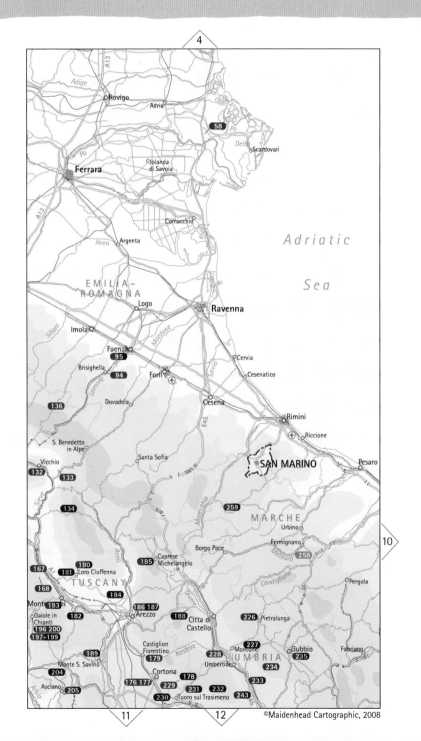

©Maidenhead Cartographic, 2008

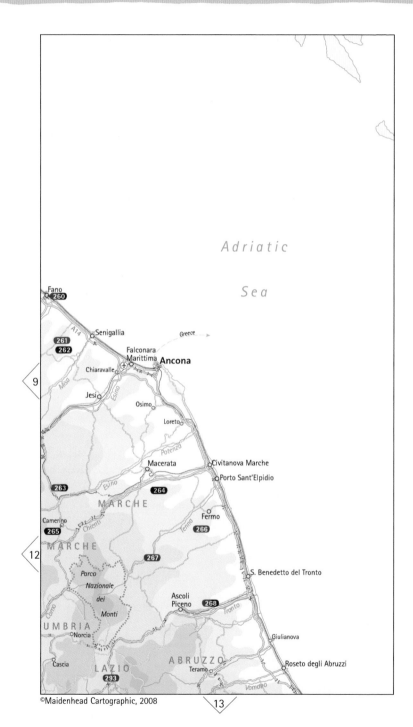

Adriatic

Sea

Fano
260

Senigallia
A14
261
262

Falconara
Marittima
Chiaravalle
Ancona

Greece →

9

Msa

Jesi

Esino

Osimo

Loreto

Potenza

Macerata
Civitanova Marche

Porto Sant'Elpidio

263

Esino

264

M A R C H E

Camerino
Chienti
265

Tenna

Fermo

266

12

M A R C H E

267

Parco

Nazionale

dei

Monti

S. Benedetto del Tronto

Ascoli
Piceno
268

Tronto

Corno

U M B R I A
Norcia

Giulianova

Cascia

L A Z I O
293

A B R U Z Z O
Teramo

Roseto degli Abruzzi

Vomano

Public transport is excellent in Italy. Many of our special places lie within ten miles of a bus or train station, and if owners are willing to arrange collection you may not need to hire a car.

A train journey in Italy can be as slow (and cheap) or as fast (and more expensive) as you want it to be, but one thing is sure: city-to-city travel is faster, easier and cheaper by train than by car. The state-run network *Ferrovie dello Stato* (FS) operates many different types of train: *Inter Regionale* (slow but cheap), *Intercity* (excellent) and the fast but relatively costly *Eurostar* (not to be confused with the London–Paris Eurostar). You pay per mile.

Seat reservations, compulsory on *Eurostar*, are strongly recommended on all routes at peak hours and in high season. Automatic ticket machines are plentiful in most major stations, but you must validate your ticket by stamping it (*convalida biglietto*), either here or in the

machines provided on platforms. If you don't, you could get a fine (*multa*) – also highly likely if you buy your ticket on board rather than beforehand.

A few mainline and most regional trains in Italy now take bikes, and you need to purchase a ticket for the bike as well as yourself. The bike ticket will be valid for 24 hours and can be used anywhere, so buy a few if you plan to travel with a cycle for several days. Usually there's a bike symbol on the bike carriage and, if you're lucky, a bike rack too.

Travel by train is not always the best choice though, particularly in the south where west–east networks are slow or non-existent, and you must always check times. You might be better off booking a seat on a coach; *agenzia viaggi* (travel agents) are found in nearly all towns across the country and will book coaches and trains for you.

Urban buses, metros, trains and trams are also reliable and cheap. Buy a day ticket in advance, at a ticket machine or a local news kiosk (*tabacchi*).

Driving in Italy is challenging for the British driver – Italian drivers are skilled but scary and like nothing better than to sit on your tail. Mountain roads can be steep and narrow with precarious drops and hair-pin bends; although we try to mention in our write-ups when roads are particularly difficult, please keep this in mind when choosing your hire car.

Photo: istock.com

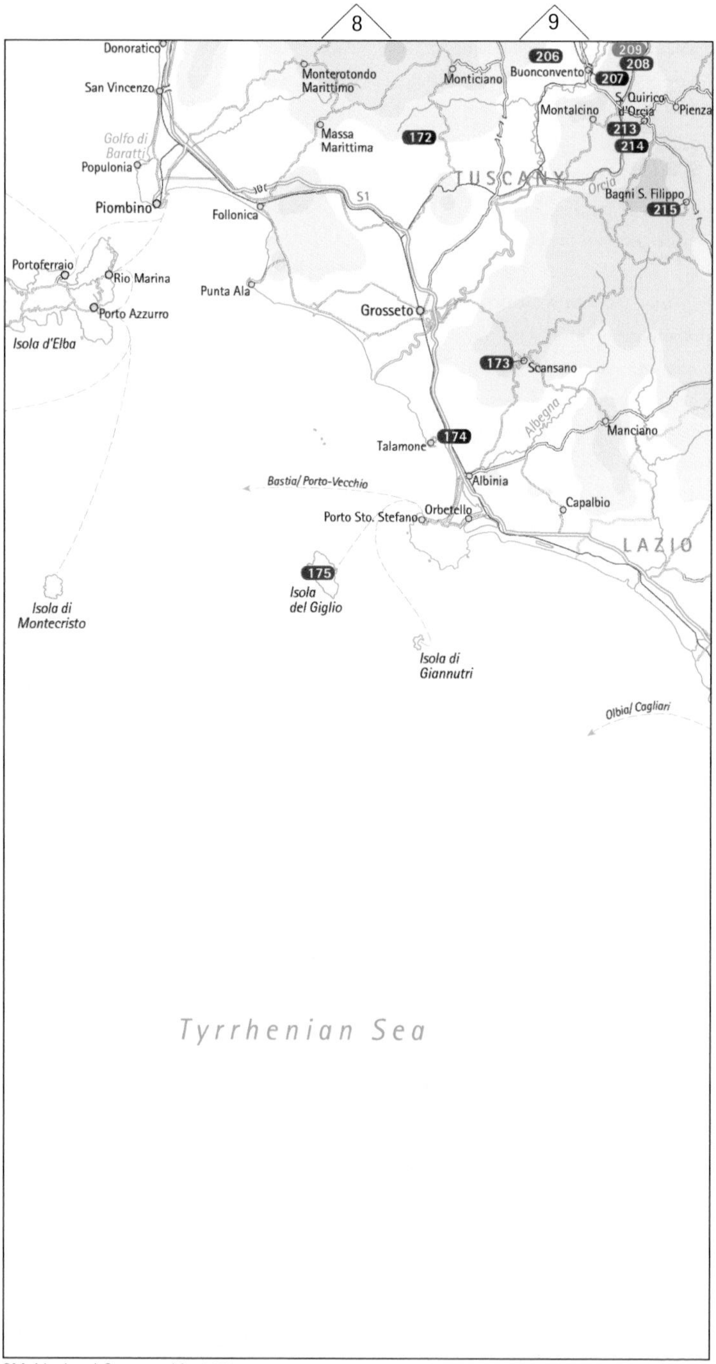

8

9

Donoratico

San Vincenzo

Monterotondo
Marittimo

Monticiano

Buonconvento

206

209
208

207

S. Quirico
d'Orcia

Pienza

Montalcino

213

Massa
Marittima

172

TUSCANY

214

Orcia

Bagni S. Filippo

215

Golfo di
Baratti

Populonia

S1

Piombino

Follonica

Portoferraio

Rio Marina

Punta Ala

Porto Azzurro

Grosseto

Isola d'Elba

173

Scansano

Albegna

Manciano

Talamone

174

Bastia/ Porto-Vecchio

Albinia

Porto Sto. Stefano

Orbetello

Capalbio

LAZIO

175

Isola
del Giglio

Isola di
Montecristo

Isola di
Giannutri

Olbia/ Cagliari

Tyrrhenian Sea

©Maidenhead Cartographic, 2008

Map 12

33

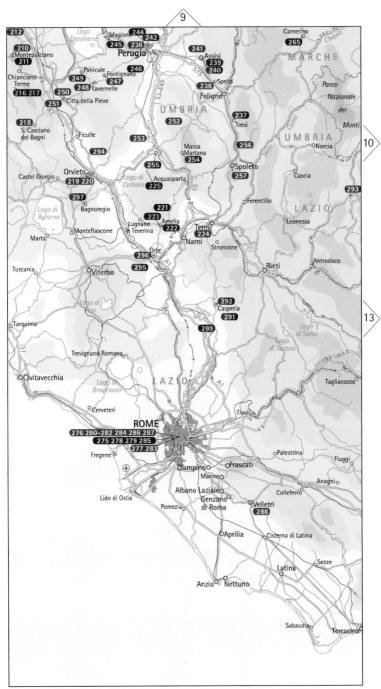

©Maidenhead Cartographic, 2008

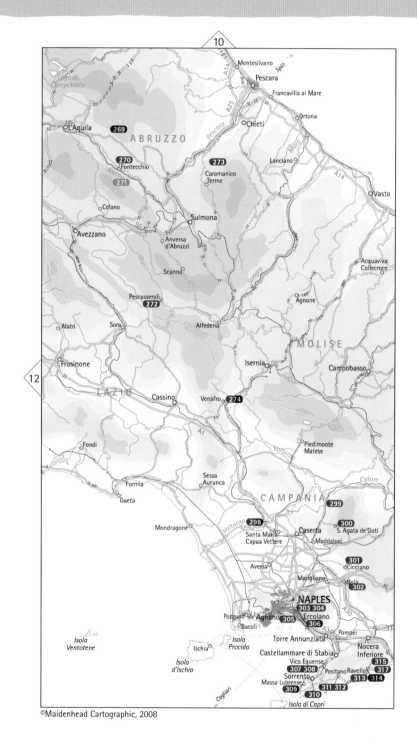

©Maidenhead Cartographic, 2008

Map 14   35

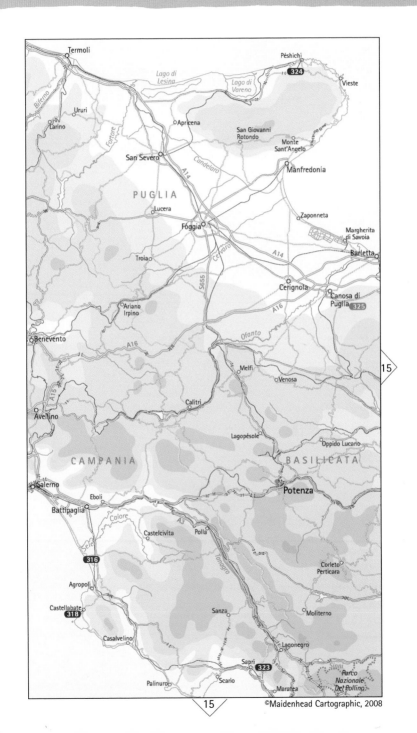

©Maidenhead Cartographic, 2008

Map 16   37

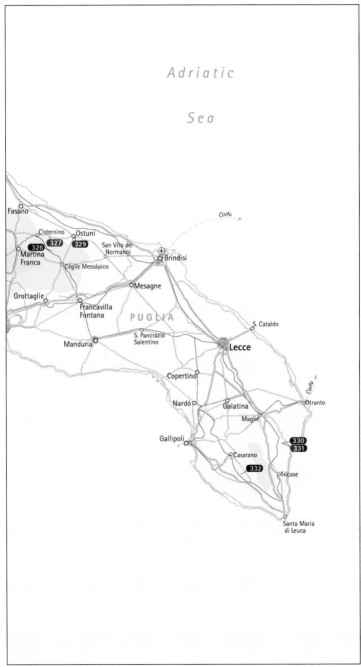

Adriatic

Sea

Corfu

Fasano
Cisternino   Ostuni
328 327   329
Martina   San Vito dei
Franca   Normanni
Céglie Messápico   Brindisi

Grottaglie   Mesagne

Francavilla
Fontana   PUGLIA

Manduria   S. Pancrazio   S. Cataldo
             Salentino
                          Lecce

             Copertino

Nardó   Galatina   Corfu
                   Maglie   Otranto

Gallipoli
                330
         Casarano   331

            332   Tricase

                      Santa Maria
                      di Leuca

©Maidenhead Cartographic, 2008

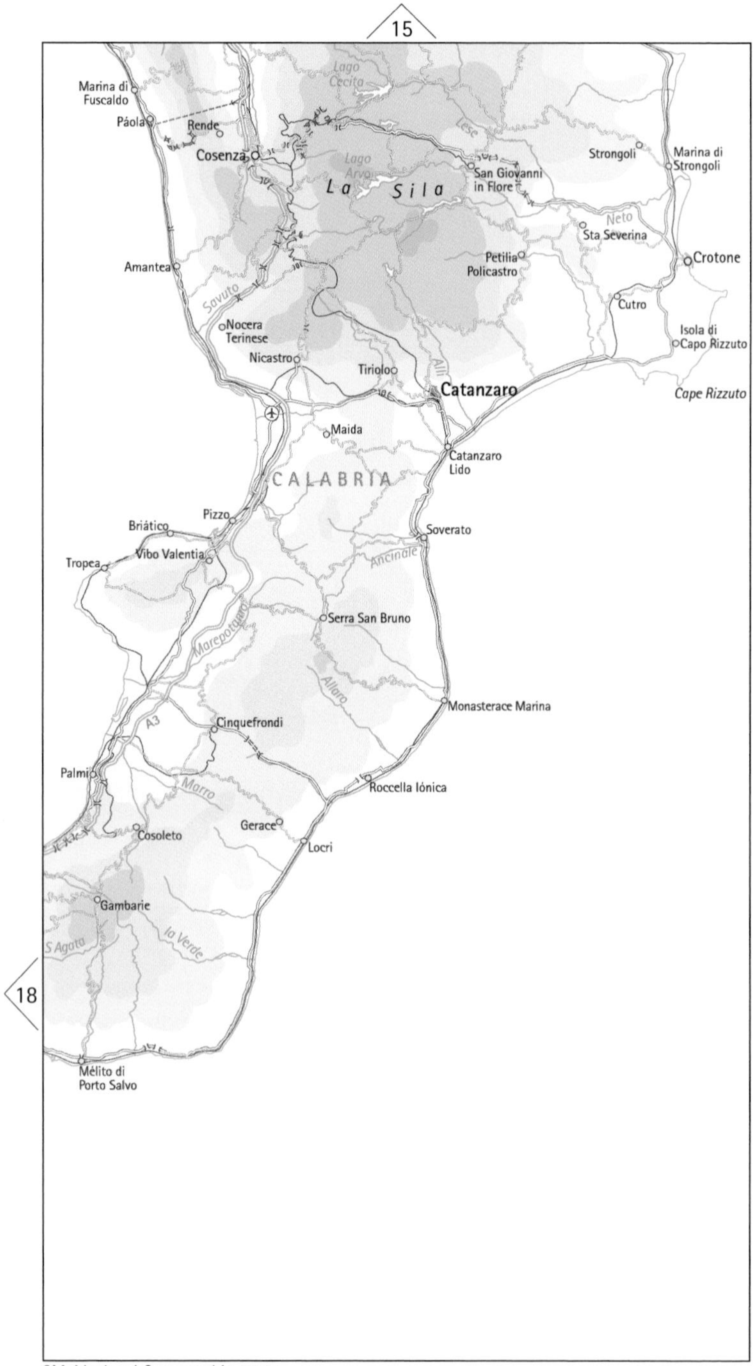

15

Marina di
Fuscaldo
Páola
Rende
Cosenza
Lago
Cecita
Lago
Arvo
La   Sila
San Giovanni
in Flore
Strongoli
Marina di
Strongoli
Neto
Sta Severina
Crotone
Amantea
Petilia
Policastro
Cutro
Savuto
Nocera
Terinese
Nicastro
Tirioló
Catanzaro
Maida
Catanzaro
Lido
CALABRIA
Isola di
Capo Rizzuto
Cape Rizzuto
Pizzo
Briático
Vibo Valentia
Tropea
Soverato
Ancinale
Serra San Bruno
Marepotam
Alloro
Cinquefrondi
Monasterace Marina
Palmi
Marro
Roccella Iónica
Cosoleto
Gerace
Locri
Gambarie
la Verde
S Agata
18
Mélito di
Porto Salvo

©Maidenhead Cartographic, 2008

Map 18   39

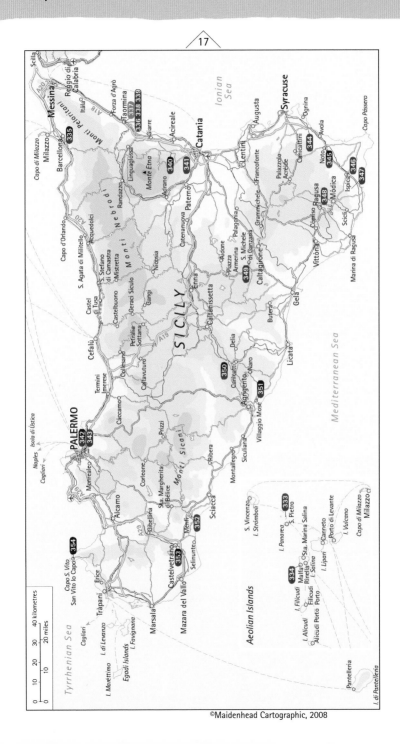

©Maidenhead Cartographic, 2008

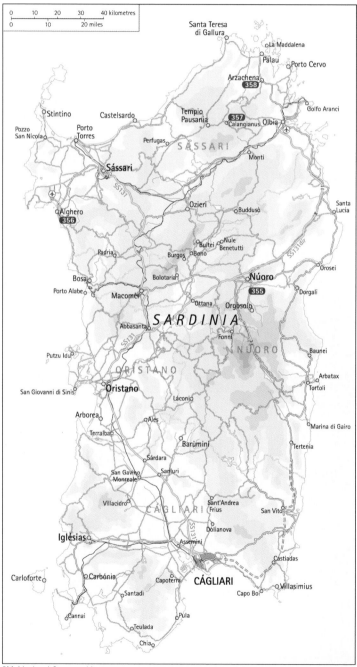

| 0 | 10 | 20 | 30 | 40 kilometres |
| 0 | | 10 | | 20 miles |

Santa Teresa
di Gallura

La Maddalena

Palau
Porto Cervo

Arzachena
358

Golfo Aranci

Stintino
Castelsardo
Tempio
Pausania
357
Calangianus
Olbia

Pozzo
San Nicola
Porto
Torres
Perfugas
SÁSSARI

Sássari
Monti

Alghero
356
Ozieri
Buddusò
Santa
Lucia

Padria
Bultei
Nule
Benetutti
Burgos
Bono

Bosa
Bolotaria
Núoro
Orosei

Porto Alabe
Macomer
355
Dorgali

Ottana
Orgòsolo

SARDINIA

Abbasanta
Fonni

NNUORO

Putzu Idu
Baunei

ORISTANO

Arbatax
Tortoli

San Giovanni di Sinis
Oristano

Láconi

Arborea
Ales
Marina di Gairo

Terraloa
Tertenia

Barùmini

Sárdara

San Gavino
Monreale
Sanluri

Villacidro
Sant'Andrea
Frius
San Vito
CAGLIARI

Dolianova

Iglésias
Assemini

Castiadas

Carloforte
Carbónia
Capoterra
CÁGLIARI
Villasimius

Santadi
Capo Boi

Cannai
Pula

Teulada

Chia

©Maidenhead Cartographic, 2008

Valle D'Aosta • Piedmont

Photo: istock.com

Auberge de la Maison

What a setting! You're in the old part of the village of Val Fenet, three kilometres from Courmayeur, in sight of Mont Blanc, surrounded by gentle terraces, gardens, meadows and majestic views. The Auberge has a quietly elegant and exclusive feel yet is not in the least intimidating, thanks to the cheerful (and efficient) staff. Bedrooms are uncluttered, stylish and comfortable with mellow colours. Many have a third bed disguised as a sofa; nearly all have balconies and the views ranging from good to superb. A Tuscan influence is detectable in the décor; the owner is from Florence. His impressive collection of images of the Valle d'Aosta, from old promotional posters to oil paintings, makes a fascinating display, while a reassembled wooden mountain house is a most unusual feature of the reception and sitting area. There's a fitness centre, too, with a sauna and hydromassage. Come in any season: to fish for trout or play a round of golf, or to ski (right to the ski lift) or don crampons for a winter ascent.

Price	€140-€310. Half-board €195-€340.
Rooms	33: 14 doubles, 13 triples, 3 family rooms, 3 suites.
Meals	Dinner €38. Wine €12.
Closed	May-mid-November.
Directions	From the south, direction Entreves; signed. From France, signed after Mont-Blanc tunnel.

Alessandra Garin
fraz. Entrèves,
11013 Courmayeur

Tel	+39 0165 869811
Fax	+39 0165 869759
Email	info@aubergemaison.it
Web	www.aubergemaison.it

Les Écureuils Agriturismo

No designer chic here, but a hard-working farm, at the end of a long mountain road, specialising in goat's cheese. In the 14th century, the building was a half-way house between the valley and the high alpine pastures for grazing animals. Now the bedrooms are quaint and homely with patterned walls, knotted pine, linen window-hangings and photos showing the farm in different seasons. Showers are private but wcs are shared. In the bistro-like dining room, crochet-trimmed shelves carry books and ornaments. Excellent food is presented in a stylish, rustic fashion with everything, apart from the bread and wine, home-grown or homemade. (There's a little farm shop, too, where you can stock up on goat's cheese if you haven't overdosed already.) Outside the garden is steep but the odd chair or bench on the small terraces makes a marvellous place to sit and absorb the glorious views across the Valle d'Aosta. Three generations of the family live here. They are quiet, friendly and immensely committed to what they do; given time, they'll talk to you about their way of life. *Children over ten welcome.*

Price	€50-€60. Triple €65-€75. Single €25-€30.
Rooms	5: 1 double, 2 twins/doubles, 1 triple, 1 single; shared wcs.
Meals	Dinner €15-€22.
Closed	Rarely.
Directions	From Aosta SS26 for M. Bianco. At Sarre right up hill to Ville-sur-Sarre; left signed to Les Écureuils.

Famiglia Gontier-Ballauri-Moniotto
fraz. Homené Dessus 8,
11010 Saint Pierre

Tel	+39 0165 903831
Fax	+39 0165 909849
Email	lesecureuils@libero.it
Web	www.lesecureuils.it

Hotel Bellevue

Lay inhibitions aside: this is a place to be pampered in style. Laura grew up in the hotel and considers guest indulgence a matter of family pride. From the chalets to a delicious Wellness Centre – perhaps a bath of milk and honey? – is an underground tunnel so you can arrive bath-robed. The public rooms are gracious and hospitable, from the bar with its red velvet upholstery to the woody sitting room where afternoon tea is served in front of the fire, and the panoramic restaurant that is Michelin-starred. Everything has been designed with pleasure in mind. Each bedroom is cosy, traditional, lavish with Alpine antiques, local woodcarvings and lace work, and white cotton piquet. Choose from a choice of wood and stone floors, an array of balcony views, soft green or raspberry tones, and, for true sybarites, a sauna. No. 70 has an in-room spa bath – not for the shy, but you are rewarded with a great view from the bubbles. All around you are protected meadows, villages and the mountains of Gran Paradiso National Park. Superb. *Minimum stay three nights; supplements for shorter stays.*

Price	€170–€330. Suites €330–€390. Chalets €240–€390.
Rooms	35 + 3: 28 twins/doubles, 7 suites for 2–4. 3 chalets: 2 for 2–4, 1 for 2–6.
Meals	Half board extra €50 p.p. Dinner €60–€80. Wine from €25. Restaurants in Cogne.
Closed	October–November.
Directions	From motorway Aosta Ovest-Saint Pierre, direction Cogne. Right at piazza; 100m.

Family Jeantet & Family Roullet
rue Grand Paradis 22,
11012 Cogne

Tel	+39 0165 74825
Fax	+39 0165 749192
Email	bellevue@relaischateaux.com
Web	www.hotelbellevue.it

La Miniera

Having wound your way up the ferrous mountainside, it's a delight to reach Roberta's garden which sits on top of the old mine spoil – a perfect setting for some fabulous, Jewish-Italian cooking. Wild funghi and berries picked from the woods above find their way into the seasonal menus. Hard to believe these former headquarters of a iron-ore mine were once completely derelict. Roberta, her husband and dogs, live in the former mine office. There are also two B&B rooms, and more in the director's house, and a kitchen and a dishwasher for guests. The bedrooms, which vary in size, are light and airy and simply decorated with old-fashioned "grandmother's furniture". A further, smaller house in the garden, cosy with heating and open fire, is for self-caterers. The Anaus are also steadily assembling a museum on the history of the mine. There are shady terraces with deck-chairs, ruins to explore and even Napoleonic mule tracks. Nature abounds: you may spot owls in these 40 wooded acres, while wild boar wander round the garden from time to time.

Price	€58-€68. Triple €64-€96. Quadruple €64-€104. Cottage €76-€86 (€500 per week).
Rooms	5 + 1: 1 double, 1 triple, 1 quadruple; 2 doubles sharing bath. Cottage for 2-3 + cot.
Meals	Breakfast €8-€14. Dinner €24-€35. Wine from €6. Restaurant 2km.
Closed	Rarely.
Directions	From Ivrea to Lessolo for 6km. Ignore 1st sign for Lessolo, on for 1.5km, left for Calea. Signed to green iron gates.

Roberta Anau
via Miniere 9,
10010 Calea di Lessolo

Tel	+39 0125 58618
Fax	+39 0125 561963
Email	roberta@laminiera.it
Web	www.laminiera.it

Cascina Motto

Flowers everywhere: spilling from the balcony, filling the patio, clasping the walls of the cottage... wisteria, vines, azaleas, roses. It's an immaculate garden, with lawns, spreading trees, boules court and a discreet summer pool. Roberta's lovely, too, so warm and friendly you are made at once to feel part of the family. They came here years ago – she and David, their daughters, Roberta's parents Sergio and Lilla, four dogs. They clearly love the house, which they've restored and filled with paintings and beautiful things. In a quiet street, in a quiet village, this is a happy and restful place to stay. The twin room, named after Roberta's grandmother, has windows facing two ways – over the garden and towards Monte Rosa – plus whitewashed walls, blue cotton rugs, blue-painted iron beds, books, a comfy sofa, a big bathroom. The cottage, its bedroom in the hayloft, is bright, airy, charming, with country furniture, a well-equipped kitchenette, a balcony; it's completely independent of the main house. Breakfast is a feast, and the lakes of Orta and Maggiore are a 20-minute drive. *Minimum stay two nights.*

Price	€75. Cottage €85–€150.
Rooms	1 + 1: 1 twin. 1 cottage for 2-4.
Meals	Restaurants 1km.
Closed	December-February.
Directions	From Milano A4 (Laghi); after Gallarate A26 for Alessandria exit Castelletto Ticino. Signs for Novara SS32, 3rd exit for Divignano (via Boschi di Sopra). At Divignano, 2nd left for via Marzabotto.

	Roberta Plevani via Marzabotto 7, 28010 Divignano
Tel	+39 0321 995350
Fax	+39 0321 995350
Email	cascinamotto@interfree.it
Web	www.cascinamotto.com

Cascina Alberta Agriturismo

This attractive hilltop farmhouse in this famous wine-producing area. Marked by two stately cypress trees, the house is two kilometres from the town centre and has 360° views of the surrounding vineyards and hills – sensational. The business is run on agriturismo lines by smiling, capable Raffaella, who lives just across the courtyard with her town-planner husband and their 16 year-old son. Tiled guest bedrooms are extremely pretty: an old marble-topped table here, a country wardrobe there, beds painted duck-egg blue, walls in soft pastel and many pieces beautifully painted by Raffaella. Both the bedrooms and the frescoed dining room lie across the farmyard from your hosts; if you choose to eat in, you dine at your own table on local dishes at reasonable prices, with wines from the estate – some of them have been aged in wooden barrels and are hard to find outside the area. Raffaella speaks excellent English and is happy to help guests get the most out of this enchanting area. Just an hour's drive from the coast.

Price	€64–€75. Triple €80–€90.
Rooms	5: 4 twins/doubles, 1 triple.
Meals	Dinner with wine, €16–€22.
Closed	20 December–February; August.
Directions	From Vignale, follow signs to Camagna. After 2km left at roadside shrine. Cascina Alberta is 400m on right.

	Signora Raffaella de Cristofaro
	loc. Ca' Prano 14,
	15049 Vignale Monferrato
Tel	+39 0142 933313
Fax	+39 0142 933313
Email	cascinalberta@netcomp.it

Agriturismo Tenuta la Camilla

Bowling along flat agricultural land, with crops as high as an elephant's eye... then the high faded ochre walls and the great open gate of the *tenuta* rise to welcome you. Once a refuge for soldiers fleeing the battle of Marengo, the family *masseria* with a hacienda-like feel now offers escape of a different sort. Pia, as warm and hospitable as her parents, oversees the apartments. Heavy front doors lead to light, airy rooms kept cool by ancient walls. Eclectic family furniture, cheerful contemporary cottons, tiled and speckled stone floors, firm beds and immaculate, old-fashioned bathrooms, welcome and satisfy. Jugs of flowers and comfortable old sofas and extra beds (some in the sitting rooms) feel homely and uncontrived. As you might expect from the marriage of a young cookery journalist and venerable farm buildings, well-kitted kitchens range from enormous to bijou. En route to the shady garden, a pedigree herd welcomes you with soft sighs and organic charms. Swap deep peace and country rusticity for jaunts to Milan or the coast. Wonderful. *Minimum stay two nights. No laundry.*

Price	€400-€800 per week.
Rooms	4 apartments for 2-12.
Meals	Breakfast €5. Dinner on request, groups only. Restaurants 3km.
Closed	Rarely.
Directions	A7, A21, A26 - exit Alessandria or Novi Ligure; follow signs for Bosco Marengo & Frugarolo; to Mandrino; just past Mandrino, signed.

Pia Scavia
strada Mandrino 40,
15065 Frugarolo

Tel	+39 0131 296691
Mobile	+39 338 5001239
Email	info@agricamilla.com
Web	www.agricamilla.com

Agriturismo Cascina Folletto

A smiling elf sitting on top of a strawberry is an apt house emblem for Cascina Folletto: once you have tried the *fragola profumata* you will vow never to try another type of strawberry again. Producing also organic saffron and chickpeas, this Tortonese farmhouse, dating from the late 18th century and made from rammed earth, faces a wisteria-filled courtyard. Maria Rosa, who was born in the house, has lovingly displayed collections of her grandmother's copper moulds in the kitchen and antique plates and tureens in the sober dining room; here breakfast is served with homemade jams, and dinner with the hosts (but book first) – a wholesome four-course affair of freshly harvested produce. Take tea and coffee in the cheerful front parlour or in the upstairs sitting room with its balcony views of the fields. A mellow brick archway frames the stone staircase to bedrooms that hold fine country antiques, iron and walnut beds, brocade spreads, a rocking cot. 'Folletto', with elf-green creeping into tartan curtains and cushions, is the only room with a private bathroom. *Minimum stay two nights.*

Price	€80–€100. Single €50. Triple €110–€120.
Rooms	4: 1 double with separate bath; 1 double, 1 single, 1 triple, all sharing bath.
Meals	Dinner with wine, €22–€25.
Closed	Rarely.
Directions	A7 Milan-Genoa exit Tortona. At Rivalta Scrivia, chapel on left, sign to Bettole di Tortona; 3km chapel on right; into Strada Veneziana, signed.

Maria Rosa Milanese
strada Veneziana 9/1,
fraz. Bettole, 15057 Tortona

Tel	+39 0143 417224
Fax	+39 0143 417224
Email	info@cascinafolletto.com
Web	www.cascinafolletto.com

La Traversina Agriturismo

Come for the roses, the irises, the hostas! You'll find over 230 different varieties of plant here – they are Rosanna's passion. With drowsy shutters, buzzing bees and walls festooned in roses, the house and outbuildings appear to be in a permanent state of siesta. As do the seven cats, basking on warm window sills and shady terraces. There's a touch of *The Secret Garden* about the half-hidden doors, enticing steps and riotous plants, and the air is fragrant with lavender, oregano and roses, many from France. The house and farm, on a wooded hillside, have been in Rosanna's family for nearly 300 years; she gave up a career as an architect to create this paradise 40 minutes from Genoa. Homely, imaginatively decorated, bedrooms have handsome furniture, books, pictures; bathrooms come with baskets of goodies. Everyone eats together at a long table in the conservatory or outside, where lights glow in the trees at night. Rosanna, Domenico and young Vijaya are the most delightful hosts and the home-grown food is a revelation: agriturismo at its best. *Children over 12 welcome. Courses on roses February-May.*

Price	€88-€110. Half-board €66-€77 p.p. Apartments €120-€140.
Rooms	2 + 4: 1 double, 1 family room. 4 apartments: 3 for 2, 1 for 4.
Meals	Dinner €22-€28, by arrangement. Wine €6. Restaurant 6km.
Closed	Rarely.
Directions	A7 Milan-Genova exit Vignole Borbera for Stazzano; 4km; signed.

Rosanna & Domenico Varese Puppo
Cascina La Traversina 109,
15060 Stazzano

Tel	+39 0143 61377
Fax	+39 0143 61377
Email	latraversina@latraversina.com
Web	www.latraversina.com

La Granica

When Karen, with Mark, went in search of her Italian roots, their adventure ended in an 18th-century grain barn in a secluded dell surrounded by rolling vineyards. Enter the beautifully renovated *granica* through a foyer of limestone floors, a wet bar and exposed brick walls: to the left is the library with deep leather sofas and chocolate and lime colours; to the right is the dining room, sleekly minimalist with polished marble floors and Lithuanian oak chairs. Here, fresh buffet-breakfasts and seasonal four-course dinners are served. Beneath a high cathedral ceiling, the four bedrooms are luxuriously furnished with lashings of silk, velvet chenille armchairs (or chaise-longue), splashes of raspberry tones, Egyptian cotton sheets. In the more traditional rooms are mahogany sleigh beds and resplendent bohemian chandeliers. The self-catering terrace house holds a diminutive sitting room, a fully equipped kitchen and double and twin bedrooms in house style – the former with a 'Jacobean' four-poster. Trees and lawns neatly frame the discreet swimming pool. *Minimum stay two nights in cottage.*

Price	€110–€180. Cottage €150–€200 (€770–€1,100 p.w.).
Rooms	4 + 1: 4 doubles. Cottage for 2-4.
Meals	Dinner with wine, €25–€30. Buffet supper €10. Snacks €5–€8.
Closed	Rarely.
Directions	From A26 exit Alessandria Sud (or from A21 Asti Est) towards Nizza-Monferrato. Follow signs for Fontanile.

Karen Langley
Cascina Mulino Vecchio 5,
reg. Mulino Vecchio,
14044 Fontanile

Tel   +39 0141 739105
Email   info@lagranicahotel.com
Web   www.lagranica.com

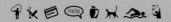

Entry 10 Map 7

Villa Sampaguita

Laze in the garden and listen to the crickets. Potter in the woods or orchards and search for fossils. Then, when you're thoroughly rested, sally forth to explore the region's vineyards and wonderful, baroque Turin, a 30-minute drive. The Villa is a modernised 19th-century *cascina* on an 11-hectare organic farm and vineyard in a national park. Standing on a ridge just outside medieval Asti, it has fine views of the Monferrato hills — and, on a clear day, the Alps. Tim and Rina have converted the hayloft into a pleasant guest wing, furnished with fine period pieces. The bedrooms have French windows and a private balcony; the apartments, on the ground floor, open to verandas. There's also a large guest salon with a wood-burning stove and big windows overlooking the terrace. The area is full of fabulous restaurants but, if you don't feel like eating out, Rina loves cooking (she holds classes on request) and uses seasonal home-grown organic produce in her contemporary Piedmontese dishes, served with the villa's wines. She's kind and charming; Tim is a friendly and well-travelled host. *Minimum stay three nights.*

Price	€90–€110. Apartments €125–€160 (€700–€1,050 p.w.).
Rooms	4 + 2: 4 doubles. 2 apartments for 2–3.
Meals	Dinner with wine €35.
Closed	15 December–15 March. Apartments open all year.
Directions	A21 Torino–Piacenza, exit Asti Ovest; 2km in opp. direction to Asti; just after Palucco, right at sign 'Valcoresa'; under autostrada to top of hill; signed right.

Tim Brewer
Bricco Cravera, Valleandona 117,
14100 Asti

Tel	+39 0141 295802
Fax	+39 0141 295970
Email	timbrewer@tele2.it
Web	www.villasampaguita.com

La Violina Agriturismo

A frantic twist of the steering wheel, up a narrow winding road, past a few houses and you're there. This rather grand old farmhouse owns all that it surveys: vineyards, olive groves, orchards and, down in the valley, century-old woodland. What to discover first? The exquisite family chapel, the lawns, beds and urns sweeping up to the tennis court and pool? Or the rambling delights of the house: the sitting room with its acres of comfy sofas, thick Persian rugs, billiard table and magazines; the gilded, garlanded music room; the playroom, exercise room and sauna? The food is delicious, a resident chef cooking what is seasonal and best, fresh from the market or organically grown on the estate. The cellars groan with home-produced olive oil and Barbera d'Asti wine, made from the grapes that swell on the sunny hillside. Energetic, artistic, friendly Davide and Carla dine with you. They love antiques, books and art, and the traditional bedrooms, with charming wallpapers and comfortable rugs, reflect their eclectic tastes. Shower rooms are well-equipped. A charming, peaceful haven.

Price	€130. Half-board €100 p.p.
Rooms	6: 4 doubles; 1 double, 1 single sharing shower room.
Meals	Dinner with wine, €35-€40.
Closed	Never.
Directions	Exit Asti/Ovest; follow SS458 Asti-Chivasso; 7km; at roundabout, signed Valmonasca; house signed suddenly on right; climb narrow hill; on right.

Davide & Carla Palazzetti
fraz. Mombarone 115,
Monferrato,
14100 Asti
Tel   +39 0141 294173
Email   info@laviolina.it
Web   www.laviolina.it

Entry 12 Map 7

Cascina Piola Agriturismo

Raffaella and Piero are former teachers who left Turin some years ago to bring up their children in the country. Their village home is a late 19th-century farmhouse that hides in a walled garden right next to the church. The two guest bedrooms have their own entrances so feel nicely private; they're also warm, cheerful and homely with a country farmhouse feel. Meals are served in a large guests' dining room at one table, and the food is as generous as your hosts. Raffaella describes her style as regional home cooking and emphasises vegetarian dishes; both food and wines are organic, and with the produce from their smallholding they also make and sell large quantities of chutneys, preserves and jams. Surrounded by flat farmland this feels well off the beaten tourist track but there's still plenty to do: walking, biking, horse riding, culture (there are some lovely old churches and castles to visit). It would be a shame to make this house a mere pit-stop – delightful hosts and delicious meals ensure guests return again and again.

Price	€65-€70. Half-board €55-€60 p.p.
Rooms	2: 1 double, 1 twin/double, each with separate bath & shower.
Meals	Lunch & dinner, 5 courses, €27. Wine €6.
Closed	8 December-8 February.
Directions	A21 exit Villanova d'Asti towards Buttigliera d'Asti to Colle Don Bosco Santuario, then towards Montafia for 1km. House in Serra di Capriglio, by white church.

Signora Raffaella Firpo
via Fontana 2, fraz. Serra,
14014 Capriglio

Tel	+39 0141 997447
Fax	+39 0141 997447
Email	cascinapiola@inwind.it

Cascina Papa Mora Agriturismo

Come for authentic agriturismo in northern Italy. Adriana runs grandmother's old house with her sister, speaks fluent English and makes you really welcome. The farm produces wine, vegetables and fruit; the pantry overflows with bottles of oil, wine, chutneys and jams. (This is one of Italy's top wine regions for Barbera, Dolcetto, aristocratic Bracchetto, cheap and cheerful Spumante.) We can't say that the farmhouse has been lovingly restored – more razed to the ground and rebuilt, then bedecked with simple stencils of flowers. Bedrooms have no-nonsense 1930s furniture and light floral spreads; those in the roof area, hot in summer, are the nicest. Shower rooms are spotless. Outside, a garden with roses, lavender and herbs slopes to the new pool and the stables. The sisters also run a restaurant here and are passionate about their organic credentials. Dinner is a feast of gnocchi and tagliatelle, pepperoni cream puffs, anchovies in almond sauce; all delicious, and fun. Breakfast on the veranda where the blossom is pretty, the hills surround you, the bread comes fresh from the wood oven.

Price	€60–€70. Triples €70–€85. Quadruples €80–€95. Singles €35–€40. Half-board €55–€65 p.p.
Rooms	6: 3 twins/doubles, 1 triple, 2 quadruples.
Meals	Lunch or dinner with wine, €25–€30.
Closed	December-February.
Directions	A21 exit Villanova d'Asti & for Cellarengo. On outskirts of village left into via Ferrere, past small chapel to farm.

Adriana & Maria Teresa Bucco
via Ferrere 16,
14010 Cellarengo

Tel	+39 0141 935126
Fax	+39 0141 935444
Email	papamora@tin.it
Web	www.cascinapapamora.it

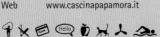

Agriturismo Erbaluna

On a hot summer's day the old cellars have a musty but blissful perfume, redolent of decades of good red wine. This working vineyard is run by the Oberto family and guests are capably and sensitively looked after by two husband and wife teams: Severino and Carla, and Andrea and Monica. Mama Letizia makes sure everything is as it should be. The house is a typical late 1800s cascina, a long, two-storeyed white building fronted by a paved and gated courtyard, across from which are the cellars; all state-of-the-art and, work permitting, open for guided viewing. Begin the day with a homemade breakfast in country surrounds, retreating later, once the sun has softened, to the shared roof terrace for an aperitif over the balustrade. Immaculately clean bedrooms hold a collection of rustic and antique walnut furniture, faux-brocade bedspreads and old family photographs. The two-storey apartments have tiled and beamed living areas with extra sofabeds, well-equipped kitchens and dining tables that seat up to eight. In every room, wine, bottle-opener and glasses come as standard – naturally.

Price	€70-€85 (€450 per week). Apartment €550 per week.
Rooms	5 + 2: 5 doubles. 2 apartments for 2-4.
Meals	Restaurant 1km.
Closed	Rarely.
Directions	A21 Torino-Piacenza exit Asti east. Follow m'way for Alba, dir. Barolo. 2nd sign for La Morra, fraz. Annunziata.

Carla Vada
fraz. Annunziata, 43,
12064 La Morra

Tel	+39 0173 50800
Fax	+39 0173 509336
Email	agriturismo@erbaluna.it
Web	www.erbaluna.it

Il Gioco dell'Oca Agriturismo

People love Raffaella: her home is full of tokens of appreciation sent by guests. She spent much of her childhood here – the farm was her grandparents'. She is happy to be back, looks after her guests beautifully, feeds them well, and has tampered with the pretty, 18th-century farmhouse as little as possible. The well-worn, welcoming kitchen, much as it must have been 50 years ago, is for you to use as and when you like – the warm hub of a sociable house. Next door is a breakfast room set with little tables, but if it's fine you'll prefer to breakfast under the portico in the garden, which is big enough for everyone to find their own secluded corner. The bedrooms are simple and cosy, with family furniture and wooden beds, one with a hob, sink and fridge – a bonus if you have little ones. Bathrooms are bright and new. The farm, up in the hills near Barolo – a wonderful area for cheeses and wines – produces wine, fruit and hazelnuts. A pity the road is so close but you'll forgive that for the pleasure of staying at such a relaxed, welcoming and thoroughly Italian agriturismo.

Price	€65–€75. Triple €75–€85.
Rooms	7: 6 twins/doubles, 1 triple.
Meals	Restaurant 500m.
Closed	January.
Directions	From Asti (east) exit autostrada TO-PC. Follow sign for Alba & Barolo. Left 2km before village, 50m on right sign for house.

Raffaella Pittatore
via Crosia 46,
12060 Barolo

Tel	+39 0173 56206
Fax	+39 0173 56206
Email	gioco-delloca@piemonte.com
Web	www.gioco-delloca.it

Hotel Castello di Sinio

Sitting atop the tiny village of Sinio surrounded by rolling hillsides, hazelnut plantations and a multitude of vineyards, this 12th-century castello belonged to the noble Carretto family for some 600 years. On the village side, the stone façade appears impregnable, but move to the courtyard and a different mood prevails: lush green lawn, colourful flower beds, cascades of geraniums falling from windows boxes…a delicious little swimming pool has been tucked to one side of the castle. Americans Denise and Jay (Giacomo to the locals) have done a tremendous job of restoration, at the same time becoming ardent Piemontesi exponents of the region's wines, gastronomic delights and traditions. Denise is the chef, personally creating the memorable meals, while Jay holds court in the dining room. Good-sized bedrooms have terracotta floors, many with exposed stonework, beams and individual examples of beautiful vaulted stonework and fine Barocco furniture. Bathrooms are equipped with shower cabins and handy magnifying mirrors. Stunning. *Minimum stay two nights at weekends in October.*

Price	€150-€325.
Rooms	18 doubles.
Meals	Dinner, four courses, €45, by arrangement. Wine from €15.
Closed	8 January-February; 2 weeks mid-August.
Directions	From Alba direction Cuneo, Barolo & Gallo. At Gallo, direction Grinzane Cavour; immediately left for Sinio, 7km. Signed.

Denise Pardini
vicolo del Castello, No.1,
12050 Sinio

Tel	+39 0173 263889
Fax	+39 0173 263958
Email	reservations@hotelcastellodisinio.com
Web	www.hotelcastellodisinio.com

Cascina Adami

An exquisite panorama unfurls before you, and there's a hillside for children to run wild on. (An Australian family came to stay one Christmas and discovered snow.) Now Flavia and Paolo – he a professional house restorer – live in Torino and the keyholder is a Dutch lady who speaks three languages and lives up the lane. Inside the long, lovely, L-shaped building are stone and brick floors, exposed stone walls, niches, beams and a stunning modern-rustic décor. 'Casa Rossa' and 'Casa Blu' are delightful spaces for small families; both have the bedroom, with small balcony, upstairs and the single sofabed below. 'Casa Arcobaleno' (rainbow house) is furnished with a brilliantly eclectic mix of modern and antique – bright stripes and crocks in the kitchen, a ceiling fan to match – yet the overall mood is classy and restful. Casa Bianca has a more sophisticated feel; be inspired by sweeping white walls, chunky stone arches and modern art, plump off-white sofas around an open fire, a long table set with cream china, a stone stair, an antique cupboard, a ladder to the mezzanine twin. Superb! *Min. stay two nights. Pool for 2008.*

Price	€600 per week. Heating extra.
Rooms	4 apartments: 2 for 2-3, 1 for 4-6, 1 for 7-9.
Meals	Dinner €40, by arrangement. Wine €12. Restaurants in Murazzano, 1.5km.
Closed	10 January-15 March.
Directions	A6 from Turin exit Carrù; right, dir. Clavesana, then Murazzano; right, 1.5km before village; on for 600m.

Paolo & Flavia Adami
fraz. Mellea 53,
12060 Murazzano

Tel	+39 0118 178135
Fax	+39 0118 178135
Email	flavia.adami@yahoo.it
Web	www.cascinaadami.it

Cascina Adami - Il Nido

A short drive down a country lane, the 17th-century farmhouse is set into its hill with superb views over gentle hills patchworked with wheat fields and vineyards – leading the eye to snowy peaks beyond. This is the best wine-producing area of Italy, and opposite the lane is a dairy where you can stock up on the sheep's cheese – soft, mild, delicious – Murazzano. Discreetly distant from the main house, down a steep unpaved track – watch your wheels! – is a four-square, two-storey stone structure, once a goats' shed. Il Nido (the nest) is a delicious bolthole for two. Owner Paolo is a master at putting salvaged finds to unusual use so expect pale new stone floors and chunky old rafters, a delicate wooden fretwork door, a stylish steel table and chairs, a charming kitchen tucked under a chunky white stone stair, a bedroom with a big cream bed and small blue shutters, driftwood and pebbles prettifying quiet corners. Outside is smart wooden furniture from which to gaze on the views and a huge linen parasol. Contemporary rusticity, ancient peace. *Minimum stay two nights. Shared pool planned for 2008.*

Price	€550 per week. Heating extra.
Rooms	House for 2.
Meals	Dinner €40, by arrangement. Wine €12. Restaurants in Murazzano, 1.5km.
Closed	Never.
Directions	A1 exit Fabro, dir. Abro. On to Allerona Scalo. Keep right for 5km until turning on left.

Paolo & Flavia Adami
fraz. Mellea 53,
12060 Murazzano

Tel	+39 0118 178135
Fax	+39 0118 178135
Email	flavia.adami@yahoo.it
Web	www.cascinaadami.it

Lombardy • Trentino–Alto Adige

Photo: istock.com

Polidora

From the botanical garden on the shores of Lake Maggiore, where islands hover on the glistening water and the Alps stand protectively in the distance, you will feel at total peace with the world. The changing light mischievously catches rare species of plant, flower and tree in moods you would not think possible, in supernatural shades. What luck that GianLuca decided to convert the stables in the grounds of his elegant 1900s villa into a spacious and stylish B&B. Now the WWF-protected acres are yours to explore: with lonely benches, pebble beaches and shady patches inviting you to unwind, we defy you to read a book without being distracted by the beauty – or to not swim in the cool waters of the lake the moment you see their enticing ripples. While GianLuca is away, Barbara and Alan are on hand for breakfasts and conversation; following careers in gardening for the National Trust and running a heritage house, the care of Polidora and guests was too good an opportunity to miss. Lunch in the nearby village of Cerro or picnic in the grounds; the great thing is, you can stay here all day.

Price	€120–€240.
	Whole house €3,780 per week.
Rooms	3: 2 doubles, 1 suite for 4.
Meals	Restaurants 1-3km.
Closed	Rarely.
Directions	From Milan, A8 exit Sesto Caleride; follow the shores of Lake Maggiore, through Angera. Entrance is before Laveno Mombello.

GianLuca Sarto
via Pirinoli 4,
21014 Cerro di Laveno Mombello

Mobile	+39 348 5113600
Fax	+39 0247 719725
Email	info@polidora.com
Web	www.polidora.com

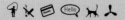

Villa Simplicitas & Solferino

The presiding genius behind this quaint, wonderful place is Ulla. Everything about her 19th-century villa is a reflection of her human approach; she is imaginative, unconventional, serene. Bedrooms, in the villa or annexe, are decorated with murals, soft browns and wrought-iron or brass beds; all draw in the grand old sweet-chestnut trees that survey the garden and seem to be a part of the rooms. There's a warm sense of fun glowing in every corner, whether from a dotty old lamp stand – not the prettiest – or from the antique piano and the billiard table that's as old as the house. The food (four courses, no choice), served with understated elegance in the handsome conservatory or on the candlelit terrace, is superb. Here, at the end of the long rugged track, is an abiding impression of deep tranquillity; it's worth sacrificing a couple of days of sun-baking on the lake shores to stay. Strike out from the door on wonderful walks, reach Como in 15 minutes by car. The lakes, with the mountains, are irresistible – and due to the high altitude, you never get too hot at night.

Price	€94–€140.
Rooms	10 doubles.
Meals	Half-board €60–€90 p.p. Full-board €70–€100 p.p.
Closed	Mid-October to April.
Directions	From Como, north for Argegno; left thro' San Fedele. After 1st bus station bear left; follow winding road for 2km. Invest in a good map!

Signora Ulla Wagner
22028 San Fedele d'Intelvi
Tel +39 0318 31132
Fax +39 0318 30455
Email info@villasimplicitas.it
Web www.villasimplicitas.it

Alberghetto La Marianna

On the banks of Lake Como, this family-run hotel is housed in a villa simply modernised and redecorated with a relaxing feel. Bedrooms are strictly functional, with cheery tiled shower rooms, most have lakeside views. Some have balconies, one has its own little terrace (but no lake view). A road runs between you and the busy lake, so if you're a light sleeper, it might be worth giving up those beautiful watery views for a room at the back, at least in summer. Paola is a delight and, in her own words, treats guests as friends. Breakfasts include homemade bread, cakes and jams; she's also a good cook and a "mistress of desserts" – try them out in the restaurant for dinner, run by husband Ty. You can eat inside and admire the ever-changing local art work lining the walls or outside where you can embrace the lake views on the terrace that juts onto the shimmering water. You won't be short of advice here on things to do: visits to gardens and villas, boat tours to Isola Comacina, day trips to St Moritz and the Engadine.

Price	€85-€95. Single €60-€65.
Rooms	8: 7 doubles, 1 single.
Meals	Dinner with wine, €40.
Closed	Mid-November to mid-March (open 26 December-6 January).
Directions	From Como direction Menaggui on west lakeside road to Cadenabbia 30km, 300m after ferry port.

Paola Cioccarelli
via Regina 57,
22011 Cadenabbia di Griante

Tel/Fax	+39 0344 43095
Mobile	+39 333 9812649
Email	inn@la-marianna.com
Web	www.la-marianna.com

Villetta Il Ghiro & Villetta La Vigna

Wisteria was growing *through* the old convent when Ann and her husband fell in love with it. The roof had fallen in too but, undeterred, they went ahead and turned it into the lovely place it is today. Though you can't see the lake from here, you do get a glimpse of the championship golf course Ann's father-in-law once part-owned – the second oldest in Italy. The apartments are old-fashioned, comfortable, homely and quiet, with large, airy rooms and outside stairs. Il Ghiro is on the first floor of a former hay barn; La Vigna, above the garages, has a second bedroom opening off the first and a little balcony to catch the afternoon sun. Children are welcome but must be supervised in the immaculate lawned gardens because of the pool (which is fenced). There's tennis too. Birdsong is all you hear, vistas all you see, yet you are a short drive from the tourist bustle of Menaggio and Como. The position is wonderful, on the isthmus between Lakes Lugano and Como, on the edge of a cobbled village, encircled by mountains, meadows, hamlets and winding country lanes. *Minimum stay one week.*

Price	Apt for 2, €516-€1,032; Apt for 4-8, €1,032-€2,064. Prices per week.
Rooms	2 apartments: 1 for 2, 1 for 4-8.
Meals	Restaurants 5-minute walk.
Closed	October-April.
Directions	From Menaggio N340 for Porlezza to Grandola, towards Porlezza & Lugano. Right at bakery; immediately right for Cardano. Right into via al Forno.

Mrs Ann Dexter
via al Forno 5, Cardano,
22010 Grandola ed Uniti

Tel	+39 0344 32740
Fax	+39 0344 30206
Email	ann.dexter@libero.it

Entry 23 Map 2

Casa dell'Ava

The 19th-century 'Sublime' resides here: in dazzling peaks, fresh air, wild snowy caps and an ever shifting spectrum of colours. Only 25km from the northern shores of Lake Como, Casa dell'Ava clings to the side of a steep valley in the tiny untouched village of Pianazzola; leave your car at the top and descend the labyrinthine paths. The comforting smell of woodsmoke welcomes you to the door of your slate-roofed, fairytale cottage with its wood-pellet burner already stoked in the hall; Richard and Lucy, explorers of the great outdoors, have restored their second home with every comfort in mind. Return exhausted from the Alps – skiing perhaps, or trekking past ice falls and through spectacular gorges where golden eagles and ibex soar – to hot showers and beds with duvets as soft as clouds. Wake at the crack of dawn to ponder the purples of the craggy peaks from your balcony before the sun rises and shines directly into the sitting room on the first floor. Great for families: there are bunk beds for children, and they'll love the cave restaurants of Chiavenna as much as you do. *Min. stay one week high season. 5% of income donated to local national park.*

Price	£494–£790 per week.
Rooms	Cottage for 6.
Meals	Restaurants 4.5km.
Closed	Never.
Directions	SS36 Lecco-Chiavenna; through Chiavenna onto SS37 to Maloja; left to Pianazzola. Follow winding road up hill, through vineyards to end.

Richard & Lucy Pash
Pianazzola 167,
23022 Chiavenna

Tel	+44 (0)1672 870665
Email	info@casadellava.com
Web	www.casadellava.com

Albergo Olivedo

Laura's Liberty-style hotel, soft orange-hued with balconies and Art Nouveau lamps, has a jaunty, independent air. The little reception with burr maple counter and speckled floor could grace a French pension; a chessboard waits on the quaint little landing. There are polished parquet floors, grandmother's furniture, starched cotton on firm upright beds and, from many rooms, wonderful views over the lake. Excellent shower rooms are strictly modern. Just a few steps away is the family's latest acquisition, a classic, 19th-century villa, the Toretta, that overlooks the harbour. Here, frescoes, decorative iron staircase and lofty ceilings have been carefully restored, while traditional tiles, handsome beds and fine old furniture give the lakeside rooms a distinguished air. Stroll back to the Olivedo for meals – Laura's brother is the chef. Fresh, local food is served on the pavement outside or in the dining room overlooking the harbour and the breezy little Como ferry. The halcyon days of 'afternoon tea' may be gone, but the staff welcome is warm and timeless.

Price	€100–€145.
Rooms	14 doubles. Villa Torretta: 5 doubles.
Meals	Half-board €150–€190 for two.
Closed	2 November–20 December.
Directions	From the north, SP72 from Colico to Varenna.

Laura Colombo
Piazza Martiri 4,
23829 Varenna

Tel	+39 0341 830115
Fax	+39 0341 830115
Email	info@olivedo.it
Web	www.olivedo.it

Albergo Milano

Colourwashed houses cluster round the church on a little, rocky promontory. The lake laps gently on three sides; on the fourth, mountain slopes rear steeply upwards. Wander along a cobbled street, catching glimpses of the lake down every side alley, and you come to Albergo Milano, smack on the waterfront. It's pretty, traditional, disarmingly small, and Bettina and Egidio are engaging people, thrilled to be running their own little hotel. Everywhere is freshly and stylishly furnished, with dashes of colour to add warmth and some lovely country furniture, and each bedroom with a balcony or terrace and a lake view. The dining room's big new windows open onto a wonderful wide terrace where you eat out on fine days, the lake stirring beside you. The food is divine gourmet-Italian, the wine list heavenly. A step away, in the old part of town, is a charming suite with great views and an apartment with kitchenette and living room. Bettina is a mine of information about this area and there's a regular train service into Bergamo and Milan. A little gem. *Book garage parking in advance.*

Price	€125–€180. Apartment €115–€250.
Rooms	11 + 1: 8 doubles, 2 doubles, 1 triple. Apartment for 2-5.
Meals	Dinner €27. Wine from €16.
Closed	December–February.
Directions	From Lecco SS36 for Sondrio; 1st exit for Abbadia Lariana. After 15km, before tunnel, left for Varenna. Park in Piazza San Giorgio. 150m to hotel (map in piazza).

Bettina & Egidio Mallone
via XX Settembre 35,
23829 Varenna

Tel	+39 0341 830298
Fax	+39 0341 830061
Email	hotelmilano@varenna.net
Web	www.varenna.net

Castello di Vezio – Casa Pupa

The *castello* of Vezio, a must-see for visitors to the area and with 360° panorama of the lake, belongs to the Greppi family; everyone staying here has free and private access. So here you have it all: activities for the family, well-kept gardens and a pool with views over what is debatably Italy's most beautiful lake; and a slice of history to boot. The castle goes back to the Middle Ages and stands high above the shore, with a sheer drop down to lovely Varenna. Admire the owls and hawks who reside in the battlements; imagine barbaric invaders approaching from Como, or aggressors advancing from Lecco. When you've had your fill of history, return to Casa Pupa to rest and unwind. The Greppi family themselves lived in the house in the 1970s and photos of their sailing days line walls. There's a light-hearted boating theme throughout, even a rope to help you up the spiral stair. At the top: light-filled, slightly faded bedrooms. A great place to stay for a large party; the two simple *mansarde* (loft-apartments) have their own kitchens. *Minimum stay three nights.*

Price	€1,900-€5,100.
Rooms	Sleeps 7-15 (min. of 8 in high season).
Meals	Breakfast €15, by arrangement.
	Restaurant 100m.
Closed	Never.
Directions	Directions on booking.

	Maria Manuela Greppi
	via del Castellano 16,
	23828 Vezio di Perledo
Tel	+39 0258 190940
Fax	+39 0258 190932
Email	vezio@robilant.it
Web	www.agriturismocastellodivezio.it

Castello di Vezio - Casa Milena & Casa Giovanni

Spectacularly secluded from the other houses inside the entrance gates of Castello di Vezio (and 700 metres down a steep path) your two-up, two-down cottage crouches in a cliff yards from the craggy edge and then... there's the lake, inviting deep breaths and wide eyes every time you open the front door. Casa Milena is one of the most romantic places to stay in this guide and it would be impossible not to feel inspired here: your gaze falls on that dazzling lake from wherever you are: bed or kitchen sink. One of the bedrooms has a terrace for those who wish to share the experience – but you'll feel alone with those views. Back up the path and you can play a spot of tennis with the other guests staying in the castle grounds. There are also secret spots for those who like their privacy. Casa Giovanni is set in its own orchard below the castle; it, too, feels private and is suitable for a family of four. The grey granite of both these new buildings is softened inside by floral bed spreads and friendly, modern kitchens. The setting is a dream. *Minimum stay one week Oct-May. Over 8s welcome at Casa Milena.*

Price	€1,000-€1,400 per week.
Rooms	Both Casa Milena & Casa Giovanni sleep 4.
Meals	Breakfast €15, by arrangement. Restaurant 100m.
Closed	Rarely.
Directions	Directions on booking.

Maria Manuela Greppi
via del Castellano 16,
23828 Vezio di Perledo

Tel	+39 0258 190940
Fax	+39 0258 190932
Email	vezio@robilant.it
Web	www.agriturismocastellodivezio.it

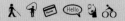

Castello di Vezio - Casa Cima & Casa Selva

With views stretching over Lake Como from your dining room, a balcony hugging the outside of the house and sun-trapped terraces at every turn, Casa Cima is a delightful family getaway high up in the historic hamlet of Vezio. Behind the entrance gates, the lake far below, is a small, friendly holiday village. Shared by just five places to stay are a tennis court and a huge games room with table football. And space! The children may play football or rounders on the lawn while you doze in the shade of one of numerous trees, or sunbathe in peace beside your very own pool (Casa Cima); you also have access to the 12th-century castle. If the party is a large one, you can rent its ground-floor companion, Casa Selva, too. Both apartments have 18th-century floral designs in pretty bedrooms and simple but functional bathrooms. There are eating areas inside and out, and heaps of storage. Shop in the delicatessens of Perledo, dine in the neighbouring restaurant, or motor down to beautiful Varenna below. A superb place for families. *Minimum stay three nights.*

Price	Cima €2,000-€2,800.
	Selva €800-€1,200.
	Whole house €2,800-€4,000.
	Prices per week.
Rooms	Cima sleeps 8. Selva sleeps 4.
	The apartments can be rented
	together (sleeps 12).
Meals	Breakfast €15, by arrangement.
	Restaurant 100m.
Closed	Never.
Directions	Directions on booking.

	Maria Manuela Greppi
	via del Castellano 41,
	23828 Vezio di Perledo
Tel	+39 0258 190940
Fax	+39 0258 190932
Email	vezio@robilant.it
Web	www.agriturismocastellodivezio.it

Il Torchio

Marcella's happy personality fills the house with good cheer. She and Franco are artists – she an animator, he a painter; if you like the bohemian life you will like it here. Franco also has an antiquarian bookshop in Milan, which explains all the shelves in the sitting room. Their home began life in 1600 as the stables of the noble Calchi family; you enter through a fine stone archway into a courtyard. Franco's bold paintings adorn the walls and every corner is crammed with curios that Marcella has picked up on her flea market forays. Bedrooms are endearingly old-fashioned – no frills but good, comfortable beds. The big, private suite, entered via French windows, has green views down to Calco, a great big bed, family photos on the walls, and a cabinet filled with children's old toys. The bathrooms are basic but have lovely hand-painted tiles. The whole family is a delight – including the cats – and Marcella's cooking is superb. Active types can canoe in summer and ski in winter (just a one-hour drive); or visit Verona, Lake Como and the stunning shops of Milan.

Price	€50.
Rooms	3: 1 suite with bath; 2 doubles sharing bath.
Meals	Dinner €15, by arrangement.
Closed	Rarely.
Directions	From Calco right at r'bout after garage for Corso Italia. Right via Ghislanzoni. At top; 100m, 2nd left (signed Vescogna). On right.

Signora Marcella Pisacane
loc. Vescogna 24,
23885 Calco

Tel	+39 0399 274294
Mobile	+39 339 5426841
Fax	+39 0395 08724
Email	il_torchio@hotmail.com

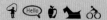

Agriturismo Casa Clelia

The hotel has been sculpted out of the 11th-century convent, using the principles of eco-bio architecture. Cows peer from sheds as you arrive, chickens, geese and sheep bustle – this is a working farm. The main house stands proud against wooded hills and beyond are convent, outhouses, orchards and barns. Rosanna is a dear and looks after you as well as she looks after her large family. She is a talented cook and has taught a fantastic team of local cooks everything she knows; one of her treats is her taster menu, your chance to sample – guilt-free – several delicacies all at once. The bedrooms, a good size, are stunning and warmly original, all wood, stone and bold colours; bathrooms are modern, lighting subtle. Heat comes from a wood-burner integrated with solar panels; cork and coconut ensure the sound-proofing of walls. Children will be welcome, free to run wild in the gardens, orchards and eight hectares of woods. Hard to imagine a more wonderful place for families... or for a get-away-from-it-all weekend. There's horse riding nearby, too, and Bergamo, mid-way between Lake Como and Lake Iseo, is a cultural treat.

Price	€95–€125.
Rooms	10: 6 doubles, 2 triples, 2 doubles/quadruples.
Meals	Lunch & dinner, with wine, €20–€35. Restaurant closed Monday.
Closed	Never.
Directions	From A4 exit Capriate. Signed.

Rosanna Minonzio
via Corna 1/3, 24039
Sotto il Monte Giovanni XXIII

Tel	+39 0357 99133
Fax	+39 0357 91788
Email	info@casaclelia.com
Web	www.casaclelia.com

Entry 31 Map 2

Agriturismo Cervano B & B

Surrounded by wild orchids and violets at the highest point of the garden, the sun splashing colour across the sky as it sets over majestic Lake Garda, you could be fooled into believing you were a 19th-century wine merchant returning from Milan for the harvest of your country estate. What a pleasant surprise you would have on entering your house if that were true. Anna and her husband Gino have mastered the restoration of Gino's once-crumbling family home, a fine example of Lombard 'fort' design, and the interior is stylish and contemporary: bathrooms are slick Italian, new beds are dressed in handmade linen, there's a marble breakfast bar in the luminous kitchen and a huge American-style fridge packed with breakfast goodies. Despite the modernity, Anna and Gino have constantly kept the 1800s in mind: exposed beams have been perfectly restored, floors imitate the original style and the marble is Verona's most rare: speckled pink and red. Wine is still produced on site but now it's organic, and solar panels heat water. A superb restoration in a beautiful and peaceful setting.

Price	€110-€150. Whole house €300 per night.
Rooms	3: 1 double, 1 double & sofabed, 1 triple.
Meals	Restaurant 1km.
Closed	Never.
Directions	From Gargnano, right towards golf club. Signed.

Anna Massarani
via Cervano 14,
25088 Toscolano Maderno

Tel +39 0365 548398
Email info@cervano.com
Web www.cervano.com

Tara Verde

Roberta's chosen name for her B&B is well deserved. In Tibetan Buddhism 'Green Tara' is the female buddha of enlightened activity, representing refuge and protection. As for the experience itself: it is vibrant, memorable, modern, artistic and there is nothing else quite like it in Milan. Only 20 minutes from the centre, Tara Verde is hidden down an elegant and surprisingly quiet street in an early 20th-century house surrounded by its own garden (great for breakfast in the summer). Inside, Roberta has combined Eastern exoticism with the characteristics of Green Tara in a rich décor where swooping silk curtains, ceramic tiles and dancing mosaic patterns, large, comfortable beds and deep-glowing intricate lamps express the warmth, compassion and energy of the tantric deity. Fantastic colours: crimson reds, verdant greens, royal purples are infinite and all consuming — even the doors are honeyed gold. Help yourself to coffee in the morning, browse through Roberta's fascinating collection of books on the orient and western literature. A wonderful way to enhance your experience of Milan.

Price	€160–€180.
Rooms	3: 2 doubles, 1 twin.
Meals	Restaurants 100m.
Closed	August & Christmas holidays.
Directions	From Corso Vercelli & Ammendola Fiera underground, a 5-minute walk.

Roberta Polverini
via Delleani 22,
20149 Milan
Tel   +39 0236 534959
Email   info@taraverde.it
Web   www.taraverde.it

Antica Locanda dei Mercanti

Entering the gloomy, cavernous courtyard, you wouldn't imagine the lightness and charm of this small, discreet boutique hotel on the second floor of an 18th-century building in the heart of Milan. Heavy glass doors slide open to a simple reception where chic Italians and visitors mingle; young staff whisk you off to rooms whose individuality and style promise country-house comfort rather than the spartan modernity associated with this energetic city. This is an enterprise run by real people with passion. From the smallest room with its elegant Milanese fabrics and wicker chair with cherry striped and piped cushions to the largest, airy room with its muslin-hung four-poster, terrace, olive tree and scented climbers, each space surprises. Fine linen, deep mattresses, dramatic murals, fresh posies, stacks of magazines, small, gleaming shower rooms – and, soon, ceiling fans giving way to air conditioning: each room bears the distinctive hallmark of Paola, the engaging and energetic owner. No communal space, so breakfast is delivered to your room. Chic simplicity, and La Scala a heart beat away.

Price	From €165.
	Double with terrace from €275.
Rooms	14: 10 doubles,
	4 doubles with terrace.
Meals	Breakfast €15. Restaurants nearby.
Closed	Rarely.
Directions	Via S. Tomaso is a small street off via Dante, halfway between the Duomo and Piazza Castello. No sign, just a brass plate.

	Bruce Scott
	via San Tomaso 6,
	20121 Milan
Tel	+39 0280 54080
Fax	+39 0280 54090
Email	locanda@locanda.it
Web	www.locanda.it

Hotel

Lombardy

Hotel du Lac

The hotel oozes old-fashioned charm. A 1900s townhouse, it shares the same street as the villa from which D H Lawrence eulogised about the "milky lake" of Garda. The ox-blood façade with white relief and green shutters is as striking as the view from the patio that overhangs the water; you can swim from here. Valerio's grandparents owned a piano shop in Milan and lived in the house until 1959; much of their furniture remains. The family could not be more helpful. Roomy bedrooms are wonderfully old-fashioned with big beds and wardrobes, thirties' lights and polished terrazzo floors; beds are deeply comfortable and dressed in crisp cotton. Six rooms look onto the lake and have small balconies or terraces. The dining room, around a central courtyard with a palm that disappears into the clouds, looks directly onto the water. You can also dine upstairs on the open terrace, where metal tables and chairs are shaded by an arbour of kiwi – a magical spot at night, the water lapping below, the lights twinkling in the distance. There's even a small music room with a piano to play – guests sometimes do.

Price	€90–€126.
Rooms	12 doubles.
Meals	Restaurant à la carte, from €30. Wine from €12.
Closed	First week of November; one week before Easter. Out of season call +39 0365 71269.
Directions	From Brescia to Salò, continue to Riva del Garda. After Bogliaco, 400m on right.

Valerio Arosio
via Colletta 21, 25084 Villa di Gargnano

Tel	+39 0365 71107
Fax	+39 0365 71055
Email	info@hotel-dulac.it
Web	www.hotel-dulac.it

Entry 35 Map 3

Hotel Gardenia al Lago

Jasmine-scented gardens and green lawns reach to Lake Garda's edge; an immaculate terrace makes the most of the views. The hotel stands, a feast of colour and design, against the steep, wooded foothills of Mount Baldo. It was bought by the Arosio family as a summer home in 1925. They were piano-makers from Lodi – note the original piano in the music room – and in the 1950s turned the house into a guesthouse. Today it is a small, restful, civilised hotel. The bedrooms have been renovated – some frescoes being uncovered in the process – and are beautiful, with distinctive Empire antiques, exquisite floor tiles and muslin billowing at French windows. Many have balconies or terraces; bathrooms are Edwardian-style and superior. The dining room has a more Sixties flavour and in summer you eat under the trees, by candlelight. The entire family – parents and sons – are delightful, and many guests return. Lemon and olive trees surround you – they produce wonderful olive oil – and a grassed garden hugs the lakeside. Take a dip off the small beach further along: the water is said to be the purest in Italy.

Price	€74–€210. Singles €104–€294.
Rooms	25 doubles.
Meals	Restaurant à la carte, from €30. Wine from €12.
Closed	First week of November; one week before Easter. Out of season call +39 0365 71269
Directions	From Brescia-Salò towards Riva del Garda. After Bogliaco, 400m slip road on right to via Colletta. Parking at hotel.

	Giorgio & Andrea Arosio
	via Colletta 53,
	25084 Villa di Gargnano
Tel	+39 0365 71195
Fax	+39 0365 72594
Email	info@hotel-gardenia.it
Web	www.hotel-gardenia.it

Dimora Bolsone

Film-like, the lake glitters between the cypress trees – an expanse of blue far below. Enjoy it as Catia, Raffaele and Rocky the spaniel settle you on the terrace with an elderflower cordial. Catia is slight and thoughtful; Raffaele is an importer of Amazonian fish, economist, lecturer, sailor, antique collector, big game hunter and green aficionado – and relishes showing you around the 46 acres of remarkable terraced garden. The 15th-century house reposes gracefully among its stone steps, flower-covered loggias and lemon trees; step inside to a cool, ordered calm. Big, dark, immaculate bedrooms have light polished wooden floors, soft washed walls and delicious linen. All are different – gilt cornices and flirty, feminine rococo in one, sober masculinity and a high 15th-century bed in another. Start the day feasting on almond cookies, *torte*, local cheeses, cold meats and… homemade ice cream. Later retire to a sitting room/library with green leather armchairs and vast stone fireplace. An essay in perfection and a feast for the senses: the creation of exceptional owners. *Children over 12 welcome. Minimum stay two nights.*

Price	€200. Singles €170.
Rooms	5 doubles.
Meals	Restaurants nearby.
Closed	30 November-28 February.
Directions	A4 exit Desenzano del Garda or Brescia Est. Take 45 Bis for Gardone Riviera. Left at Il Vittoriale, signed San Michaele; 2km, on left.

Raffaele & Catia Bonaspetti
via Panoramica 23,
25083 Gardone Riviera

Tel	+39 0365 21022
Fax	+39 0365 293042
Email	info@dimorabolsone.it
Web	www.dimorabolsone.it

Villa San Pietro Bed & Breakfast

A splendid 17th-century home. Annamaria, warm, vivacious, multi-lingual, is married to Jacques, French and charming; they have a young son, and Anna's mother lives in self-contained splendour at the far end. It's a rather grand name for a house that is one of a terrace, but once inside you realise why we have included it here. This is an immaculate home and no expense has been spared. There are oak beams, ancient brick floors, fine family antiques, floral fabrics, not a speck of dust. Guests have their own sitting room with a frescoed ceiling, the bedrooms are delightful and, to the excitement of Annamaria and Jacques, frescoes were discovered in the newly restored Sala di Pranzo. Another exceptional thing about the house is the large garden and terrace. There is also a pretty ground-floor loggia for memorable meals – Annamaria's dinners are sophisticated regional affairs, we are told. You are close to the town centre yet in a quiet road, and Montichiari is perfectly sited for forays into Garda, Brescia, Verona and Venice.

Price	€100–€110.
Rooms	5 doubles.
Meals	Dinner with wine, 4 courses, €30.
Closed	Rarely.
Directions	From Milan motorway A4 exit Brescia east towards Montichiari, city centre & Duomo. Via S. Pietro leads off corner of central piazza.

Jacques & Annamaria Ducroz
via San Pietro 25,
25018 Montichiari
Tel +39 0309 61232
Fax +39 0309 981098
Email villasanpietro@hotmail.com
Web www.abedandbreakfastinitaly.com

Tenuta Le Sorgive - Le Volpi Agriturismo

One cannot deny the beauty of Lake Garda, but it's a relief to escape to the unpopulated land of Lombardy. This 19th-century *cascina* has been in the Serenelli family for two generations. The exterior, crowned with pierced dovecote and flanked by a carriage house and stables, remains impressive, even if some character has been lost during restoration. Vittorio is justly proud of his 28-hectare farm: everything is organic, solar panels provide electricity, wood-chip burner the heating. Big guest rooms, with wooden rafters, are a mix of old and new. Some have attractive, metalwork beds, some a balcony, two have a mezzanine with beds for the children, all are crisp and clean. This is a great place for families to visit as there's so much to do: horse riding and mountain biking from the farm, go-karting and archery nearby, watersports, including scuba diving courses, at Garda. There are also a large gym and a well-maintained pool. Vittorio's sister, Anna, runs Le Volpi, the *cascina* only a stroll away where you can sample gnocchi, Mantovan sausages and mouthwatering fruit tarts. *Min. stay three days in high season; apartment one week.*

Price	€85–€105.
	Apartments €550–€900 per week.
Rooms	8 + 2: 8 twins/doubles.
	2 apartments for 4.
Meals	Breakfast €5 for self-caterers.
	Dinner with wine €15–€28.
	Restaurant closed January & Mon-Tues.
Closed	Never.
Directions	Exit A4 Milano-Venezia at Desenzano for Castiglione delle Stiviere; left at traffic lights ; left after 20m to Solferino. At x-roads turn left. Signed.

	Signor Vittorio Serenelli
	via Piridello 6,
	46040 Solferino
Tel	+39 0376 854252
Fax	+39 0376 855256
Email	info@lesorgive.it
Web	www.lesorgive.it

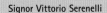

Trebisonda Country Resort

Enrico and Valeria have exchanged the rat race for the country amid olive and peach groves and three hectares of prairie. They are full of enthusiasm for this place and keen to share its beauty. The farmhouse, which dates back to the 15th century, has been renovated and decorated with understated good taste. Apartments on the first-floor of the stables (horses sometimes stabled below) are accessible directly from the garden. Big and light, they have white walls and the original tiled floors. Fabrics and towels are cream and white, the furniture a mix of antique, contemporary Conran and flea-market finds. Shower rooms are gorgeous, old railway sleepers set against white walls make for a perfect ascent to beds upstairs, kitchens are simple but well-equipped. Enrico and Valeria breed horses, and will take you to meet the foals. Breakfast is an array of organic honeys and homemade jams, served in the main house. Cycle along the Mincio river, visit Lake Garda, Mantova or Venice, play golf... or stay here and glory in the views.

Price	€80 for 2. €100 for 3. €130 for 4.
Rooms	2 apartments for 2-4; 1 for 4.
Meals	Restaurants 1-3km.
Closed	Never.
Directions	From autostrada Milano-Venezia exit Peschiera del Garda & Valeggio. Cross old bridge in Borghetto, direction Solferino. Signed, after 3km.

	Signora Valeria Moretti
	via Tononi 100, loc. Trebisonda, 46040 Monzambano
Tel	+39 0376 809381
Fax	+39 0376 809381
Email	info@trebisonda.com
Web	www.trebisonda.com

Entry 40 Map 3

B&B Antica Locanda Matilda

Home of the Gonzaga family, patrons of art and architecture during the Renaissance, Mantua is one of Italy's finest cities. Surrounded on three sides by lakes, brimming with *palazzi* that sing with intricate frescoes depicting stories from the colourful past of the Gonzagas, Mantua will elate you. The skyline of the city, with its curvaceous churches and tall narrow spires, has an oriental air, especially at night when lights reflect the exotic shapes onto the surrounding lakes. When you stay with Cristina's family (and their two gorgeous romping dogs), you'll catch that skyline every time you venture out. Cristina's B&B lies just outside the old city walls near the main road and here you experience contemporary Italian life. Lovely, bubbly Cristina has great taste. Her breakfast conservatory, overlooking the garden's infinity pool – a godsend in high summer – is stylish and cool; bedrooms are more traditional, and spacious; bathrooms are functional. Cristina is Mantuan born and bred so follow her advice on where to eat: the local cuisine is a delight.

Price	€80-€90.
Rooms	3: 1 double; 2 doubles sharing bath.
Meals	Restaurant 700m.
Closed	Never.
Directions	Modena-Brennero exit Mantova Nord; over r'bout thro' industrial area; after 500m (immed. after underpass), right; on to Ostiglia. At r'bout, straight on, over flyover; signed Castelletto Borgo, keep left; on left after 200m.

Cristina Parma
via F. Rismondo 2,
46100 Mantua
Mobile   +39 335 6390624
Fax   +39 3763 02418
Email   info@locandamatilda.it
Web   www.locandamatilda.it

Bio-hotel Hermitage

It's not often that a bio-hotel comes with such a splash of luxury. Built a century ago, the old Hermitage has been entirely refashioned – with a modern 'eco' eye and a flourish of decorative turret. A wooden floor spans the reception area; behind is a vast and comfortable living room. A Tyrolean-tiled wood-burner dominates the centre; windows open onto a balcony with the best views in the Alps. You eat at red-clothed tables on Trentino dishes and homemade pasta in the *stübe*, with its lovely panelled ceiling of old, recycled wood. The main restaurant is larger but as beautiful. Bedrooms are serene, some are under the eaves, most have a balcony and the suites are huge. Wooden floors are softened by Persian rugs or pale carpets from Argentina, curtains and bedspreads are prettily checked. There's a superb wellness centre and an indoor pool with a ceiling that sparkles. Bars and chic boutiques are a ten-minute walk, and the hotel has its own bus that shuttles you to the slopes. Santa tips up at Christmas distributing presents for the children from a little cabin at the end of the garden.

Price	Half-board €140-€340 p.p.
Rooms	25: 18 twins/doubles, 7 suites for 3-4.
Meals	Half-board only. Wine from €18.
Closed	May; October-November.
Directions	Exit A22 St Mich & Mezz for Madonna di Campiglio for 75km; At Madonna di Campiglio, bypass through mountain; take next exit. Hotel signed on left.

Barbara Maffei
via Castelletto Inferiore 63,
38084 Madonna di Campiglio

Tel	+39 0465 441558
Fax	+39 0465 441618
Email	info@biohotelhermitage.it
Web	www.biohotelhermitage.it

Schwarz Adler Turm Hotel

All around are the soaring, craggy Dolomites – nothing like them to give a sobering perspective on man's place in nature's scheme. If you do feel overawed, you'll be soothed on arrival – Manfred, Sonja and their staff are so delighted to see you, so eager to do all they can to please. Though the hotel is young, it is a faithful reproduction of a 16th-century manor house and blends in well with the village. The roomy, light bedrooms are carpeted and hotel-comfortable, with glorious alpine views; each has a loggia, a balcony or direct access to the garden. The pretty village of Cortaccia (known as 'Kurtasch' by the locals) stands at 300 metres and looks down over a wide valley floor studded with orchards. This was Austria (the area turned Italian in 1919) and the hotel's cuisine, served in the beautifully restored family restaurant opposite, reflects this – a tour de force of Italian and South Tyrolen dishes. A fascinating example of German Renaissance architecture, the restaurant has a well-stocked bar: the perfect place to gather after a day of walking and a visit to the hotel's sauna and steam room.

Price	€130–€175.
Rooms	24 doubles.
Meals	Half-board €72–€95 p.p. Dinner, three courses, €25–€40. Wine from €15.
Closed	22-27 December; 2 weeks in February.
Directions	From A22 exit Egna/Ora. On for 8km for Termeno; left for Cortaccia; immediately after church on left.

Famiglia Pomella
Kirchgasse 2,
39040 Kurtatsch/Cortaccia
Tel   +39 0471 880600
Fax   +39 0471 880601
Email   info@turmhotel.it
Web   www.turmhotel.it

Entry 43 Map 3

Hotel Berghofer

At the end of the meandering track: birdsong and fir trees, cowbells and meadows, the scent of larch and pine. The tranquillity continues: there are shelves of books and magazines beside the fire, light modern furniture, an abundance of flowers, a cuckoo clock to tick away the hours. Bedrooms, named after the peaks you can see from large windows, have glazed doors leading to a private balcony each, and breathtaking Dolomites views. Rugs are scattered, pale pine floors and light walls are offset with painted wardrobes and stencilled borders. Some rooms have an extra store room, a few can be linked – ideal for a family; all have a separate seating area and a large bathroom. Dine in the charming 1450 *stübe*, purchased from a local farmer and painstakingly moved, timber by timber, up the hill. The restaurant displays a wonderful 18th-century stove; the food is regional and stylish. Ski in winter, hike among the alpine flowers in summer, return to a massage or hay-sauna, catch the sun set over the mountain.

Price	Half-board €190–€238 for 2.
Rooms	13: 12 suites for 2, 1 chalet for 4.
Meals	Half-board only. Wine from €20.
Closed	Certain weeks in February & November.
Directions	A22 exit Neumarkt/Auer; SS48 to Kaltenbrunn; 200m after garage, left for Radein; on to Oberradein; signed.

	Zeno Bampi
	Oberradein 54, 39040 Radein
Tel	+39 0471 887150
Fax	+39 0471 887069
Email	info@berghofer.it
Web	www.berghofer.it

Hotel Cavallino d'Oro

The village is postcard Tyrolean, and Cavallino d'Oro (Little Gold Horse) has been welcoming travellers for 680 years. The market still runs every Friday in summer: farmers set up their stalls at the foot of the 18th-century bell tower (that still chimes through the night!). This was Austria not so very long ago: the local customs are still alive, and regular concerts take place at the inn over dinner. Bedrooms are mostly delightful, though a few have roof lights only. Others look onto the medieval square, the best have balconies with incredible views. There's a fascinating mix of antique country beds – some hand-decorated, some four-poster, some both. Many of the doors are painted, as are the beams in the green and peach sitting room; room 9 has the original ceiling. Dine in the sparkling dining room; breakfast in the rustic *stübe*, a wood-panelled room with geraniums at the window and check tablecloths. Susanna and Stefan are as friendly as they are efficient. Go swimming, walking and biking in summer, sleigh riding and skiing in winter, and you can take the free shuttle to the new cable car and Alpe di Siusi.

Price	€80. Singles €50. Suites €100. Half-board €55-€75 p.p.
Rooms	18: 5 doubles, 2 twins, 4 triples, 4 singles, 3 suites.
Meals	Lunch €12. Dinner €22. Wine from €14.
Closed	November.
Directions	A22 motorway, exit Bolzano Nord. Castelrotto signed at exit. Hotel in market square in town centre.

Susanna & Stefan Urthaler
Piazza Kraus 1, 39040 Castelrotto

Tel	+39 0471 706337
Fax	+39 0471 707172
Email	cavallino@cavallino.it
Web	www.cavallino.it

Relais & Châteaux Hotel Castel Fragsburg

Stay in May and you'll see and smell the glory of the wisteria that drapes itself the length of the loggia where meals are served. The Fragsburg, built as a shooting lodge for the local gentry, perches on the side of a wooded hill with a crystal-clear view across the valley – mountains and valley unfurl. Perhaps the most magnificent spot from which to enjoy the view is the pool. Sun yourself on the screened deck on a hot day, then wander the grounds, beautiful with sub-tropical trees, surrounded by vineyards. Big bedrooms and huge suites have been redecorated and the combination of rugs, wood and some antique painted headboards softens any newness. Beds are deeply inviting with piles of pillows; white bathrooms are stunning. And then there's the wellness centre, studded with treatments, purifying products, aromatic smells and white robes. The whole feel of the place is Tyrolean, from the staff costumes to the delicious teatime strüdel. The fairytale castles and scenery of this northern region are not to be missed, and the Ortner family ensure you get the most out of your stay. Truly delightful.

Price	€250-€400.
	Half-board €140-€250 p.p.
Rooms	20: 6 doubles, 14 suites.
Meals	Dinner à la carte, €40-€120.
Closed	15 November-25 March.
Directions	Exit A22 Bolzano Sud; Merano Sud. Right to Merano; 1.5km; right at Shell station to Scenna. 2.5km on, bridge on right, signed Labers; over and 5km on.

Signor Alexander Ortner
via Fragsburger Strasse 3,
39012 Merano
Tel   +39 0473 244071
Fax   +39 0473 244493
Email info@fragsburg.com
Web   www.fragsburg.com

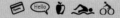

Veneto • Friuli-Venezia Giulia

Photo: istock.com

All'Eremo Relais Agriturismo

Far from the madding crowds, you are ensconced in an Italian family's solid, 1970s farmhouse overlooking Lake Garda. In true Italian style, Mamma and daughter are in the kitchen baking brioche for breakfast; Papa snoozes in the chair. The downstairs, open-plan room is the heart of the house, all chunky beams, wall paintings and agrarian artefacts. Authentically cluttered, somewhat chaotic, this is where you are welcomed by young, enthusiastic Elena, her parents and the family's cats. Bedrooms are a good size and clean, the slightly smaller one trumpeting the best view. Some are a touch 'retro' with green fabric wallpapers and the odd white plastic mirror; all have stripped floors, shutters and comfortable, crisp-cottoned beds. The parents sleep on the same level as the guests; Elena is above. One double is en suite, the others share a shower room. Take breakfast on the terrace, forget the plastic chairs and absorb the unfolding landscape that reaches from the vineyards to the hazy hills beyond. Slip off to the lake, dine on fabulous fish, sample the opera in Verona, come and go as you please.

Price	€70–€100.
Rooms	3: 1 double;
	2 twins/doubles sharing shower room.
Meals	Restaurants 1km.
Closed	November–March.
Directions	A22 exit Affi; lake road north to Garda for 3.5 km. In Albare, left at lights towards Bardolino; after 3km, 'Corteline'; 500m on right, take minor road Sem e Pigno until end; follow dirt track on left to house.

Elena Corsini Piffer
strada delle Rocca 2, loc. Casetta Rossa,
37011 Bardolino

Tel	+39 0457 211391
Fax	+39 0457 211391
Email	info@eremorelais.com
Web	www.eremorelais.com

La Foresteria Serego Alighieri

Bought by Dante's son in 1353, the estate has been in the family every since. It is vast and magnificent, a formal procession of cypresses sweeping you into a pocket of Italian history in the very heart of Valpolicella, where wine is the thing. Apartments are named after local grapes and the elegant wine shop is open six days a week with regular wine tastings to grasp the flavour of Verona's varied viticulture. The estate also produces olive oil, balsamic vinegar, grappa, honey and jam. The apartments, in a separate, carefully restored wing, are spacious and spotless with an elegant green, white and soft-yellow décor. 'Oseleta', for two, is on three floors of an old tower, its rooms linked by a narrow spiral stair. All have small kitchens, though it's hard to imagine guests here lugging plastic bags from the car to self-cater... nor is there anything so brash as a swimming pool. But breakfasts are generous and delicious, the gardens and orchards are dreamy and the all-pervading peace is a balm – even the staff, ever delightful, speak in soft voices. *Minimum stay four nights.*

Price	Apartment €127-€194 for 2. €183-€257 for 3. €205-€313 for 4.
Rooms	8 apartments: 4 for 2, 2 for 3, 2 for 4.
Meals	Breakfast included. Restaurants 3km.
Closed	January.
Directions	A22 exit Verona Nord for Valpolicella & Trento. At end left for S. Ambrogio for La Foresteria.

	via Stazione 2, 37015 Gargagnago di Valpolicella
Tel	+39 0457 703622
Fax	+39 0457 703523
Email	serego@seregoalighieri.it
Web	www.seregoalighieri.it

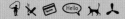

Cà del Rocolo

Such an undemanding, delightful place to be and such a warm, enthusiastic young family to be with. Maurizio ran a restaurant in Verona, Ilaria was a journalist and has three cookbooks to her name; they gave it all up for a country life for their children. Their 1800s farmhouse is on the side of a hill overlooking forested hills and the vast Lessinia National Park. Over a decade has passed since their move; Maurizio did much of the renovation himself and the result is authentic and attractive. Simple cotton rugs cover stripped bedroom floors, rough plaster walls are whitewashed, rooms are big and airy, with solid country furniture and excellent beds and bathrooms. There's also a shared kitchen. Breakfasts are at the long farmhouse table or out on the terrace, making the most of the views: delicious food, seasonal cakes, home-grown fruits, happy conversation. Dinner, mostly vegetarian, is an occasional affair. This is a seven-hectare, all-organic farm, with olives and fruit trees, hens, horses and beehives; there are nature trails galore, a saltwater pool in the offing, and always something going on.

Even in winter, when the fields are resting their agricultural heads, the place buzzes with activity, particularly in the workshops where the wood from the forests is transformed into handcrafted objects and furniture. Try to arrange your visit to tie in with one of their fairs. Here the loos are flushed with recycled rainwater, the floors heated by solar panels, and the furniture in your room and the cotton on your beds come from sustainable sources; you will sleep with a free conscience. There's also an exciting new building in the pipeline, with a grass roof to attract wildlife.

Price	€63–€70 (€390–€450 per week).
Rooms	3: 2 doubles, 1 family room. Shared kitchen.
Meals	Restaurant 4km.
Closed	Rarely.
Directions	Directions on booking.

Ilaria & Maurizio Corazza
via Gaspari 3, loc. Quinto, 37142 nr. Verona,

Tel	+39 0458 700879
Fax	+39 0458 700879
Email	info@cadelrocolo.com
Web	www.cadelrocolo.com

SPECIAL
GREEN ENTRY
see page 14

Map 3 Entry 49

La Rosa e Il Leone

Everything about La Rosa e Il Leone – from the ancient Roman columns in the flower-filled garden to the Juliet-style balcony of the marbled-floor master bedroom – breathes sentiment and romance. Named after Valeria's Milanese father and Veronese mother – the Rose of Lombardy, the Lion of the Veneto – the villa is an ode to their love both for each other and for the arts. The walls sing with framed musical scores and programmes from nights at La Scala, Milan and L'Arena, Verona, while adjoining first-floor sitting rooms celebrate the juxtaposition of the masculine (hard lines, dark colours, stacks of leather-bound books) and the feminine (curves, pastel colours, a passion for music and dance). The soft hand-woven sheets on antique-framed beds were part of Valeria's mother's dowry, the furniture part of her parent's lifetime collection. Stroll under leafy pergolas; listen to the history humming in the leaves of ancient cypresses; breakfast al fresco admiring an extraordinary replica of the Louvre's winged *Victory* of Samothrace. Like her house, Valeria is a gold-mine of high culture. A must for anyone visiting Verona.

Price	€135. Whole house €1,890 per week.
Rooms	3: 1 double; 2 doubles sharing bath.
Meals	Restaurants 1-4 km.
Closed	October-March.
Directions	From Verona dir. Vicenza to Caldiero; left for Illasi. Right after 2km, then right again, then left at end.

Valeria Poli
via Trieste 56,
37030 Colognola ai Colli

Tel	+39 0457 650123
Mobile	+39 320 9767337
Fax	+39 0457 650123
Email	vvpoli@libero.it

Agriturismo Tenuta La Pila

Raimonda and Alberto will soon have you chatting over a welcome drink in the kitchen; he speaks a clutch of languages, she's bubbly. Each B&B room is named after a fruit and smartly decorated: cream walls and exposed brick, crisp bed linen and starched towels, antique furniture to add a homely touch and sofabeds are large and comfortable. The apartments, on two floors of a separate building once used for drying tobacco, have immensely high beams and are decorated in a similar style. You get a table, chairs and sofabed in the large central living area, and neat corner kitchens. Cheerful bedrooms have flower prints and check bedspreads, and there's a large room for yoga retreats or seminars. Breakfast is a spread of home produce: kiwi jam, eggs, fruit, bread, yogurt. The farm is surrounded by fertile fields, trees and kiwi vines meandering across the plains, yet Verona, Venice, Lake Garda and Mantua are an easy drive. Then return to a peaceful patio-garden, a game of tennis, a dip in the pool, and skittles or boules beside the huge magnolia. *Minimum stay two nights.*

Price	€80. Apartments €882 per week.
Rooms	5 + 2: 5 rooms for 2-3.
	2 apartments for 4-6.
Meals	Breakfast €5 for self-caterers.
	Dinner €15. Wine €5-€10.
	Restaurants 2km.
Closed	Rarely.
Directions	From SS 434 Verona-Rovigo exit Carpi. Left at 'Stop', after 500m left onto Strada dell'Argine Vecchio della Valle & onto Via Gorgo da Bagno. After 1km along asphalt road left into farm.

Raimonda & Alberto Sartori
via Pila 42, loc. Spinimbecco, 37049
Villa Bartolomea

Tel	+39 0442 659289
Fax	+39 0442 658707
Email	post@tenutalapila.it
Web	www.tenutalapila.it

Il Castello

A narrow, winding road leads up to the *castello* at the foot of the Berici hills. Also known as the Villa Godi-Marinoni, the castle was built by Count Godi in the 15th century, on the ruins of an old feudal castle. Massive hewn walls enclose the compound of terraced vines, orchard, Italian garden and panoramic views stretching to Padua; you enter via an arched entrance, ancient cobbles beneath your feet. The villa itself is still lived in by the family: Signora Marinoni and her son, courteous and attentive, run this vast estate together. Guest apartments (one with its kitchen on the far side of the courtyard) are in an outbuilding with curious gothic details in the plastered façade; furnishings are a mix of dark antique and contemporary. Hidden below the castle walls is the garden with fish pond; in spring, hundreds of lemon trees are wheeled out to stand grandly on pedestals. The climate is mild and the hillside a mass of olive groves. Olive oil is produced on the ten-hectare estate – there's a wine cellar in the bowels of the castle, and a *cantina* where you can buy. *Minimum stay three nights.*

Price	€58.
Rooms	4 apartments for 2-4.
Meals	Restaurant 500m.
Closed	Never.
Directions	A4 exit Vicenza Est; at r'bout follow signs to Riviera Berica for 15km. In Ponte di Barbarano, at traffic lights right towards Barbarano. At main square, left to Villaga; villa 500m on left.

Signora Elda Marinoni
via Castello 6,
36021 Barbarano Vicentino

Tel	+39 0444 886055
Fax	+39 0444 777140
Email	info@castellomarinoni.it
Web	www.castellomarinoni.it

B&B Casa Ciriani

Set back from the road, the gated villa looks cool and inviting: shaded by trees, shuttered against the sun. Mariantonietta and her husband built it in 1974; now she and daughter Silvana live here and run the B&B. The entrance hall of this peaceful family home has a traditional mosaic floor that sweeps into the drawing room – designed (and partly laid!) by Mariantonietta. Upstairs, a family room with some wonderful antique pieces and paintings by nieces and nephews. In the twin, a beautiful old yellow chest catches the eye, and the private suntrap terrace. The double room is more informal and countrified, with a wicker-framed bed and a busy bookshelf. Brush up your Italian with Silvana at breakfast on the cool portico in summer, delightful with wrought-iron furniture, earthenware jars and garden views. The owners are passionate gardeners so a stroll after breakfast is rewarding. Enjoy wine tours in the lush Euganean hills, hop on a bus for Venice from town, book up the opera at Verona. Mariantonietta has also arranged special prices for guests at the exquisite thermal spa nearby. *Minimum stay two nights.*

Price	€65-€80. Singles €40-€50.
Rooms	3: 2 doubles, 1 family room.
Meals	Restaurants 2km.
Closed	Christmas & New Year.
Directions	Firenze-Venezia, exit Padova Sud after toll for Padova; 1st lights, main road left for Rovigo; 3km; 2nd lights, right for Abano; 1km; 3rd lights, right via S.Maria d'Abano; 700m, left into via Guazzi; 200m.

	Silvana & Mariantonietta Ciriani
	via Guazzi 1,
	35031 Abano Terme
Tel	+39 0497 15272
Email	bb.casaciriani@libero.it
Web	www.casaciriani.com

Villa Mandriola

A charming surprise when, after the modern village of Albinasego, the unassuming gates swing open to via San Caboto, a leafy statue-lined avenue, a peaceful pocket of 18th-century Italy. Villa Mandriola is the country home of one of the oldest families in Italy: the San Bonifacios, Earls of Padova. Thick ancient walls surround the charming park garden preserving the remarkable calmness that the San Bonifacio family would have enjoyed in the 1700s. From the vaulted vestibule of the approach to the chapel and frescoed ballroom, the landing and halls patrolled by family portraits, the panelled bedrooms with their faded bathrooms, the villa is steeped in history yet still provides comfort and relaxation. Feast on the half-board option and be treated as nobility would, retreating from town for respite. A large group may take on the whole house, a smaller group may choose between the two-floored apartment at the villa gates or the beautiful cottage overlooking the swan-sprinkled lake. Padua is the shortest of drives. *Minimum stay three nights.*

Price	€60–€150. Apt €450–€900. Cottage €600–€1,200. Whole villa €2,400–€4,000. All self-catering prices per week.
Rooms	7 + 2: 1 double, 2 twins, 2 suites for 2, 2 singles. Apartment for 3. Cottage for 2. Whole villa available (sleeps 12).
Meals	Breakfast from €10. Dinner €20. Half-board extra €30 p.p. Wine from €8.
Closed	Never.
Directions	Directions on booking.

Nicolò San Bonifacio
via S. Caboto, 10,
35020 Albignasego

Tel	+39 0496 81246
Fax	+39 4988 29616
Email	info@villamandriola.com
Web	www.villamandriola.com

Villa Selvatico Agriturismo

Live like a Venetian noble, gazing over your parkland with distant views of spires, tree-lined avenues and the vineyards of the Veneto plains. This 15th-century patrician's summer villa has been in the Da Porto family for generations. The Da Portos are kind and gracious and offer three apartments in the main house, separate from the family. (Ask to be shown round their bit: wonderful paintings, wonderful history.) Rooms are airy and traditionally furnished – often family antiques – with tiled or stripped wood floors. Portraits of the Da Portos add a personal touch. The largest, 'Le Magnolie', includes a grand Venetian carved bed and elegant sitting room scattered with Persian rugs. 'Il Fogher' has dark beamed ceilings and country style furniture while 'Il Portico', accessed from the garden, is full of light. 'La Serra', the summer house by the river, has glorious views and an outside eating area. Apart from Le Magnolie's kitchen, cooking areas are tucked into living rooms. Help yourself to fruit and vegetables from the garden. There are shady garden spots, walks along the river and, of course, Padua. *Minimum stay two nights; one week in high season.*

Price	Apts €70-€80 for 2. €90-€170 for 4. €140-€210 for 6. €180-€240 for 8.
Rooms	4 apartments: 2 for 2-4, 1 for 4-6, 1 for 4-8.
Meals	Restaurants 1-8km.
Closed	Never.
Directions	A4 exit Padova Est. After lights into SR308 to Castelfranco Veneto; 4th exit, Reschigliano; left at r'bout to Sant'Andrea; right at T-junc.; 200m after church right into via Selvatico; 2nd gate at end on right.

Antonio & Vittoriana Da Porto
via Selvatico 1,
35010 Codiverno di Vigonza

Tel	+39 0496 46092
Fax	+39 0496 46092
Email	villaselvatico@tiscali.it
Web	www.villaselvatico.com

Entry 55 Map 4

Gargan L'Agriturismo

Such a surprise: behind the austere façade lies a sophisticated interior and some very good food. Elegant rooms, delightful antiques, pale-painted beams, tables laid with linen and silver… such are the rewards for those who cross the uneventful landscape of the Veneto to get here. Bedrooms are old-fashioned and pretty, with iron bedheads and cotton quilts, mellow brick floors and Persian rugs, fine pieces of family furniture (Grandma was from Tuscany, Grandfather from Veneto) and armchairs to sink into. The several rooms on the ground floor given over to dining, one with a fine old chimney-piece, indicate the importance attached to food. Tables are immaculate and the food well-presented; it is gentle Signora's passion, and she is aided by a team of chefs. Children will enjoy the park-like gardens and resident donkey and dogs. Venice, Padua, Vicenza and Treviso are an easy drive so this would be a good base for those planning to explore, then retreat to the countryside and the agriturismo's delights.

Price	€65. Suite €85.
Rooms	6: 4 doubles, 2 suites.
Meals	Lunch or dinner €20, by arrangement. Wine from €8.
Closed	January; 15-31 August.
Directions	A4 exit Padova Est, SS515 for Treviso. After Noale & level crossing for Badoere, Montebelluna. After S. Ambrogio left at lights. In Levada di Piombino, right at church; farm 100m.

Signor Alessandro Calzavara
via Marco Polo 2,
35017 Levada di Piombino Dese

Tel	+39 0499 350308
Fax	+39 0499 350016
Email	gargan@gargan.it
Web	www.gargan.it

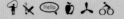

Ca' Marcello

Venice owes her history of great Renaissance naval battles partly to the long line of military Captains in the Marcello family: many lead the fleet to victory, thus securing Venice her wealth and beauty. Ca'Marcello, a magnificent Palladian-style villa set in a perfectly manicured and historic garden, represents the Marcello legacy. Stroll around the peaceful, statue-lined park; take a private tour of the main house and its fresco-filled ballroom; peer in awe at the ancestral portraits of the Marcellos. Despite its history and significance Ca'Marcello is still the family home – and behind the formal façade the atmosphere is wonderfully relaxed. Kind, softly spoken Jacopo grew up here and will ensure a luxurious stay: you have the whole west wing at your disposal. Expect beeswax-polished wooden stairs and floors; rooms over two floors, virtually untouched since the 18th-century yet in perfect condition; a well-equipped kitchen (but do ask if you'd prefer meals cooked for you); a sitting room; and an exquisite pool in a private garden. Unique. *Minimum stay one week in high season.*

Price	€2,250–€3,500 per week.
Rooms	Apartment for 8.
Meals	Breakfast €10. Dinner €30–€40. Wine from €10. Children's menu €15.
Closed	Never.
Directions	From Venice-Treviso airport, left until Quito; right & follow signs to Badoere. Signed from Badoere.

Jacopo Marcello
via dei Marcello 13,
35017 Levada di Piombino Dese

Tel	+39 0499 350340
Fax	+39 0499 350340
Email	info@camarcello.it
Web	www.camarcello.it

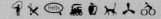

Agriturismo La Presa

The agriturismo is Lucia's baby – she looks after both farm and guests wonderfully. So bowl along the flatlands of the Po delta, pass the chicken factory by, approach the silver poplar lined drive – Lucia has planted hundreds – and sweep through open gates to a peaceful farmstead scented with jasmine. These 400 acres of maize, soya, wheat and cattle have been in the family for 30 years; Lucia has received guests for three. Brick pathways link the main house (two bedrooms) to the rest which lie in a converted farm building. Inside, all feels clean, simple, spacious and cool. Shower rooms are new, floors are wooden or tiled and softened by rugs, walls are light green, and the 'single' beds in the annexe – two beds up, two down – are more like small doubles. The beamed dining room, where meat roasts on the fire before supper, is most inviting. Breakfasts promise homemade tarts and the chestnut table seats 16. Friend Alberto's knowledge of the delta is superb – let him take you up the river and catch oysters. Or borrow the bikes: this flat reclaimed countryside is brilliant for cycling. *Minimum stay two nights.*

Price	€80. €130 for 4.
Rooms	8: 1 double, 1 suite for 2 + cot; 2 doubles sharing bathroom. Annexe: 4 mezzanine suites for 4-6.
Meals	Dinner with wine, €30. Restaurant 5km.
Closed	Never.
Directions	From Taglio di Po follow right bank of river Po for 5km until the poplar lined driveway of La Presa.

Lucia La Presa
via Cornera 13, Taglio di Po,
45019 Rovigo

Tel	+39 0426 661594
Fax	+39 0426 661772
Email	info@lapresa.it
Web	www.lapresa.it

Entry 58 Map 9

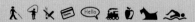

Villa Rizzi Albarea

Hidden behind the house is the loveliest wild garden. Exciting pathways thread their way past statues and trees; there are bridges of Murano glass and a romantic lake with an island and swans. To the front, a lawn next to the art-filled chapel, roses in the cloisters, pines, palms, peonies and ancient magnolias. The house is intriguing, too: the oldest Palladian villa between Venice and Padua. Once a convent for the Giudecca nuns, it goes back ten centuries. Though wars and fire have meant much restoration, it's a beautiful place, deep in the country but not isolated, barely touched by the nearby motorway. The bedrooms are a fresh mix of traditional and flounced, with delectable antiques and comfortable beds, some with old frescoes, others with stunning rafters. Shower rooms sparkle, Persian rugs glow on stone or wooden floors. Be charmed by birdsong and roses in summer; in winter, by Vivaldi and a big fire. In spite of breakfasts served by gloved butlers – and sauna, gym and two pools – the atmosphere is personal, thanks to these generous hosts. *Minimum stay two nights.*

Price	€180–€280. Apt €200–€280.
Rooms	7 + 1: 7 suites. 1 apartment for 2-4.
Meals	Restaurants nearby.
Closed	Rarely.
Directions	From Autostrada A4 Milano-Venezia, exit Dolo, over lights, 1.5km. Right at Albarea sign, 1km; signed.

Aida & Pierluigi Rizzi
Via Albarea 53,
30030 Pianiga di Venezia

Tel	+39 0415 100933
Fax	+39 0415 132562
Email	info@villa-albarea.com
Web	www.villa-albarea.com

Entry 59 Map 4

Villa Colloredo

Handsomely ranged around a courtyard, these 18th-century Venetian buildings – all peachy stone and olive green shutters – hold a cool surprise. Bold paintings, modern sculptures and colourful collages dot the interiors: part of the private collection of the Meneghelli family. Architecturally, the converted stables and grain stores behind the family villa fuse modern styling and original features. Beamed ceilings, wooden or tiled floors and family antiques contrast with white walls, streamlined kitchens, simple rustic furniture and colourful artworks. Spaces have been imaginatively used – a shower, perhaps, in a glass-topped cube – to maximise the open, airy feel. Upper floors have lovely low windows, with views to fields, orchards or courtyard. Two of the larger apartments can be joined together – great for families. You can breakfast in the arched portico, lined with shrubs and fruit trees, and there's a statue-strewn garden behind the villa. Drop in on Padua; borrow a bike and cycle to Venice along the Brenta river. Family-run with a welcoming, homely feel. *Minimum stay three nights.*

Price	€60–€80. Apartments €80–€110.
Rooms	2 + 4: 2 doubles. 4 apartments for 4.
Meals	Breakfast €7.50. Restaurant 200m.
Closed	Never.
Directions	From A4, exit Dolo & follow to Sambruson; turn right opposite church.

	Andrea Meneghelli
	Brusaura 24,
	30030 Sambruson di Dolo
Tel	+39 0414 11755
Mobile	+39 348 2102337
Email	info@villacolloredo.com
Web	www.villacolloredo.com

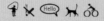

Hotel Villa Alberti

Pluck fruit from the orchard, wash it in the fountain, pick a quiet spot in the walled garden; you could get used to the aristocratic life. This 17th-century villa, once the summer residence of Venetian nobility, has been restored by the Vio family to combine grand features with a warm and unstuffy mood. A family of architects, the Vios have rescued original shutters and flooring, Murano glass lights and chandeliers, decorative ironwork lamps and balconies. Father is proud of the Italian garden with its box hedge lined paths, statues and century-old trees. The reception hall – a sweep of dark polished wood, rich rugs and deep sofas – leads to three floors of bedrooms furnished in a simple but refined style: wooden or stone floors, a few antiques, silky bedspreads. Ask for one overlooking the garden rather than the road. The rooms in the *barchessa* (the workers' house) are more rustic with beams and terracotta floors. Feast on polenta dishes and risottos on the terrace in the summer. A delightful, knowledgeable family and a refreshing alternative to Venice, 15km away.

Price	€90–€130.
Rooms	20 doubles.
Meals	Dinner €25. Wine €12.
Closed	Rarely.
Directions	A4 exit Dolo-Mirano. At traffic lights in Dolo, left, direction Venice. 2km along river, over bridge & cont. in same direction along opp. bank for 1.5km. Hotel on right.

	Anna Vio
	via E Tito 90,
	30031 Dolo
Tel	+39 0414 266512
Fax	+39 0415 608898
Email	info@villalberti.it
Web	www.villalberti.it

Madonna

Bliss to escape the Venetian crowds and return to a friendly little ground-floor apartment with an entrancing walled garden in a peaceful and pretty part of town. Passionflowers climb the warm brick walls; there are chairs and a table, roses and hydrangeas. Close by is the Madonna dell'Orte Church (known as Tintoretto's church) and the area is beautifully quiet, with – for Venice – a rare feeling of space. The owner is an American and comes to Italy whenever she can but lets her apartment at other times. It has all the attraction of a real home. Though the rooms aren't large they are furnished with style and individuality; interesting pictures hang on white walls, terracotta floor tiles are dotted with rugs. The bedroom is cool and airy with muslin curtains; the living room has two large, elegant day beds piled high with cushions. A big gilt mirror and plenty of books make this a charming and restful room. At one end is a kitchen, equipped with hob, microwave and fridge (no oven but loads of restaurants nearby) and French windows door opening into that lovely garden.

Price	£550 per week.
Rooms	Apartment for 2-4.
Meals	Restaurants nearby.
Closed	Rarely.
Directions	Nearest water bus stop: Madonna dell'Orta line 42 or 52.

Susan Schiavon
Campiello Piave,
Cannaregio, 30121 Venice

Tel	+44 (0)207 7225060
Mobile	+44 (0)7971 378608
Email	susan@apartments-venice.com
Web	www.apartments-venice.com

Miracoli

This must be one of the most beautiful balconies in Venice, perched over a canal with soaring Gothic window arches, Corinthian capitals and wrought-iron balustrade tangled in jasmine. It's a perfect spot to sit and gaze languidly at the gondolas floating below – but be prepared to pose for the odd photo by a passing tourist. Through the arches and you enter the vast salon of a 16th-century palazzo (some parts of the building go back to the 11th century). Chandeliers are suspended from the original high wooden ceilings, beautiful antiques rest on polished marble floors, dark grey sofas entice the weary sightseer, and those beautiful arches flood the room with sunlight. Bedrooms are large; one has an original painted ceiling, another a fireplace, another full-length curtains framing a scene of little stone bridges hopping over the canal. There's a well-equipped kitchen, of course, and plenty of restaurants on the doorstep – just in case the thought of cooking on holiday has little appeal. *Minimum stay one week. Children over 12 welcome.*

Price	From £1,800 per week. Additional £100 p.w. over Christmas, New Year, Easter & Carnival.
Rooms	3: 2 doubles, 1 twin.
Meals	Restaurants within walking distance.
Closed	Never.
Directions	Vaporetto to Rialto; 100m from Miracoli Church.

Susan Schiavon
calle Larga Giacanta Gallina 5401/A,
Cannaregio, 30121 Venice

Tel +44 (0)207 7225060
Email susan@apartments-venice.com
Web www.apartments-venice.com

Locanda ai Santi Apostoli

You could walk straight past without even noticing that there is a hotel within this palazzo – and miss the nicest surprise. The Locanda is on the third floor of the Bianchi Michiel, known locally as the Palazzo Michiel del Brusà on account of its having burnt down three centuries ago. Nor does the courtyard, through which you pass, give any clue as to what is in store. The next minute, you're in a Henry James novel… a Venetian palace close to the Rialto on the Grand Canal. Public rooms, opening off a central salon, are still hung with the fabrics and papers of grander days; each room has been furnished differently with all the comforts, atmosphere and hospitality are of an elegant Venetian home. Ask for a room with a view: the two at the front, looking across the Grand Canal to the fish markets, are wonderful. Ludovica is delightful, keen to update the 15th-century palazzo that her family has owned since it was built. The private dock, a minute away, allows direct access to water taxis and gondolas. There is some noise, but this is Venice. A marvellous little find.

Price	€120-€300. Singles €100-€160. Family room €200-€340.
Rooms	10: 9 doubles, 1 family room for 4.
Meals	Restaurants 3-minute walk.
Closed	January; 2nd & 3rd weeks of August.
Directions	Water bus stop: Ca'd'Oro (line 1). Private dock for water taxis.

Ludovica Bianchi-Michiel
strada Nova 4391,
30121 Venice
Tel   +39 0415 212612
Fax   +39 0415 212611
Email aisantia@tin.it
Web   www.locandasantiapostoli.com

B&B Corte 1321

Down a narrow alleyway, through a large and lovely courtyard, tall walls towering above, and enter a 15th-century palazzo. The apartment is on the ground floor, the B&B on the first. Catch your breath inside, at this calm, eclectic décor of Persian rugs, silk curtains, fresh flowers and influences from Bali and Morocco. Amelia is a Californian artist and her paintings hang on every wall. She and her mother Deborah live nearby, so there's no need to tiptoe around your hosts. Most guests are English speaking and bedrooms have been designed to meet American expectations: the best linen, mattresses and showers; hand-crafted beds; the internet. One room looks onto the canal, the other two onto the courtyard. In the apartment downstairs the style is uncluttered, the whitewashed walls making the most of the light. Breakfast is a pretty basket of brioche and bread in the courtyard. The little vaporetto is five minutes away – no bridges! – the local shop is across the square and the Rialto, markets and Accademia are nearby. *Minimum stay two nights.*

Price	€125-€175 for 2; €150-€190 for 3; €175-€220 for 4. Apt €125-€220.
Rooms	3 + 1: 2 family rooms for 2-3, 1 family room for 2-4. 1 apartment for 4.
Meals	Restaurants nearby.
Closed	Rarely.
Directions	From Piazzale Roma, water bus towards Lido; exit San Silvestro; walk towards Campo San' Aponal; 3rd left; 3rd right.

	Amelia Bonvini
	San Polo 1321,
	30125 Venice
Tel	+39 0415 224923
Email	info@cabernardi.com
Web	www.cabernardi.com

Casa San Boldo - Grimani & Loredan

Your own tennis court – in Venice. Enjoy a game or settle with a picnic beneath the jasmine-covered bandstand in the garden. Francesca's parents live on the ground floor and share the court and garden. These very well-restored apartments are smart yet cosy: family antiques, fresh flowers, new sofas, Persian rugs on parquet floors. There are intriguing quirks too: an original window and its glass preserved as a piece of art, a 1756 dowry chest from Alto Adige. And you're never far from a window with bustling canal views. The smaller apartment on the first floor has a sweet twin/double tucked away beneath the rafters, and a larger double room downstairs with modern paintings by a local artist. The little kitchen is beautifully equipped, the dining room has high ceilings and a Venetian marble floor. 'Grimani' has a bedroom on the ground floor with garden views and another up, with iron-framed beds and a lovely old desk. Multi-lingual Francesca who lives nearby is kind, friendly and runs cookery courses that include buying the produce from the Rialto market, just around the corner.

Price	Grimani €1,550-€1,950. Loredan €1,150-€1,550. Prices per week.
Rooms	2 apartments: 1 for 4-6, 1 for 4.
Meals	Restaurants nearby.
Closed	May.
Directions	Park at Piazzale Roma nearby. Details on booking.

Francesca Pasti
San Polo 2281,
30125 Venice

Tel	+39 0452 41070
Fax	+39 0421 66156
Email	venezia@adriabella.com
Web	www.adriabella.com

Pensione La Calcina

Catch the sea breezes of early evening from the terrace butting out over the water as you watch the beautiful people stroll the Zattere. Or gaze across the lagoon to the Rendentore. Ruskin stayed here in 1876, and for many people this corner of town, facing the Guidecca and with old Venice just behind you, beats the crowds of San Marco any day. The hotel has been discretely modernised by its charming owners; comfortable bedrooms have air con, antiques and parquet floors. Those at the front, with views, are dearer; the best are the corner rooms, with windows on two sides. A small top terrace can be booked for romantic evenings and you can breakfast, lunch or dinner at the delightful floating restaurant, open to all – simple dishes are available all day and the fruit juices and milkshakes are delicious. Pause for a moment and remember Ruskin's words on the city he loved: "a ghost upon the sands of the sea, so weak, so quiet, so bereft of all but her loveliness, that we might well doubt, as we watched her faint reflection on the mirage of the lagoon, which was the City and which the shadow."

Price	€99-€210. Singles €96-€110.
Rooms	29: 20 doubles, 7 singles.
Meals	Lunch or dinner €22-€40.
Closed	Never.
Directions	Water bus line 51 or 61 from Piazzale Roma or railway station; line 82 from Tronchetto.

	Signor Alessandro Szemere
	Fondamenta Zattere ai Gesuati,
	Dorsoduro 780, 30123 Venice
Tel	+39 0415 206466
Fax	+39 0415 227045
Email	la.calcina@libero.it
Web	www.lacalcina.com

Pensione La Calcina - Apartments

A two-minute stroll from the hotel of the same name, a clutch of beautiful apartments on the fashionable Zattere. Though they vary in size and in feel, each has a sitting room, a double bedroom and a bathroom; three have kitchens, all are named after flowers. 'Giglio' is large and lovely, with a white-walled sitting room, exposed beams in a vaulted ceiling and a view onto a garden. 'Rosa' is deliciously rustic, with lovely old pieces of furniture and colourful rugs, and a fabulous kitchen. Marble-floored 'Viola' feels Venetian, with its white drapes, fragments of Istrian stone and glimpse of church and small square; 'Iris' looks onto an elegant well with a little fountain and has a modern air. 'Dalia', the smallest, is designed by the Italian architect Scarpa. Inspired by views that sail over the boat-busy lagoon he has created a nautical den — wooden panelling, padded seating, latticed windows, a boatish door; views skim the water and the sunlight dances on the ceiling. All have fridges, and you breakfast at the hotel (see above). Deep comfort in one of the greenest, quietest corners of Venice.

Price	€136–€239.
Rooms	2 + 3: 1 suite for 2, 1 suite for 4. 3 apartments for 3.
Meals	Lunch or dinner €22–€40. Wine €15.
Closed	Never.
Directions	Water bus line 51 or 61 from Piazzale Roma or railway station; line 82 from Tronchetto.

Signor Alessandro Szemere
Fondamenta Zattere ai Gesuati,
Dorsoduro 780, 30123 Venice

Tel	+39 0415 206466
Fax	+39 0415 227045
Email	la.calcina@libero.it
Web	www.lacalcina.com

Fujiyama Bed & Breakfast

Jasmine, wisteria, shady trees – hard to believe this pool of tranquillity is minutes from the hurly-burly of Venice's streets and the grandeur of the Rialto and St Mark's Square. Even more unusual – for this city – to step through an oriental tea room to reach your bedroom. The four rooms are on the upper two floors of this tall, narrow 18th-century townhouse and continue the gentle Japanese theme. Carlo worked in Japan for eight years – also Algeria, Egypt, Holland – and his love of the Far East is evident throughout the house. Rooms, with views over the garden or Venetian rooftops, exude a light, airy and ordered calm with polished dark wood floors, cream walls, Japanese prints and simple oriental furnishings. Shower rooms are small but neat and spotless. Breakfast on the terrace in summer or in the tea room in winter. A charming and warm host, full of stories and happy to chat, Carlo will recommend good local restaurants – especially those specialising in fish. Retreat here after a busy day exploring this magical city and sip a cup of jasmine tea on the shady terrace.

Price	€70–€140.
Rooms	4 doubles.
Meals	Restaurants next door.
Closed	Never.
Directions	From station, take water bus line 1. Get off at stop Cà Rezzonico & walk to end of Calle Lunga San Barnaba.

Carlo Errani
Calle Lunga San Barnaba 2727A,
Sestiere Dorsoduro, 30123 Venice

Tel	+39 0417 241042
Fax	+39 0412 771969
Email	info@bedandbreakfast-fujiyama.it
Web	www.bedandbreakfast-fujiyama.it

Hotel Locanda Fiorita & Ca' Morosini

A low-budget option for those who have neither boundless wealth nor the inclination to spend their time lounging around a grand Venetian hotel. Tucked away behind the Campo Santo Stefano, close to the Accademia Bridge, this is a sweet, peaceful place, and a convenient base (near the vaporetto) from which you may head off in all directions. It is a faded russet palazzo hung with vines, in a tiny square which somehow contrives to look green in an area without gardens. The terrace at the front is a charmingly ramshackle affair, from which people spill out onto the *piazzetta* for cappuccini and newspapers. Bedrooms vary in size and have pleasantly faded Venetian-style tables and chests and some antique mirrors. Annexe rooms are on two floors in a separate building, newly decorated in bold colours and with slightly bigger showers. No restaurant, but there are plenty of places to eat nearby, and an internet café round the corner. Cross the Accademia Bridge and dive into the network of alleyways on the far side, trailing a thread like Ariadne so that you can find your way back again.

Price	€70–€165. Singles €50-90–€120. Ca' Morosini: €120–€230.
Rooms	16: 4 doubles, 6 twin/doubles. Ca' Morosini: 4 twins/doubles, 2 triples.
Meals	Restaurants nearby.
Closed	Never.
Directions	Vaporetto 1 to Sant'Angelo. Walk until tall red-brick building, then 1st right (Ramo Narisi); on until small bridge then left. Along Calle del Pestrin until courtyard on right (Campiello Nuovo); hotel just in front.

Renato Colombera
Campiello Nuovo, San Marco 3457A,
30124 Venice

Tel	+39 0415 234754
Fax	+39 0415 228043
Email	info@locandafiorita.com
Web	www.locandafiorita.com

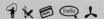

Terrazza Veronese

You're in a creative corner of 'La Serenissima' – the City otherwise known as Venice. In fact, you would be forgiven for missing the little red door altogether, hemmed in as it is between one art gallery (parading a mouthwatering collection of Venetian treasures) and another. Inside, at the top of the staircase, awaits a delightful top-floor flat. In the little red sitting room are glistening crystal chandeliers, their reflections bouncing off pretty mirrors; in the bedroom, ornate French armoires and matching side tables; in the bathroom, pretty blue and white tiling from top to toe. Striking orange walls express the colours of the Mediterranean in the kitchen, and then it's out onto a narrow terrace where window boxes perch on sills, spilling red geraniums in summer – a sunny spot for a morning coffee. It's very central here, yet quiet; the street leads to a vaporetto stop so there's no through traffic, and the Rialto is five minutes away. Sara has compiled a bumper pack of information: essential reading for the first time visitor and Venice buff alike. *Minimum stay three nights. Cot available.*

Price	€150.
Rooms	1 apartment for 2-4.
Meals	Restaurants nearby.
Closed	Never.
Directions	Vaporetto 82 to San Samuele; up calle delle Carozze (Palazzo Grassi on left) into Salizzada San Samuele; house between Profumo Santa Maria Novella & Venice Design Art Gallery, on right.

Sara Tidy
3147 Salizzada San Samuele, San Marco,
30124 Venice

Tel	+44 (0)1484 435974
Mobile	+44 (0)7973 560142
Email	sara.tidy@btinternet.com
Web	www.terrazzaveronese.com

Entry 71 Map 4

Locanda al Leon

Such friendly people, such a perfect spot: three minutes walk from the Basilica end of St Mark's Square, and the same from the airport bus and the vaporetto stops. This small, unpretentious, family-run hotel, its characterful old entrance down a tiny alley, is an excellent choice if you're visiting Venice on a tightish budget but want to be at the centre of it all. It's been modestly modernised: all is spotless, everything works, and there's heating for winter stays. Clean, carpeted bedrooms (the biggest on the corner of the building, looking onto the Campo San Filippo e Giacomo and the Calle degli Albanesi) have Venetian-style bedheads with scrolled edges and floral motifs; there are matching striped counterpanes and curtains, modern Murano chandeliers and neat shower rooms. Breakfast is taken at little tables on the big, first-floor landing (no lift) buffet-style: breads and croissants, yogurts and fruit juice – what you'd expect for the price. And there's no shortage of advice – one or two members of the delightful Dall'Agnola family are always around.

Price	€80–€210. Triple €100–€250. Singles €60–€130.
Rooms	11: 8 doubles, 1 triple, 2 singles.
Meals	Restaurants nearby.
Closed	Rarely.
Directions	Water bus line 1 or 82 to San Zaccaria. Follow Calle degli Albanesi until last door on left; signed.

Marcella & Giuliano Dall' Agnola
Campo Santi Filippo e Giacamo 4270,
Castello, 30122 Venice

Tel	+39 0412 770393
Fax	+39 0415 210348
Email	leon@hotelalleon.com
Web	www.hotelalleon.com

Giudecca Mare Riva

On the site of an old gondola boathouse, on the southern side of the island of Guidecca, is a luxurious new waterfront development with spectacular views. Life's quieter this side of the lagoon, but there are still plenty of trattorias, shops and bars, the vista of islands is a dream and in eight minutes you can be stepping out of the vaporetto and onto the square of San Marco. If you have your own boat, you'll be glad of the private jetty. Inside: huge sheets of glass pulling in water and sky, polished marble sweeping from living room-kitchen to bathroom, Italian furniture, clean lines, white walls and pictures in gold frames. White and duck-egg blue is the kitchen, contemporary and cool. In the bedroom, the floor is of pale ash, the wardrobe of fitted glass and the bed is vast. Almost every modern luxury you can think of is here: air conditioning, underfloor heating, American style fridge freezer, electric sun blind, DVD and CD players, flat-screen TV. Outside, a courtyard from which a metal stair spirals its way up to a roof terrace and two perfect loungers... the sunsets are fabulous.

Price	€1,795 per week.
Rooms	Apartment for 2.
Meals	Restaurants within walking distance.
Closed	Rarely.
Directions	Private water taxi from Marco Polo airport or vaporetto from Piazzale Roma to Zitelle; walk from Calle Michelangelo to lagoon end.

Nick & Wendy Parker
D3 Giudecca Mara Riva,
Calle Michelangelo, 30133 Venice

Mobile	+44 (0)7805 066891
Email	info@venicefortwo.com
Web	www.venicefortwo.com

Castello di Roncade Agriturismo

An imposing entrance, a garden full of statues and roses and a grand 16th-century villa do not mean impossible prices. Three beautiful double rooms, furnished with antiques, are available in the house itself and — ideal for families — three vast and simply furnished apartments in the corner towers, the largest with a very good kitchen. All have big wardrobes and dark wooden floors, central heating in winter, air con in summer, thick walls keep you cool. Surrounding the castle and the village are the estate vineyards which produce some excellent wines; try the Villa Giustinian Rosso della Casa or the Pinot Grigio and you'll be sorely tempted to take a case home. Or sample them at dinner in the villa, an occasional rather than a regular event but a fabulous experience, with everyone seated at one table in a magnificent family dining room. The owners and their son Giorgio are helpful hosts who love meeting people and are proud of their wines. Don't take the car to Venice; instead catch the bus to Treviso — an ancient place of cloisters and canals, frescoes and churches — and then the train.

Price	€83–€93. Apartments €31–€36 p.p.
Rooms	3 + 4: 3 doubles.
	4 apartments for 4-6.
Meals	Occasional dinner, €50.
	Restaurants 500m.
Closed	Rarely.
Directions	Exit A4 Venice-Trieste at Quarto d'Altino, follow Roncade. You can't miss the castle's imposing entrance and magnificent gardens.

Barone Vincenzo Ciani Bassetti
via Roma 14, 30156 Roncade

Tel	+39 0422 708736
Fax	+39 0422 840964
Email	vcianib@tin.it
Web	www.castellodironcade.com

Maso di Villa Relais di Campagna

Under an hour from Venice, high up on a hill, Maso di Villa is a world away from the usual Italian agriturismo set-up. Chiara Lucchetta, the owner, has renovated this glorious old farmhouse with breathtaking attention to detail. Everything, from the beautifully restored Veneto furniture and the stripped wooden beams to the light switches – in the original style, salvaged from antique shops – has been put in place to produce a quiet symphony of rural Italy. Although grand and imposing on the outside, the house couldn't be more homely and cosy within. The bedrooms are comfortable and painted in warm colours, some with stunning ornate headboards designed by Chiara's father and carved locally. Knotted old wooden pillars shore up the ceiling in the sitting room, which is scattered with armchairs and bathed in sunlight. And everywhere in the house there are astonishing views; on one side, the Dolomites, on the other, the unbroken expanse of vineyards and woodland that is the Prosecco wine region. Enjoy abundant breakfast on the terrace, wander in the gardens: this is a magical place.

Price	€120-€160. Singles €105.
Rooms	6: 4 doubles, 2 twins.
Meals	Trattoria 300m (closed Mon/Tues).
Closed	Rarely.
Directions	A4 Venice-Trieste; dual c'way 10km; A27 for Belluno; past Treviso Sud; exit Treviso Nord; right for Treviso-Conegliano, SS13 Pontebbana; 18km; in Susegana left at lights for Collalto, 5km; on left, entrance in via Morgante II, green gate.

Chiara Lucchetta
via Col di Guarda 15, loc. Collalto,
31058 Susegana

Tel	+39 0438 841414
Fax	+39 0438 981742
Email	info@masodivilla.it
Web	www.masodivilla.it

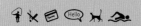

Il Giardino Segreto

During the Second World War, residents of Tovena fled for their safety into France. Many settled and never returned (those who did return brought the French language back with them). When Janine and Angelo found their dream house, it stood untouched, cobwebs lining the antique furniture. The hamlet is surrounded by mountains, the house with its little garden is hidden behind green gates. A great deal of work has gone into restoring the place and keeping as much of the 18th-century feel as possible; in the Casa Padronale the stairs creak charmingly, the chestnut floorboards show the cracks of age and you get a delightful living room/kitchen with big French windows and an open fire. Right next door in the old *cantina* where grappa was once made is a bedroom up and a living room down. In Casa Vecchia there are two twins upstairs and a cheery dining room/kitchenette down; furniture includes junk shop finds, colours are pleasing, there's no TV but hundreds of books. The village is a great starting point for walks and mountain bike rides.

Price	Casa Padronale & Casa Vecchia from €420 each. Annexe from €273. Whole property from €1,100. Prices per week.
Rooms	Casa Padronale & Casa Vecchia sleep 4-5. Extra annexe for 2-3 (no kitchen).
Meals	Dinner with wine, €15-€20. Osteria (lunch) next door. Restaurants 5km.
Closed	Rarely.
Directions	A27 exit Vittorio Veneto Nord for centre, right for Cison/Passo san Boldo, 10km. Green gate set back from main square by side of Locanda Bar Al Bàkaro.

	Janine Raedts & Angelo Vettorello Piazza della Vittoria 22, 31020 Tovena
Mobile	+39 320 0525289
Email	giardinosegreto@tiscali.it
Web	www.giardino-segreto.it

Hotel Villa Luppis

Still the grand country mansion it became in the early 1800s, when Napoleon secularised the monastery that had been here for centuries; the present owner's ancestors later made it a base for diplomatic activities. Geographically, it feels in limbo, too – on the border between Veneto and Friuli and surrounded by acres of flat farmland. The hotel, all creamy peeling stucco and terracotta roof tiles, is reached via an imposing gateway. Twelve acres of grounds include lawns and venerable trees, gravel paths and a fountain. Inside, the various formal reception and dining areas are graced with antiques and presided over by dignified staff. Bedrooms are elegantly old-fashioned, with comfortable beds and excellent bathrooms. You can go for walks along the river bank but really this place works best as a centre for day excursions. There's a daily shuttle into Venice and the staff will organise trips to other towns and cities, as well as to the Venetian and Palladian villas along the river Brenta. Cookery courses are on offer – and wine tastings in what was once the monks' ice-cellar.

Price	€215-€265. Single €115-€125. Suite €280-€320.
Rooms	38: 26 doubles, 2 singles, 10 suites.
Meals	Dinner from €55. Wine from €15.
Closed	Never.
Directions	From Oderzo towards Pordenone. Right at Mansue, signed. From A4, exit Cessalto (12km) for Motta di Livenza & Meduna di Livenza. Hotel before village of Rivarotta.

Signor Giorgio Ricci Luppis
via San Martino 34, 33080
Pasiano di Pordenone

Tel	+39 0434 626969
Fax	+39 0434 626228
Email	hotel@villaluppis.it
Web	www.villaluppis.it

Tenuta Regina Agriturismo

Views stretch to Croatia on a clear day. Great for a family holiday: an hour to Venice, Treviso, Trieste and Austria, 30 minutes to the sea, and a pool with snazzy loungers and a big garden with volleyball. The owners have children themselves, are wonderfully easy-going and proud of their new restoration; the breakfast room was completed in 2005. Now grandfather's farmhouse and grain store look spanking new outside and in, but the lovely old ceiling rafters remain. The most homely apartment is the largest, on the western end of the farmhouse: two storeys of laminated-wood floors and gleaming doors, a pristine white kitchen, four immaculately dressed beds and a sprinkling of attractive family pieces. Perhaps even a bunch of fresh roses – Giorgio's passion. The other apartments, three in front of the pool, two just over the road, feel more functional. Comfortable and open-plan, they come with new mattresses, spotless showers, dishwashers and safes; two are wheelchair-friendly. *Minimum stay two nights; July & August one week.*

Price	€75–€100. €400–€1,500 per week.
Rooms	8 apartments for 2-7.
Meals	Breakfast €7. Restaurants 1.5km.
Closed	Rarely.
Directions	A4 Venezia-Trieste, exit Latisana; signs for Trieste. At Palazzolo, right at 1st lights for Piancada; continue for 7km.

Alessandra Pasti
Casali Tenuta Regina 8,
33056 Palazzolo dello Stella

Tel	+39 0431 587971
Fax	+39 0431 587972
Email	tenutaregina@adriabella.com
Web	www.adriabella.com

Agriturismo La Faula

An exuberant miscellany of dogs, donkeys and peacocks on a modern, working farm where rural laissez-faire and modern commerce happily mingle. La Faula has been in Luca's family for years; he and Paul, young and dynamic, abandoned the city to find themselves working harder than ever. Yet they put as much thought and energy into their guests as into the wine business and farm. The house stands in gentle countryside at the base of the Julian Alps – a big, comfortable home, and each bedroom delightful. Furniture is old, bathrooms new. There is a bistro-style restaurant where wonderful home-reared produce is served (free-range veal, beef, chicken, lamb, just-picked vegetables and fruits); on summer nights there may be a barbecue. An enormous old pergola provides dappled shade during the day; sit and dream awhile with a glass of estate wine or acquavita. Or wander round the vineyard and *cantina*, watch the wine-making in progress, practice your skills with a golf club on the residents' driving range, cool off in the river, visit the beaches of the Adriatic. Perfect for families. *Minimum stay two nights.*

Price	€40–€45. Half-board €56–€66. Apartments from €65.
Rooms	9 + 4: 9 twins/doubles. 4 studio apartments for 2-4.
Meals	Lunch or dinner €15. Wine €9.
Closed	Rarely.
Directions	A23 exit Udine Nord dir. Tarvisio/Tricesimo. From SS13 'Pontebbana' dir. Povoletto-Cividale. At r'bout turn right dir. Povoletto. Follow signs for Attimis then Attimis/Ravosa. At Attimis pass Trattoria Al Sole on left. Signed.

Paul Mackay & Luca Colautti
via Faula 5, Ravosa di Povoletto,
33040 Udine

Tel   +39 0432 666394
Fax   +39 0432 647828
Email   info@lafaula.com
Web   www.faula.com

Casa del Grivò Agriturismo

This is the house that Toni built – or, rather, lovingly revived from ruin. The smallholding sits in a hamlet on the edge of a plain; behind, wonderful, high-wooded hills extend to the Slovenian border, sometimes crossed to gather wild berries. Your lovely hosts have three young children. Simplicity, rusticity and a 'green' approach are the keynotes here; so you'll sample traditional wool-and-vegetable-fibre-filled mattresses. Beds are comfy and blanketed, some with wonderful quilts. Your children will adore all the open spaces, the animals and the little pool that's been created by diverting a stream. Adults can relax with a book on a bedroom balcony, or in a distant corner of the garden. Maps are laid out at breakfast, and there are heaps of books on the region; the walking is wonderful, there's a castle to visit and a river to picnic by. Paola cooks fine dinners using old recipes and their own organic produce. There's a lovely open fire for cooking, and you dine by candlelight, sometimes to the gentle accompaniment of country songs: Paula was once a singer. *Minimum stay two nights; five nights in high season.*

Price	€55. Half-board €45 p.p.
Rooms	4: 1 double, 2 family rooms sharing 2 bathrooms; 1 family room with separate bathroom.
Meals	Dinner with wine, from €25. Lunch in summer only. Picnic by arrangement.
Closed	Mid-December-April.
Directions	From Faédis, via dei Castelli for Canébola. After 1.5km right, over bridge; 2nd house on left.

	Toni & Paola Costalunga Borgo Canal del Ferro 19, 33040 Faédis
Tel	+39 0432 728638
Email	casadelgrivo@libero.it
Web	www.grivo.has.it

Golf Hotel Castello Formentini

A wild boar prances on a weathervane above a creeper-covered tower. The medieval, hilltop castle near the Slovenian border – one-hour drive – surrounded by rolling hills and vineyards, is a very comfortable, very stylish place to stay, whether your room is in the castle itself or in the mellow, friendly little inn across the way. The Formentini have been here since 1520 and the wild boar motif, in triplicate on the family coat of arms, recurs throughout – on fine porcelain, damask linen, white sheets. Amoretti biscuits, candles, a bottle of Prosecco and a note from the Contessa welcome you to a pleasant and generous bedroom. Enjoy a candlelit bath and sleep deeply – you won't oversleep: the church clock begins its routine at 7am and continues until ten at night. Breakfast is on a stone terrace looking down over the village rooftops – a lavish affair that should fuel you through the most energetic day. The hotel has a couple of tennis courts, a superb pool and private park with views stretching to vineyards and castles beyond. There's also a nine-hole golf course – and discounts for four more in the area.

Price	€225. Single €135-€175. Suite €325.
Rooms	14: 6 doubles, 5 twins, 2 singles, 1 suite.
Meals	Restaurants 1km. Cold buffet free to guests. Wine from €30.
Closed	December-March.
Directions	From Goriza, 6km. Signed.

Contessa Isabella Formentini
via Oslavia 2,
34070 San Floriano del Collio

Tel	+39 0481 884051
Fax	+39 0481 884052
Email	isabellaformentini@tiscali.it
Web	www.golfhotelformentini.com

Entry 81 Map 5

Emilia-Romagna

Photo: istock.com

Antica Torre Agriturismo

Two golden labradors ambling across the pristine gravel paths in the lee of the 14th-century tower and enormous colonnaded barn, covered in vines, exude a peaceful contentment – which belies the energy that the family pour into this enterprise. From sweeping flagstones at dawn to the final flourish of a delicious bottle at dinner, this family is devoted to agriturismo. Don't expect to stumble across farm machinery or be set upon by winsome lambs: Antica Torre, with its many buildings, has the air of a model farm. The big rooms in the *casa rustica*, with their ancient polished brick and tile floors, have strange and wondrous rustic furniture, and curly metal bedheads inject a light-hearted air. Otherwise, expect simple bathrooms, immaculate housekeeping and an honest rurality. With its huge fireplace and long tables covered in red gingham, the barn, where generous breakfasts are served, has a distinctly alpine air. In the evening, deep in the ancient Cistercian cellar, to the strains of plain chant and Puccini, feast with locals and guests on Vanda's astonishingly good cooking.

Price	€110. Half-board €75 p.p.
Rooms	8 twins/doubles.
Meals	Dinner with wine, €25.
Closed	December-February.
Directions	From Salsomaggiore centre, SP27 for Cangelasio & Piacenza. Fork left (signed Cangelasio); 1.5km; left for Antica Torre. Driveway left after 1.5km.

	Signor Francesco Pavesi
	Case Bussandri 197, loc. Cangelasio,
	43039 Salsomaggiore Terme
Tel	+39 0524 575425
Fax	+39 0524 575425
Email	info@anticatorre.it
Web	www.anticatorre.it

Villa Bellaria

Off the track, but not isolated, tucked under a softly green hillside, this cream-painted *casa di collina*, with its wide hammock'd veranda and well-established garden, has been a retreat from summer heat since 1900. Having moved here 15 years ago, Marina, warm and kind, herself a keen traveller, decided to throw open its doors and share her enthusiasm for this lovely, little-known area with its medieval villages, castles and thermal cures. On the stairs, etchings of The East India Company recall the Raj. A much-loved, ornately carved mirror, made by her cabinet maker father at his renowned atelier in Milan, graces a wall. Immaculate bedrooms are a happy mix of wrought-iron bedsteads, delicately embroidered blinds, tile floors and contemporary art. After breakfast alfresco – and delectable homemade tart – head off through leafy lanes to the walled hill town Castel Arquato, or Piacenza and Parma. After a hard day exploring or being sporty, contemplate the area's gastronomic delights: nothing sums up Emilia-Romagna so well as its food. This is a comfortable, civilised bolthole – and great value.

Price	€60-€70. Singles €40-€50.
Rooms	3 doubles.
Meals	Restaurant 300m.
Closed	Rarely.
Directions	At traffic lights in Alseno head for Vernasca. On for 5km, right into small street for Cortina; house 2km with green gate on left.

Sig.ra Marina Cazzaniga Calderoni
via dei Gasperini,
29010 Cortina di Alseno

Tel	+39 0523 947537
Mobile	+39 338 6925674
Email	info@villabellariabb.it
Web	www.villabellariabb.it

Villa Gaidello

A neat, pretty pattern of vineyards and fields edged with cypresses, two infant canals and a lake with swans: an unexpected find just off the main Modena-Bologna road. Paola's restaurant in a stone barn serves the most wonderful organic dishes and looks like an old oil painting – a long table bright with flowers, expectant rows of chairs, shadowy, arched ceilings, shelves of gleaming jars. There are four old farmhouses on the estate: 'Casa Padronale' and 'Case del Contadino' overlooking the garden and the lake, and, further along the winding, tree-lined road, green-shuttered 'Gaianello' and 'San Giacomo'. The apartments range from old, thick-walled rooms with dark, period furniture to slightly more modern spaces with lighter furnishing and pale floor tiles. Bathrooms and kitchens are basic and functional. 'San Giacomo' also has two independent double rooms with wrought-iron beds, fresh colours, matching friezes and wooden stable doors. Paola is the hard-working genius behind it all, a relaxed and charming hostess. *Ask about gastronomic visits & cookery courses.*

Price	€65–€93. Apartments €86–€228.
Rooms	2 + 6: 2 doubles.
	6 apartments for 1–6.
Meals	Dinner €50. Wine €8. Restaurant
	closed Sunday evenings & Mondays.
Closed	August.
Directions	From Modena, via Emilia to
	Castelfranco Emilia. Left at hospital
	lights for Nonantola, right from
	Bologna. Under bridge, immed. right;
	3rd left onto via Gaidello, 500m; signed.

Signore Paola Bini & Marta Sexton-Masotti
via Gaidello 18,
41013 Castelfranco Emilia

Tel	+39 0599 26806
Fax	+39 0599 26620
Email	info@gaidello.com
Web	www.gaidello.com

Art Hotel Commercianti

The Basilica of San Petronio, one of the greatest churches of the Catholic world, is on the other side of the street; opposite its west front is the Piazza Maggiore, Bologna's great square. You are in the heart of it, and yet there is little noise and barely any traffic. The Commercianti is, astonishingly, a restored 12th-century building whose conversion has managed to avoid the errors of many. Bedrooms are magnificent, many with their massive old (and low!) beams exposed and six with little terraces overlooking the gothic Basilica. The suites are particularly impressive, with lovely sloping beamed ceilings. One room has the exposed remnants of an early fresco but all have a slightly medieval feel, with white, rough-plaster walls, some wrought-iron furniture, wooden floors and Persian rugs. The marble, blue-carpeted staircase leads down past a fine marble bust to the breakfast room, where the first meal of the day does full justice to its impressive setting. Magnificently central, and if you don't wish to walk, take a bike instead: they're free for guests.

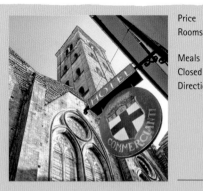

Price	€210–€378. Suites €305–€492.
Rooms	34: 22 doubles, 7 singles, 3 suites for 3, 2 suites for 4.
Meals	Restaurants nearby.
Closed	Rarely.
Directions	Hotel in centro storico, in pedestrianised area. Garage.

Signor Mauro Orsi
via dei Pignattari 11,
40124 Bologna

Tel	+39 0517 457511
Fax	+39 0517 457522
Email	commercianti@inbo.it
Web	www.bolognarthotels.it

Art Hotel Orologio

Just off the Piazza Maggiore – one of Italy's most beautiful medieval squares – is the Orologio, a tall, narrow slice of building, its glass and brass entrance guarded by small shrubs; so discreet it's easy to miss. Immediately above the door, plants trail through a pretty, latticed railing in front of a green-shuttered window. Step into a reception hall hung with clocks and big mirrors, and make your first acquaintance with the delightful Cristina and her kind, friendly, multi-national staff. Above are the tranquil sitting and breakfast rooms (breakfast is an excellent spread), then the well-decorated bedrooms with their padded headboards, soft carpets and papered walls. Bathrooms are immaculate and generous, suites come with sitting areas, sofabeds and statues, and well-dressed windows look over a fascinating maze of terracotta rooftops or across to the piazza and the Duomo. You are wonderfully central yet this delightful hotel is surprisingly quiet. Outside the entrance is seating so you can watch the comings and goings of the square before joining the glorious fray.

Price	€200–€378. Suite €295–€492.
Rooms	34: 26 doubles, 2 singles, 5 suites.
Meals	Restaurants nearby.
Closed	Rarely.
Directions	From station, buses 25 or 37 stop in Piazza Maggiore, 70m from hotel. Parking.

Cristina Orsi
via IV Novembre 10,
40123 Bologna
Tel   +39 0517 457411
Fax   +39 0517 457422
Email   orologio@inbo.it
Web   www.bolognarthotels.it

Art Hotel Novecento

Another Art Hotel, another lovely old townhouse in the centre of Bologna. But this one has been refitted in a style that has echoes of 1930s Viennese Secession. Bedrooms are black, red, white and beige, smart and minimalist, with low-slung beds, Asian-inspired furniture, marble bathrooms, expensive linen. A central staircase with wrought-iron railings climbs past the several floors to the top, where a grand suite presides with an arched triple window and a balcony overlooking the pedestrianised street below. The place runs on perfectly oiled wheels, the staff are helpful, the bikes are free and breakfast – taken in your room – is unusually good. Like Art Hotel Orologio round the corner, this fabulous hotel is very central. The delights of the city, with its markets, theatres, palazzi and seemingly endless network of beautiful porticoes to stroll through, are yours, and if you long to see something lush and splendid after the Novecento's clean lines, there's the Palazzo Communale right behind, whose fine collection of miniatures and paintings from the Bolognese School awaits your discovery.

Price	€210–€378. Suite €305–€492.
Rooms	25: 15 doubles, 9 singles, 1 suite.
Meals	Restaurants nearby.
Closed	Never.
Directions	In centro storico, 300m from Piazza Maggiore. Garage.

Signor Mauro Orsi
Piazza Galileo 4/3,
40123 Bologna

Tel   +39 0517 457311
Fax   +39 0517 457322
Email   novecento@inbo.it
Web   www.bolognarthotels.it

Hotel Corona d'Oro

The palazzo, with its glorious 14th-century wooden portico, is full of history. And the Liberty-style interiors are spectacular. A lavish plastered frieze runs round the glass-roofed central hall; two columns tower above the patterned wall-seats. Old-fashioned gold-striped sofas and armchairs, slightly formal, are entirely fitting. Huge potted plants stand on a marble floor, there are Venetian wall lights and Art Nouveau glass; the effect is opulent and makes the Corono d'Oro special. Just off the hall is a charming little bar/breakfast room, a mirror reflecting light off the whole of one wall. Bedrooms are not large but solidly comfortable, in a rather traditional 'hotel' style, with brass-edged sockets and light fittings, heavy curtains and built-in desks. Some have tiny terraces or balconies overlooking the glass roof of the central hall; bathrooms are impeccable. Breakfast is a huge treat, the staff are charming and you are as central as it gets, just off a pedestrian street 200 metres from Bologna's two leaning towers.

Price	€220–€378. Suite €315–€492.
Rooms	40: 22 doubles, 14 singles, 3 suites.
Meals	Restaurant next door.
Closed	August.
Directions	In centro storico, in little street off via Rizzoli. Parking.

Signor Mauro Orsi
via Oberdan 12,
40126 Bologna

Tel	+39 0517 457611
Fax	+39 0517 457622
Email	corona@inbo.it
Web	www.bolognarthotels.it

Entry 88 Map 8

B&B a Bologna

Before it became a B&B, nuns lived here – but don't expect cloisters. This is a modern Italian city apartment block with a central lift and a winding stair. The position, not the street, is the thing: Davide offers a clean, no-frills place to stay in the heart of the city. A long, narrow, white-painted corridor, enlivened with the occasional picture, leads to bedrooms cool with tiled floors and blinds. The furniture is plain, beds are floral and there's lots of space. Two of the bedrooms share a huge bathroom and a washing machine – ideal for a family. Basic breakfast is in your room or in the dining area but, if you prefer it earlier or later than the norm, Davide will give you vouchers for the bar round the corner. It's all very flexible, you have your own keys so you may come and go as you please, and there are plenty of good restaurants to choose from. The Piazza Maggiore is a ten-minute walk and a bi-weekly market is a short stroll. Davide, when he pops by, is very friendly.

Price	€65–€110. Triple €95–€120.
Rooms	4: 1 double, 1 triple; 2 doubles sharing bath.
Meals	Restaurants nearby.
Closed	Never.
Directions	Right out of train station; 1st left onto via Amendola; 2nd right onto via Milazzo; 100m, left onto via Cairoli. On 2nd floor; ring bell.

Signora de Lucca
via Cairoli 3,
40121 Bologna

Tel	+39 0514 210897
Fax	+39 0514 210897
Email	takakina@hotmail.com
Web	www.traveleurope.it/bolognabb

Agriturismo Cavaione

A tranquil, undemanding place to return to after a day of metropolitan bustle. Gaze down over the vineyards for a different perspective on the rooftops and towers of Bologna – then turn your back on the city and rest your eyes on meadowfuls of wild flowers. For the house is on a hill and the views are a delight in both directions. The family bought the place in the 1950s and it has been a B&B for over ten years – one of the first near the city, just 15 minutes away. The family do not live here but friendly owner Davide pops by. What you get is an unpretentious farmhouse with thick walls, a red-tiled roof, a balcony shielded by brown blinds. Inside is dark and cool and the rooms functionally decorated; bedrooms are painted in light colours and plainly furnished with dark country furniture. Two open to the balcony and look across the valley to the rolling hills; the new, simple-style apartment just behind the house sleeps a family. Once you've tired of cultural pleasures, there are some lovely walks in the hills close by – and a basic restaurant next to the park opposite.

Price	€50–€130.
Rooms	5 + 1: 3 doubles; 2 doubles sharing bathroom. Apartment for 5-6.
Meals	Restaurant within walking distance.
Closed	Never.
Directions	From Bologna Porta San Mamolo, signs to San Mamolo: via dei Colli. Continue but keep to your right; right at sign for Casaglia. House opp. Parco Cavaione.

Faccioli de Lucca
via Cavaione 4,
40136 Bologna
Tel   +39 0515 89006
Fax   +39 0515 89371
Email   tcavaione@iol.it
Web   www.agriturismocavaione.it

La Fenice Agriturismo

A place for all the family. Remo and Paolo are brothers and farmers (the farm has been in the family for five generations) and are constantly restoring and renovating their beloved Fenice – in true Romagna style. This is Rustic with a capital R: guest bedrooms in the old house have a hotchpotch of furniture but lovely big rafters, some very low; rooms are darkish, windows small, and most have their own entrances. Some rooms have fireplaces and logs on the house – super-cosy in winter. More low rafters in the recently renovated, cloister-like building next door where five new bedrooms lie. Active teenagers will be happy: there are mountains bikes, quad bikes, archery and a pool, and horse riding a five-mile drive. La Fenice's restaurant is another reason to stay; the food is locally sourced, reasonably priced and truly delicious. You are 800m above sea level so all that fresh air and outdoor living should build up an appetite. Visit the stones of Rocca Malatina, the waterfalls of Labante, the restaurants of hilltop Zocca – but be careful on those windy roads. *Minimum stay three nights for half-board.*

Price	€80. Half-board €120 for 2.
Rooms	8: 4 doubles/twins, 4 family rooms.
Meals	À la carte from €25. Wine €10-€25.
Closed	7 January-6 February.
Directions	From Bologna SS64 south 30km, right to Tole, then towards Cereglio. After 1.5km, right. La Fenice 5km from Tole on right.

	Remo & Paolo Giarandoni via S. Lucia 29, Ca' de Gatti, 40040 Rocca di Roffeno
Tel	+39 0519 19272
Fax	+39 0519 19024
Email	lafenice@lafeniceagritur.it
Web	www.lafeniceagritur.it

La Piana dei Castagni Agriturismo

Write, paint, read or potter: here, deep in the woods, there's nothing to distract you. This is a secret little Hansel and Gretel house with a vegetable patch, demure shutters and lace-trimmed curtains. It stands isolated among chestnut and cherry trees, reached via a long, wriggling track; below are bucolic meadows, falling to a farm or two, and a further distant descent along the yawning valley. An old stone farmhouse converted and adapted for B&B, La Piana is a modest place to stay. The bedrooms, named after local berries, are a good size and painted in clear pastel colours; tiny pictures hang above beds and little windows set in thick walls look out over the glorious valley. The shower rooms – one of them a restyled chicken shed! – are simply tiled. Valeria lives ten minutes away at La Civetta. She is gentle, kind, spoiling; even the breakfast *torte di noci* are homemade. She will also help organise everything, from trekking to truffle hunting. An ideal spot for those who love the simple pleasures of life: good walks by day, good food by night.

Price	€60–€90. Singles €40.
	Triple €80–€100.
Rooms	5: 2 doubles, 2 triples, 1 single.
Meals	Dinner €17. Wine €8–€15.
	Restaurant 3km.
Closed	December–March.
Directions	From Tolè, follow signs for S. Lucia &
	Castel d'Aiano. Signed.

Signora Valeria Vitali
via Lusignano 11,
40040 Rocca di Roffeno

Tel	+39 0519 12985
Fax	+39 0519 12717
Email	info@pianadeicastagni.it
Web	www.pianadeicastagni.it

B&B Valferrara

On an ancient road between Canossa and Carpineti, this 17th-century travellers' lodge sits in the silent hamlet of Valferrara. Weary merchants would rest their heads in peace – and absorb the calm and protection of the surrounding forested hills and distant castle of Carpineti. Ruined when Giuliano and Cosetta discovered it in 1994, the *casa di scale* ('tiered house'), complete with flat-roofed Emilian tower – where a clutch of apartments are almost ready – has been completely and masterfully restored with local materials, and parquet flooring fashioned from recycled beams of oak. Cosetta restores local antique furniture and the house is full of it; crisp cotton envelops large, beautifully framed beds and an eye-catching walnut writing desk stands elegantly near one of her several finely polished wardrobes. Expect a warm welcome and a delicious breakfast – under the cool portico, in the walled garden or in the dining room: a fabulous conversion of the old stables. Fresh parmesan can be sampled locally and smiling Cosetta, also a great cook, provides dinner on request.

Price	€76-€90.
Rooms	3: 1 double;
	2 doubles sharing bathroom.
Meals	Restaurants 1-4km.
Closed	Rarely.
Directions	A1 Bologna-Milano exit Modena Nord. SS via Emilia to Reggio Emilia, exit Scandiano to Viano; to Carpineti, dir. Casina, thro' Cigarello. After 1.5km, right at small Valferrara sign; 100m on left.

Cosetta Mordacci & Giuliano Beghi
via Valferrara 14, Pantano,
42033 Carpineti

Mobile	+39 340 1561417
Email	info@bb-valferrara.it
Web	www.bb-valferrara.it

Relais Varnello

Just above the pretty town of Brisighella, but you'll need the car – it's quite a hike! In young gardens, the brick buildings stand sparklingly clean and tickety-boo. Nicely-furnished rooms have views across the valley or garden; the suites are in a separate building, with a sauna. The farm produces Sangiovese DOC wine and olive oil, which you can buy along with Faenza pottery showing the family crest. Giovanni has been producing oil and wine all his life and you won't leave here without a bottle or two – its delicious. If you speak a little Italian, pick his brains, he has a vast knowledge of Italian grapes (over 1,000 varieties) and will happily tell you about some of the best wines available. Spend your days lounging by the pool: there are wide views over the Padana and to the Adriatic, and there's a private wild park – Giovanni's pride and joy – just a stroll away: a lovely place for a picnic and a book. Higher up the hill is the Pacro Carné, with Club Alpino Italiano (CAI) walking trails. *Minimum stay two nights.*

Price	€130. Suites €180.
Rooms	6: 4 twins/doubles, 2 suites.
Meals	Dinner from €20. Restaurant 300m.
Closed	January-15 March.
Directions	From Brisighella on SP23 Montecino & Limisano road, signed to Riolo Terme. After 3km, left after Ristorante Manicômi, signed to Rontana. Relais 1st building on left.

	Signor Giovanni Liverzani
	via Rontana 34,
	48013 Brisighella
Tel	+39 0546 85493
Fax	+39 0546 83124
Email	info@varnello.it
Web	www.varnello.it

Azienda Vitivinicola e Agrituristica Trerè

Braided vines stretch as far as the eye can see… in the middle of this flat green patchwork is a compact grouping of rosy buildings and a clump of tall trees to one side. The entertainingly angular farmhouse is surrounded by barns and stables – now modern apartments and a conference room. This is very much a wine-producing estate – around the house are certificates and awards, a shop and a little rose-and-gold wine museum – but in spite of all this, there's a family feel; toys are scattered around and the atmosphere is easy. The bedrooms in the house have a light and pretty elegance, all beamed ceilings, pastel walls, lovely old family furniture and memorable touches – the deep lace trim of a white sheet folded over a jade bedcover, a wall full of books. The apartments are attractive but more functional in feel. Each has French windows opening onto a private patio and a mezzanine with an extra bed tucked under a skylight – fun for kids. The restaurant is only open on weekend evenings, but there are other places to eat nearby. *Air conditioning in apartments only.*

Price	€64-€74. Singles €42-€52. Suite €135-€150. Apts €78-€88 for 2; €175-€190 for 6.
Rooms	7 + 4: 3 doubles, 2 twins, 1 triple, 1 suite for 2-5. 4 apts: 3 for 2-6, 1 for 3-6.
Meals	Breakfast €6.50. Dinner €23 (not Jan/Feb or Mon-Thurs). Wine €7-€22. Restaurants 2km.
Closed	Rarely.
Directions	From Faenza via Emilia SS9 for Imola/Bologna; 3km left after Subaru garage on via Casale; signed.

Morena Trerè & Massimiliano Fabbri
via Casale 19,
48018 Faenza

Tel	+39 0546 47034
Fax	+39 0546 47012
Email	trere@trere.com
Web	www.trere.com

Liguria

Photo: istock.com

Villa Elisa

The climate is kind: visit at any time of the year. The hotel was created in the 20s when Bordighera, a pretty town with sloping tree-lined roads and pastel houses, became a winter retreat. Rita's father-in-law, who ran it for years, was a painter and had artists to stay – bedroom walls are still hung with the works they left him. Some still come, following in the steps of Monet. Your hosts are the nicest you could wish to meet. Rita and husband Maurizio take groups off into the Maritime Alps in their minibus and guide them back on three-hour walks, Rita likes to spoil – she has even provided a playroom for children, and special activities for summer. Bedrooms have parquet floors and are dressed in blue; bathrooms are white-tiled with floral friezes and heated towel rails; larger rooms have terraces with views to the hills. There's a courtyard garden scented with bougainvillea, oranges and lemons, and a wonderful pool area with plenty of quiet corners. The pebbled beach is a ten-minute dash down the hill and the restaurant is charming; fresh fish is on the menu and the wine list is long.

Price	€120–€180. Singles €80–€110. Suite €200–€250. Apt €220–€300. Half or full-board option for week-long stays.
Rooms	34 + 1: 30 doubles, 3 singles, 1 suite. Apartment for 4.
Meals	Lunch & dinner from €40. Wine €16–€50.
Closed	5 November–22 December.
Directions	Via Romana parallel to main road through town (via Aurelia), reachable by any crossroad that links the two. Villa at western end of via Romana.

Signora Rita Oggero
via Romana 70,
18012 Bordighera

Tel	+39 0184 261313
Fax	+39 0184 261942
Email	info@villaelisa.com
Web	www.villaelisa.com

Casa Villatalla Guest House

Revel in the peace – and the views: they sweep across the wooded valley to the blue-grey mountains beyond. Roger (British) and Marina (Italian-Swiss) moved not long ago to Liguria and had the delightful Casa Villatalla built in traditional style, ochre-stuccoed and green-shuttered. They are wonderfully welcoming hosts – and the cheerful, eclectic décor of the house reflects their warm personalities and love of travel. Through the brick archway, a Swiss armoire presides over a dining room furnished with rustic wooden tables on which seasonal breakfasts and dinners (do book) are served. Upstairs, charming modern bedrooms, some lead to balconies and those views. All are different – in 'Quercia', a bedstead woven from banana tree fronds, in 'Corbezzolo', rose tones and a flowery patchwork quilt. Marina, a keen horticulturist, nurtures her fledgling garden full of roses, and there's a swimming pool terrace which is crowned by a fine oak tree, beautifully illuminated at night. Together they organise occasional painting and yoga courses: another reason to stay. *Min. stay two nights July & August.*

Price	€80–€100.
Rooms	5: 1 double, 4 twins/doubles.
Meals	Dinner from €25. Wine €6.
Closed	Never.
Directions	Follow Val Nervia road from coast. 1km after Dolceacqua, left to Rocchetta Nervina. After 3km, left to 'La Colla'. Villatalla on right, after 2km.

Roger & Marina Hollinshead
loc. Villatalla,
18035 Dolceacqua

Tel	+39 0184 206379
Fax	+39 0184 205975
Email	info@villatalla.com
Web	www.villatalla.com

Casa Cambi

Casa Cambi

You can hardly believe that such a village has survived unspoilt into the 21st century. It's a fairytale tangle of winding cobbled streets and medieval stone houses on a green and rocky hilltop. All around are dramatic mountains and stupendous views. A square, uncompromising castle dominates the hill; right below is Anna's entrancing house. A tiny front door (the house is 700 years old, after all) takes you straight into a delightful, vaulted room – a soothing mix of creams and whites, ochres and umbers. Pale walls contrast with a gleaming wooden floor and old polished furniture; its subtle, restrained country charm sets the tone for the rest. All the rooms are a delight, all full of unexpected touches – jugs of fresh wild flowers, hessian curtains on wrought-iron poles, a rack of old kitchen implements stark against a white wall... vivacious Anna adores her house and has lavished huge care on it. She's bubbly and friendly and loves cooking; her kitchen is a delight. Breakfast out in the pretty terraced garden among olive and fig trees, revel in those mountain views.

Price	€90-€110.
Rooms	4: 2 doubles, 1 twin, 1 family.
Meals	Dinner with wine, €25-€30.
Closed	5 November-March.
	Out of season fax +39 010 812613.
Directions	A10 exit Albenga. S582 for Garessio for Castelvecchio di Rocca Barbena, 12km. Free car park outside pedestrianised Borgo, 5-minute walk.

Anna Bozano
via Roma 42, 17034
Castelvecchio di Rocca Barbena

Tel	+39 0182 78009
Fax	+39 0182 78009
Email	casacambi@casacambi.it
Web	www.casacambi.it

Palazzo Fieschi

The name of this elegant townhouse near Genoa commemorates former owners, the distinguished Fieschi family, once a power in the land. Now it belongs to Simonetta and Aldo Caprile, who left the world of commerce for a life of hotel-keeping. They have carefully renovated the old palazzo, adding modern comforts to its *cinquecento* grandeur. The oldest working hotel in Liguria, it overlooks a square and is a short walk to the centre; there's also a shuttle service for guests. The surrounding countryside is steep and wooded, away from the autostradas and with walking nearby. Bedrooms are white-walled and spotless, many with lovely antiques and fabulous carved or painted bedheads. Rooms vary but those on the mezzanine floor in the oldest section of the house have the most character: beautiful tiles, grand doorways, low ceilings. One has access to the tower from where you can peep out over the square. The dining room, with its chandeliers and sweeping red drapes, is popular for weddings. The Capriles are courteous hosts, and you may encounter the odd musical evening in winter.

Price	€118-€150. Singles €73-€98. Triples €135-€180. Family room €150-€190.
Rooms	24: 3 doubles, 10 twins/doubles, 2 triples, 1 family, 8 singles.
Meals	Lunch & dinner €26-€50.
Closed	24 December-February.
Directions	From A7 exit to Busalla. In Busalla for Casella; 3.5km, left for Savignone. Hotel in village centre.

Aldo, Simonetta & Sara Caprile
Piazza della Chiesa 14,
16010 Savignone

Tel	+39 0109 360063
Fax	+39 0109 36821
Email	info@palazzofieschi.com
Web	www.palazzofieschi.com

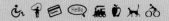

Villa Gnocchi Agriturismo

Once you negotiated the steep, windy and poorly maintained access drive, you are rewarded with fantastic views over Santa Margherita. Roberto, a farmer, trained at Pisa University and inherited the house from his grandfather in a dilapidated state; he's made a few changes! He loves it here, deep in the country but within sight of the sea... so sip a glass of wine from the terrace and gaze down the coast. The views are spectacular. Each bedroom is different: white, ochre or saffron; all are simply furnished and decorated with dried flowers. Bright bedcovers dress Grandfather's beds, muslin curtains flutter at windows, old framed prints hang on the walls and many shower rooms are tiny. Apart from the hoot of the train and the faint hum of the traffic below, the only sound to break the peace is birdsong. Santa Margherita – a 15-minute walk downhill, a bumpy bus or taxi up – is a charming little town, with beach, fishing boats, shops, bars and restaurants. Paths lead to most of the villages and buses from the gate. *Strict check-in/out times.*

Price	€105.
Rooms	9: 5 doubles, 2 twins, 2 family.
Meals	Restaurant 500m.
Closed	Mid-October to Easter.
Directions	From Santa Margherita for S. Lorenzo, 4km. Pass big sign 'Genova & S. Lorenzo' on left, Rapallo & A12 on right, 50m ahead, left down narrow road. At red & white barrier ring bell.

	Signor Roberto Gnocchi
	via Romana 53, San Lorenzo della Costa, 16038 Santa Margherita Ligure
Tel	+39 0185 283431
Fax	+39 0185 283431
Email	roberto.gnocchi@tin.it
Web	www.villagnocchi.it

Monte Pù

The farm stands, remote and blissfully silent, on the site of a ninth-century Benedictine monastery whose tiny chapel still survives. The cherry and pear orchards and trout ponds are surrounded by woods; dogs and cats doze, the donkey brays. Pù (from the Latin *purus*) means pure, referring to the quality of the air and natural spring water and harking back to the importance of purification in monastic life. Organic produce is served in the restaurant – rabbits, goats, hens, cows contribute in their various ways – and Aurora may find time to sit with guests on summer evenings, to gaze at the stars and the lights of fishing vessels on the sea far below. Rooms are simply furnished; one has an optional kitchen, well-equipped but, understandably, seldom used. Provided you can face negotiating the steep road, this makes a good base; if you prefer, a minibus to Genoa can be arranged, which can also call at Sestri Levante station. Archery, flower arranging and cookery lessons are offered, and there's a huge sitting room in the hayloft. The chapel can even be used for weddings.

Price	€82. Half-board €70 p.p. Apartment €125.
Rooms	10 + 1: 5 doubles, 3 triples, 2 family. 1 apartment for 6.
Meals	Dinner €25-€32. Wine €10. Restaurant 12km.
Closed	November-Easter.
Directions	From Sestri Levante for Casarza. Approx. 1km beyond Casarza, left to Massasco & Campegli. Monte Pù on left just before Campegli, up 4km of private road.

Signora Aurora Giani
loc. Monte Pù,
16030 Castiglione Chiavarese

Tel	+39 0185 408027
Fax	+39 0185 408027
Email	montepu@libero.it
Web	www.montepu.it

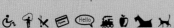

Entry 101 Map 7

Hotel Villa Edera

The villa is perched above the beautiful town of Moneglia and is the quintessential, beautifully run, family owned hotel. Orietta, the elder daughter, is manageress – businesslike yet approachable. She is a mine of information about Ligurian art and history, sings in the local choir and loves meeting people who share her interest in music. Her husband and her sister's husband are waiters; mother Ida is a brilliant cook, preparing Ligurian dishes, some vegetarian, with the freshest organic produce, and fabulous breakfasts; sister Edy is a cake-making genius; and father Lino ensures that it all runs like clockwork. Orietta is a keen walker who may take guests out for real hikes – though you can always catch a boat to Portofino and explore the Cinque Terre by sea. You are fairly close to the railway here (a significant part of the landscape, threading the Cinque Terre villages together) but you'd never know. Lots of treats to come back to: a fitness room, sauna, spa, lovely pool, and the beach a ten-minute walk. *Minimum stay three nights. Gluten-free meals available.*

Price	€130-€210. Singles €85-€135. Suites €170-€280. Half-board €75-€125 p.p.
Rooms	27: 21 doubles, 2 family, 2 singles, 2 suites.
Meals	Lunch or dinner €28-€35. Wine €5.
Closed	10 November-15 March.
Directions	Exit A12 at Sestri Levante; signs for Moneglia tunnel. Immed. after 5th tunnel right (at sports field); signed. Free parking.

Signora Orietta Schiaffino
via Venino 12,
16030 Moneglia

Tel	+39 0185 491119
Fax	+39 0185 490270
Email	info@abbadiasangiorgio.com
Web	www.villaedera.com

Abbadia San Giorgio

Sublimely romantic and peaceful, this 15th-century monastery recalls the life of St Francis in frescoes and sculptures overhung by vaulted ceilings. You can almost hear the sandaled Franciscans padding around the cloistered garden. Dipping into a delicious spread for breakfast – served in the refectory by candlelight – evokes a further monastic air. As for the bedrooms, Orietta and Francesca, a mother and daughter team, have searched Italy for antique furniture and sensual fabrics to make them both sumptuous and individual. Many of the beds are wrought-iron; one's a four-poster. Floors are of original octagonal terracotta or terrazzo tiles. 'Benefica Mulier' is the large and ethereal honeymoon suite, swathed and festooned with gauze and ivory soft furnishings. Elsewhere, tones range from lavish-red to green, apricot and gold, all opulently matched. Neat marble bathrooms sport spa shower cabins with pretty olive oil based toiletries. An amorous evening might begin with wine tasting in the cellar, then stepping out for dinner. A haven of peace in the centre of a beautiful Moneglia. *Minimum stay three nights.*

Price	€150–€180. Suites €170–€270.
Rooms	6: 3 doubles, 1 twin/double, 2 suites for 4.
Meals	Restaurants 80m.
Closed	Rarely.
Directions	A12 exit Sestri Levante dir. Moneglia; under bridge towards town centre, immed. left down palm tree lined street, right at end after pharmacy; entrance to Abbadia next to church. Or 5-min walk from station.

Signora Orietta Schiaffino
Piazzale San Giorgio,
16030 Moneglia
Tel +39 0185 491119
Fax +39 0185 490270
Email info@abbadiasangiorgio.com
Web www.abbadiasangiorgio.com

Agriturismo Giandriale

Once city dwellers in Milan, Giani and Lucia have made the restoration of what was a very run-down property their life's work. The house is isolated, reached up a long, windy road, but the surroundings are heavenly: high pastures dotted with trees, dense woods beyond, alpine views. The Val di Vara is a completely protected environmental zone, where hunting is forbidden and only organic farming allowed. You may join in with the farm activities if you wish, or doze off with a book. Simple bedrooms (no hanging space) are in the house and outbuildings: thick stone walls, wooden furniture, colourful rugs, cane and bamboo. Traditional farm furniture, much of it chestnut, stands alongside the modern. Your hosts have young children and will be happy to meet yours — there's so much space to run around in, and Lucia will help children identify flowers, trees and wildlife. There's even an adventure park in the trees. Breakfasts are sociable affairs around the big table, a feast of home-grown, home-reared produce. Beware the rough and narrow track, leave the low-slung Morgan behind! Tranquillity is your reward.

Price	€70–€80.
	Apartment €40-45 p.p. (incl. breakfast).
Rooms	6 + 2: 3 doubles, 3 triples.
	2 apartments: 1 for 4, 1 for 5.
Meals	Dinner €15.
Closed	Rarely.
Directions	From Sestri Levante N523 for Parma. On for 14km thro' tunnel & immed. right before 'Torza' for Tavarone then Giandriale. Steep, pot-holed track to top.

Giani & Lucia Nereo
loc. Giandriale 5, 19010
Tavarone di Maissana

Tel	+39 0187 840279
Fax	+39 0187 840156
Email	info@giandriale.it
Web	www.giandriale.it

Hotel Stella Maris

A grand villa of 1870, oozing character and largesse. The frescoed ceiling in the entrance is a dream, a mere hint of what is to come. Bedrooms have frescoed or stuccoed ceilings, some of which depict the activities carried out in each when the place was a private villa. Every room is tall and splendid; antiques and chandeliers are de rigeur, décor is wine-red and cream. White bathrooms are perfectly proportioned and planned, with delicious linen; rooms in the annexe navy and modern. Ask on booking for one of the quieter rooms. Renza is adorable; she has an eye for comfort and has thought of everything, even a washing machine for long-stay guests. She genuinely loves looking after people. Indulge in occasional dinners served al fresco with music then sink into an armchair in the cosy sitting room. The restaurant is classically elegant and, though tables are separate, Renza is happiest when guests link up. Breakfast is a simple buffet and fresh coffee served in the Winter Garden. The town is lovely, full of activity and character, and with a good beach. *Minimum stay two nights.*

Price	Half-board €200–€252. Singles €120–€126. Suites €300.
Rooms	9: 4 doubles, 1 single, 4 suites for 3-4.
Meals	Half-board only.
Closed	November.
Directions	Via Marconi lane off via Jacopo da Levanto. Hotel above Banco Chiavari bank. Entrance around corner, use 1st-floor bell.

	Signora Renza Pagnini via Marconi 4, 19015 Levanto
Tel	+39 0187 808258
Fax	+39 0187 807351
Email	renza@hotelstellamaris.it
Web	www.hotelstellamaris.it

Villa Margherita by the Sea B&B

Federico, the young, understated owner of this family hotel, assures us that if you want to explore his native Cinque Terre, the train and a pair of walking boots are the answer. (Or hop on a boat.) He himself will shuttle you to the local station of this old-fashioned seaside town. Built in 1906, the villa once mingled with the smart set and played her part in the summer seasons between the wars, when Levanto was seriously fashionable. Fishermen still fish, children build sandcastles but the glitterati have moved on. Sensitively renovated in classic Liguria ochre and decorative fresco, the house sits in leafy, terraced gardens with tall palms. White walls, muslin-clad windows and deep armchairs welcome. Charm abounds – in each marble stair, graceful iron banister and decorative floor tile. Simply furnished, flowery bedrooms, family bathrooms and unfussy style imbue the house with the spirit of a well-loved, long-established *pensione*. And if you and your family stay in the comfortable garden flat, join the others for breakfast in the traditional blue and yellow breakfast room.

Price	€85–€125. Apartment €400–€1,100 per week.
Rooms	7 + 1: 7 doubles. 1 apartment for 4.
Meals	Restaurants nearby.
Closed	Never.
Directions	From A12 exit Carrodano & Levanto; right after station; left onto main street; right onto Corsa Italia up hill; hotel on left; parking; signed.

Federico Campodonico
via Trento e Trieste 31,
9015 Levanto

Tel	+39 0187 807212
Fax	+39 0187 807212
Email	info@villamargherita.net
Web	www.villamargherita.net

Agriturismo Villanova

Villanova is where Barone Giancarlo Massola's ancestors spent their summers in the 18th century; it has barely changed. The villa is a mile from Levanto yet modern life feels far behind as you wind your way up the hills through olive groves. The red and cream villa with its own chapel stands in a small, sunny clearing. Giancarlo, quiet, charming, much-travelled, loves meeting new folk; his cat and golden retriever will welcome you too. Guest bedrooms are in the main house and in a small stone farmhouse behind; all have an elegant, country-house feel and rooms are large, airy, terracotta tiled. Furniture is of wood and wrought iron, beautiful fabrics are yellow and blue. All have private entrances and terraces with pretty views. Two of the apartments are separate, a third is in the farmhouse. Giancarlo grows organic apricots, figs and vegetables and makes his own wine and olive oil; breakfasts are delicious. This is a great place to bring children: swings and table tennis in the garden, space to run around in, the coast nearby.

Price	€90–€120. Triples €130–€160. Suites €120–€170. Apartments €600–€1,400 per week.
Rooms	9 + 4: 4 doubles, 3 triples, 2 suites for 3. 4 apartments for 3-6.
Meals	Breakfast €10 for self-caterers. Restaurants 1.5km.
Closed	January.
Directions	Exit A12 at Carrodano Levanto towards Levanto. Signs from junction before town (direction Monterosso & Cinque Terre).

Barone Giancarlo Massola
loc. Villanova,
19015 Levanto

Tel	+39 0187 802517
Fax	+39 0187 803519
Email	info@agriturismovillanova.it
Web	www.agriturismovillanova.it

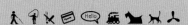

Entry 107 Map 7

La Sosta di Ottone III

Legend has it that Otto III stayed here on his way to his coronation in Rome in 996, creating La Sosta, a 'stopover' of some magnificence. Now a listed building, the house's unadorned stone façade stands proudly over the hamlet of Chiesanuova, scanning a vista from all rooms of olive groves, village and vineyard-clad hills, before dropping down to Levanto and the sea. The terrace is a superb breakfast and dinner setting, perfect too at sunset with a glass of chilled vermentino. At night, the glow from a host of illuminated bell towers is enchanting. Angela has taken great care to gather the best local slate, marble and wood in the renovation of dining and sitting rooms. Bedrooms, named after Otto and his family members, come in an elegant range of neutrals and corals in parquet floors, antique pieces, indoor shutters and iron beds graced by fine bedspreads... take time to pamper in stylish marble and slate bathrooms. Aficionados of all things Ligurian, Angela and Fabio can be depended on for local information, the freshest ingredients and one of the best wine cellars around. Superb.

Price	€160-€180.
Rooms	4: 1 double, 2 family rooms for 2-4, 1 suite for 4.
Meals	Breakfast €10. Dinner €35. Restaurant 5km.
Closed	November-February.
Directions	From Levanto follow signs to Cinque Terre. Ignore signs on right for Chiesanuova. Continue for 100m passing signs on left. After 400m park on left near cement watertank. Follow path for 150m.

	Angela Fenwick
	loc. Chiesanuova 39,
	19015 Levanto
Tel/Fax	+39 0187 814502
Mobile	+39 338 1369602
Email	lasosta@lasosta.com
Web	www.lasosta.com

L'Antico Borgo

High in green hills and along a winding road is the tiny hamlet of Dosso. Leave the car in a little car park and make the short but intrepid journey by foot down to the hotel. Surrounded by olive groves and pocket vineyards, it's hard to believe you are only four kilometres from Levanto. A pretty pebble-paved square and a stone archway form the entrance to the building, a 1700s *casa padronale* fully restored with a soft-ochre façade and dark green shutters so typical of Liguria. A panoramic terracotta-tiled terrace is a fine place to take breakfast or an aperitif and Cecilia is happy for guests to eat their own food here. Relax in the sitting room with a book from the small library, or breakfast at round tables in the rustic taverna. Bright and generous bedrooms are framed by wooden beamed ceilings, two with sea views; all are comfortably furnished with wrought-iron beds warmed by shades of gentle yellow. Modern bathrooms employ solar-heated water. Siblings Cecilia and Carlo are natural hoteliers, he a local surfing hero, both supporters of the Slow Food movement…they know the best places for dinner.

Price	€70–€105. Triple €90–€130. Family €100–€140.
Rooms	7: 1 double, 1 twin/double, 3 triples, 2 family rooms for 4.
Meals	Restaurant 15-minute walk.
Closed	Rarely.
Directions	A12 Genova–Livorno exit Carrodano–Levanto. On for Levanto. Left after gallery, follow signs for Dosso; free parking at entrance.

Cecilia Pilotti
loc. Dosso,
19015 Levanto

Tel	+39 0187 802681
Fax	+39 0187 802681
Email	antico_borgo@hotmail.com
Web	www.anticoborgo.net

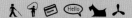

Tuscany

Photo: istock.com

Villa Mimosa

In a tiny, lovely, medieval village, a few steps down from road and church, is a handsome, well-proportioned house – once a flour mill. Now it is is a warm and open-hearted retreat run by people for whom hospitality is second nature. The flagged dining room is cool and inviting, the reading room is stuffed with good books, the first-floor drawing room is a joy: light and airy, with original patterned tiles, pretty vaulted ceiling, big cotton sofas and grand piano. Views stretch over the richly wooded hills of the Apennines, topped with snow in winter. Comforting bedrooms are in old-fashioned English-style with no shortage of chintz and wash basins in the corners; those in the attic get hot in the summer. Shower rooms are simple. Jennie and Alan are well-rooted here, love Italian life and their food is worth climbing the hills for. The absurdly picturesque fishing villages of the Cinque Terre are a drive away; Lerici has a castle and a lovely sandy bay; and elegant, beautiful, musical Parma is an hour away. Return to a pretty back garden with an above-ground pool. *Aga cooking & art courses in low season.*

Price	€90–€110. Singles €60.
Rooms	4: 3 doubles, 1 family room for 4.
Meals	Dinner with wine, 4 courses, €45.
Closed	Mid-November to mid-February. Open Christmas & New Year, by arrangement.
Directions	From A15 exit Aulla & Pontremoli. SS62 for Villafranca & Bagnone. Through archway, left into via Niccolo Quartiere (signed Carabinieri). Left at 1st fork. At r'bout to Corlaga. Park behind church; walk back 50m. 2nd on left.

Jennie & Alan Pratt
Corlaga Bagnone,
54021 Bagnone
Tel   +39 0187 427022
Fax   +39 0187 427022
Email   mimosa@col.it
Web   www.villamimosa-tuscany.com

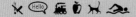

Dimora Olimpia

When they came here it was a ruin; eight years on, Olimpia and Gaetano's 16th-century farm house is an exquisitely restored home. For the full force of its charm, approach via the cobbled back street where chickens potter and an archway leads to a neighbouring farmer's house. This is a verdant, very unspoilt part of Tuscany – country roads, tiny villages, good walks, fine wines. Passionate lovers of old things, your hosts are also fluent guides to the region; there are uninterrupted views of fields, woods and rumpled hills from elegant terrace and pool. Gorgeousness abounds: bare beams and exposed brickwork have been lovingly preserved, there are old wall hangings, very fine, early country furniture and, in the snug bedroom, original shutters at tiny windows. The apartments are small, simple and charming, peaceful and cool, their beds aligned with the Earth's magnetic field to ensure perfect sleep. Shower rooms are first-class, kitchens are tiny, pillow cases are lined with lace. You will dine well in nearby restaurants and are most welcome to join B&B guests round the antique Indian table. Special. *Minimum stay two nights.*

Price	€70–€75. Apt €350–€450 per week.
Rooms	2 + 1: 1 double, 1 suite. 1 apt for 4.
Meals	Breakfast for self-caterers €5. Restaurants 4km.
Closed	Never.
Directions	From Aulla SS62 to SS665, then Monti & Amola. Right for Dimora Olimpia in middle of village; on right.

Olimpia De Caro & Gaetano Azzolina
via Molesana,
54017 Licciana Nardi

Tel	+39 0187 471580
Fax	+39 0187 472977
Email	olimpia.decaro@virgilio.it
Web	www.dimoraolimpia.it

Fosdinovo Bed & Breakfast

You really are on top of the hill here and the views are wonderful. From the terrace you look over Castle Fosdinovo (one of over 100 castles in the area, flood-lit at night) to the Bocca di Magra estuary and Monte Marcello; on a clear day you can see Elba and Corsica. The house was built in the early 1960s and is open plan. Slate steps lead up to a pleasant sitting area, with a teak-deck floor (reclaimed from an old boat), a rough-cut stone fireplace and comfortable leather sofas with views. The bedrooms are white-walled, attractive, super-clean; new beds wear embroidered linen sheets that belonged to Lidia's mother. Lidia and Andrea, friendly, enthusiastic and speaking excellent English, give you your own key so you can come and go as you please. There's a wonderful restaurant a five-minute drive away but you're welcome to bring your own drinks and snacks to eat on the terrace in the evening; you're also encouraged to help yourself to fruit from the orchard in front of the house. Breakfasts are a surprise each day, and Lidia's cakes are delicious.

Price	€80.
Rooms	2 twins/doubles.
Meals	Restaurant 5-minute drive.
Closed	November.
Directions	From A12 exit Sarzana; SS1 for 3km for Carrara-Massa; left SS446 for Fosdinovo. Pass village & castle. Right at x-roads for Carrara. 150m on, left on via Montecarboli. After 400m track right. On left.

Lidia & Andrea Fabbretti
via Montecarboli 12,
54035 Fosdinovo

Tel	+39 0187 68465
Email	info@fosdinovo-bb.com
Web	www.fosdinovo-bb.com

La Cerreta

Be different and head for the hills. The chestnut-covered slopes of the Garfagnana region are less well-known, more remote and somewhat wilder than the southern Tuscany everyone knows and loves, but no less captivating. Wind up through the Serchio Valley from Lucca, up and up, until you reach this secluded hideaway with views of the breathtaking variety. Inside it's typical rustic simplicity with beams, open fireplace in the kitchen and a traditional stove in the sitting-room. Sybarites might want to bag the cool (in both senses) third bedroom which has its own entrance and shower room and one of those vast beds that you just have to dive on. There's a pretty terrace at the front for breakfast, but you'll more than likely fancy the shady deck round the back for lunch and supper – you'll feel as if you're dining in the tree tops. If all gets too relaxing, you can always pop down the road to the six-hole golf course with its dinky clubhouse, or pack a picnic and stride off in any direction. Jazz and opera fans can head for arty Barga – an irresistible medieval hilltop town where there's always a festival in the offing.

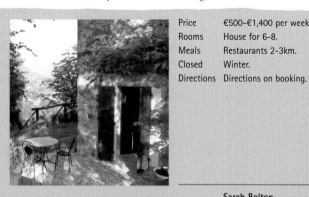

Price	€500–€1,400 per week.
Rooms	House for 6-8.
Meals	Restaurants 2-3km.
Closed	Winter.
Directions	Directions on booking.

Sarah Bolton
Castelnuovo di Garfagnana
Tel   +44 (0)117 9260867
Email   info@lacerreta.co.uk
Web   www.lacerreta.co.uk

Peralta

Peralta is precariously perched on the foothills of Mount Prana. The sculptress Fiore de Henriquez took it on 30 years ago, a labyrinth of ancient dwellings connected by steep steps and sun-dappled terraces. Lemon trees, jasmine and bougainvillea romp on every corner, a sculpture peeps from every cranny, the chestnut-groved valley swoops to the sea. The whole place hums with creativity. Rooms are properly rustic, not luxurious but full of charm, some light, some less so; all have vibrant walls, breathtaking views, perhaps an old red sofa, a simple bed covered in a striped cover, a rag rug on a terracotta floor. Four of the apartments have dishwashers, a rare concession to modernity. British Dinah and her team of international helpers draw you together like one big family: there's a panoramic terrace where guests gather to swap stories, a light-filled studio for courses (art and writing), a log-fuelled sitting room, a small pool. The approach road will thrill you: it is an adventure to get here, and an adventure to stay. *Minimum stay two nights. Children over 10 welcome.*

Price	€350–€2,125 per week.
Rooms	3 apts for 2, 2 apts for 3, 1 house for 4-5, 1 house for 7-8.
Meals	Restaurants 2km.
Closed	Never.
Directions	From A12 Livorno & Genoa, exit Camaiore. Left after Camaiore for Pieve, uphill, signs for Peralta. Left at fork for Peralta, pass blue sign & onto Agliano. Unsigned. Parking 200m.

Kate Viti & Dinah Voisin
Pieve di Camaiore, via Pieve 321,
55041 Camaiore

Tel	+39 0584 951230
Mobile	+39 349 3597900
Email	peraltusc@tiscali.it
Web	www.peraltatuscany.com

Casa Gialla - La Bergenia

Laura describes the style here as 'allegro': light, breezy, full of zing. She's a prestigious sculptress, and her artistic touches are everywhere. Take the open-plan sitting room: dried lavender and colourful pictures, wicker chairs elbow-deep in cushions, exposed brickwork around columns and archways. All three bedrooms link you to the lovely gardens; look out on lemon trees from the citrus-themed room, inhale the scent of roses from the rose room. All are serene in cream with one or two splashes of colour – a sprig of purple flowers on a wardrobe, an old print hand-tinted by Laura's grandmother. Immaculate white bathrooms have big showers. Breakfasts are an array of homemade cakes and breads, cheese, ham, eggs, most of it from a friend's organic *orto*; on fine days you eat on the rose-strewn pergola to a panorama of the Apennines, the hills sprinkled with villages down to the sea. Hidden up a private lane, five minutes from Camaiore, the peace is delicious. Later, join your charming hostess for an aperitif or a glass of fresh, cold peach juice. Handy for the Puccini festival. *Minimum stay two nights.*

Price	€130.
Rooms	3 doubles.
Meals	Dinner on request.
Closed	Rarely.
Directions	Exit motorway at Camaiore & phone owner.

Laura Frigerio
via di Contra 38,
55041 Camaiore

Tel	+39 0584 984035
Mobile	+39 335 6180878
Email	info@labergenia.it
Web	www.labergenia.it

Albergo Villa Marta

The huge table in reception, fashioned from an Indonesian bed, sets the mood: elegant yet unstuffy. The villa-hotel is the creation of the young Martinellis who personally welcome you and attend to your every whim… a Tuscan Christmas, a wine and chocolate tour, riding in the hills. With two flights of steps leading to an entrance on either side, the elegant, loftily positioned 19th-century villa stands in sweeping lawns enfolded by the Monti Pisani (from whose verdant hills you can spot Pisa's leaning tower). The whole feel is intimate yet there's masses of space, and a wonderful terrace for summer surrounded by camellias, magnolias, jasmine and pines. Bedrooms ooze subtlety and comfort: fabrics with flowers and stripes, peach and grey walls, modern art. Bed linen is delicious, walk-in showers luxurious, views bucolic. Return after a day in Lucca (just three miles) to cocktails in the Renaissance-style garden and a dip in the pool. In winter you breakfast by an open fire, on yogurts, jams, cold cuts, fresh fruits and breads and brioche straight from the oven. *Min. two nights in high season.*

Price	€120–€200. Singles €90–€160.
Rooms	11 doubles.
Meals	Restaurant à la carte, €28–€40. Wine €20–€80.
Closed	January.
Directions	A11 Firenze-Mare exit Lucca Est; signs for Pisa onto SS12; signs to Albergo Villa Marta; after 250m, left into via del Ponte Guasperini; entrance 500m on left. Can be tricky, ask for detailed directions on booking.

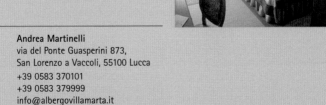

	Andrea Martinelli
	via del Ponte Guasperini 873,
	San Lorenzo a Vaccoli, 55100 Lucca
Tel	+39 0583 370101
Fax	+39 0583 379999
Email	info@albergovillamarta.it
Web	www.albergovillamarta.it

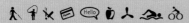

Entry 116 Map 8

Villa Alessandra

They ask that you stay for at least three nights, so do – it is worth every penny. You will be a guest in a beautiful country house close to one of Italy's most perfect towns. Despite a touch of formality the setting seems to have been designed to help you relax: take your own picnic into one of the gardens, cool off in the pool. The road to the house is a country lane, the countryside gentle and very lovely, the house within distant sight of Lucca (a seven-minute drive). The two sitting rooms are stylish and welcoming with big floral sofas, *terre cuite* floors, beautiful murals and attractive little touches. All but one of the bedrooms has a view, all are appealing: white walls and open stonework, wicker armchairs, generous fabrics, splendid bathrooms. One has a four-poster. There are three bikes for you to borrow, walks into the hills, medieval Lucca to explore and the fashionable seaside resort of Forte dei Marmi to discover. Your cultivated hosts are very proud of their villa and breakfasts are quite a spread. *Minimum stay three nights.*

Price	€125-€155.
	Whole villa €8,000 per week.
Rooms	6: 5 doubles, 1 twin.
Meals	Restaurants nearby.
Closed	Christmas.
Directions	From Lucca north on Camaiore road; cross River Serchio right to Monte S.Quirico; 1.5km right; left to Arsina (via Billona) to via Arsina on right; after 1.1km drive on right.

Signora Enrica Tosca
via Arsina 1100b,
55100 Lucca

Tel	+39 0583 395171
Fax	+39 0583 395828
Email	villa.ale@mailcity.com
Web	www.villa-alessandra.it

Da Elisa alle Sette Arti

Some cities are to be escaped – for cooler breezes, respite from the crowds. Lucca isn't like that. It is more serene than its Tuscan cousins and it is the locals, not the tourists, who set the pace and create the atmosphere. The elegant shop fronts – dark wood, gold lettering, sparkling windows – are piled high with cheeses, bread, wines; much is pedestrianised and the entire city is encircled by a wide city wall along which you may walk, car-free. Da Elisa sits within the embrace of the walls feels like a comfortable youth hostel for grown ups (good beds, the odd flourish in décor and furnishings) – unusual. A big wooden door on the street leads to an unprepossessing staircase; through a little hall are six rooms and a shared kitchen, a blessing for those on a budget; a note says 'help yourself to supplies and leave something for others, too'. Breakfast is DIY – nip up to the bakery while the coffee brews. Expect the faintest whiff of luxury and you will be disappointed: this is frill-free, functional and easy. And you are in one of the most beautiful and beguiling medieval cities in Italy.

Price	€45-€70.
Rooms	10: 4 doubles; 6 doubles sharing bath.
Meals	Breakfast €7.
Closed	Never.
Directions	Follow signs to railway station, around walls; after 1st bend, through Porta Elisa gate; on for 50m.

Andrea Mencaroni
via Elisa, 25,
55100 Lucca

Tel	+39 0583 494539
Fax	+39 0583 471609
Email	info@daelisa.com
Web	www.daelisa.com

Villa Michaela

A lifetime's treat. Writers, celebrities and a First Lady have all stayed here, in the opulent Tuscan villa with its *House & Garden* interiors. You can even make it your own: indulge family and friends and get married in its chapel. You may have the best luck booking out of season. Come for a few days, join a Slow Food house party, sample local wines, listen to opera. An interior designer has worked his magic on every room, mingling fine English furniture with classic Italian style, while Puccini, Verdi and Dante lend their names to the grander bedrooms, awash with frescoed ceilings, lavish fabrics, king-size beds and double sinks. Also: a family kitchen, a formal dining room, a library and a room for TV, tennis and an outdoor pool. Dine al fresco, on culinary artist Luca's divine concoctions, and let your gaze drift over the floodlit gardens, heady with gardenias, to the 50 acres of pine forests and olive groves beyond. You are bathed in tranquillity yet it's a five-minute walk to the delightful village of Vorno, and unspoilt Lucca is a ten-minute drive. *Coach house for six occasionally available. Minimum stay two nights.*

Price	€200–€300. Entire villa on request.
Rooms	10 doubles.
Meals	Dinner with wine, €50.
Closed	Never.
Directions	SS12 from Lucca to Guamo. Follow signs for Vorno. Villa behind church.

Vanessa Swarbreck
via di Valle 8,
55060 Vorno

Tel	+44 (0)1428 683815
Fax	+39 0583 971292
Email	vanessaswarbreck@yahoo.co.uk
Web	www.villamichaela.com

Fattoria di Pietrabuona

Hide yourself away in the foothills of the Svizzera Pesciatina – Tuscany's 'Little Switzerland'. Home to a beguiling brood of ancient breed Cinta Senese pigs, this huge estate immersed in greenery is presided over by the elegant Signora – an unlikely pig farmer. The farm buildings have been cleverly divided into apartments that fit together like a puzzle; we liked the three oldest best, near the main villa and each very private. The rest – and the communal pool – are quite a drive up winding hills and some of the roads, though well-maintained, are precipitous in parts: not for the faint-hearted nor those worried about heavily-laden hire cars. All have gardens, outside seating and stupendous views. The exteriors are full of character, the interiors are simple and some of the newer apartments have steep stairs. Bring a Tuscan cookbook: the kitchens, some with old sinks but with new everything else, ask to be used, and there's a small shop next to the office selling estate produce. The views are amazing, particularly from the pool, and the villages are worth a good wander. *Minimum stay one week.*

Price	€400–€1,200 per week.
Rooms	14 apartments: 5 for 2, 5 for 4, 3 for 6, 1 for 8.
Meals	Restaurants nearby.
Closed	November-February, but open Christmas & New Year.
Directions	Exit A11 at Chiesina Uzzanese towards Péscia, then Abetone & Pietrabuona. After P. left for Medicina; left again. After 500m road becomes an avenue of cypresses. Villa & Fattoria at end.

Signora Maristella Galeotti Flori
via per Medicina 2, Pietrabuona,
51010 Péscia

Tel	+39 0572 408115
Fax	+39 0572 408150
Email	info@pietrabuona.com
Web	www.pietrabuona.com

Poderino Lero

An old farmhouse up in the hills with beautiful views over olive groves and Montecatini – a perfect place to unwind. There's a homely atmosphere here, with family, cats, dogs – and Maria Luisa and Lucia, who love having people to stay. Built against a hill centuries ago, a lemon tree clambering up its front, the house is cool in summer and warm in winter. The bedroom in the main house has a stone floor, white walls and is furnished with country antiques; it's slightly dated but in a nice way, and has a relaxed feel. The other rooms to the side of the house have been done in a modern style, and have walk-in showers. There's good, homemade breakfast from Maria Luisa, while dinner, up in the hills, is a ten-minute drive. Downstairs is a large open room with fireplace and comfortable sofas which opens onto the garden – relax on sunloungers and drink in the views: you are surrounded by tumbling olive groves and vines. Chimes and mosaics in the garden, small pieces of Lucia's artwork inserted into the masonry, serene sculptures dotted around – a deeply relaxing place.

Price	€70. Singles €45. Triple €90. Apartment €450 per week.
Rooms	3 + 1: 2 doubles, 1 triple. Apartment for 2-4.
Meals	Dinner with wine, €30-€35. Restaurants 2km.
Closed	Rarely.
Directions	A11 Firenze-Pisa exit Montecatini Terme, follow signs to Pescia. At Montecatini towards Massa e Cozzile. After Cozzile, 2 curves, follow yellow arrow down to Poderino Lero, signed.

Signora Maria Luisa Nesti
via in Campo 42,
51010 Massa e Cozzile

Tel	+39 0572 60218
Mobile	+39 338 6340152
Fax	+39 0572 60218
Email	poderinolero@yahoo.it

The Lance Manor Castle

The name is grand, the reality is cosy – and marvellously peaceful. Come to escape the world and get drunk on the views, which sweep over the tree-lush valley to three villages in the hills… catch them from the garden, the pool, the terrace and every little window. Here you have two 18th-century stone cottages: one, The Tale, originally the gatehouse, the other, down a steep path and divided into two, with one huge terrace. (Aptly named The Elf and The Fairy, these are best rented together, with the option of a connecting door upstairs.) The Tale is a nest for a nimble pair, its bedroom on a mezzanine up a spiral stair; its quaint 'crazy paving' shower is downstairs. Cute interiors are stuffed with antique beds and bolster pillows, walls are rag-rolled with Tuscan colours, floors are ancient tiled and drapes flow. Artificial flowers decorate lovely old beams, the kitchens remain simple and all is pleasantly cool in summer. Your English-speaking hostess lives nearby, a baker calls every day in summer (otherwise it's a trek down to the village), there are two hot tubs and one pool. *Min. stay three to seven nights.*

Price	€350–€500 for 2–3; €500–€700 for 4–5; €950–€1,350 for 8–9.
Rooms	Cottage for 2–3; 2 apartments for 4. Can rent whole place.
Meals	Restaurant 1km.
Closed	Rarely.
Directions	A1 exit Chiesina Uzzanese, on to Pescia; phone from Esselunga (no signal for 12km).

Gloria Wainwright Ciofi
via di Pontito 19,
51010 Lanciole

Mobile	+39 333 3759100
Fax	+39 0572 429639
Email	gloria.ciofi@tin.it
Web	www.thelancemanor.it

Antica Casa "Le Rondini"

Imagine a room above an archway in an ancient hilltop village, within ancient castle walls. You lean from the window and watch the swallows dart to and fro; there are *rondini* inside too, captured in a 200-year-old fresco. The way through the arch – the via del Vento ('where the wind blows') – and the front door to this captivating house await just the other side. Step into a lovely room, a study in white – fresh lilies and snowy walls and sofas – dotted with family antiques and paintings. Fulvia and Carlo are warm, interesting hosts who have lovingly restored the house to its original splendour. The delightfully different bedrooms have wrought-iron bedheads, big mirrors and some original stencilling. Several, like the Swallow Room, have pale frescoes. All have good views. The little apartment, too, is simple, charming, peaceful. Just across the cobbled street is a walled garden with lemon trees – an idyllic place for breakfast on sunny mornings. A short walk brings you to the square where village ladies sit playing cards, children scamper and the church bell rings every hour, on the hour.

Price	€75-€115. Apartment €65 for 2.
Rooms	5 + 1: 5 doubles. Apartment for 2-4.
Meals	Restaurant 200m.
Closed	November-February.
Directions	A11 Firenze-Pisa Nord. Exit Montecatini Terme. Follow signs to Pescia. Left after 2nd set of traffic lights. Right after petrol station. Follow sign "Colle-Buggiano". Up hill to parking area.

	Fulvia Musso
	via M Pierucci 21,
	51011 Colle di Buggiano
Tel	+39 0572 33313
Fax	+39 0572 905361
Email	info@anticacasa.it
Web	www.anticacasa.it

Tenuta di Pieve a Celle

Fiorenza welcomes you with coffee and homemade cake, Julie – the retriever – escorts you round the garden, and there are freshly-laid eggs for breakfast. This is pure, genuine hospitality. Off a country road and down a cypress-lined drive, the shuttered, ochre-coloured *colonica* sits amid the family farm's olive groves and vineyards. The Saccentis (three generations) live next door but this house feels very much like home. Bedrooms (one downstairs) are furnished with well-loved antiques, rugs on tiled floors and handsome wrought-iron or upholstered beds. Cesare, Fiorenza's husband, designed the fabrics – pretty country motifs – and his collection of African art is dotted around the rooms. Books, flowers, soft lighting give a warm and restful feel. There's an elegant but cosy sitting room, with fireplace, where you eat breakfast if it's too chilly on the patio, and dinner is by request. Sometimes the Saccentis join you: a real family affair. Laze by the pool with views to distant hills, walk in the woods, borrow bikes or visit nearby Lucca.

Price	€120–€140.
Rooms	5 twins/doubles.
Meals	Dinner €30, by arrangement. Wine €8.50–€10.
Closed	Rarely.
Directions	A11 for Pisa Nord. Exit Pistoia; signs for Pistoia Ovest to Montagnana; 2km, Tenuta on right. Ring bell at gates.

Cesare & Fiorenza Saccenti
via di Pieve a Celle 158,
51030 Pistoia

Tel	+39 0573 913087
Fax	+39 0573 913087
Email	info@tenutadipieveacelle.it
Web	www.tenutadipieveacelle.it

Villa Anna Maria

The wrought-iron gates swing open to reveal a strange and atmospheric haven. You feel protected here from the outside world, miles from the heat and bustle of Pisa. It is an intriguing place. Secret rooms lurk behind locked doors; some bedrooms seem untouched since the 17th century. They are all different, themed and with high ceilings, the most curious being the Persian and the Egyptian. The entrance hall is splendidly marble, graced with columns and chandeliers ; the library – a touch over the top for some – is nevertheless in tune with the rest, and in tune, it must be said, with its eccentric, jolly owner. Claudio and his wife collect anything and everything and rooms are crammed with curios and collectibles. Yes, it is shambolic – but your host cares more about people than about money and there are no rules, so treat it as your home. There's a game room with billiards and videos (3,000 of them), table tennis, woodland paths, a pool with piped music issuing from clumps of bamboo, a barbecue area for those who choose to self-cater, and a romping dog. *Minimum stay two nights.*

Price	€120–€150. Singles €90. Apartments €800–€2,000 per week. Cottage €1,000 per week.
Rooms	6 + 1: 6 doubles/triples (or 2 apartments for 2-8). 1 cottage for 2-3.
Meals	Dinner with wine, €40.
Closed	Rarely.
Directions	From Pisa SS12 for Lucca. At S.Giuliano Terme, SS12 left down hill; after Rigoli to Molina di Quosa. On right opposite pharmacy.

Signor Claudio Zeppi
SS dell'Abetone 146,
56010 Molina di Quosa

Tel/Fax	+39 0508 50139
Mobile	+39 328 2334450
Email	zeppi@villaannamaria.com
Web	www.villaannamaria.com

Agriturismo Fattoria di Migliarino

On 3,000 farmed hectares fronting the sea is an agriturismo run on immaculate wheels. This is due to the charm and indefatigable energy of Martino and Giovanna, a young couple with four children who understand perfectly the needs of families. The B&B rooms are in the main house: Tuscan beds, soft wall lights and prints, mosquito-proofed windows, big arched sitting areas and a raftered dining room with two sociable tables. In the buildings beyond are 13 apartments of every shape and size. Most are two-storey, all have terraces divided by hedges of jasmine – you may be as private or as gregarious as you like. There's a family pool open from June to September, a new 'quiet' pool too, neatly gravelled pathways and lawned spaces with loungers, a well-being centre brimming with treatments, a farm shop for meat, wine and olive oil, football, tennis, ping-pong and sporting activities you can book yourselves into, including riding and sailing. It's five miles to Pisa, elegant Lucca is not much further and the sandy beaches are a bike ride away – you can hire a bike, too. *Dinner (min. 15) on request.*

Price	€100-€160.
	Apartments €350-€1,500 per week.
Rooms	10 + 13: 10 doubles.
	13 apartments for 2-10.
Meals	Breakfast €5 for self-caterers.
	Restaurants 200m.
Closed	Never.
Directions	Exit A11-A12 Pisa Nord, left for Pisa; 1st lights right under r'way bridge to viale dei Pini. Left after 800m; in via del Mare.

Dott. Martino & Giovanna Salviati
viale dei Pini 289,
56010 Migliarino

Mobile	+39 348 4435100
Fax	+39 0508 03170
Email	info@fattoriadimigliarino.it
Web	www.fattoriadimigliarino.it

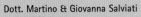

Antica Dimora Leones

A labyrinth of vaulted ceilings, stone fireplaces and original frescoes in the heart of the medieval *borgo* of Palaia. The palazzo was restored in the 1800s but goes way back to AD1000, when it formed part of the castle. Now it is an antique collector's paradise – which is no surprise: the owner's grandparents were antique dealers. It almost feels as though they are still here, wandering the historic corridors and rooms. Specialness is everywhere, from the high frescoed ceilings of the 'noble floor' to the bare beams and rooftop views of the characterful servants' quarters. Every floor has a wonderful sitting room or library, with books, comfy chairs and something precious in each corner. A tray of drinks awaits your arrival; the buffet breakfast (salami, cheeses, homemade cakes) is served in the beamed dining room or under wisteria in the pretty garden. So much history, yet there are some winning modern touches – notably the seven-person hydropool. Restorative, soothing, special – and don't miss the lovely Etruscan town of Volterra.

Price	€95-€120.
Rooms	13: 12 doubles, 1 single.
Meals	Lunch or dinner with wine €35, on request. Restaurants 100m.
Closed	Rarely.
Directions	Superstrada Firenze-Pisa-Livorno, exit Pontedera, follow signs for Palaia centre. Just beyond clock tower on the corner.

Andrea Soldani
via della Rocca 2,
56036 Palaia

Tel	+39 0587 622024
Fax	+39 0248 14736
Email	info@leones-palaia.it
Web	www.leones-palaia.it

Relais Guado al Sole Agriturismo

Bump down a lazy track to electric gates and this huge estate of forest and groves, once the hunting lodge of nobility. This is a quiet part of Tuscany, with fewer crowds, where peace reigns in rolling hills and renovated stone buildings, and the views exude serenity. For those seeking solitude it is bliss. Terraces and gardens for strolling give way to tough, hilly walking country: ideal for ramblers and birdwatchers. The apartments here are spacious, spotless and traditional in décor with wooden furniture and neutral washes on walls, well-tiled bathrooms and bedrooms in golds, browns and beiges. Most have open fires in their sitting rooms and almost all the bedrooms have those glorious views. Kitchens are bursting with equipment but if you can't be bothered to use it, wander up to the brick-arched dining room of the big house for local food and wine (served in summer on the terrace). Heaven to laze away a hot afternoon by the infinity pool; there's enough space to feel private, and masses of lush greenery. Laziness may get the better of you: take plenty of novels. *Minimum stay three nights.*

Price	€60–€100. Apartments €80–€180. Linen & cleaning extra.
Rooms	5 + 6: 3 doubles, 2 triples. 6 apartments: 3 for 2-4, 2 for 3-5, 1 for 4-6.
Meals	Breakfast for self-caterers €7. Dinner, 4 courses, €25, by arrangement. Wine €6.
Closed	November-March.
Directions	From SS68 direction Volterra exit Casole D'Elsa- San Dalmazio. At X-roads tirm left direction Montecerboli. Signed.

Annalisa Buzzichelli
loc. S. Ippolito,
56045 Pomarance

Tel	+39 0588 65854
Fax	+39 0588 67854
Email	info@relaisguadoalsole.com
Web	www.relaisguadoalsole.com

Monsignor della Casa Country Resort

It could be a Giotto landscape: the view of Monte Senario has not changed for 500 years. But the old buildings in the hamlet where estate workers once lived have become an upmarket resort, wonderful for all ages. Run by the charming Marzi family, the complex has a warm, inviting feel. Bay hedges and big terracotta pots of herbs scent the courtyards, there are cherry and olive trees everywhere, established gardens, a playground and two safely fenced pools. The apartments, mostly on two floors, are stylish and uncluttered, with fireplaces, stonework, beams; all have little gardens; the villas have private pools; one is in the old tower with views over the landscape. Airy bedrooms are painted in soft colours; some have four-posters with fine linen drapes, others wrought-iron beds. You can eat in the restaurant-bar where hams hang from the beams – the menu is Tuscan, the wine list long. Then burn off the calories in the Wellness Centre, splendid with sauna, jacuzzi and gym. Close by is the Renaissance villa where Monsignor Giovanni Della Casa, a descendant of the Medici, was born in 1503.

Price	€160-€360. Apt €800-€2,200. Villa €2,000-€6,000. Self-catering prices per week.
Rooms	26 apartments: for 2, 4, 6 or 8. 2 villas: 1 for 8-12, 1 for 12-16.
Meals	Dinner €35-€50. Restaurants 5km.
Closed	9 January-9 March.
Directions	From m'way exit A1 Barberino di Mugello; signs to Borgo San Lorenzo; signs to Faenza; right after 2.7km , signs to Mucciano and Corniolo. After 1km left to villa.

Alessio Marzi
via di Mucciano 16,
50032 Borgo San Lorenzo

Tel	+39 0558 40821
Fax	+39 0558 408240
Email	booking@monsignore.com
Web	www.monsignore.com

Casa Palmira

A medieval farm expertly restored by charming Assunta and Stefano who, being Italian, have a flair for this sort of thing. You are immersed in greenery yet half an hour from Florentine bustle. The views on the road to Fiesole are stunning; Stefano will ferry you around neighbouring villages in his mini-van, or you could hire mountain bikes and take one of Assunta's wonderful picnic baskets with you. The log-fired sitting room sets the tone: the *casa* has a warm, Tuscan feel, and bedrooms open off a landing with a brick-walled 'garden' in the centre – all Stefano's work. Two have four-poster beds dressed in Florentine fabric, all have polished wooden floors and pretty views, either onto the gardens where Assunta grows her herbs and vegetables or onto vines and olive trees. You are 500 metres above sea level so... no need for air conditioning, no mosquitoes! Breakfast on apricots and home-produced yogurt; dine on Tuscan food. There is also an excellent restaurant up the road. *Minimum stay two nights. Ask about cookery classes.*

Price	€85–€100. Single €65–€75. Triple €120–€125. Family €130. Apt €135–€145 (€750–€950 per week).
Rooms	7 + 1: 4 twins/doubles, 1 twin, 1 triple, 1 single. Apt for 3-4.
Meals	Dinner with wine, €30. Restaurant 700m.
Closed	10 January–10 March.
Directions	From north, A1 exit Barberino del Mugello for Borgo S. Lorenzo. Follow 302 via Faentina dir. Florence. 3km after Polcanto, left at "Feriolo" sign; house on left.

Assunta & Stefano Fiorini-Mattioli
via Faentina 4/1, loc. Feriolo, Polcanto,
50030 Borgo San Lorenzo

Tel	+39 0558 409749
Fax	+39 0558 409749
Email	info@casapalmira.it
Web	www.casapalmira.it

La Campanella

The impressive green gates are a welcoming sight after the steep crawl up the unmade road, but the views across the valley and the inviting breeze on a hot day are worth every bump. The delightful Jill will soon have you seated in her lovely farmhouse kitchen (or under the parasol on the patio): a glass of homemade lemonade, a slice of something sweet perhaps; you can't help but feel there's nowhere else you'd rather be. The airy sitting room has high ceiling arches interrupted by the odd beam, and deep window sills; white walls are busy with paintings, puffed-up white sofas sit under mounds of embroidered cushions, big lamps and fresh flowers rest on polished tables; there's more than just a touch of Englishness about the place. Pretty bedrooms have terracotta floor tiles, patchwork quilts and fine views. Children will entertain themselves for hours in the young garden, on the swing under the mulberry tree or in the pool. Adults may flop into the hammock with some of Jill's homemade wine. The peace is broken only by the faint shuffles of next door's hens – source of your breakfast eggs. *Cot available.*

Price	€75–€95.
Rooms	2: 1 twin/double, 1 family suite for 2-4.
Meals	Lunch €12. Dinner with wine, €30.
Closed	Rarely.
Directions	Exit A1 at Barberino di Mugello; signs for Borgo San Lorenzo; SP41 to Sagginale; 1st right into Via di Zeti. Follow track up & fork right; 1st yellow house on right at top.

Jill Greetham
via Romignano 9, Località San Cresci,
50032 Borgo San Lorenzo
Tel/Fax +39 0558 490373
Mobile +39 333 1923031
Email info@atuscanplace.com
Web www.atuscanplace.com

Villa Campestri

High in the Tuscan hills, at the end of an avenue of cypresses, surrounded by parkland, olive groves and verdant lawns… a 13th-century dream. Pass the frescoes by a pupil of Giotto and the 14th-century chapel; observe the wooden ceilings and the time-worn terracotta tiles; contemplate the indoor well, the ultimate in medieval 'mod-cons'. Renaissance-style bedrooms come with antique furniture, rich fabrics and country views; the honeymoon suite has an unbelievably grand 18th-century canopied bed. On each floor is a welcoming sitting room, each with a massive stone fireplace and plump sofas. The light, Tuscan food has a serious local following, and the dining room, with its glittering Murano chandelier, 17th-century frescoes and Art Deco windows, is a spectacular setting for dining on homemade, home-grown delicacies. Try the olive oil menu (every course includes it) or visit the *oleoteca* in the cellar; you can attend courses, tastings and visit the mill. The peace here is a testament to Viola's gentleness and to her diligent, contented team.

Price	€120-€310.
Rooms	25: 12 doubles, 2 triples, 1 single, 10 suites.
Meals	Dinner €52.
Closed	15 November-15 March.
Directions	For Borgo San Lorenzo/Viccho; through Sagginale; after 2 km, right for Cistio & Campestri; signed.

Viola Pasquali
via di Campestri 19/22,
50039 Vicchio di Mugello

Tel	+39 0558 490107
Fax	+39 0558 490108
Email	villa.campestri@villacampestri.it
Web	www.villacampestri.com

Entry 132 Map 9

Le Due Volpi

Twenty miles from Florence, yet utterly unspoilt: the gentle hills of the Mugello valley have escaped development and the drive from Borgo is truly lovely. At the end of a long white track is a big house strewn with ivy; outside two snazzy little foxes – 'le due volpi', – splash water into a trough. Step into spaciousness and light and a charming Tuscan interior. Heidi is Italian, well-travelled and speaks perfect English; Lorenzo has a passion for old radios and antiques They are naturals at looking after guests, love cooking on their Aga, dispatch meals to the loggia in summer and are embarking on a greener lifestyle, introducing solar panels and wood-fired central heating. The bedrooms, with their wooden floors and chunky rafters, couldn't be nicer. Beds are large and lighting soft, wood-burners keep you cosy in winter, Chini-tiled shower rooms have a stylish rusticity. Note that the two top-floor rooms are reached via several stairs. Vicchio, full of history, is a ten-minute drive and there's a riding stables down the road. Bliss. *Minimum stay two nights. Pool planned for 2008.*

Price	€75–€95. Extra bed €20–€30. Half-board option.
Rooms	3 doubles (one with kitchenette). Extra beds.
Meals	Dinner €20. Picnic, with wine, €15.
Closed	Rarely.
Directions	A1 exit Barberino; SS551 to Vicchio. From town square, take Molezzano & Caselle road. 2km after Caselle, over bridge; at x-roads, right up track signed Villa Poggio Bartoli for 800m; cypress trees on right.

Heidi Flores
via di Molezzano 88,
50039 Vicchio del Mugello

Tel/Fax	+39 0558 407874
Mobile	+39 338 6220160
Email	info@leduevolpi.it
Web	www.leduevolpi.it

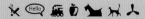

Il Casellino

Traditional Tuscan interiors and a country rusticity beautify this 17th-century farmstead 350 metres above sea level and beset with views. Once the buildings belonged to the Abbey Saint Maria of Vallombrosa, now they form part of a working organic olive farm with a stunning garden. Only guests from the three houses share the 800 rose bushes, the orchard and cutting garden, the courtyards with their potted lemon trees, the loungers around the landscaped pool, the glorious views over olive groves. Each house is individual; each has a feeling of space. There are fireplaces and cosy corners with window seats, tapestry cushions and books written in several languages. Bedrooms have ragged walls, fresh flowers, patchwork bedspreads; kitchens get top gadgets and all the basics. The quietest rooms are away from the pool, but all are serene. At the bottom of the road you can catch the bus to Florence... or hop in the car for endless unspoilt villages. As well as producing organic olive oil, the farm is devoted to discovering rare animal breeds, including the endangered black chicken – the symbol of Chianti Classico.

Price	€800-€5,000 per week.
Rooms	3 houses: 1 for 2, 2 for 4-6.
Meals	Breakfast €7. Restaurant 1km.
Closed	Never.
Directions	Pontassieve dir. Rosano, Volognano & Torri; through Torri, past bar on right, on for 1km then 2nd right; up track, through olive groves to house.

Eduardo Salvia
Torri Villa 49,
50067 Rignano sull'Arno

Tel	+39 0558 305320
Fax	+39 0248 12754
Email	info@casellino.com
Web	www.casellino.com

Casa Valiversi

The old pharmaceuticals laboratory, perched on a hill, painted in pretty pink, has become a distinctive, distinguished B&B. Just four rooms – one with a balcony, one with an open fire – and Mirella, warm, friendly and living next door. Tired of commuting to Florence every day she has opened her Casa to guests, popping in to serve a generous breakfast. Inside are 20th-century antiques from her years of dealing, sprinkled over three floors with originality and taste. Armchairs range from cream Thirties' Art Deco to Sixties' bubblegum pink, bold art beautifies pale walls, a white 50s lamp dominates a glass dining table, six dining chairs are immaculately upholstered. Bedrooms are serene spaces that ooze comfort and class and monogrammed linen, big arched windows overlook groves of olives. For self-caterers, the kitchen is fitted in contemporary style (plus one perfect antique cupboard from France), opening to garden, pergola and large terrace. Here in the hillsides of Sesto Fiorentino, five miles from Florence's centre, a relaxing, refreshing and peaceful place to stay. *3km from airport.*

Price	€100-€120.
	Whole house €3,000-€5,000 per week.
Rooms	4 twins/doubles.
Meals	Use of kitchen €10.
	Restaurants nearby.
Closed	Never.
Directions	A1 exit Sesto Fiorentino dir. Centro & Colonnata; signed. Ring for further directions.

Mirella Mazzierli
via Valiversi 61,
50019 Sesto Fiorentino

Tel	+39 0553 850285
Fax	+39 0553 850285
Email	mirella@casavaliversi.it
Web	www.casavaliversi.it

Locanda Senio

Food is king here: genuine home cooking from Roberta, and, in the restaurant, much gastronomic enthusiasm from Ercole. Echoing a growing movement to bring lost medieval traditions back to life, they are passionate about wild herbs and 'forgotten' fruits. Enrol on one of their cookery courses (stay three nights and join one at no extra cost). The prosciutto from rare-breed *maiale medievale* is delicious; breakfast is a feast of homemade breads, cakes, fruits and jams; dinner a leisurely treat served in the restaurant with nine tables and cosy log fire. The little inn occupies a stunning spot in a quiet town in the Mugello valley, surrounded by rolling hills... there are guided walks through the woods, gastronomic meanders through the valley. Bedrooms are comfortable and cosy and it is worth paying extra for the suites if you can; they're in the 17th-century building with original fireplaces. There's a relaxation centre of which Roberta and Ercole are very proud – the jacuzzi, sauna and Turkish bath have a delicious aroma. Steps lead up to a pool with blue loungers; body and soul will be nurtured.

Price	€115-€200. Suites €190-€230. Half-board €100-€145 p.p.
Rooms	8: 6 twins/doubles, 2 suites for 2-3.
Meals	Dinner from €45. Wine from €10.
Closed	6 January-13 February.
Directions	From Bologna A14, exit Imola for Rimini; 50m; for Palazzuolo (40 mins). House in village, right of fountain & Oratorio dei Santi Carlo e Antonio.

	Ercole & Roberta Lega
	via Borgo dell'Ore 1,
	50035 Palazzuolo sul Senio
Tel	+39 0558 046019
Fax	+39 0558 043949
Email	info@locandasenio.com
Web	www.locandasenio.com

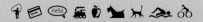

Residenza Casanuova

Live like a Florentine in the heart of the city, high above the madding crowds. The top floor of this handsome palazzo belonged to Beatrice and Massimiliano's grandmother, and is filled with her elegant taste. There are panelled doors and parquet floors, creamy walls and tall windows. Light-filled rooms are furnished with antiques, grand mirrors and pretty chandeliers, polished surfaces are dotted with china vases, walls hung with engravings, portraits and a collection of oils by great-grandfather. Calm, uncluttered bedrooms are soft and spacious, each with an amusing theme: a collection of umbrellas, hats or tin boxes. One has a magnificent Murano mirror. Breakfast on beautiful china in the handsome dining room or on the terrace before plunging into the hubbub of the city's museums, galleries and churches. The owners, with an apartment on the same floor, will help with tours, museums and shopping trips. Friendly and easy going, they're on hand when you need them or happy to leave you alone. Return to a private terrace for a glass of wine and rooftop views.

Price	€160–€180.
Rooms	5: 4 doubles, 1 single.
Meals	Restaurants within walking distance.
Closed	Never.
Directions	Exit Firenze sud. Follow directions to city centre and S. Ambrogio market.

Beatrice & Massimiliano Gori
via della Mattonaia 21,
50121 Florence

Tel	+39 0552 343413
Fax	+39 0552 343413
Email	info@residenzacasanuova.it
Web	www.residenzacasanuova.it

Palazzo Niccolini al Duomo

One minute you're battling with tourists in the Piazza del Duomo, the next you're standing inside this extraordinarily lovely palazzo. The *residenza* is on the second floor (with lift); two small trees, a brace of antique chairs and a brass plaque announce that you've arrived at the friendly reception. Ever since it was first built by the Naldini family in the 16th century, on the site of the sculptor Donatello's workshop, the building's grandeur has been steadily added to. And the recent restoration hasn't detracted from its beauty, merely added some superb facilities. It's all you hope staying in such a place will be – fabulously elegant and luxurious, with 18th-century frescoes, trompe-l'oeil effects, fine antiques and magnificent beds… but in no way awesome, thanks to many personal touches. Relax in the lovely drawing room and look at family portraits, books and photos. Two signed photos are from the King of Italy, sent in 1895 to Contessa Cristina Niccolini, the last of the Naldini. She married into the current owner's family, bringing the palazzo as part of her dowry. A gem.

Price	€200–€380. Singles €190–€220. Suites €270–€650.
Rooms	10: 5 doubles, 5 suites.
Meals	Dinner, by arrangement. Restaurants nearby.
Closed	Rarely.
Directions	In Florence centro storico. A1 exit Firenze south; head for town centre & Il Duomo; via dei Servi off Piazza del Duomo. Park, unload & car will be taken to garage: €25–€30.

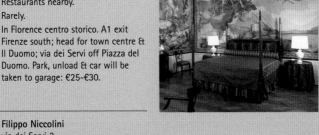

	Filippo Niccolini
	via dei Servi 2,
	50122 Florence
Tel	+39 0552 82412
Fax	+39 0552 90979
Email	info@niccolinidomepalace.com
Web	www.niccolinidomepalace.com

Palazzo Bombicci Pontelli

Those huge, handsome doors on the streets of Florence – what lies behind them: a cool hallway, a fountained courtyard? This one, on the banks of the Arno, heaves open to a marbled hall guarded by concièrge Maurio (on duty: 8am to 7pm) and an impressive stairway (no lift) leading to a large, luminous apartment on the first floor. Enter a small hall, then a sitting/dining room with divans for four, a new kitchen with oven, a furnished terrace (what a treat), a vast bedroom with contemporary wicker armchairs, a stunning stone fireplace – pure 16th-century palazzo – and a terrace with a view that sweep towards the Piazzale Michelangelo (where the photographer stands). The second apartment on the second floor, reached via an open staircase, has much the same; no terrace, but long views and a large glazed room overlooking the courtyard below. Next door, at no 19, but on the third floor (with a lift), is a simple but comfortable and cool apartment for two with views down to Piazza Santa Croce. It all feels so central – and special.

Price	€114–€140. €700–€900 per week.
Rooms	3 apartments: 2 for 2-6, 1 for 2 + children.
Meals	Restaurants nearby.
Closed	Never.
Directions	In Florence centro storico. No parking in central Florence, ask about garage on booking.

Signor Tuccio Guicciardini
corso dei Tintori 21,
50122 Florence

Tel/Fax	+39 0577 907185
Mobile	+39 329 2273120
Email	info@guicciardini.com
Web	www.guicciardini.com

Albergotto Hotel

You are an awfully long way from *The Mill on the Floss* but George Eliot once stayed here – as did Verdi and Donizetti. Peeking between two Gucci shops on one of Florence's swankiest streets (once described as 'the drawing room of Europe') the hotel still has an air of glamour though inside all is quiet; bustle quickly recedes behind the double glazing, the big fresh flowers and the old prints of Florence. Immaculate, traditional bedrooms have warm parquet floors, flowers, a military print or oil, the odd antique. There are good city views from large windows: rooms at the front overlook the beautiful Palazzo Strozzi; from the huge window in the fourth-floor suite you can see as far as Fiesole. Spotless bathrooms are mosaic-tiled with big white fulsome towels. There's a smart sitting room to return to, and the breakfast room is elegant: royal blue and gold curtains frame large windows, plates adorn walls, fresh flowers fill corners. Museums, galleries, restaurants and shops abound and you can walk to them all.

Price	€117–€310. Suite €335.
Rooms	22: 18 doubles, 3 singles, 1 suite.
Meals	Restaurants nearby.
Closed	Never.
Directions	In Florence centro storico. Short walk from Santa Maria station. Secure parking €27 per day – ask on booking.

Carlo Martelli
via dé Tornabuoni 13,
50123 Florence
Tel   +39 0552 396464
Fax   +39 0552 398108
Email info@albergotto.com
Web   www.albergotto.com

Casa Howard Guest House

A five-minute walk from the bus and train station is this handsome palazzo, the talk of the town. No reception staff, no communal space, just a big fur throw on a welcoming divan and smiling housekeepers who serve breakfast in your room. On each floor, too, an honesty fridge stocked with soft drinks, wine and champagne. But best of all are the bedrooms, designed with style, originality and humour. If you can splash out on a larger, more lavish room, do, though all are delightful. One, with a sunken bath and Japanese prints on the walls, is a deep sensual red; another is 18th-century elegant, with a black velvet sofa and gold taffeta curtains. The apartment, its queen-size bed residing at the top of a spiral stair, is ultra-moderne. There's a room specially for those who arrive with their pooches (dogs' beds, baskets, large terrace), and another, the 'Play Room', for families (Disney videos, a climbing wall!). Bathrooms are memorable; nights are air-conditioned and peaceful, providing you keep windows shut. A breath of fresh air, and decent value for the heart of old Florence. *Minimum stay two nights at weekends.*

Price	€160–€250.
	Apartment €1,800–€2,700 per week.
Rooms	12 + 1: 10 doubles, 2 suites.
	1 apartment for 2-3.
Meals	Breakfast €15. Restaurants nearby.
Closed	Never.
Directions	50m from Santa Maria Novella train station.

	via della Scala 18, 50123 Florence
Tel	+39 0699 24555
Fax	+39 0667 94644
Email	info@casahoward.it
Web	www.casahoward.com

Residenza Johanna I

Astonishingly good value in the historic centre of Florence – and what an attractive, friendly place to be. You really feel as though you have your own pad in town, away from tourist bustle. Lea's other *residenze* (see overleaf) have been such a success that she and Johanna have opened this one in a lovely 19th-century palazzo, shared with notaries and an embassy. Up the lift or marble stairs to a big welcome on the second floor. Your hosts are charming, keen to make your stay a happy one. Graceful arches, polished parquet floors and soft colours give a feeling of light and space to the two parallel corridors, classical music wafts in the background and there are plenty of books and guides to browse through on rainy days. The bedrooms are big, airy and cool, silk drapes beautify beds (some four-posters) and give the rooms a feeling of charm and elegance. All have excellent, stylish bathrooms. There's a new breakfast room, too. Slip out to a bar for a cappuccino and a panino before wandering happily off to the Duomo, the San Lorenzo market and the Piazza della Signora.

Price	€90–€120. Single €65–€80.
Rooms	10: 9 doubles, 1 single.
Meals	Restaurants nearby.
Closed	Never.
Directions	In Florence centro storico. You cannot park in central Florence; ask about garage on booking.

Lea Gulmanelli c/o Eduardo Vitta
via Bonifacio Lupi 14,
50129 Florence

Tel	+39 0554 81896
Fax	+39 0554 82721
Email	lupi@johanna.it
Web	www.johanna.it

Antica Dimora Firenze

Ring the buzzer and up you go – via the small lift or the wide stone stair. Enter the relaxed *residenza* where you come and go as you please; friendly reception is manned until 7pm. A treat to come back here, to a decanter of Vin Santo and a book of love stories by your bed. Perhaps even a four-poster or a jasmine-scented balcony... Italian love of detail is revealed in walls washed rose-pink and pistachio green, in fabrics woven by local artisans, in striped sofas, silk curtains and little vases of dried lavender. Black and white 19th-century prints and antique *cotto* floors combine beautifully with waffle towels and walk-in showers, modems and satellite TV: it's the best of old and new. Settle down in the guest sitting room, dip into almond biscuits and a cup of tea and plan where to have dinner; there's all the info. Browse a glossy book or a magazine, choose a favourite DVD, be as private or as sociable as you like. There are homemade cakes and jams at breakfast, you are on a quietish street near the university area and it's brilliant value for the centre of Florence.

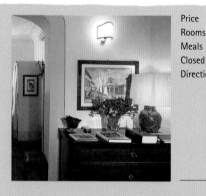

Price	€100–€145.
Rooms	6: 3 doubles, 3 twins.
Meals	Restaurants nearby.
Closed	Rarely.
Directions	In Florence centro storico. You cannot park in central Florence, ask about garage on booking.

Lea Gulmanelli
via San Gallo 72, 50129 Florence
Tel   +39 0554 627296
Fax   +39 0554 634450
Email   info@anticadimorafirenze.it
Web   www.anticadimorafirenze.it

Residenza Johlea

Experience living in a real Florentine *residenza*... a particularly charming home. The restored, late 19th-century building is in an area well-endowed with musuems (the Museum of San Marco and Michelangelo's David are just around the corner). It has good access to train and bus stations, and Laura, Giovanna or Anna will be there to greet you until 8.30pm. A lift transports you up to big bedrooms with long, shuttered windows, subtle colours and lovely fabrics. All are different and all are comfortable, with settees, polished floors and rugs, super bathrooms; all friendly and cosy. There are antiques and air conditioning, books, a shared fridge. There's no breakfast room, but you can enjoy buffet-style breakfasts in the seclusion of your own room. And there's a well-stocked honesty bar available throughout the day. Like the rest of Lea's *residenze* (there are four altogether in this book and Antica Dimora Johlea, is right next door — see overleaf), this is excellent value considering its closeness to the city centre.

Price	€90–€120.
Rooms	8: 5 doubles, 2 twins.
Meals	Restaurants nearby.
Closed	Rarely.
Directions	In Florence centro storico. You cannot park in central Florence, ask about garage on booking.

	Lea Gulmanelli
	via San Gallo 76,
	50129 Florence
Tel	+39 0554 633292
Fax	+39 0554 634552
Email	johlea@johanna.it
Web	www.johanna.it

Antica Dimora Johlea

A cross between a B&B and a hotel – no room service but a friendly face on reception throughout the day – the *residenza* idea is perfect for the independent traveller. Lea Gulmanelli has got her *residenze* down to a fine art – and what's special about this one is that it has its own roof terrace. Weave your way past antique pieces tucked under sloping ceilings and up to a wide, sun-flooded, pergola'd terrace for breakfasts and sundowners and a panorama of Florence. Now that it has been redecorated, the entire top floor of this restored 19th-century palazzo feels bright, light and inviting. Furnishings are colourful and fresh; bedrooms – intimate not huge – have beautiful silk-canopied four-poster beds, delicate prints on walls and mosquito nets at windows so you can open the windows. Luxurious extras include mini fridges and radios, WiFi and satellite TV, there's an honesty bar for drinks and polished tables for breakfast. Michelangelo's David is at the Accademia round the corner; the Duomo is a ten-minute walk.

Price	€120–€170. Single €90–€120.
Rooms	6: 3 doubles, 2 twins, 1 single.
Meals	Restaurants nearby.
Closed	Never.
Directions	Directions on booking.

Lea Gulmanelli
via San Gallo 80,
50129 Florence

Tel	+39 0554 633292
Fax	+39 0554 634332
Email	anticajohlea@johanna.it
Web	www.johanna.it

Villa La Sosta

It's a 15-minute walk to the Duomo, yet the 1892 villa on the Montughi hill stands in large landscaped gardens where songbirds lull you to sleep. The mansard-tower sitting room with sofas, books and views is a lofty place in which to relax, and there's billiards. Bedrooms, with large windows and wooden shutters, are equally stylish with striking Toile de Jouy or checks and dark Tuscan pieces. Interesting, too, are the artefacts – ivory carvings and wooden statues – gathered from the Fantonis' days in Africa; the family ran a banana plantation there. Simple breakfast is served outside under an ivy-covered pergola in summer or in the dining room, just off the family's bright sitting room; over coffee the young, affable Antonio and Giusi – a brother-and-sister team – help you plan your stay. If the city's treasures start to pall they will organise a day in the vineyards or local pottery villages. There's parking off the main road and the number 25 bus, which stops outside the gates, will ferry you into the city or up into the hills. *Gluten-free breakfasts available.*

Price	€95–€130. Singles €85–€105. Triple €130–€160. Quadruple €160–€190.
Rooms	5: 3 doubles, 1 triple, 1 quadruple.
Meals	Restaurants 800m.
Closed	Rarely.
Directions	Signs for Centro & Piazza della Libertà, then via Bolognese; villa on left. Bus 25 bus from r'way station; get off 800m after via Bolognese begins, just before Total Petrol. Parking.

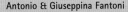

Antonio & Giuseppina Fantoni
via Bolognese 83,
50139 Florence

Tel	+39 0554 95073
Fax	+39 0554 95073
Email	info@villalasosta.com
Web	www.villalasosta.com

Classic Hotel

The hubbub of the city is so overwhelming at times that it is sheer heaven to enter the shaded, gravelled driveway of the Classic. It lies just beyond the old town gate, the Porta Romana, where Florence seems to begin and end. The area is leafy and residential, the Uffizi is a 20-minute roadside walk. The Classic is cool, friendly, secluded – elegant in a low-key way. Much of the furniture has come from the owner's parents' house in town (once a famous old hotel): interesting paintings and handsome Tuscan pieces. Its greatest charm, though, is the shaded courtyard garden with trees, shrubs and little corners where you may sit peacefully with a cappuccino and an unlavish, typically Florentine, breakfast. In winter there's a breakfast room in the basement. Bedrooms are parquet-floored and modestly attractive; some are lovely, especially those in the attic, with their heavily-beamed, sloping ceilings. Altogether an easy-going and comfortable place to stay (lift, air con, TV) for anyone visiting Florence – the feel is more villa than hotel and you're in the countryside in minutes.

Price	€150–€200. Singles €110.
Rooms	20: 17 doubles, 1 suite, 2 singles.
Meals	Breakfast €8.
Closed	Occasionally.
Directions	Directions on booking. Private parking.

Dottoressa Corinne Kraft
viale Machiavelli 25,
50125 Florence

Tel	+39 0552 29351
Fax	+39 0552 29353
Email	info@classichotel.it
Web	www.classichotel.it

Entry 147 Map 8

Villa Poggio San Felice

The moment the gates open and you drive up past the roses, you sense this will be a special stay. Livia inherited the house from her grandparents: it's in a bewitching garden high on a hill overlooking Florence. Narrow paved paths wend their way between shrubs and tall trees, wisteria graces the walls, foxgloves border a flight of old stone steps...The villa itself, tall and immaculate, dates back to 1427. Despite its beautiful, high-ceilinged rooms, it is a friendly and approachable house. The dining room is so light and airy that it makes you smile just to be there; the drawing room has a grand piano you're welcome to play, alongside fresh flowers, big mirrors and interesting books, paintings and engravings. All the bedrooms are big, light and serene, with glossy parquet floors, family antiques, exquisite attention to detail, and views. There's also a super, well-equipped apartment right at the top, with its own terrace and lift. Livia and Lorenzo are young, hardworking and delightful. They even offer a daily 'shuttle' into Florence, to save you the hassle of driving and parking.

Price	€200–€250.
Rooms	5: 3 doubles, 1 twin, 1 suite.
Meals	Lunch from €15. Dinner from €30. Wine from €12. Restaurants 1km.
Closed	January–February.
Directions	Directions on booking.

Livia Puccinelli Sannini & Lorenzo Magnelli
San Matteo in Arcetri 24,
50125 Florence

Tel	+39 0552 20016
Fax	+39 0552 335388
Email	info@villapoggiosanfelice.com
Web	www.villapoggiosanfelice.com

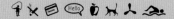

Torre di Bellosguardo

Breathtaking in its beauty and ancient dignity. The entrance hall is cavernous, glorious, with a painted ceiling and an ocean of floor; the view reaches through a vast, plaster-crumbling sun room to the garden. Imposing, mellow buildings, georgous gardens fashioned by a friend of Dante, magical views of Florence. A water feature meanders along a stone terrace, a twisted wisteria shades the walkway to a kitchen garden, there are goats, ponies and rabbits. A pool, gym and cane tables and chairs occupy the old orangery while another pool settles into a perfect lawn. Most of the bedrooms can be reached by lift but the tower suite, with windows on all sides, demands a long climb. The bedrooms defy modern convention and are magnificent in their simplicity, the furniture richly authentic, the views infinite. But do ask for a room with one of the newer beds. Signor Franchetti is often here, and his manners and his English are impeccable – unlike those of the irrepressible pink parrot. All this, and Florence a 30-minute walk, or a 10-minute cab ride, down the hill.
Telephone and internet connection in each room.

Price	€290. Singles €160. Suites €340-€390.
Rooms	16: 8 doubles, 7 suites, 1 single.
Meals	Breakfast €20-€25. Supper €12. Trattoria 1km.
Closed	Rarely.
Directions	A1 exit Firenze Certosa for Porta Romana/Centro; left at Porta Romana on via Ugo Foscolo; keep right & take via Piana to end; right into via Roti Michelozzi.

Signor Amerigo Franchetti
via Roti Michelozzi 2,
50124 Florence

Tel	+39 0552 298145
Fax	+39 0552 29008
Email	info@torrebellosguardo.com
Web	www.torrebellosguardo.com

Relais Villa L'Olmo

With a bit of luck you will be greeted by Claudia, a lovely German lady of considerable charm, married to a Florentine whose family have owned the property since 1700. The Relais is a clutch of immaculately converted apartments, all looking down over the valley, all shamelessly *di lusso*. Imagine softly-lit yellow walls beneath chunky Tuscan beamed ceilings, nicely designed kitchenettes, white china on yellow cloths, smartly checked sofas, glass-topped tables, fresh flowers – even a private pool (and plastic loungers) for the two villas if you can't face splashing with others in the main one. And there's a new communal barbecue, so you can mingle if you wish. Claudia runs a warmly efficient reception and rents out mountain bikes and mobile phones; she organises babysitting, cookery classes and wine tastings, too. There's a cheerful restaurant and a pizzeria, and farm products for sale, Florence is 20 minutes away by car or bus and it's heaven for families. *Special rates for local golf, tennis & riding clubs.*

Price	Villas €160-€285. Apts €90-€240. Farmhouse €180-€380.
Rooms	11: 2 villas for 2-4; 8 apartments for 2-5; 1 farmhouse for 6-8.
Meals	Breakfast €10. Dinner with wine, €20-€40. Restaurants 200m.
Closed	Never.
Directions	A1 exit Firenze-Certosa; at r'bout, signs for Tavarnuzze; there, left to Impruneta. Track on right, signed to villa, 200m past sign for Impruneta.

	Claudia & Alberto Giannotti via Impruneta per Tavarunzze 19, 50023 Impruneta
Tel	+39 0552 311311
Fax	+39 0552 311313
Email	florence.chianti@dada.it
Web	www.relaisfarmholiday.it

Dimora Storica Villa Il Poggiale

This 16th-century villa is so lovely it's impossible to know where to start. Breathe in the scent of old-fashioned roses from a seat on the Renaissance loggia. Wander through the olive trees to the pool (note: some traffic hum from the next-door road). Retreat into the house for some 1800s elegance. Much loved, full of memories, this is the childhood home of two brothers, Johanan and Nathanel Vitta, who devoted two years to its restoration. Rooms are big, beautiful, full of light, and everything has been kept as it was. An oil painting of the Vittas' grandmother welcomes you as you enter; another, Machiavelli by Gilardi, hangs in the salon. Bedrooms are all different, all striking. Some have frescoes and silk curtains, others have fabrics commissioned from a small Tuscan workshop. The attention to detail is superb but in no way overpowering. The independent apartment is a restored farmhouse with original fireplace and stunning views over the rose garden. The staff really make you feel like wanted guests, breakfast is buffet, dinner is in the restored olive store and Florence is a 20-minute drive.

Price	€130–€230. Suites €195–€230. Apartment €300.
Rooms	24 + 1: 21 doubles, 3 suites. Apartment for 5.
Meals	Dinner €28. Wine from €12.
Closed	February.
Directions	Rome A1 exit Firenze-Certosa; superstrada Firenze-Siena, exit San Casciano; signs for Cerbaia-Empoli. After 3km, signs on left.

Monica Cozzi
via Empolese 69,
50026 San Casciano

Tel	+39 0554 633292
Fax	+39 0554 634552
Email	johlea@johanna.it
Web	www.villailpoggiale.it

Il Poggetto

A deliciously green and sunny Tuscan hilltop, surrounded by vineyards and olive groves. Once through the electronic gates, you'll be captivated by the views. The gardens are delightful, too: three hectares of rose-ridden lawns, fruit trees, azaleas and heather (always something in flower), with pines and cypresses for shade and a terrace dotted with lemon and mandarin trees. Ivana and her family moved to the 400-year-old *casa colonica* in 1974 and have renovated beautifully, using original and traditional materials. The apartments are attractive, uncluttered and full of light. All have big comfortable beds, antique furniture and private patios. 'La Loggia' was once a hay barn; the huge, raftered living/dining area is superb and the old triangular air bricks are still in place. 'La Cipressaia', characteristically Tuscan in style and very private, is a conversion of the stable block, and sleeps five. 'Il Gelsomino', named after the jasmine outside the door, and 'La Pergola' join each other. Everyone has use of the pool, which is set apart in a stunning position: you can watch the sun rise and set from your lounger.

Price	€70-€90 (€355-€1,120 per week).
Rooms	4 apartments for 2-5.
Meals	Restaurants 1km.
Closed	Rarely.
Directions	Milano-Roma A1 exit Scandicci; take Pisa-Livorno exit Ginestra; right for Montespertoli. In Baccaiano left uphill; left for Montagnana; signed after 1km. 1st left into via Montegufoni, left at the church into via del Poggetto.

Andrea Boretti & Ivana Pieri
via del Poggetto 14,
50025 Montespertoli

Mobile	+39 339 3784383
Fax	+39 0270 035890
Email	info@poggetto.it
Web	www.poggetto.it

Locanda le Boscarecce

A sparkling star in Tuscany's firmament. Susanna is full of life and laughter, her daughter Swan is equally warm – and an accomplished sommelier. Swan's husband, Chef Bartolo from Sicily, concocts dishes that people travel miles to discover. Fruits, vegetables, herbs and olive oil come from the grounds, there are 450 wines in the cellar and, outside, the biggest pizza oven you will ever see. The 200-year-old *locanda* is on a ridge, embracing fields and farms and heavenly sunsets. Bedrooms in the farmhouse are part rustic, part refined, with bold colours and pretty lace at the windows, each space unique. Beds are modern and comfortable, furniture 18th and 19th-century, bathrooms have bath tubs *and* showers, and some rooms have kitchenettes. Tennis, cycling, swimming – all are possible – or you may relax under the dreamy gazebo and dip into a book on art history from the library. Even the location is enticing, in a charmed triangle formed by Florence, Siena and Pisa. Heart-warming, creative, special. *Ask about cookery courses, wine, cheese and olive oil tastings.*

Price	€100–€145.
Rooms	12: 8 doubles, 3 triples, 1 quadruple.
Meals	Dinner €35.
Closed	20 November–26 December.
Directions	From Castelfiorento, via A. Vivaldi for Renai; right after dirt road, signed. Over bridge road curves left, stay on paved road for 'di Pizzacalada'; T-junc left; signed.

Susanna Ballerini
via Renai 19,
50051 Castelfiorentino

Tel	+39 0571 61280
Fax	+39 0571 634008
Email	info@leboscarecce.com
Web	www.leboscarecce.com

Fattoria Barbialla Nuova

A 500-hectare organic farm specialising in Chianina cattle, olive oil and, above all, white truffles. Guido, Gianluca and Marco have worked hard to provide somewhere beautiful to stay in this glorious nature reserve. Three farmhouses here, all with sweeping views, all on the top of a hill; 'Le Trosce' has several levels but is all on one floor. 'Doderi' is divided into three apartments, simple and minimalist; Gianluca's joyous bedcovers and 60s-style furniture in Tuscan colours add style, originality and colour. The apartments in 'Brentina', deeper in the woods, are a touch more primitive, though many will love the simplicity of the whitewashed walls and the handmade staircase; all have delicious bathrooms. Outside: pergolas, patios and pools, cheerful with deckchairs and decking, and orchard and hens. Marco or Guido is always around to help if you need anything, and September to December are the times to go if you fancy a spot of truffle-hunting: you will be accompanied by an expert and his dog. We love this place. *Minimum stay two nights.*

Price	Apts for 2: €440–€570. Apts for 4: €740–€940. Apts for 6: €950–€1,250. Farmhouse €1,400–€1,900. Prices per week.
Rooms	7 apartments: 2 for 2, 3 for 4, 2 for 6. Farmhouse for 8.
Meals	Self-catering. Restaurant 3km.
Closed	10 January–10 March.
Directions	From A1, exit Firenze Scandicci, follow signs to 'S.G.C. FI-PI-LI' direction Pisa, exit San Miniato up hill to Montaione; 4km after Corazzano, on right opp. white 6km sign.

Àrghilo Società Agricola
via Castastrada 49,
50050 Montaione

Tel/Fax	+39 0571 677004
Mobile	+39 335 1406575/6
Email	info@barbiallanuova.it
Web	www.barbiallanuova.it

Fattoria Le Filigare

Overlooking vineyards, surrounded by green-cloaked hills, pretty gardens, shady patios and a statue-strewn terrace, this is an attractive Tuscan estate. Now the Burchis have converted part of the main villa and farm buildings into stylish apartments with an authentic feel, architect Deborah working hard to combine traditional materials with a modern love of space. Beams, raftered ceilings, archways, terracotta floors, cool white walls set the tone, rustic furniture does the rest – simple wrought-iron or wooden beds (some four-poster), painted wardrobes, copper pans. Modern sofas and art works add elegance; living areas are open-plan with smart kitchens tucked into corners. Some apartments have patios, others a mezzanine level, others jacuzzi baths. Choose 'Girasole' up the hill for romance and a private garden. You get a summer swimming pool, a tennis court, peacocks, wines on tap… shops and restaurants are down a bumpy track, then a ten-minute drive. Florence and Siena are under an hour and your energetic hosts are very welcoming. *Minimum stay one week.*

Price	€650–€890 per week.
Rooms	12 apartments for 2, 4 or 6.
Meals	Restaurant 3km.
Closed	Rarely.
Directions	A1 exit Certosa; superstrada for Siena; exit San Donato in Poggio; well signed from Panzano road.

Alessandro Cassetti Burchi
loc. Le Filigare,
50020 Barberino Val d'Elsa

Tel	+39 0558 072796
Fax	+39 0558 072128
Email	info@lefiligare.it
Web	www.lefiligare.it

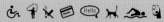

Fattoria Casa Sola Agriturismo

Count Giuseppe Gambaro and his wife Claudia tend the wine and olive oil production as the family has done for generations. The estate grows a variety of grapes (and the gates are shut at night to prevent wild boar from snaffling them!). The two-storey apartments, 700 metres from the main house and pool, are cool, fresh, comfortable with whitewashed walls, tiled floors, traditional country bedspreads and vineyard views. Named Red, White and Yellow, each has a garden with roses to match. Your hosts are charming and courteous and passionate about their wine, and give you a bottle on arrival. Once a week they take guests round the vineyards and wine-making facilities, rounding off the visit with a glass of Vin Santo and *cantucci* biscuits. Claudia is very fond of children and often organises races and games. There are cookery and watercolour classes for grown-ups, and you can play tennis and ride nearby. Sample the creations of a personal chef; eat out in Barberino and San Donato. Or drive the 30 minutes to Florence or Siena. *Minimum stay two nights.*

Price	€770–€2,430 per week.
Rooms	6 apartments: 1 for 2-3, 2 for 4, 2 for 4-6, 1 for 8.
Meals	Chef available, by arrangement. Restaurant 5km.
Closed	Rarely.
Directions	Firenze-Siena exit San Donato in Poggio; SS101 past S. Donato church; 1.5km, right to Cortine & Casa Sola.

Conte Giuseppe Gambaro
via Cortine 5,
50021 Barberino Val d'Elsa

Tel	+39 0558 075028
Fax	+39 0558 059194
Email	vacanze@fattoriacasasola.com
Web	www.fattoriacasasola.com

Sovigliano

A stone's throw from Tavarnelle, down a country lane, this ancient farmhouse stands among vineyards, olives, cypresses and pines. Though the setting is secluded you are in the middle of some of the most popular touring country in Italy; on a clear day, you can see the towers of San Gimignano. Every view is breathtaking. Sovigliano has been renovated by the family with deep respect for the architecture and traditional materials. The self-catering apartments – one palatial, with a glorious stone fireplace – are most attractive, all white walls, ancient rafters, good beds and country antiques. If you choose to go B&B, the double rooms are equally charming. The big rustic kitchen, with a private fridge for each guest, makes it easy to meet others should you wish to do so; and dinner can be arranged. Relax under the pines in the garden, take a dip in the pool, work out in the exercise area (here children must be supervised), enjoy a pre-dinner drink. Vin Santo, olive oil and grappa are for sale, Signora is most helpful and will insist you return!

Price	€130-€160. Apartments €150-€390.
Rooms	4 + 4: 2 doubles, 2 twins.
	4 apartments for 2-4 (some rooms combine to make an apt for 8).
Meals	Dinner with wine, €35.
Closed	Rarely.
Directions	SS2 Firenze-Siena exit Tavarnelle; on entering town, right & follow Marcialla. Sovigliano just out of town: left at 4th r'bout down lane signed Magliano; follow signs.

Signora Patrizia Bicego
Strada Magliano 9,
50028 Tavarnelle Val di Pesa

Tel	+39 0558 076217
Email	info@sovigliano.com
Web	www.sovigliano.com

Il Borghetto Country Inn Agriturismo

A tall hedge, private gates, lofty cypress trees – you could drive past and miss this. Slip inside and you feel you've stumbled on a lost world. The 15th-century building, all sloping pantiled roofs around a central tower, was rescued by the Cavallini family and restored, along with the olive groves and vineyards. Step into rooms of timeless elegance, rich but welcoming. The airy dining room opens onto a covered veranda, perfect for breakfasts of brioche, local cheeses and homemade jams. Dinner – from a fine Tuscan chef – is by request. Bedrooms, with their tiled floors and beamed ceilings, are understatedly luxurious with soft colours, antiques, fresh flowers and individual touches; perhaps a pretty wallpaper or a sleigh bed, a writing desk or a hand-painted wardrobe. Florence and Siena are close: borrow a bike and explore. Or wander the gardens with their terraces, pond, orchard and Etruscan tomb. The Cavallinis are quiet and easy-going while Tim, the UK wine-maker, is happy to explain his work. Raise a glass of chianti from the pool to far-reaching Tuscan views. *Ask about cookery courses. Min. stay two nights.*

Price	€130–€260.
Rooms	8: 3 doubles, 5 suites.
Meals	Dinner, 3 courses, €50. Wine €12–€80. Light lunch €15–€35.
Closed	November–April.
Directions	A1 exit Firenze-Certosa; after toll, Firenze-Siena exit Bargino; right; 200m, then left for Montefiridolfi; 500m after church, leave gate with columns on right; 20m signed.

Roberto Cavallini
via Collina S. Angelo 23,
50020 Montefiridolfi

Tel	+39 0558 244442
Mobile	+39 338 4498407
Email	info@borghetto.org
Web	www.borghetto.org

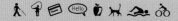

La Canigiana Agriturismo

With Florence's Duomo glistening in the distance across a carpet of olive groves, this Tuscan farmhouse has the best of both worlds. Set amongst the sparkling air of the Chianti hills, it is 15 minutes from that glorious city. Producing organic olive oil, the farm has been in Alessandra's family for over 100 years. Her family and father still live on the estate – let yourself to be swept into their warm embrace. The apartments (with private entrances) share those glorious views. A cut above those of the average agriturismo, the bedrooms here are country comfortable with colourful bedspreads, wrought-iron beds, posies of fresh flowers and prints on white walls. Traditionally tiled floors, beams and shuttered windows add charm. Kitchen areas incorporated into the living room are fine for holiday cooking and there are pretty tablecloths for dinner; choose the ground-floor apartment for its lovely terrace, or take the two together. Those Tuscan jewels – Pisa, Lucca, Siena, Florence – are under an hour away, and there's an orchard-enclosed pool for your return. Bliss. *Minimum stay three nights.*

Price	€550–€750.
	Whole house €1,200–€1,400.
	Prices per week.
Rooms	2 apartments for 3.
Meals	Restaurant 2km.
Closed	December–February.
Directions	From A1 exit Firenze-Certosa towards Firenze. At lights turn left for Montespertoli. Junction after 6km, right to La Romola. House after 1km on left. Signed.

Alessandra Calligaris
via Treggiaia, 146,
50020 La Romola

Tel/Fax	+39 0558 242425
Mobile	+39 339 4463483
Email	info@lacanigiana.it
Web	www.lacanigiana.it

Palazzo Malaspina B&B

A special find. The medieval walls of San Donato are tucked away behind an arch, while the Renaissance façade belies a modern and spacious interior. Enter the big hall with its fine wooden doors and stylish staircase: sense the history. The palazzo is a listed building and Maria is enthusiastic about all she has to offer. She was born here, in Room 3, and now lives in the apartment downstairs with her pet dog. Breakfast, in your bedroom – or set by Maria at a huge table on white runners and china – includes fruits, cheeses, croissants, jams. (Do try her delectable chocolate cakes.) Each of the bedrooms has a classic Tuscan charm with family antiques and fabrics from the House of Busatti in Anghiari. Luxurious bathrooms have mosaic tiles and huge white towels bearing the palazzo's emblem; three have a jacuzzi. From some of the rooms you can just glimpse the towers of San Gimignano, from others, little gardens that guide the eye to the countryside beyond and its treasures. There's a very small garden to the rear. Drop your baggage off outside; car parks are a five-minute walk.

Price	€85-€120.
Rooms	5: 3 doubles, 2 twins/doubles.
Meals	Restaurant next door.
Closed	Occasionally.
Directions	A1 exit Firenze-Certosa; SS Firenze-Siena for Siena; exit San Donato; signs for San Donato; thro' arch into centro storico; via del Giglio, on left.

Maria Pellizzari
via del Giglio 35,
50020 San Donato in Poggio

Tel	+39 0558 072946
Fax	+39 0558 092047
Email	info@palazzomalaspina.it
Web	www.palazzomalaspina.it

Corte di Valle Agriturismo

The British ambassador in the 1920s, Sir Ronald Graham (a reputed pro-fascist) lived here, and what was good enough for him… But it did go downhill, and Marco, who left banking after 35 years to pursue this dream, has had to pour money into it as well as affection. He has succeeded brilliantly: the old Tuscan farmhouse is a handsome, even stylish, place to stay and has not lost any of its dignity and character. Bedrooms are large, the décor is uncluttered but lovely, the shower rooms are immaculate and the beds very comfortable. The room at the top has its own terrace – an idyllic spot from which to watch the sun set and rise. Downstairs is a huge sitting room where you can gather with your friends and a cavernous hall; outside is a pool with a view. Occasional dinner is served in their hunting lodge restaurant across the yard. Marco enjoys food and wine and may offer tastings of his own vintage; Irene, gentle and shy, is proud of the herbs and saffrons she sells. All around you lies the lush and lovely Chianti countryside, and the idyllic little town of Greve is five kilometres away.

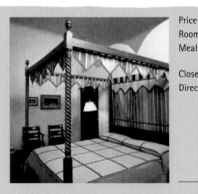

Price	€95–€115.
Rooms	8: 7 doubles, 1 twin.
Meals	Dinner €25–€30, on request. Wine €7–€9.
Closed	Rarely.
Directions	5km north of Greve in Chianti, on west side of S222, north of turning to Passo dei Paccorai. House visible from road.

Marco & Irene Mazzoni
via Chiantigiana, loc. Le Bolle,
50022 Greve in Chianti

Tel	+39 0558 53939
Fax	+39 0558 544163
Email	cortedivalle@cortedivalle.it
Web	www.cortedivalle.it

Poggio all'Olmo Agriturismo

A small, ten-hectare Tuscan farm, six kilometres from Greve, where wine and olive oil are produced in the traditional way. Three generations of Vannis still toil, grandfather tending fat tomatoes in the kitchen garden and pruning the vines. Francesca loves having people to stay and looks after you as she would a friend. The farmhouse, which goes back to the 17th century, has two guest bedrooms, each with a simple kitchenette, while the old hay barn has been converted into a couple of simple but comfortable apartments, all beams and terracotta. The lower of the two has an extra bed and its own patio; the views, across vineyards and olive groves to the hills beyond, are superb. The undulating landscape is typical Chianti, the air is as pure as can be, the swimming pool, fragrant with the scent of herbs and roses, is a delight. Witness the day-to-day activities of a working farm without stirring from your chair – though there is a guide in nearby Lamole who can take you out on trails. Peace and tranquillity, genuine family life, home-produced wine and olive oil. *Minimum stay three nights in apartments.*

Price	€75. Apartments €90-€110.
Rooms	2 + 2: 2 doubles.
	2 apartments: 1 for 2-3, 1 for 2-4.
Meals	Breakfast €10, by arrangement.
	Snacks possible. Restaurants 6km.
Closed	Rarely.
Directions	From Greve in Chianti SS222 for
	Panzano. After 2km, left for Lamole &
	on for 5km. House between
	Vignamaggio & Lamole, signed.

Francesca Vanni
via Petriolo 30,
50022 Greve in Chianti

Tel	+39 0558 549056
Fax	+39 0558 53755
Email	olmo@greve-in-chianti.com
Web	www.greve-in-chianti.com/olmo.htm

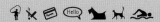

Podere Torre Agriturismo

At the end of a long bumpy track, a little farmstead that exudes contentment; no wonder the roses do so well. They are coaxed and charmed by Cecilia, who has the same effect upon her guests. Hers is no run-of-the-mill B&B: here everything is intuitively presented. Next to the main house is 'La Stalla', a cool, ground-floor bedroom in the watchtower. 'Concimaia' (the name referring to its unpoetical origins as a manure store) is reached across a flowery terrace with table and chairs for two, and interconnects with 'Fienile', an apartment in the small barn – a useful set-up for a party of four. Cecilia gives you fluffy towels, cotton bed linen, blocks of Marsiglia soap, lavender bags and candles for evening relaxation. Swallows nest in the laundry room, where you can wash and iron, and you get the basics needed to rustle up a picnic supper and eat outside. Cecilia and Paolo run a small vineyard producing good-quality wine and olive oil. There is a taverna a mile away that you can walk to; at breakfast time we advise you stay put and be spoiled.

Price	€70 (€450 per week). Apartment €85 (€550 per week).
Rooms	2 + 1: 2 doubles. 1 apartment for 2.
Meals	Breakfast €10. Restaurants 2km.
Closed	Rarely.
Directions	From Greve in Chianti for Pieve di San Cresci; 3km on minor road, signed.

Signora Cecilia Torrigiani
via di San Cresci 29,
50022 Greve in Chianti

Tel	+39 0558 544714
Fax	+39 0558 544714
Email	poderetorre@greve-in-chianti.com
Web	www.greve-in-chianti.com/poderetorre.htm

Hotel Villa Bordoni

Who could resist the vegetables and fruits from the walled garden, the olive oil from the estate, the fish and meat from the market? The hotel's kitchen is a passionate celebration of regional produce and the handsome chef's style is creative and refined. Your base: a 16th-century patrician villa, painted the palest blue, planted above the town of Greve (Chianti Classico headquarters and member of *Citta Slow*) overlooking olive groves, vineyards and hills. Understated and cleverly designed bedrooms have a theme that reflects – in sumptuous fabrics and carefully chosen pieces – the vibrant colours of the antique Vietri tiles in the bathrooms. All mod cons are hidden and yet they are there; perfect. And when you've eaten to your heart's content, and made a dent in David's wine cellar (he's a sommelier), you may take a book to your pergola'd terrace by the pool-with-a-view, in a garden where tortoises roam. In autumn the colours are glorious and fires burn brightly indoors. A special place – and you can trot back down the bumpy track to town in ten minutes flat. *Ask about cookery courses.*

Price	€180-€480.
Rooms	10 doubles.
Meals	Lunch €25-€40. Dinner €40-€50. Wine from €14.
Closed	6 January-March.
Directions	Hotel signed from Greve in Chianti. See website for detailed directions.

	David & Catherine Gardner
	via San Cresci 31/32, loc. Mezzuola,
	50022 Greve in Chianti
Tel	+39 0558 840004
Fax	+39 0558 840005
Email	info@villabordoni.com
Web	www.villabordoni.com

Castello di Lamole

Heavy rafters, tiny windows, floors of granite, stunning old stone walls – history seeps from every cranny. The 13th-century fortress is an intriguing, stepped maze of nooks and alleys, arches and passageways, trailing vines and dripping wisteria. You are surrounded by 13 hectares of ancient chestnut woods, a small vineyard and olive groves; lovely views sweep down terraces past rosemary and lavender to a pool and across the valley. The apartments vary in size and character and have patios and much rustic charm. Expect good solid furniture and pretty fabrics, tapestry cushions, rush mats, perhaps a sink decorated with straw hats or a noble old fireplace. Jacopo's grandfather bought the castello years ago; now it has been restored and your young host is relaxed among guests. A grocer's shop is a walk away, the castle sells wine, grappa and olive oil, and a bus transports you to Greve. In the hayloft restaurant there's good farmhouse cooking, the estate's fine wines and the background music of Riccardo Marasco – famous folk singer and Jacopo's dad. *Minimum stay two nights. Tricky parking some distance away.*

Price	€120-€200. Self-catering: €680-€1,050 per week.
Rooms	9 apartments: 2 for 4, 7 for 2.
Meals	Breakfast €9. Dinner with wine, €30. Restaurant 1km.
Closed	January-February.
Directions	From Florence SS222 for Greve in Chianti; 1km after Greve left for Lamole; follow signs for Castello di Lamole.

Jacopo Marasco
via di Lamole 82, Lamole,
50022 Greve in Chianti

Tel	+39 0556 30498
Fax	+39 0556 30611
Email	info@castellodilamole.it
Web	www.castellodilamole.it

Fattoria Viticcio Agriturismo

You're on a hill above Greve, in Chianti Classico country. Alessandro's father, Lucio, bought the farm in the 1960s and set about producing fine wines for export. It was a brave move at a time when people were moving away from the countryside. Now the vineyard has an international reputation. Visit the vaults and taste for yourself. Nicoletta (also a sommelier) runs the agriturismo, helped by their daughters. The apartments are named after them – Beatrice, Arianna, Camilla – and lie at the heart of the estate. Much thought has gone into them. Plain-coloured walls, brick arches, beams and terracotta floor tiles give an attractively simple air, furniture is a charming blend of contemporary and antique pieces; kitchens are superb. One pool rests in a walled garden, with a small play area for children; a second lies withing the olive groves. You may hear the occasional tractor – this is a working estate – but the farmyard is tidy and well-kept, with tubs of flowers everywhere. There's a family atmosphere, too, and wonderful views. *Minimum stay two nights; one week in apartments.*

Price	€100. Apartments €683–€970.
Rooms	3 + 5: 2 doubles, 1 twin.
	5 apartments: 3 for 2-4, 2 for 4-6.
Meals	Breakfast €5 p.p.
	Restaurants 15-minute walk.
Closed	Rarely.
Directions	A1 exit Firenze Sud; via Chiantigiana SS222. In Greve, signs for pool (piscina): over small bridge past pool on right; take track for Viticcio, signed.

Alessandro Landini & Nicoletta Florio Deleuze
via San Cresci 12/a,
50022 Greve in Chianti

Tel	+39 0558 54210
Fax	+39 0558 544866
Email	info@fattoriaviticcio.com
Web	www.fattoriaviticcio.com

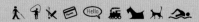

Podere La Casellina Agriturismo

Come here for life's slow rhythm – and for the gentle family. The Bensi grandparents moved here in 1936 (see picture below), when the local church put the *podere* into their careful hands; the family and young Michelangelo have worked the land ever since. Anyone wishing to experience the 'real' side of peasant life (*vita del contadino* – and learn something of its history – should come here; so little has changed at La Casellina, inside or out, and there are few concessions to modernity. Guest bedrooms are in the old hayloft and stables, simple but comfortable, with views of the little San Pietro al Terreno church. The landscape, between Chianti and Valdarno, is exquisite; you have the chestnut woods of the Chianti mountains to one side, and oaks, cypresses and olives to the other. Learn to prune vines and pick olives on the farm; gather chestnuts and wild mushrooms in the woods. Go riding or biking, then return to Grandma's recipes – the grape flan is delicious. There's passion fruit for breakfast, and Michelangelo is a dear who speaks brilliant English. *Minimum stay two nights.*

Price	From €76.
Rooms	3 doubles.
Meals	Lunch with wine, €18.
	Dinner with wine €24.
Closed	Never.
Directions	Leave A1 at Incisa; Figline road. Just before Figline, right to Brollo & Poggio alla Croce; 4km, on right.

Michelangelo & Silvia Bensi
via Poggio alla Croce 60,
50063 Figline Valdarno

Tel	+39 0559 500070
Email	poderelacasellina@tin.it
Web	www.poderelacasellina.it

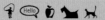

Locanda Casanuova

Ancient, in spite of its name, Casanuova was once a monastery, then an orphanage, then a farmhouse… Ursula and Thierry took it on 20 years ago, rescuing the house and returning the land to organic use. They're a very generous couple – Ursula may invite you to join her at yoga – and the whole place exudes an air of serene simplicity. Meals are sociable affairs in the lovely refectory, off which is a library where you can pore over trekking maps at a big round table. (No TVs here!). The bedrooms, attractive, minimalist and furnished with natural fabrics, have a serenely monastic air, while bathrooms are charming and unfussy. As well as being a talented cook, Ursula is an imaginative gardener; green secret corners, inviting terraces and unusual plants abound. Just a short walk from the house, in a clearing in the woods, is an enchanting swimming 'pond', a natural, self-cleansing pool with lily pads, surrounded by decking. (But unfenced, so children must not visit alone.) By the old mulberry tree 800m from the house are two pleasing apartments, one on the ground floor.

Price	€90. Half-board €65 p.p. Apartments €60-€85.
Rooms	18 + 2: 12 doubles, 2 suites, 4 singles. 2 apartments: 1 for 2, 1 for 4.
Meals	Dinner €25-€30. Wine €8-€35.
Closed	November-March.
Directions	A1 from Rome exit Incisa Valdarno. Follow signs to Figline, right for Brollo; left before Brollo for San Martino; on for 2km.

Ursula Gromann-Besançon
San Martino Altoreggi 52,
50063 Figline Valdarno
Tel +39 0559 500027
Fax +39 0559 500211
Email locanda@casanuova-toscana.it
Web www.casanuova.info

Villa Le Barone

The Marchesa, who has now passed away, wrote a delightful book about her passion for the countryside and the lovely old manor house that has been in the family for 400 years. It's a gorgeous place, with old-fashioned comforts and no TVs: truly unspoiled. Staff bustle with an easy-going friendliness under the supervision of the owners, a charming couple who spend part of the year here. Bedrooms vary, some in the villa, others in outbuildings around the estate; some are small, others on a grand scale; most have a warm Tuscan style and some charming pieces of furniture. The sitting room has an irresistible comfort, with a log fire for chilly nights and vast coffee-table books to whet your appetite for Italy. The airy dining room – once the wine cellar – is a fitting setting for leisurely Tuscan dinners and local wines. The gardens are no less appealing, full of roses, olive trees and lavender; you have tennis for the active, a parasoled terrace for the idle and a pool that is far too seductive for anyone intent upon a cultural holiday. That said, do visit the exquisite church of San Leolino, a step away.

Price	€170-€320. Half-board €100-€135 p.p.
Rooms	28: 27 twins/doubles, 1 single.
Meals	Light lunch €20. Dinner €39. Wine from €20.
Closed	November-March.
Directions	Panzano (not marked on all maps) 7km from Greve in Chianti; hotel signed from Greve.

Conte & Contessa Aloisi de Larderel
via San Leolino 19,
50020 Panzano in Chianti
Tel   +39 0558 52621
Fax   +39 0558 52277
Email info@villalebarone.com
Web   www.villalebarone.com

Villa di Riboia

Step over the threshold and into the arms of this Italian family. Three generations live in the 16th-century villa; you will be welcomed as friends and children will be adored. Wander where you will, among the comfy sofas and antiques of the sitting room, where doors open to the garden, beneath the frescoes (the work of Elisabetta's uncle) of the formal dining room, or over a cup of coffee in the rustic kitchen. For peaceful moments there's a guest sitting room at the top of the grand stone staircase. Beamed and tiled bedrooms ooze traditional comfort with their dark chests and iron bedsteads, patterned rugs and woodland murals, bathrooms are old-fashioned but spacious, fresh flowers abound. There are walks and cycle routes from the house, and the treasures of medieval Impruneta just up the road. Return to an Italian garden with steep steps in parts, a play area, a pool and views towards Florence. Dine on produce from their small organic farm under the gazebo in the summer. Embrace for a brief while Italian family life. *Minimum stay two nights. Welcome dinner with family for four-night stays.*

Price	€80–€90. Triple €110–€120.
Rooms	2: 1 double, 1 triple.
Meals	Dinner with wine, €20.
Closed	Never.
Directions	A1 exit Certosa dir. Firenze; right at lights in Galluzzo main square onto viale Gherardo Silvani dir. Impruneta; pass Pozzolatico, then Mezzomonte; after Monteoriolo 1st sharp right onto via di Riboia; on right.

Elisabetta Renzoni
via di Riboia 2a,
50023 Monteoriolo
Tel/Fax	+39 0552 374038
Mobile	+39 333 3154788
Email	info@villadiriboia.it
Web	www.villadiriboia.it

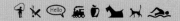

Podere Le Mezzelune

A treat to find this house in the north Maremma. After a long, winding track, two big wooden gates; ring the bell and they swing open to reveal a tree-lined drive. The Chiesa Alfieri family have turned their home into a delightful B&B where you feel as though you are visiting friends. Downstairs, a huge dining table for breakfasts of fresh, home-baked pastries and seasonal fruits, and an open fire for winter. Upstairs are the bedrooms, two looking out to sea, all with their own terrace and a view. Painted white and cream, they have linen curtains, wooden floors, furniture made to Luisa's design, candles, fresh fruit and vintage wooden pegs hung with an antique shawl. Bathrooms, too, are perfect. For longer stays there are two little private cottages in the garden, comfortable with open fires, dishwashers and beams. You are surrounded by cypresses, vines, flowers, herbs, 2,000 olive trees and seven hectares of woodland. This is a magical place, five minutes from the historic centre, 15 minutes from the sea and blissfully free of newspapers and TV. *Minimum stay two nights.*

Price	€166–€176. Cottages €166–€176.
Rooms	4 + 2: 4 twins/doubles.
	2 cottages for 2.
Meals	Breakfast for self-caterers €13–€15, by arrangement. Restaurants 3km.
Closed	10 December–March.
Directions	Exit SS1 at La California towards Bibbona. Just before village, signs for Le Mezzelune on left. Follow for approx 2km to farm gate.

Luisa Chiesa Alfieri
via Mezzelune 126,
57020 Bibbona

Tel	+39 0586 670266
Fax	+39 0586 671814
Email	relais@lemezzelune.it
Web	www.lemezzelune.it

Pieve di Caminino

A fallen column lying deep in the grass, woods, a quiet lake... so peaceful it's hard to believe what a history this settlement has had since it was first recorded in 1075. It is set in a huge natural amphitheatre, ringed by hills and medieval fortresses, and has its own magic spring. Once you've driven through the big rusty gates and down the tree-lined drive, you'll be greeted by your hosts in an 11th-century church – part of their private quarters. It's the most lovely, airy space, with battered columns, soaring arches and elegant furniture – a subtle study in cream, gold and brown. The suites (one a romantic cottage) and the apartments are beautiful too. Each has its own terrace or balcony and is simply furnished with family antiques and fine old paintings. Enchanting windows look over the grounds, the massive walls are rough stone or plaster, the ceilings beamed or vaulted. The 500-hectare estate has been in Piero's family since 1650 and produces its own olive oil and wine. The beautiful panoramic pool has distant views to the isle of Elba. *Min. stay three nights in high season.*

Price	€120-€160. Apts €200-€240 (€900-€1,300 per week).
Rooms	4 suites for 2-3, 2 apartments for 4, 1 apartment for 5.
Meals	Breakfast €10. Restaurant 6km.
Closed	Never.
Directions	From Milan m'way Bologna-Firenze exit Firenze-Certosa, for Siena-Grosseto, exit Civitella Marittima for Follonica. 5km before Montemassi right for Sassofortino. On right 1km.

Piero Marrucchi & Daniela Locatelli
via prov. di Peruzzo,
58028 Roccatederighi
Tel +39 0564 569736
Fax +39 0564 569736
Email caminino@caminino.com
Web www.caminino.com

Antico Casale di Scansano

The food is delicious and breakfasts are quite a spread – and the restaurant gets full marks for not overwhelming you with a long menu. Be idle, by all means – but when you see your fellow guests scooting off to various parts of this mini-resort to ride, hike or cook the day away, you may wish to join them. There are morning courses in Tuscan cookery with Mariella Pellegrini, while down at the stables lessons and pony treks take place under the watchful eye of Athos. The bedrooms in the old building vary in size while those in the new are large, light, fresh and clean, with balconies and breathtaking views; the cheapest lie closest to the road. There's satellite TV for the evenings and air con for sultry nights. In the restaurant, picture windows pull in the light and the views, the sitting room is welcoming with big sofas, open fire and games, there's a super outdoor pool and a wellness centre dedicated to relaxing treatments and enhanced by delightful perfumes. The Pellegrini family and their staff are warm and gracious; this is a happy place, wonderful for families. *Oriental spa.*

Price	€130–€190. Singles €80–€100. Suites €195–€260.
Rooms	32: 21 doubles, 5 suites, 6 singles.
Meals	Dinner €27.50. Wine from €7.50.
Closed	Never.
Directions	From Scansano towards Manciano (SS322). House 2.5km east of Scansano.

Signor Massimo Pellegrini
loc. Castagneta,
58054 Scansano

Tel	+39 0564 507219
Fax	+39 0564 507805
Email	info@anticocasalediscansano.it
Web	www.anticocasalediscansano.it

Villa Bengodi

A house that matches its owners: family orientated, gentle and with old-fashioned charm. Great-aunt Zia Ernesta lived in the room with the angel frescoes for most of her life; now Caterina shares the running of the B&B with her brothers and their wives. The villa and its gardens are their pride and joy. Bedrooms are generous, light and spotless and house a hotchpotch of furniture from past decades; some have ceilings painted in 1940, another a terrace; all have original floor tiles in varying patterns. Modern bathrooms are excellent, views are to the garden or sea. While away the days in the enchanting palm-fringed garden, or on the terrace where views reach to Corsica on a clear day. Beaches and mile upon mile of surf are a hop away – or you could walk the full mile to Talamone, where a family friend takes you out on his boat to fish and to swim; eat what you catch. The apartments sit on terraces below the villa and have their own gardens. Dine al fresco in summer; in winter under a chandelier made of antlers and pine cones. A personal home and a magical setting. *Minimum stay three nights.*

Price	€110–€170.
	Apartment €800–€1,500 per week.
Rooms	6 + 2: 6 doubles.
	2 apartments for 2-4.
Meals	Dinner with wine, €30, by arrangement.
Closed	Rarely.
Directions	From Grosseto-Roma superstrada, towards Talamone. First left & where road ends near station right into via Bengodi. First right again.

Famiglia Orlandi
via Bengodi 2, loc. Bengodi,
58010 Fonteblanda

Mobile	+39 335 420334
Fax	+39 0564 885515
Email	info@villabengodi.it
Web	www.villabengodi.it

Il Pardini's Hermitage

The quickest way to get here from the port is by sea; the trip around the coast, often choppy, takes 20 minutes. If the seas are too rough, your mode of transport is on foot or by donkey, and it's quite a hike up to the villa (with plenty of little areas to sit and catch your breath along the way!). The island is a wonder of flora and fauna – peregrine falcons, kestrels and buzzards if you're lucky, gorgeous wild flowers.... This once-hermitage, now a 50-year old villa, is far from any village or coastal resort: perfect seclusion. Bedrooms are simple, pale-walled and delicious, the doubles with stunning sea views. Find a quiet spot in the well-kept gardens, all cacti and flowers, or indulge in a bout of sea-water therapy – there's a beautiful platform to dive from and the water is crystal-clear. Paint or pot, play an instrument or a game, ride a donkey, visit a beach on the other side. And dress up for dinner, a formal affair of stiff white napery and hushed conversation. Unusual, and special. *Minimum stay three nights. Watercolour & pottery courses available. Health & beauty weeks.*

Price	Half-board €95–€155 p.p.
	Full-board €130–€180 p.p.
Rooms	13: 10 doubles, 2 singles, 1 suite.
Meals	Half-board or full-board only.
	Wine from €15.
Closed	October–March.
Directions	Ferry from mainland to Giglio Porto takes half an hour. From there, 20-min boat trip; if seas rough, go on foot: 1.5 hours. Full details on booking.

Federigo & Barbara Pardini
loc. Cala degli Alberi,
58013 Isola del Giglio

Tel	+39 0564 809034
Fax	+39 0564 809177
Email	info@hermit.it
Web	www.hermit.it

Villa Marsili

Always refreshing to come to Cortona, set so magnificently on the top of a hill. And the site of this beautifully run palazzo-hotel is steeped in history: in the 14th century the church of the Madonna degli Alemanni stood here, built to house the miraculous image of the Madonna della Manna. Beneath, an Oratory was linked by a flight of stairs (still to be seen in the breakfast room); in 1786 the church was demolished and an elegant mansion built on the site. The owners have carefully preserved many of the original architectural features hidden over the centuries, and the hall and the light-filled bedrooms are immaculately and individually decorated with trompe l'œils and hand-painted borders. Colours are gentle yellows, bathrooms are gorgeous, most rooms are large, some are tiny, all windows have views. The front of the house looks onto a garden with a pergola where an excellent breakfast buffet is enjoyed – along with a stunning panorama of the Valdichiana and Lake Trasimeno. On the northern side is a winter garden, with the Borgo San Domenico a mesmerising backdrop. *Complimentary evening aperitif.*

Price	€130–€230. Singles €80–€130. Suites €250–€340.
Rooms	26: 18 doubles, 3 suites, 5 singles.
Meals	Restaurants 10-minute walk uphill.
Closed	9 January-February.
Directions	Leave A1 at Val di Chiana, take Siena/Perugia m'way; 2nd exit for Cortona. Follow signs for Cortona Centro. Parking nearby.

Stefano Meacci
viale Cesare Battisti 13,
52044 Cortona

Tel +39 0575 605252
Fax +39 0575 605618
Email info@villamarsili.net
Web www.villamarsili.net

Casa Bellavista

A glass of wine at a table in the orchard. Birdsong for background music – or occasionally foreground, if the family rooster is feeling conversational. And a panorama of Tuscan landscape. Bellavista is well-named: its all-round views take in Monte Arniata, Foiano della Chiana and the old Abbey of Farneta. There was a farm here for 200 years but the house was extensively restored about 30 years ago. It still has the original brick exterior, now softened by creepers, and a welcoming, family atmosphere (Simonetta and her husband, Guido, have two teenage children). There's an assured, uncluttered country elegance to the rooms, and pretty, airy bedrooms are furnished with family antiques and interesting textiles; two have their own balcony with views onto the garden. Simonetta's kitchen has a huge marble table top for kneading bread and she cooks farmhouse food for her guests: it is delicious; breakfasts are lavish, cookery lessons are a treat. Roam the Arezzo province in true Italian style: vespas and bikes are free! Italian family B&B of the very best sort.

Price	€120-€140.
Rooms	3: 1 double, 2 twins/doubles.
Meals	Dinner €35, by arrangement. Wine from €19.
Closed	Rarely.
Directions	Autostrada Valdichiana exit Perugia; exit Foiano. After 400m, right for Fratta-S.Caterina. On for 2.8km, right next to ruined building. After 1km, right at junc.; keep to left-hand road. After 600m, right onto a dirt road.

Simonetta Demarchi
loc. Creti C.S. 40,
52044 Cortona

Tel	+39 0575 610311
Fax	+39 0575 610749
Email	info@casabellavista.it
Web	www.casabellavista.it

La Palazzina

There is an English inflection to La Palazzina, with its quirky 14th-century watchtower planted inexplicably beside the main house. And it makes a most unusual self-contained retreat with luscious views across the wooded valley. You get a well-equipped kitchen, a wood-burner for cosy nights, a winding stair to a half-moon double and, at the top, a twin with a stunning, brick-beehive ceiling. The honeysuckle-strewn terrace is just as you would wish, with cypress trees marching sedately up the hill alongside, and birdsong to disturb the peace. The grounds, including a saltwater swimming pool with views, are for you to explore, and lead to some of the loveliest walks in the valley. David and Salina are great company and will prepare dinner for you on your first evening, left in the fridge for your arrival. Hannibal defeated the Roman army at nearby Lake Trasimeno and there is little that David doesn't know about the historical importance of this area – his enthusiasm is contagious. The garden is a delight; the tower magical. *Minimum stay one week.*

Price	£650-£895 per week.
Rooms	Tower for 2.
Meals	Dinner first evening, with wine, €30, by arrangement.
	Restaurants 15-min drive.
Closed	Rarely.
Directions	Directions on booking.

David & Salina Lloyd-Edwards
Sant'Andrea di Sorbello,
52040 Mercatale di Cortona

Tel/Fax	+39 0575 638111
Mobile	+39 335 5727812
Email	italianencounters@technet.it
Web	www.palazzina.co.uk

Relais San Pietro in Polvano

Our readers love this place, it is a paradise high in the hills. The adorable Signor Protti and his wife run this enchanting hotel with their son and daughter-in-law and the care they lavish on the place is apparent at every turn. Bedrooms have shutters and gorgeous old rafters, wide wrought-iron beds, elegant painted wardrobes, rugs on tiled floors, straw hats on white walls. For cool autumn nights there are cream sofas and a log fire. The pool, on a terrace just below, must have one of the best views in Tuscany: keep your head above water and you are rewarded with the blue-tinted panorama for which Italy is famous. There is a restaurant for guests serving delicious local food and their own olive oil; bread comes fresh from the bread oven. In summer you dine at beautifully dressed tables on a terrace overlooking the gardens, full of cool recesses and comfy chairs, and the olive-grove'd valley beyond. An atmosphere of luxurious calm and seclusion prevails, and your hosts are a delight. For those who choose to venture forth, note that gates close at midnight. *Children over 12 welcome. Minimum stay two nights.*

Price	€230–€260. Single €150–€170. Suites €270–€300.
Rooms	10: 4 doubles, 1 single, 5 suites.
Meals	Dinner €25–€40. Wine from €16.
Closed	November–March.
Directions	A1 Rome-Milan exit Monte San Savino for Castiglion Fiorentino. At 3rd lights, left for Polvano. After 7km, left for Relais San Pietro.

Signor Luigi Protti
loc. Polvano 3,
52043 Castiglion Fiorentino

Tel	+39 0575 650100
Fax	+39 0575 650255
Email	info@polvano.com
Web	www.polvano.com

Entry 179 Map 9

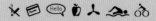

Relais Villa Belpoggio

There's a monastic, simplistic feel to this 19th-century Italian aristocrat's country pad high in the Chianti hills, with bucolic views of the Arno valley, redolent with olive and lemon groves. Yet the train gets you to Florence in half an hour. On arrival you will be greeted by Maria, charming and helpful, then shown to perfect big bedrooms with interesting antiques, cooling floors and wafting curtains at large windows. Bathrooms are marble tiled and soap-scented. Maria's mum and daughter are in the kitchen, where they dream up divine Tuscan dinners of bruschetta, pasta al pomodoro, lemon chicken, fresh strawberries: the olive oil is local and so is the red wine; the dining room is vaulted with brick walls. Tempting to fill up and flop, but the garden is crammed with fragrant white roses, jasmine and honeysuckle, so couples beware – a dewy-eyed stroll around it could induce a proposal. A swimming pool sits high in the garden for lazy bobbing on hot afternoons, by evening it's cool enough to walk the hills; you shouldn't have a care in the world after time spent here. *Ask about cookery courses.*

Price	€126-€220.	
	Apts €650-€1,400 per week.	
Rooms	10 + 2: 6 doubles, 2 twins, 2 triples.	
	2 apts: 1 for 2-3, 1 for 4-5.	
Meals	Dinner, 4 courses with wine, €25,	
	by arrangement. Restaurant 2.5km.	
Closed	8 January-15 March.	
Directions	From Loro Ciuffenna to Castelfranco.	
	After 5km, blue sign on right.	

Maria Ventrone
via Setteponti Ponente 40,
52024 Loro Ciuffenna
Tel/Fax   +39 0559 694411
Mobile   +39 338 5960812
Email   info@villabelpoggio.it
Web   www.villabelpoggio.it

Odina Agriturismo

You are 650 metres above sea level and feel on top of the world – the Arno valley reaches out before you and the air is pure. Paolo is a talented gardener and each bush, tree and herb has been chosen with care, posing magnificently next to the solid, blue-shuttered house. The interiors of the house and apartments are delightfully rustic and contemporary. Each is different: kitchen surfaces are of granite, or local *pietra serena*, bathroom walls are softly ragged in varying shades. All have French windows to a patio with wooden outdoor furniture. Oil, vinegar, sugar, coffee, salt and washing-up liquid are provided; ask in advance and they'll provide more (for which you pay). The reception is in a beautifully restored, de-consecrated chapel, with an old bread-making chest and a 'shop' selling Odina olive oil, honey, lavender and beans. Take a dip in the pool, go for long, lazy walks in the olive groves and chestnut woods, prepare a barbecue. Garden courses and visits – highly recommended – are held here in May. *Minimum stay one week; three nights in low season. Private chef available.*

Price	€525–€945 for 2. €800–€1,750 for 4-5. Farmhouse €2,100–€3,700. Prices per week.
Rooms	4 apartments for 2, 5, 6, 7. Also farmhouse for 8-10.
Meals	Restaurants 5km.
Closed	Mid-January to mid-February.
Directions	Florence-Roma A1, exit Valdarno. In Terranuova, follow Loro Ciuffenna.

Signor Paolo Trenti
loc. Odina,
52024 Loro Ciuffenna

Tel	+39 0559 69304
Fax	+39 0559 69305
Email	info@odina.it
Web	www.odina.it

Borgo Iesolana Agriturismo

At the centre of an immaculate patchwork of fields, vineyards and woods, this irresistible group of old buildings. Mellow stone and warm brick blend, flowers tumble from terracotta pots, arches invite you in out of the sun, a pool beckons. Giovanni and Francesco inherited the estate from their grandfather and live here with their young families. They have created nine apartments, all different, from the farm buildings, and it is a solid, sensitive conversion. The décor is an upmarket, uncluttered mix of traditional and new: good beds and fabrics, super kitchens, thoughtful lighting. And if you prefer not to self-cater, you can breakfast in the 'wine bar' across the way. This, too, is an impeccable restoration, with modern Italian furniture and big windows. Lunch and dinner are available on request: local produce and traditional Tuscan fare. The farm is beautifully run (the very vines are edged with roses) and produces wine, olive oil, grappa and honey. It lies alongside an old Roman road that once linked Siena with Florence, with views on all sides of Chiantishire. *Min. stay two-seven nights depending on season.*

Price	€785–€2,395 per week. €260 2 nights low season.
Rooms	11 apartments: 3 for 2, 3 for 4, 3 for 6, 2 for 8.
Meals	Breakfast €10. Lunch or dinner €25–€30, by arrangement.
Closed	Never.
Directions	A1 Firenze-Roma exit Valdarno; at toll, right for Montevarchi; dir. Levane/Bucine; thro' Bucine; left to Pogio; left for Iesolana; 150m left; over narrow bridge; cont. to Borgo.

Giovanni & Francesco Toscano
loc. Iesolana,
52021 Bucine

Tel	+39 0559 92988
Fax	+39 0559 92879
Email	info@iesolana.it
Web	www.iesolana.it

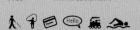

Entry 182 Map 9

Rendola Riding Agriturismo

One of the forerunners of agriturismo in Tuscany, Jenny started Rendola back in the 70s and gives you the best possible way of seeing Chianti – on horseback. You need to be able to ride, and the minimum age for riders is ten. Equestrians may expect excellent conditions and an English (not western) style. Choose between lessons with set timetables, relaxed treks and three-day forays. How wonderful, after a long sticky day in the saddle, to return to showers and homely rooms! Then, at the rustic ring of a cow bell, guests, family and stable workers gather in the dining room for dinner, where sprightly Pietro serves wholesome organic Tuscan dishes washed down with Chianti – and regales the assembled company with many a tale. It's all delightfully laid back: chickens, ducks, turkeys, horses, dogs in the courtyard; music, books an open fire in the sitting room; jackets on the backs of chairs... Non-riders will appreciate generous Jenny's advice on what to see and do in the area. *Minimum stay two nights. Pick-up from Montevarchi train station.*

Price	€90. Single €50. Half-board €65 p.p. Full-board €85 p.p.
Rooms	6: 3 twins/doubles, 2 family rooms, 1 single.
Meals	Lunch or dinner €15-€20, with wine.
Closed	Rarely.
Directions	From autostrada del Sole exit 25 for Montevarchi & Mercatale Valdarno. After 5km right for Rendola; house 200m from village.

Jenny Bawtree
Rendola 66, Montevarchi,
52025 Arezzo

Tel	+39 0559 707045
Fax	+39 0559 707045
Email	info@rendolariding.it
Web	www.rendolariding.it

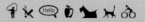

Galealpe Agriturismo

Alessandra and Andrea work their organic olive farm themselves. They have also fully restored their house, laying tiles, rescuing beams, fitting bathrooms. The two apartments (each with its own entrance and seating area in the garden) have ivory walls and are bright and country simple with well-stocked kitchens, comfortable sitting rooms and wood-burners for chillier evenings. Bedrooms are a good size, rather charming, spanking new. Your young hosts are also passionate about nature, the environment, the great outdoors. Come for their guided tours of the Prato Magno range, the wild flowers, the wildlife – on horseback or in your walking boots. Mountain bikes are free to hire too; there are trails nearby. A short drive brings you to Arezzo, where you can stock up at the Saturday market with gorgeous cheeses, local hams, crusty bread, rich tomatoes, fresh herbs, then head for the hills and a picnic. Or take it back to your terrace overlooking the pretty garden and breathe in the peace. Florence is an hour away – perfect for a day trip if the peacefulness overwhelms you! *Minimum stay two nights.*

Price	€21–€31 p.p.
Rooms	2 apartments: 1 for 2-3, 1 for 4-6.
Meals	Breakfast €6, by arrangement. Restaurant 9km.
Closed	Never.
Directions	Directions on booking.

Alessandra Cerulli & Andrea Pesce
Pieve San Giovanni 76,
52010 Arezzo

Tel/Fax	+39 0575 451309
Mobile	+39 338 9975376
Email	info@galealpe.it
Web	www.galealpe.it

Casa Simonicchi

After a blissful drive through the Casentino National Park you arrive at a hamlet of stone houses. This one is a farmhouse with a barn attached, carefully restored over 20 years by sculptress Jenny. Warm, generous, knowledgeable, she can tell you about the historic towns to visit; the countryside of Michelangelo and St Francis of Assisi; the friendly taverna down the road. In the top barn (six entrance steps only) is a family apartment simply and charmingly furnished with natural colours, Italian and English pieces, paintings and sculpture. The two bedrooms, each with a shower, are placed at either end, with the spacious sitting room and well-equipped kitchen in between. Best of all is the walk-on roof terrace – and its breathtaking panorama of sweet-chestnut forests. Bask in the sun or the shade, take a cool shower, dine al fresco, stargaze (there's a reflector telescope). Below are flowery terraces, lavender and olives. Jenny also does B&B in her farmhouse and gives you two bedrooms, one romantically over the arch. Beams, antiques, a huge fireplace – and a vine-draped pergola for breakfasts in the sun. *Minimum stay two nights.*

Price	€175 for 2, €350 for 4. €675–€975 per week.
Rooms	1 + 1: 1 suite for 4 (2 doubles). Apartment for 4 (1 double, 1 twin).
Meals	Dinner with wine from €30, by arrangement. Restaurant nearby.
Closed	Christmas–April.
Directions	Exit A1 Arezzo; north for Sansepolcro; signs for Caprese Michelangelo; left for Lama; right for Chiusi della Verna; after cypress-filled cemetery, house on 3rd right-hand bend; sharp descent.

Mrs Jennifer Frears-Barnard
via Simonicchi 184,
Caprese Michelangelo, 52033 Arezzo

Tel	+39 0575 793762
Fax	+39 0575 793762
Email	jenniferbarnard@libero.it
Web	www.simonicchi.com

Fattoria La Striscia

Arty, dramatic, vibrant. Hidden among vineyards, the villa dates back to the 1500s; Alexandra, a screen writer, is the youngest generation of her family to live here. You stay in one of the outbuildings of which there are five. Alexandra calls them 'homes' and very lovely they are too, filled with gorgeous objects and antiques from India and France, beautiful fabrics and tiles from Mexico. All are individual, all have up-to-the-minute TVs and DVDs but it is the quirkiness that is charming: canopied beds, a lavish gilt mirror, a fresco on a wall. In some the feel is elegant, in others 'shabby chic'. Kitchens are generously equipped, some with limited cooking facilities, but breakfast is served every morning at the villa and supper three times a week – in summer by candlelight in the gardens. Outside, several lazy cats saunter through the lush garden, there are covered pergolas with floating muslin curtains and hammocks by the pool, wrought-iron furniture by a fountain, terracotta pots with scented flowers. Expect no rules: come with an open mind and you'll have a lovely time. *Minimum stay four nights May-Sept.*

Price	€120-€300. €900-€1,500 per week (May-September only).
Rooms	5 apartments: 2 for 2, 1 for 2-4, 1 for 3, 1 for 4-5.
Meals	Dinner with wine, €50. Barbecue €35. Buffet €35, all by arrangement. Restaurant 1km.
Closed	Rarely.
Directions	A1 Florence-Rome exit for Arezzo. Follow signs for stadium, then signs for Fattoria. Directions on booking.

	Alexandra La Capria
	via dei Cappuccini 3,
	52100 Arezzo
Tel/Fax	+39 0575 26740
Mobile	+39 340 0630192
Email	occhini@hotmail.it
Web	www.lastriscia.com

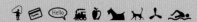

Villa i Bossi

Fifty people once lived on the ground floor of the old house and everything is still as it was – the great box which held the bread, the carpenter's room crammed with tools, the rich robes hanging in the sacristy, the old oven for making charcoal… Francesca loves showing people round. Her husband's family have lived here since 1240 and the house is full of their treasures. There's even a fireplace sculpted by Benedetto da Maiano in the 1300s – his 'thank you for having me' to the family. Sleep in faded splendour in the main villa or opt for the modern comforts of the orangery: simple yet beautiful. This really is a magical place, full of character and memories, with lively, friendly hosts. The park-like gardens, set among gentle green hills, are a delight, and have been altered and enriched over the centuries. To one side of the pool, a hill covered in rare fruit trees; to the west, Italian box hedges and camellias, peonies and old-fashioned roses, avenues, grassy banks and shady trees, a pond and enticing seats under arching shrubs, olives and vines: they make their own chianti and oil. *Ask about cookery courses.*

Price	€125–€165.
Rooms	10 + 1: 2 doubles, 2 twins. Orangery: 2 doubles, 2 triples, 2 quadruples. Apartment for 2.
Meals	Dinner, 4 courses with wine, €30, by arrangement. Restaurant 2km.
Closed	Never.
Directions	In Arezzo follow signs to stadium. Pass Esso garage & on to Bagnoro. Then to Gragnone. 2km to villa.

Francesca Viguali Albergotti
Gragnone 44-46,
52100 Arezzo

Tel	+39 0575 365642
Fax	+39 0575 964900
Email	franvig@ats.it
Web	www.villaibossi.com

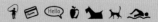

Villa Buta

Amble up the sweet-scented drive, pert with statuesque cypresses, bright with broom, to this almost monastic stone house, its olive-green shutters enhancing its nobility. You are high up in the hills with a good breeze blowing and there's cool water in the pool; the hottest summers are bearable here. Local artisans have teased the interiors to show off their best; chestnut beams, terracotta floors, stone or limewashed walls. Brush up your cooking skills in an enormous, modern kitchen whose French windows lead to a covered terrace for bright lunches and candlelit dinners; views take you all the way to Umbria along the Tiber valley. Light rushes in from every side to an elegant dining room with a marble topped table and Regency chairs, then a sitting room with green and gold fauteuils, gilt-framed paintings and a beautiful Tuscan fireplace. Two bedrooms are downstairs and two up, along with another, small sitting room; bathrooms, too, are understated and stylish. Swoon over Norcia ham, salami, truffles and funghi; taste the sunshine in the local wine, then collapse on a shady lounger. *Minimum stay one week.*

Price	£1,450-£2,500 per week.
Rooms	House for 10 (3 doubles, 2 twins).
Meals	Restaurant 6km.
Closed	Rarely.
Directions	Leave Monterchi on Lippiano road. After Rossi supermarket, right to Ripoli. At Ripoli keep on white road for 3km.

Ian Abercrombie
52037 Monterchi

Tel	+44 (0)1738 840372
Mobile	+44 (0)7779 780573
Email	ianabercrombie@gmail.com
Web	www.tuscan-villa-holidays.com

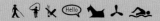

Castello di Gargonza

A fortified Romanesque village in the beauty of the Tuscan hills, whose 800-year-old steps, stones, rafters and tiles remain virtually intact. Today it is a private, uniquely Italian marriage of exquisitely ancient and exemplary modern. Seen from the air it is perfect, as if shaped by the gods to inspire Man to greater works: a magical maze of paths, nooks and crannies, castellated tower, great octagonal well, a heavy gate that lets the road slip out and tumble down, breathtaking views. You're given a map on arrival to help you navigate your way round. No cars, no shops, but a chapel, gardens, pool and old olive press for meetings, concerts and breakfasts by the fire. A restaurant sits just outside the walls. The Count and Countess and their staff are passionate about the place and look after you well. Bedrooms and apartments are 'rustic deluxe' with smart modern furnishings, white-rendered walls, superb rafters, open fireplaces, tiny old doors reached up steep stone staircases. There's an ancient ambience, as if time has stood still. Intriguing, delightful. *Min. stay two nights; apartments one week.*

Price	€110–€171. Suites €163–€181. Apartments €840–€1,960 per week.
Rooms	24 + 8: 21 doubles, 3 suites. 8 apartments for 2-10.
Meals	Breakfast €9 for self-caterers. Lunch & dinner, with wine, €25–€35.
Closed	10 January-1 March; November.
Directions	Exit A1 at Monte S. Savino; SS73 for Siena. Approx 7km after Monte S. Savino right for Gargonza; signed.

Conte Roberto Guicciardini
loc. Gargonza,
52048 Monte San Savino

Tel	+39 0575 847021
Fax	+39 0575 847054
Email	gargonza@gargonza.it
Web	www.gargonza.it

Fortezza de' Cortesi

Restoring the ruins of this lovely place was a labour of love for Cledy. The project took nine years, the results are stunning. An actress, Cledy has given the 10th-century *fortezza*-turned-villa a charm and distinction all of its own. Captivating features – vaulted ceilings, arched windows, rich stone, chestnut beams – mix with fabrics and colours in the most harmonious manner. The five double rooms, all different, have sumptuous bathrooms and unforgettable views; up in the tower is the most tempting of suites, with a big fireplace and a bath from which you gaze on the hills as you soak. There's a tiny kitchen area, too, for hot drinks. Come for two nights of perfect B&B – or rent the entire lovely place. And if you're into self-improvement, Cledy can rustle up a course or two, on cookery, ceramics or wine tasting. The house stands high in 12 hectares of land, with a terraced garden, gazebo, pool and views of the celebrated towers of San Gimignano. Worth the drive to get here, but leave the children behind: this place is exquisite! *B&B minimum stay two nights.*

Price	€160-€180. Suite €240-€260. Whole villa €6,500-€7,500 per week.
Rooms	6: 5 doubles, 1 suite.
Meals	Good restaurant 5km.
Closed	Rarely.
Directions	Exit Florence-Siena m'way at Poggibonsi Nord; signs for San Gimignano; after 8km, road forks, right for San Gimignano; 50m left into gravel road; signed.

Cledy Tancredi
loc. Monti 26,
53037 San Gimignano

Tel	+39 0577 940123
Fax	+39 0577 940123
Email	info@fortezzacortesi.com
Web	www.fortezzacortesi.com

Hotel L'Antico Pozzo

Step inside – and the hustle and bustle of San Gimignano vanishes. It's like entering another era: one of grace, elegance and calm. The interiors of the hotel, a medieval house bang in the heart of the city, are a study in soft Tuscan colours. The cool bedrooms are restrained, luxurious, inviting, all with fine fabrics and special ceilings, some frescoed, others vaulted or white-painted wood. The wrought-iron bedsteads are exquisite, the bathrooms are excellent. Breakfast is in the 'Sala Rosa', a ballroom in its heyday, renowned for 18th-century society gatherings. The old well that gives the place its name is still here, too, secure, water-filled and artfully lit by concealed lighting. Approach it via a sequence of little passageways and stairs and note the holes in the walls – the 15th-century equivalent of air con! Outside, the pretty terracotta terrace, bright with scarlet geraniums, has shady arches for escaping the sun. Emanuele and his sisters are in charge and run the hotel with youthful charm and efficiency. It is deliciously soothing to return to after busy forays into town.

Price	€125–€160.
Rooms	18: 17 doubles, 1 single.
Meals	Restaurants nearby.
Closed	Rarely.
Directions	A1 exit Firenze-Vertosa for Siena; exit Poggibonsi-Nord; follow signs for S. Gimignano; use car park no. 3 in *centro storico*.

Emanuele Marro
via San Matteo 87,
53037 San Gimignano

Tel	+39 0577 942014
Fax	+39 0577 942117
Email	info@anticopozzo.com
Web	www.anticopozzo.com

Fattoria Guicciardini

A visit to San Gimignano is a must and this makes a charming base: eight self-catering apartments right in the centre, immaculately converted from a 15th-century complex of farm buildings. Two were granaries in a former life (their bedrooms on a mezzanine floor), another was the farm cook's house. Lovely cool rooms have huge raftered ceilings, others arched windows or original fireplaces and tiles; all have been furnished in a contemporary style with new sofas, kilim-style rugs, white curtains and the occasional antique. There are entrances from both outside the city walls and from the Piazza S. Agostino (and do sneak a look at the church's altar frescoes by Benozzo Gozzoli). Get up early and watch the mists fall away to reveal the vineyards all around, then drink in the astonishing art of San Gimignano before the army of tourists descends. Evening in the city is magical, too, when the city's fairytale towers are floodlit. This is the time of day at which San Gimignano – honey pot of Tuscan tourism, deservedly so – is at its most lovely.

Price	€120-€187 for 2-6 per night. (€800-€1303 per week).
Rooms	8 apartments: 5 for 2-4, 3 for 4-6.
Meals	Restaurants nearby.
Closed	Rarely.
Directions	Leave Florence-Siena m'way at S. Gimignano & Poggibonsi Nord exit. Fattoria in centre of S.Gimignano.

Signor Tuccio Guicciardini
viale Garibaldi 2/A, Piazza S. Agostino 2,
53037 San Gimignano

Tel/Fax	+39 0577 907185
Mobile	+39 329 2273120
Email	info@guicciardini.com
Web	www.guicciardini.com

Fattoria Tregole

A vineyard and a private family chapel. What could be more Italian? The delightful Kirchlechners – he an architect, she a restorer – make Chianti Classico, grappa and olive oil from their Tuscan manor farm. They spent seven years restoring the buildings, keeping original features – raftered ceilings, terracotta floors, large fireplaces – and furnishing with a light, country-house touch. The airy apartments and the bedrooms, including a ground-floor suite with a terrace, feel like the family's rooms; all are lovely. Walls are eye-catching with Edith's hand-painted stencils, painted brass bedsteads are cleverly restored; there are traditional lampshades, dried flowers, patchwork quilts and crochet cushions. It is light, warm and inviting. Breakfast in the sunny dining room or on the patio; twice a week Edith cooks a Tuscan dinner, accompanied by the wine from the Tregole cellars. A beautiful pool, quiet views over olive groves and vine-clad hills, a garden with shady nooks, a tiny Renaissance chapel – it is intimate and homely. *B&B: over 12s welcome. Apartments minimum stay three nights.*

Price	€130. Suite €180. Apartments €200-€320.
Rooms	5 + 2: 4 doubles, 1 suite for 2. 2 apartments: 1 for 4, 1 for 5.
Meals	Dinner €35, book ahead. Wine from €10. Restaurants 4 km.
Closed	January to mid-March.
Directions	From Florence SS222 for Greve-Panzano-Castellina; 5km after Castellina in Chianti; sign for Tregole; 1km.

Edith Kirchlechner
loc. Tregole 86,
53011 Castellina in Chianti

Tel	+39 0577 740991
Email	fattoria-tregole@castellina.com
Web	www.fattoria-tregole.com

Palazzo Leopoldo

In a corner of the hall is a stone carving of a swaddled baby – 14th-century evidence of the hospital this once was. For the last few centuries Palazzo Leopoldo has been a manor house. It's surprisingly peaceful here, in the middle of beautiful, hilltop Radda, and it's walking distance to several *enoteche* nearby to taste the finest chiantis. The whole house, on different levels teeming with nooks and crannies, has a delightful feel: the hall is light, with white-painted arches, an old tiled floor, the occasional bright rug, and fresh flowers. Stroll onto the terrace and gaze over the lovely hills. Bedrooms range from suites to doubles in the eaves; all are big, generously equipped and have a rustic Tuscan feel. Some have the old bell-pulls for service, others the original stoves and frescoes; the owner has preserved as much as possible. A remarkable breakfast is served in a remarkable kitchen, replete with 18th-century range. Add to that an indoor pool and spa, a restaurant serving delicious food and truly delightful staff. Worth the steep and winding road to get here. *Ask about cookery classes.*

Price	€160–€230. Suites €230–€390.
Rooms	17: 12 doubles, 5 suites.
Meals	Lunch €25. Dinner €35.
Closed	January-February.
Directions	Signed in centre of Radda in Chianti.

	Martina Rustichini
	via Roma 33, Radda,
	53017 Radda in Chianti
Tel	+39 0577 735605
Fax	+39 0577 738031
Email	info@palazzoleopoldo.it
Web	www.palazzoleopoldo.it

La Locanda

Admire the view from the pool – both are stunning. This is a magical place; a soft green lawn edged with Mediterranean shrubs slopes down to the pool, a covered terrace overlooks medieval Volpaia. (Some of the best chianti is produced here; the village itself is a 20-minute walk.) The house vibrates with bold colour and lively fabric. The beautiful raftered living room, with open fireplace, big, stylish sofas and pale terracotta floor, reveals photos of Guido and Martina, he from the South, she from the North. They scoured Tuscany before they found their perfect inn, renovated these two houses and filled them with fine antiques, delightful prints, candles and fun touches. There's a library/bar where you can choose books from many languages and where Guido is generous with the grappa. The bedrooms, some with their own terraces, are in a separate building and have big beds, great bathrooms and whitewashed rafters, as was the custom here. Martina cooks and gardens while Guido acts as host – they are a charming pair. Once settled in you'll find it hard to stir. *Minimum stay two nights.*

Price	€200–€280. Singles €180–€250. Suite €300.
Rooms	7: 3 doubles, 3 twins, 1 suite.
Meals	Dinner €35 (not Thurs & Sun). Wine €18–€70. Restaurants 4km.
Closed	November to mid-April.
Directions	From Volpaia village square take narrow road to right which becomes track. On for 2km past small sign for La Locanda to left; 1km further to group of houses.

Guido & Martina Bevilacqua
53017 Radda in Chianti

Tel	+39 0577 738833
Fax	+39 0577 739263
Email	info@lalocanda.it
Web	www.lalocanda.it

Hotel Villa la Grotta

There are many treats in store. The first, glimpsed on your way in, is the marvellous Castello di Brolio. The second is the hotel itself, on the castle's 4,000-acre estate. Originally a ninth-century manor house and later a nunnery, it has been restored and converted into a delightful small hotel by its Swiss owner. A bottle of wine will be waiting to welcome you in a cool, inviting bedroom – all pastel walls, soft lighting, lovely old beds, colourful kilims on terracotta-tiled floors. All have four-posters and many have vineyard views, making this a popular honeymooners' retreat. General manager Doogie runs it all with panache and her own inimitable style – it's informal and fun. You're pampered, too, with a Turkish bath, jacuzzi baths and two swimming pools, the outdoor one with pillars sculpted by a famous artist. But perhaps the biggest treat of all is the restaurant, where fish and meat dishes are cooked to perfection, accompanied by well-priced wines and served in a stylish dining room (or al fresco, under an ancient walnut tree). No surprise that people travel from as far as Florence. *Minimum stay two nights.*

Price	€260-€280. Suites €340-€360.
Rooms	12: 10 doubles, 2 suites.
Meals	Dinner €35-€45. Wine €25- €320.
Closed	December-March.
Directions	From Gaiole to Castello di Brolio; left of castle for Castelnuovo Berardenga, signs 1km, hotel up dirt track for 1km with Lucignano Hotel in front.

Doogie Morley-Bodle
Brolio, 53013 Gaiole in Chianti

Tel	+39 0577 747125
Fax	+39 0577 747145
Email	info@hotelvillalagrotta.it
Web	www.hotelvillalagrotta.com

Borgo Argenina

Weeds smothered the stone walls and there was no running water or electricity. When Elena found it, the tiny hamlet of Borgo Argenina had been abandoned for 20 years. Much hard labour has gone into restoration and the results show all the creativity you'd expect from a former fashion designer. Elena's exquisite artistry appears in patchwork tablecloths and delicately stencilled arches and ceilings, rooms are scented with lavender, sage and roses, bedrooms have quilts and cushions made from fabrics found in antique markets, and furniture is hand-painted by Elena in Tuscan colours. In the pretty breakfast room, old grilled doors open on to a bright garden. The house and villa, set slightly apart, are equally refreshing, full of imaginative detail, and have plenty of privacy; you may prepare your own meals if you wish. Elena is an engaging hostess and she and her daughter Fiorenza look after you well; if you're a castle enthusiast, she'll draw you a map of all the castles in the area (and there are many!). An unusual place – tucked well away from the rest of Chianti. *Minimum stay three nights.*

Price	€170. Suites €180-€200. Villa €400-€480. House €240.
Rooms	6 + 3: 4 doubles, 2 suites. Villa for 4; 2 houses for 2-3.
Meals	Occasional dinner. Restaurants 5 minute drive.
Closed	November-March.
Directions	From Gaiole towards Siena follow signs for San Marcellino Monti. Left to Argenina.

Elena Nappa
loc. Argenina, San M. Monti,
53013 Gaiole in Chianti

Tel	+39 0577 747117
Fax	+39 0577 747228
Email	info@borgoargenina.it
Web	www.borgoargenina.it

Borgo Casa Al Vento Agriturismo

Comfortable agriturismo in green Chianti; the approach to the hamlet down the long, sandy track is stunning. Proceed to your airy rooms and prepare to unwind in this secluded retreat, surrounded by wooded hills, tree-fringed lake, olives and vineyards. The property is made up of a hotch-potch of old buildings, medieval in origin, that were given a makeover some years ago and are now packed with contented families. Exposed beams, stone walls and red-tiled floors create a rustic mood, while the décor, though not stylish – dralon and velour are in much evidence – is as neat as a new pin and as comfortable as can be. Each apartment is different, a little dated but with a certain charm. Some have patios and all are a short walk from a lake. The B&B rooms are in two separate houses and share a beamy lounge; the cellar restaurant is jolly with red tablecloths and Italian radio. Come for the gardens and terraces, ducks, geese, goats, mini-playground, tennis and pretty pool. Trace your steps back down the bumpy, twisted track to Gaiole for good, well-priced restaurants. *Minimum stay three nights.*

Price	€110–€250. Apts €700–€1,700 per week. Villa €4,200–€5,000 per week. Half-board €32 p.p. extra.
Rooms	7 + 8: 7 doubles. 7 apartments: 2 for 2, 2 for 4, 3 for 6. Villa for 8.
Meals	Breakfast €10. Dinner, 5 courses, €30, by arrangement. Wine €8.
Closed	Never.
Directions	Exit A1 at Valdarno. Follow signs for Siena & Gaiole in Chianti, about 20km. At Gaiole, signs to Barbischio. Signed.

Signor Giuseppe Gioffreda
loc. Casa al Vento,
53013 Gaiole in Chianti

Tel	+39 0577 749068
Fax	+39 0577 744649
Email	info@borgocasaalvento.com
Web	www.borgocasaalvento.com

Castello di Tornano

The first thing you see is the ancient stone tower, peeking above the wooded hills and vineyards. Inside, a beautiful restoration that has enriched the glorious stonework, the spaciousness and the sense of history. Rooms are positively regal with deep rugs on tiled floors, sparkling chandeliers and richly coloured drapes and linen (plum, raspberry, royal blue, vermilion). The opulent Tower Room has its own jacuzzi and a terrace with stunning views. Self-catering apartments are uncluttered with exposed beams and stone walls, some with lovely vaulted ceilings. Bathrooms are a treat: neutral-toned mosaics blend in with the original stone, there are big mirrors and fluffy white towels and robes. Relax downstairs in the living room with its old font, soft-lighting and plush red drapes; request dinner and you are served fine Tuscan food. The hotel is also an agriturismo so chianti, olive oil, grappa and sweet Vin Santo are all produced here. Come for the friendly atmosphere and the lovely pool and garden, the wine tastings, the riding on the estate, the luxuriousness of it all, and the peace.

Price	€215-€495.
Rooms	11 + 7: 7 doubles, 2 triples, 2 suites. 7 apartments.
Meals	Dinner €36, on request. Wine from €14.
Closed	10 January-10 February.
Directions	A1 exit Valdarno for Cavriglia-Gaiole on road 408. Pass Gaiole, cont. for Siena for 5km; signed on left.

Patrizia & Francesco Gioffreda
loc. Tornano,
53013 Gaiole in Chianti
Tel   +39 0577 746067
Fax   +39 0577 746094
Email info@castelloditornano.it
Web   www.castelloditornano.it

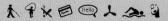

L'Ultimo Mulino

The sense of space is stunning – the vast, medieval hall, the lofty ceilings, the stone walls, the flights of stairs… Original arches give glimpses of passageways beyond and many of the rooms are connected by little 'bridges' from which you can see the millstream far below. Outside the restored watermill is a large terrace for delicious breakfasts, a lovely long pool, and a small amphitheatre where occasional concerts are held. In the middle of nowhere you're surrounded by trees and it's immensely quiet – just the sound of water and birds. All feels fresh and clean, the atmosphere is welcoming and informal, and nothing is too much trouble for the staff. Sparsely, elegantly and comfortably furnished, the great hall makes a cool, beautiful centrepiece to the building – and there's a snug with a fireplace where you can roast chestnuts in season. Excellently equipped bedrooms have terracotta tiled floors and good, generously sized beds. You dine in the conservatory overlooking the stream, on mainly Tuscan dishes – be tempted by truffles and local delicacies. Historic Radda is a ten-minute drive.

Price	€175–€232. Suite €230–€284.
Rooms	13: 12 doubles, 1 suite.
Meals	Dinner €35–€45. Wine list €15–€80. Restaurant closed Mondays.
Closed	Mid-November to mid-March.
Directions	From Gaiole in Chianti 1st right on road to Radda. Mill on right after bend. Signed.

Lorenza Padoan
loc. La Ripresa di Vistarenni,
53013 Gaiole in Chianti

Tel	+39 0577 738520
Fax	+39 0577 738659
Email	info@ultimomulino.it
Web	www.ultimomulino.it

Entry 200 Map 9

Antico Borgo Poggiarello

The 17th-century farm buildings in the woods – the *borgo* – have been transformed into holiday homes and linked by a circuit of well-considered paths. Poggiarello is a family set-up. Signora Giove does the cooking, son Roberto does front of house (he once worked in a tax office and has no regrets); Nino, Paolo and Ciro – the perfectly behaved English setters – are there when you need them. You can self-cater or do B&B here: arrangements are flexible. Most apartments are for two; some interconnect and are ideal for eight. Rooms are big and comfortable with wrought-iron beds, cream curtains and covers, tiled floors; all have patios and great views. One is excellent for wheelchair-users. Days are spent lolling by the pool, evenings sunset-gazing on the terrace. Though the treasures of Siena, Monteriggioni and Volterra lie a short drive away, it's hard to leave: there's a beautifully lit bath housed in a cave that's heated all year to 38 degrees (extra charge), and a terraced restaurant in the old stables where you can sample the best of Tuscan home cooking. *Minimum stay three nights.*

Price	Suites €140-€190. Apartments €115-€160 for 2.
Rooms	2 + 13: 2 suites. 13 apts: 9 for 2-4, 3 for 4-6, 1 for 6-8.
Meals	Breakfast €9. Dinner, 5 courses, €29 by arrangement. Wine from €11.
Closed	November-February.
Directions	From Florence-Siena m'way exit Monteriggioni. Right after stop sign, 1.4km, left for Abbadia a Isola & Stove. After 6km, left for Scorgiano. On for 4km, left at 'Fattoria di Scorgiano'. Signed for 2km.

Roberto Giove
strada di San Monti 12,
53035 Monteriggioni

Tel	+39 0577 301003
Fax	+39 0577 301003
Email	info@poggiarello.com
Web	www.poggiarello.com

Frances' Lodge

You stay in a converted hilltop lemon house, a ten-minute bus ride into the city. Catch your breath at views that soar across olive, lemon and quince groves to the Torre del Mangia of Siena. The old farmhouse was built by Franca's family as a summer retreat. Now she and Franco – warm, charming, intelligent – have filled the lofty, light-filled *limonaia* with beautiful things: an oriental carpet, a butter-yellow leather sofa, vibrant art by Franca. Guests may take breakfast in this lovely room, divided by a glass partition etched with a lemon tree from the kitchen, Franca's domain. And the first meal of the day – on the loggia in summer – is to be lingered over: Tuscan salami and pecorino, fresh figs, delicious coffee. Bedrooms burst with personality and colour – one, funky, cosy and Moroccan, another huge, white and cream, with a terrace. Chic coloured bed linen, huge walk-in showers, a fridge stocked with juice and water, towels for the pool. And what a pool – curved, it lies on the edge of the house, filled with views. A special place with a big heart. *Minimum stay two nights. Over 18s only.*

Price	€180-€220. Suites €240.
Rooms	4 + 2: 4 doubles. 1 suite for 2-3, 1 suite for 4, each with kitchenette.
Meals	Restaurants 1-2km.
Closed	10 January-20 February.
Directions	Pass by Siena on Tangenziale (ring road) for Arezzo-Roma; exit Siena Est to big r'bout 'Due Ponti'; road to S. Regina; 1st right Strada di Valdipugna; signed on right.

Franca Mugnai
strada di Valdipugna 2, 53100 Siena

Tel	+39 0577 281061
Fax	+39 0577 281061
Email	prenotazioni@franceslodge.it
Web	www.franceslodge.it

Campo Regio Relais

Bustling, beautiful Siena. Step straight in from a quiet cobbled street to marble floors, frescoed walls and heavy antiques. A first-floor sitting room gleams with leather sofas and huge vases of fresh flowers, there are striped tablecloths on the breakfast tables and the terrace looks over rooftops to the Duomo. This building, which dates from the 16th-century, is known locally as 'stick of the parrot' thanks to its particular architectural structure: one bedroom has the view and a private terrace, another a window onto the view from its bed. All are generously sumptuous with monogrammed linen sheets, taffeta curtains, soft creams and pale lilacs, big buckets of scents and soaps and large-mirrored bathrooms; thoroughly pampering. It's strolling distance to restaurants, shops, street life. Then back for a nightcap from the honesty bar in the candlelit salon, as you watch the twinkling lights of the city below. Honeymooners will find it irrresistible, architecture buffs will swoon, children may prefer somewhere a touch more robust.

Price	€150–€650.
Rooms	6 twins/doubles.
Meals	Restaurants nearby.
Closed	Rarely.
Directions	From m'way exit Siena west. Follow signs for stadium until x-roads with la Basilica di San Domenico.

Livia Palagi
Residenza d'Epoca,
via della Sapienza, 25, 53100 Siena

Tel	+39 0577 222073
Fax	+39 0577 237308
Email	relais@camporegio.com
Web	www.camporegio.com

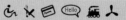

17 via dei Goti

Just south-east of Siena, this medieval hill town buzzes with its weekly market and year-round inhabitants. Catch brilliant views of surrounding hills through entrance arches in ancient walls; Porta dei Tintori is a fine place to sit with a glass of wine in the evening. Your perfect townhouse is tall and narrow, on four floors, cool in the summer yet cosy in winter; rusts, blues and whites bathe its walls. You enter the open-plan dining area off the street; through an arched wall is a fully-stocked kitchen. (Take what you need – wine included – then simply replace.) On the first floor are a double bedroom and an elegant living room with a beamed ceiling, an open fireplace, a cream sofa and chairs, lovely art work and books galore. A second salon and another bedroom are on the third floor, then right at the top (not for the un-nimble) is the master bedroom, splendid with its French antiques and embroidered linen curtains and sheets. The bathroom has a claw-foot bath from which you may gaze over rooftops, and candles are waiting to be lit. Fabulous.

Price	€650–€970 per week.
Rooms	House for 6
	(2 doubles, 1 twin/double).
Meals	Restaurant 50m.
Closed	Rarely.
Directions	Directions on booking.

Sheri Eggleton & Charles Grant
53040 Rapolano Terme

Tel	+44 (0)117 9081949
Mobile	+44 (0)7932 166096
Email	sherieggleton711@googlemail.com
Web	www.17viadeigoti.co.uk

Hotel Borgo Casabianca

A medieval hamlet on top of a hill, meticulously restored. In theory a farm, this has more the feel of a country estate. In the 'Villa Padronale'- with a tiny chapel standing alongside – are terracotta-floored bedrooms grandly endowed with elaborate ceilings and rich drapes and chandeliers; some have their 18th-century wall decorations. The surrounding stables and barns have become 20 self-contained, individually furnished apartments, nicely rustic with white walls, old beams and chunky terracotta. Each has its own little garden; many have balconies or terraces with stupendous forest views over the estate. You will find everything you need in the farm's on-site shop, from wine to olive oil and homemade biscuits: this is an ideal set-up for self-caterers and families. There are wonderful walks in the surrounding countryside and bikes for further afield; you can meander down to the lake to fish, relax at the poolside bar or hide away in the secluded cloister garden. The bright and inviting restaurant is in the old wine cellars, still with its vats and press.

Price	€170-€198. Suites €240-€360. Apts €245-€420 (€950-€1,995 per week).
Rooms	9 + 20: 3 doubles, 6 suites. 20 apartments: 15 for 2, 5 for 4-6.
Meals	Breakfast €12 for self-caterers. Dinner €35. Wine from €10.
Closed	January-March.
Directions	A1 exit 28 for Valdichiana, Sinalunga, Asciano. After Asciano, 9km on right.

Signor Luigi Scaperrotta
SP 10, loc. Casabianca,
53041 Asciano

Tel	+39 0577 704362
Fax	+39 0577 704622
Email	casabianca@casabianca.it
Web	www.casabianca.it

Bosco della Spina

The road sign for 'pizzeria' is misleading: nothing so mundane here. Tables overlook a magical garden of pergolas, waterfalls, vines and wisteria; Castle Murlo hangs in the distance. Imaginatively restored and landscaped, these former farmhouse cellars in medieval Lupompesi have strikingly modern interiors and old Tuscan beams and terracotta; it is an arctitecturally interesting restoration. The restaurant, a cool space of open arches, raftered ceiling and sleek furniture, serves classic regional dishes (pizza in the summer only) accompanied by 180 wines. The minimalist mini-apartments, each with fridge, sink and dual hob, have terraces and big divans and furniture made by local craftsmen. Blankets are neatly rolled, colours are white and conker brown, beds hi-tech four-poster, bedcovers faux suede, shower rooms designer-special. All this and a wine bar, library, small gym, slimline pool (suitable for lengths only) and garden spots filled with tinkling water and views. A chic family affair, where Mum cooks and daughter is professional manager. Popular with wedding parties, too.

Price	€120–€200.
Rooms	14 apartments: for 2-4, 4-6, 4-8.
Meals	Dinner €30. Wine from €7.
Closed	Rarely.
Directions	A1 for Siena; exit Siena south; SS2 for Rome; 15km; Monteroni d'Arbia; right to Vescovado di Murlo just before Lucignano d'Arbia; 8km; right for Casciano di Murlo; 1km; in Lupompesi, on left, signed 'Residence'.

Brigida Meoni
Lupompesi,
53016 Murlo

Tel	+39 0577 814605
Fax	+39 0577 814606
Email	bsturist@boscodellaspina.com
Web	www.boscodellaspina.com

Entry 206 Map 11

Azienda Agricola Podere Salicotto Agriturismo

Watch sunsets fire the Tuscan hills; catch the sunrise as it brings the valleys alive. Views from this hilltop farmhouse roll off in every direction. It is peaceful here, and beautiful. Breakfast is a feast that merges into lunch, with produce from the organic farm, and Silvia and Paolo, a well-travelled, warm and adventurous couple, are happy for you to be as active or as idle as you like. Eat in the big farmhouse kitchen or under the pergola, as deer wander across the field below. Paolo is full of ideas and will take you sailing in his six-berth boat that has crossed the Atlantic – or organise wine-tasting and cycling trips. The beamed and terracotta tiled bedrooms are airy and welcoming, full of soft, Tuscan colours and furnished with simplicity but care: antiques, monogrammed sheets, great showers. B&B guests are in the main house (private entrance) while the apartment is in the converted barn. Visit Siena, medieval Buonconvento, Tuscan hill towns. Come back, rest in a hammock, laze around the pool with a glass of wine and a fabulous view.

Price	€130–€150 (€840–€980 per week). Studio €1,330 per week.
Rooms	6 + 1: 6 doubles. 1 studio for 2-4.
Meals	Breakfast for self-caterers, €10. Lunch or dinner €15–€20, on request. Restaurants 3km.
Closed	Mid-November to mid-March.
Directions	From Siena via Cassia to Buonconvento; with the Consorzio Agraria on your left, turn immed. left; follow road to Podere on right.

Silvia Forni
Podere Salicotto 73,
53022 Buonconvento

Tel	+39 0577 809087
Fax	+39 0577 809535
Email	info@poderesalicotto.com
Web	www.poderesalicotto.com

La Locanda del Castello

Antique clocks and white truffles are just two of the treats here; the former are collected by your excellent host Silvana, the latter are a rare delicacy for which the region is famous. The hilltop village of San Giovanni d'Asso acts as a bridge between the Val d'Orcia (home of the celebrated truffle) and the breathtaking countryside of the Crete Senesi. At the heart of the town is an imposing 16th-century castle, and tucked into its walls lies La Locanda Del Castello. There are only nine bedrooms in this lovely hotel; all are beautifully decorated and furnished with Silvana's family hierlooms. Bathrooms are luxurious and, as with everything in the hotel, built into the original shape of the castle. But the jewel in this particular crown is the restaurant – open to the public – where the chefs cook to old Tuscan recipes and guests feast on pecorino cheese, fine meats and an intoxicating selection of regional wines. And, of course, truffles. On balmy evenings, the canopy over the patio can be rolled back to allow diners to marvel at the moon. Breakfasts are every bit as delicious.

Price	€120–€160.
Rooms	9 doubles.
Meals	Lunch or dinner with wine, €35.
Closed	10 January–10 March.
Directions	Florence-Roma A1 exit Valdichiana; 5km to Sinalunga; 10km Trequanda-Montisi; 5km to hotel. Park below castle.

Signora Silvana Ratti Ravanelli
Piazza V. Emanuele II 4,
53020 San Giovanni d'Asso

Tel	+39 0577 802939
Fax	+39 0577 802942
Email	info@lalocandadelcastello.com
Web	www.lalocandadelcastello.com

Poggio Boldrini

Artists, poets, dreamers, lovers will find inspiration here, high, high up in the hills. Sue, an artist, has beautifully, sustainably restored her home... even battling with a builder to insist on geothermal heating. Enter an open-plan space with whitewashed walls, graceful arches and reclaimed stone floors, enhanced by deep aubergine sofas, pale lilac curtains and many of Sue's paintings; a charming kitchen and a salon stuffed with books and music share this floor. Stone stairs wind up to bedrooms; peek through a picture window on the way and gasp at the view to San Giovanni. Sleep will be deep in big airy rooms painted in gorgeous pinks, oranges, lilacs. Curtains are diaphanous, bathrooms large and light. Sue's artistry is not confined to painting and her terraced garden is a year-round joy filled with hidden areas and a small private studio for those who cannot be idle. One stone terrace has deeply cushioned rattan chairs and tables for reading or gazing; cool off later in the lazy pool. Beauty and serenity surround you, and you can walk to the hamlet of Chiusure. *Caretaker in neighbouring cottage.*

Sue and her husband Ryan refuse to live off the Tuscan land without ensuring they do it no harm. Everything they have done to restore their 15th-century villa has passed the 'green test'; Ryan works as an environmental engineer in London. There are rows of photovoltaic panels providing the site with electricity, the olive field at the back of the house is lined with an energy system for environmentally friendly air conditioning and underfloor heating, rainwater is harvested to feed the garden and the house has its own soft water well, for irrigation and for the pool.

Price	£900–£4,500 per week.
Rooms	House for 8.
Meals	Restaurants 2km.
Closed	Rarely.
Directions	Directions on booking.

Sue Kennington
53020 San Giovanni d'Asso,
Mobile   +39 347 8812709
Email   sookay@tin.it
Web   www.poggioboldrini.co.uk

SPECIAL GREEN ENTRY
see page 14

Map 11 Entry 209

Villa Poggiano

It's the gardens that capture the imagination – six enchanting hectares of them. Centuries-old cypresses line the paths, a stone table in a secluded alcove overlooks a breathtaking view, flowers tumble out of stately pots on the terrace. The house and gardens once belonged to a German general and it was he who imported the magnificent stone statues, dating back to the 1900s, and built the memorable pool. Austerely beautiful, it is made of travertine stone, with more statues presiding over the patio and walls. There's a fountain, too, in what was once the children's pool. Stefania's family bought the place in 2000. It is immaculately, elegantly and traditionally furnished with antiques and old paintings. The suites are luxurious and the bathrooms sumptuous – they have space and marble in plenty, some have pretty tiles from Capri. The bedrooms, in the main house or in the independent lodges in the grounds, have heaps of space, both inside and out: one has a terrace, another a garden and all have wonderful views to Monte Amiata and the Torre di Monticchiello. *Beauty treatments available.*

Price	€195-€220. Suites €235-€310.
Rooms	14: 3 doubles, 11 suites.
Meals	Light meals available. Restaurants 2km.
Closed	Mid-November to March.
Directions	From A1 exit Valdichiana for Montepulciano. After 5km left at lights in Torrita di Siena for Montepulciano. On for 8km SS146 for Pienza. 2km further left at Relais Villa Poggiano. Left to Villa after 800m.

Stefania Savini
via di Poggiano 7,
53045 Montepulciano

Tel	+39 0578 758292
Fax	+39 0578 715635
Email	info@villapoggiano.com
Web	www.villapoggiano.com

Montorio

As you pootle up the drive, you will be inspired by the Temple of San Biagio. A Renaissance masterpiece designed by Antonio Sangallo the Elder, it is an unforgettable backdrop to Montorio. The house stands on top of its own little hill, 600m above sea level, overlooking a vast green swathe of Tuscany. Made of warm stone walls and roofs on different levels, it was once a *casa colonica*. It is now divided into five attractive apartments, each named after a celebrated Italian artist or poet, each with a well-equipped kitchen and an open fire. White walls, beams and terracotta floors set a tone of rural simplicity; antiques, paintings and wrought-iron lights crafted by Florentines add a touch of style; leather chesterfields and big beds guarantee comfort. The terraced gardens – full of ancient cypress trees, pots of flowers and alluring places to sit – drop gently down to olive groves and vineyards. Stefania's other villa, Poggiano, is five minutes away and historic Montepulciano, full of shops and eating places, is close enough to walk. *Minimum stay three nights.*

Price	€120–€180 for 2 (€500–€1,200 per wk). €180–€250 for 4 (€1,100–€1,700 per wk).	
Rooms	5 apartments: 3 for 2, 2 for 4.	
Meals	Restaurants 500m.	
Closed	December-January.	
Directions	A1 exit Valdichiana for Montepulciano. In Torrita di Siena, left at lights to Montepulciano. There, follow signs to Chianciano. Right at x-roads bilvio di S. Biagio.	

	Stefania Savini
	strada per Pienza 2,
	53045 Montepulciano
Tel	+39 0578 758292
Fax	+39 0578 715635
Email	info@villapoggiano.com
Web	www.montorio.com

Residenza d'Arte

Sleep in an art gallery: a big, bold, historic space filled with big, bold, contemporary art. Around one thousand sculptures, paintings and installations litter the 14th-century Residenza's unique bedrooms, salons and terraces. They are the works of Anna Izzo, whose family spent five years restoring the mellow stone buildings. Cool spaces of vaulted and raftered ceilings, chunky stone and brick walls and elegant arches, they form the perfect backdrop for her striking work. Bedrooms range from large to vast; small shower rooms reveal ancient brickwork. Furnishings are minimal and characterful: a sleek modern sofa by an antique chest, a red glass vase filled with twigs, a fuchsia bedspread on a big bed. Breakfast on the terrace where bronze sculptures vie for attention with views of medieval Torrita di Siena on the hill. Enrico, Anna's son, can arrange riding, wine tours, cycling trips, spa treatments at Montepulciano, swimming in a nearby private pool, hot-air ballooning. Enthusiastic and friendly, the family are a delight. Not for the sedate and conventional – a place to fire the senses.

Price	€135-€270.
Rooms	8 doubles.
Meals	Restaurant 500m.
Closed	November to mid-March.
Directions	From A1 exit Valdichiana until Torrita di Siena; signed. Outside *centro storico*.

Enrico Ferretti
Poggio Madonna dell'Olivo,
53049 Torrita di Siena
Tel   +39 0577 684252
Fax   +39 3384 814384
Email   residenzadarte@fastwebnet.it
Web   www.residenzadarte.com

Il Rigo

The fame of Lorenza's cooking has spread so far that she's been invited to demonstrate her skills in the US. (She runs courses here, too.) So meals in the big, beamed dining room at pretty check-clothed tables are a treat. Irresistible home-grown organic produce, 60 local wines to choose from and a gorgeous Tuscan setting. There are two houses on the family farm, named after the stream running through it. 'Casabianca', reached via a cypress-flanked drive, is ancient and stone built. A vine-covered pergola shades the entrance; beyond the reception area is a courtyard full of climbing roses. The second house, 'Poggio Bacoca', is about 600 metres away. Once home to the farmworkers, it's red-brick built and has two sitting rooms and panoramic views. You walk (600m) to 'Casabianca' for those wonderful meals. Bedrooms are homely, pretty and inviting; all have embroidered sheets, appealing colour schemes and matching bathrooms. No televisions: it's not that sort of place. Lorenza and Vittorio hope and believe that their guests will prefer a relaxed chat over a glass of wine.

Price	€100–€110. Half-board €144–€156.
Rooms	15 doubles.
Meals	Lunch or dinner €22–€25, by arrangement. Wine from €12.
Closed	Never.
Directions	Exit A1 Certosa; follow superstrada, exit Siena South. SS.2 (via Cassia) 2km south of S Quirico d'Orcia; on left on 2km track, signed.

Signor Vittorio Cipolla & Lorenza Santo
Podere Casabianca,
53027 San Quirico d'Orcia
Tel   +39 0577 897 291
Fax   +39 0577 898 236
Email   info@agriturismoilrigo.com
Web   www.agriturismoilrigo.com

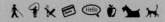

Castello di Ripa d'Orcia

As you drive up the long, white road, the castle comes into view: a thrilling sight. Ripa d'Orcia dates from the 13th century, one of Siena's most important strongholds. The battlemented fortress (closed to the public) dominates the *borgo* encircled by small medieval dwellings. The family are descendants of the Piccolomini who acquired the estate in 1484 and are hugely proud of their heritage. Grand banquets and knights in shining armour may come to mind... children will love it here. Rooms and apartments have huge raftered ceilings and are furnished simply and well; many have breathtaking views. There's also a day room, filled with lovely furniture and heaps of books to browse. You breakfast in a small annexe off the main restaurant; there's a cellar for wine tastings and a shop for you to stock up on your favourites. A pool too, and a beautiful chapel in the grounds. The area is a paradise for walkers and there is enough on the spot to keep lovers of history and architecture happy for hours – before the 'official' sightseeing begins. *Minimum stay two nights in rooms; three nights in apartment.*

Price	€110–€150. Apts €110–€155 for 2; €175–€190 for 4.
Rooms	6 + 8: 6 twins/doubles. 8 apartments: 5 for 2, 3 for 4.
Meals	Breakfast for self-caterers €12. Dinner €25. Wine from €6. Closed Mondays.
Closed	November–March.
Directions	From SS2 for San Quirico d'Orcia; right over bridge. Follow road around town walls for 700m. Right again, signed; 5.3km to Castello.

Famiglia Aluffi Pentini Rossi
via della Contea 1/16,
53027 Ripa d'Orcia

Tel	+39 0577 897376
Fax	+39 0577 898038
Email	info@castelloripadorcia.com
Web	www.ripadorcia.it

Hotel Terme San Filippo

Arthritic Pope Pio II came here in 1462. The Italians still adore hot thermal springs, and this is one of the best, sited in the gorgeous, rolling Orcia valley. People come from all over to test the healing properties of what many believe to be miraculous minerals – don't be alarmed by the occasional wafts of sulphur. There's a pool heated to 40 degrees (that's hot), a superb waterfall, cold showers and a well-being centre offering massages, mud baths, saunas and a whirlpool. Work out in the woods, stroll to the extraordinary and calcareous Fosso Bianco nearby. Bedrooms are comfortable, nothing fancy. Well-presented regional dishes are served in the yellow dining room, full of lively Italian life; friendly staff present a seasonal menu at breakfast. Walls are faux-marble – "for fun", says Gabriella, who is as delightful as her team. The atmosphere is bustling yet relaxed (quieter on weekdays), with white towelling *robes de rigeur*. A great place for a healthy, pampering weekend, and a fine starting point for an excursion to Mount Amiata, central Tuscany's most majestic peak. *Minimum stay two nights.*

Price	€100-€120. Singles €58-€78. Half-board €70-€80 p.p. Full-board €76-€86 p.p.
Rooms	27: 23 doubles, 4 singles.
Meals	Lunch & dinner €22. Wine €8.50-€38.
Closed	November-Easter.
Directions	From Siena SS2 for Rome, then to Bagni S. Filippo. via S. Filippo is main road through village.

Gabriella Contorni
via San Filippo 23,
53020 Bagni San Filippo

Tel	+39 0577 872982
Fax	+39 0577 872684
Email	info@termesanfilippo.it
Web	www.termesanfilippo.it

La Foce: Castelluccio, Montauto, Santa Maria

Open the venerable door to an arched courtyard, a thousand geraniums and, in the last week of July, a festival of chamber music. 'Castelluccio' (the 'little castle') dominates a hill of the remarkable La Foce estate, and protects two apartments within its 11th-century walls. In the walled gardens – as beautiful as all the gardens here – is a pool with a breathtaking view. 'Santa Maria', in seven hectares, once belonged to a nearby parish; now it is part of the fold. Chestnut trees behind, mushrooms in the woods, orchards tumbling down to the road; Benedetta found the setting irresistible. Inside are soft Sienese colours, simple furnishings, a few choice antiques. And then there's 'Montauto', with masses of space and sweeping views back up to 'Castelluccio' on its hill. The old stables keep their huge arches, stone fireplaces and terracotta floors; beds, sofas and super kitchen are new. The terraced garden, with pool, is full of views; walks radiate from the door. Beyond are pungent wines and white truffles, wild herbs and pecorino cheeses, the unsung hill towns of Montalcino, Monticchiello, Chiusi, and the hot springs of Vignoni. Bliss. *Minimum stay one week.*

Price	Castelluccio: €500–€1,550.
	Montauto: €3,570–€6,200.
	Santa Maria: €2,550–€4,160.
	Prices per week.
Rooms	Castelluccio: 1 apt for 2, 1 for 4–5.
	Montauto: 3 doubles, 1 twin, 2 singles.
	Santa Maria: 3 doubles, 1 single.
Meals	Restaurant 2km.
Closed	Never.
Directions	From A1 exit Chiusi towards Chianciano Terme. Before Chianciano follow signs to Monte Amiata. La Foce 5km.

Benedetta Origo
strada della Vittoria, 61,
53042 Chianciano Terme

Tel	+39 0578 69101
Fax	+39 0578 69113
Email	info@lafoce.com
Web	www.lafoce.com

La Foce: Chiarentana, Gonzola, La Sassaia

You could spend days in the generous, delightful company of Donata and Benedetta. Each property in this valley has memories of their childhoods and their love for each home is infectious. 'Chiarentana', built around a vast courtyard and a linden tree, started life as a castle where pilgrims would stop on their way to Rome; later it became a farm where 20 families and their livestock lived, up until the 50s. Now framed pictures hang on colourwashed walls, big friendly rugs cover terracotta floors and logs fill fireplaces. A tennis court, pool and playground hide in the olive tree'd gardens, a pretty restaurant serves Tuscan food… for huge gatherings this is perfect. 'Gonzola', at the end of a gravel road surrounded by fields, alone with its pool and landscaped garden, is ideal for a party of ten. And lovely old 'La Sassaia'… hard to believe it was once a barn; now the mangers tumble with cushions and the seven ground-floor windows flood it with light. A travertine spiral stair leads to a huge Tuscan kitchen where you can cook over the fire; outside are pretty pergola and fine pool. *Minimum stay one week.*

Price	Chiarentana €600–€2,260. Gonzola €3,570–€6,200. La Sassaia €4,750–€7,500. Prices per week.
Rooms	Chiarentana: 2 apts for 2, 3 apts for 4, 1 apt for 6. Gonzola for 10. Sassaia for 10 (extra double & twin in garden house).
Meals	Restaurant 2km.
Closed	Never.
Directions	From A1 exit Chiusi towards Chianciano Terme. Before Chianciano follow signs to Monte Amiata. La Foce 5km.

Donata Origo
strada della Vittoria 63,
53042 Chianciano Terme

Tel	+39 0578 69101
Fax	+39 0578 69113
Email	info@lafoce.com
Web	www.lafoce.com

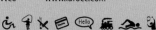

La Crocetta Agriturismo

Basking in fresh air and perfectly positioned between Siena, Perugia, Florence and Rome
are 900 farmed Tuscan acres. The land spills over with good things: cereals, wine, olive
oil… The large stone building dates from 1835 and has been completely restored. Though
next to a main road, it is shielded by oak trees and a large garden that feels wonderfully
secluded. The interior is furnished with attractively colourwashed or stencilled walls and
rush-seated chairs. Bedrooms are charming and cosy, with good modern shower rooms;
some are country-Italian in style, others traditional-English with floral fabrics. Cooking is
a strong point – mouthwatering aromas drift in from the kitchen towards mealtimes and
there's always a choice. Be sure to ask in advance to prepare dinners for you and your
family – you won't have to lift a finger and your hosts will be thrilled to serve you a feast
of culinary delights. Cristina and Andrea are engaging and conversation is easy; he's the
cook, she's the designer. There's a pool, and it's a five-minute walk to the spa of San
Casciano dei Bagni. *Minimum stay three nights.*

Price	€120. Singles €64.
Rooms	8: 4 doubles, 3 twins, 1 single.
Meals	Dinner €30, by arrangement. Wine from €11.
Closed	Mid-November to March.
Directions	Exit A1 motorway at Chiusi towards S. Casciano dei Bagni; signed.

Andrea & Cristina Leotti
loc. La Crocetta, 53040
San Casciano dei Bagni

Tel	+39 0578 58360
Fax	+39 0578 58353
Email	agriturismolacrocetta@virgilio.it
Web	www.agriturismolacrocetta.it

Umbria

Photo: istock.com

Locanda Palazzone

An imposing palazzo in the Umbrian countryside, Locanda Palazzone is full of contrasts. Built by a cardinal as a resting place for pilgrims to Rome, it was designed with an urban sophistication: buttressed walls, mullioned windows, vaulted hall. It later fell from grace and became a country farmhouse – until Ludovico's family rescued it, planting vineyards and restoring the buildings. Despite the rusticity of the setting, the interiors are cool, elegant, chic. The sitting room (once the Grand Hall) is light and airy, its huge windows overlooking the garden. Bedrooms – split-level suites, mostly – are understatedly luxurious, their modern and antique furnishings set against pale oak floors, cream walls, exposed stone. Red, claret and purple cushions add warmth; white linen sheets, Bulgari bath foams and specialist herb soaps soothe. Meals – regional, seasonal – are served on rainbow porcelain on the terrace, accompanied by the estate's wines. Your generous hosts are eager to please, the pool is surrounded by delphiniums and roses, and views sweep to vineyards and forests. A remarkable place.

Price	€156-€340.
Rooms	7: 5 suites for 2, 2 suites for 4.
Meals	Dinner, 4 courses, €34, by arrangement.
Closed	10 January-20 March.
Directions	A1 Florence-Roma, Orvieto exit; 1.8km dir. Orvieto; at bridge for funicular, right for Allerona; cont. to Sferracavallo junc.; again follow Allerona; 200m, left toward Castel Giorgio, keeping petrol station on right; 2.5km, signed.

	Lodovico Dubini
	loc. Rocca Ripesena,
	05010 Orvieto
Tel	+39 0763 393614
Fax	+39 0763 394833
Email	info@locandapalazzone.com
Web	www.locandapalazzone.com

Locanda Rosati Agriturismo

From the moment you turn off the road – whose proximity is quickly forgotten – the atmosphere is easy. The house has been gently modernised but remains firmly a farmhouse; the summer-cool rooms on the ground floor – with open fires in winter – have been furnished with an eye for comfort rather than a desire to impress, and wild flowers, books and magazines are scattered. Dinner is the thing here; it's rustic, delectable and Giampiero and Paolo are natural hosts, full of stories and enthusiastic advice on what to do and where to go. Tables are laid with simple cloths, glass tumblers and butter-coloured pottery, the recipes have been handed down the Rosati generations and the wines come from a wonderful cellar carved out of the tufa seven metres below ground. Bedrooms are simple, with new wooden beds, pristine bed linen, spotless showers. Much of the furniture comes from the famous Bottega Michelangeli in Orvieto, whose jigsaw-like carved animal shapes characterise this region. From the gardens you can see the spiky skyline of Orvieto: delightful. *Ask about cookery courses.*

Price	€110–€130. Singles €90–€110. Half-board option.
Rooms	10: 4 doubles, 5 family, 1 single.
Meals	Dinner with wine, €33.
Closed	7 January-February.
Directions	Exit A1 at Orvieto; for Viterbo, Bolsena & Montefiascone; 10km; on right.

Signor Giampiero Rosati
loc. Buonviaggio 22,
05018 Orvieto

Tel	+39 0763 217314
Fax	+39 0763 217314
Email	info@locandarosati.orvieto.tr.it
Web	www.locandarosati.orvieto.tr.it

La Palombara Maison d'Hôtes

Picture a valley in gently rolling farmland in a hidden corner of Umbria. Nothing grand or pretentious, just an 18th-century farm, an ancient mulberry tree, the nightingale's ballad… Marie France and Massimo retired here recently after running a hotel in Amelia. They live in the main house with Mouette, their bouncy young golden retriever, and are gentle, unobtrusive and charming. The old stone-built piggery has been converted into two attractive, white-shuttered apartments. The airy rooms are simply and pleasingly furnished with a mix of old and new: antique china cabinets and modern pine cupboards, marble-topped tables and the odd pretty item of painted furniture. There is a washing machine but don't expect mod cons and luxuries – it's not that sort of place, and the beds are decidedly firm! Each apartment has its outside sitting area and the pool is fringed with lavender and rosemary. The garden is still in its infancy – tiny olive trees, roses, wisteria – and there's a little orchard with apricots and peaches, cherries and figs: pick your own. *Minimum stay three nights in low season.*

Price	€900-€1,100 per week.
Rooms	2 apartments: 1 for 5, 1 for 6.
Meals	Restaurant & pizzeria 2km.
Closed	Rarely.
Directions	Exit Amelia from Terni-Perugia; follow signs to Avigliano; left to Collicello for 500m; signed left.

Massimo Ralli & Marie France de Boiscuille
strada di Collicello 34,
05022 Amelia

Tel	+39 0744 988491
Fax	+39 0744 988491
Email	info@lapalombara-umbria.it
Web	www.lapalombara-umbria.it

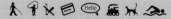

La Fontana

Your heart lifts as you approach these three small vine-clad cottages in their olive-grove setting. The outskirts of historic Amelia are not promising, but here you are enveloped by beautiful old trees. Each cottage fits two comfortably, and each has its own furnished eating out area. Indoors, furnishings are an intriguing, jostling mix of styles, as are the pictures, *objets* and many books. One cottage, 'Limonaia', has both open fire and central heating: a winter break here would be wonderfully cosy. 'Rosetto' too has an open fire, and beautiful Russian icons on its walls; 'Pergola' has a pretty sitting out area and a small double bed. Set in seven acres of hillside, the lovely mature gardens flow through a small orchard and down to a rose-strewn pergola, barbecue area and swimming pool. The drinking water, from a private source and pure enough to be bottled and sold, is yours for free – no need to lug plastic bottles from the supermarket. The English owners live in Amelia but are full of advice should you need it: the town is lively and unspoilt and one of the oldest in Italy. *Minimum stay one week.*

Price	€450–€550 per week.
Rooms	3 cottages: 2 for 2, 1 for 2-3.
Meals	Restaurants 2km.
Closed	Rarely.
Directions	Exit A1 for Orte; follow Terni; exit Amelia. In front of main walls follow Giove to 1st intersection. Left & immed. right. 1st left to strada di Palazzone.

Flavia Corsano
strada di Palazzone 8,
05022 Amelia

Tel	+39 0744 983465
Mobile	+39 335 5344767
Email	flavia.corsano@alice.it
Web	www.umbriandream.com

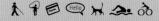

Residenza Carleni

There's such a cluster of old houses elbowing each other in this steep cobbled street that it's difficult to decide where Residenza Carleni begins and ends. It's medieval, built of golden stone and a new venture for Cate (who has also just opened a rather smart restaurant just next door). She's chatty and friendly, has lived in Italy for a number of years and her two apartments are reached via a pair of pretty brick-and-stone arches and an open-air staircase. One has its own terrace, both have marvellous views over the little town's jumble of rooftops to the hills beyond. The bedrooms are country simple and very delightful, with white or yellow walls and timbered, sloping ceilings; the kitchen/dining areas have warm yellow walls and old terracotta floors. No sofas here but you'll probably want to spend every waking moment outside. The secret garden, approached over a bridge, is unexpectedly big, entirely enclosed and has a wood-fired oven for al fresco cooking. The bells from the nearby duomo will mark the precious hours of your stay; it's all so relaxing that families will love it. *Minimum stay three nights.*

Price	€600–€1,200 per week.
Rooms	2 apartments for 4.
Meals	Restaurant next door.
Closed	Rarely.
Directions	Leave A1 at Orte for Terni; 9km, exit to Amelia; in Amelia enter *centro storico*; for cathedral & Residenza Carleni.

Cate Thomas
via Roscia, 05022 Amelia

Tel/Fax	+39 0744 978143
Mobile	+39 333 848 5803
Email	actho7@gmail.com
Web	www.residenzacarleni.com

Locanda di Colle dell'Oro

Candles flicker alongside the path, illuminating your way as you return from the garden restaurant. It's an imaginative touch, in keeping with the Locanda's ethos. Gioia delights in her family's country home and you will too, from the moment you step into the striking entrance hall and breathe in the heady scent of jasmine. In spite of occasional music and four lively dogs, the restored 19th-century house feels harmonious and calm. Large, lovely bedrooms, named after plants, have neutral colour schemes and bleached wooden furniture that Gioia has painted with flowers. Ask for a room with a view. Sheets and towels are of the purest linen and the bathrooms are beautifully planned; the luxury is real and understated. French windows lead from the breakfast room to the terrace looking down over sprawling Terni, and a garden full of birdsong and geraniums, jasmine, roses, hydrangeas; the swimming pool is hidden on a lower terrace. Yoga classes three times a week, cookery classes out of season.

Price	€70–€100. Triples €110. Suites €130.
Rooms	10: 5 doubles, 4 triples, 1 suite.
Meals	Lunch & dinner €30. Half-board €20 extra p.p.
Closed	Rarely.
Directions	From A1 Orte exit Terni Ovest. Follow signs for Norcia Cascia until signs for Locanda. Hotel on left.

Gioia Iaculli
strada di Palmetta 31,
05100 Terni

Tel	+39 0744 432379
Fax	+39 0744 437826
Email	locanda@colledelloro.it
Web	www.colledelloro.it

Entry 224 Map 12

Torre del Tenente

The medieval lieutenant's lookout tower, outwardly forbidding, is full of light and stylish comfort. It is owned by the delightful Maria, who has lived in Rome most of her life and now inhabits a small house in the grounds, with three bouncy dogs and one moody cat. All around are layer upon layer of beautiful, wooded, Umbrian hills; up the road, a three-minute walk, is the little village (two shops, one bar, one restaurant). Seemingly suspended above the countryside, the tower may be entered on any of three levels, from a steeply terraced garden smothered in summer roses. On the ground floor: a lovely big living/dining room with an open fire, a super bathroom, a kitchen that is a joy to use; on the first floor, two bedrooms and a shower; at the top, a loft-like sitting room with a kitchenette and an en suite bedroom above. White walls and peachy terracotta floors, pretty arched windows with spectacular views, antique prints in lovely gold frames, beautiful fabrics, deep sofas, a piano: rooms to linger in. But make time for Orvieto, with its jazz festival in winter. *Minimum stay three nights.*

Price	€240-€400.
Rooms	House for 6 (1 double, 2 twins/doubles).
Meals	Restaurant 5-minute walk.
Closed	May-September.
Directions	E45 exit Todi direction Orvieto; 14km, left at x-roads for Acqualoreto. Right before piazza, via del Mulino. House below village, 100m along track on right.

Maria Bolasco De Luca
Mulino 4,
05020 Acqualoreto

Tel	+39 0744 953066
Mobile	+39 348 3800190
Fax	+39 0744 953066
Email	mariabolasco@tiscali.it

Monte Valentino Agriturismo

On top of the world in Umbria. Woods fall away, hills climb to snow-scatttered heights. It's the perfect escape, the only route in a steep, winding, two-kilometre dirt track. All around you lie 60 hectares of organically farmed land – mushrooms are gathered from the woods, cereal and vegetables from the fields, fruit from the trees. These new apartments are contemporary yet cosy with simple wooden furniture, tiled floors and throws on the striped sofas. All have small balconies and kitchens and clean, fresh shower rooms; two have access to beautifully designed, red-brick terraces, where the views sweep and soar away. The swimming pool is delightful, surrounded by deck chairs and olive trees. Fabrizia, who lives next door, is enthusiastic and charming with an engaging smile, and proud of her new venture – meet her over simple breakfast in her homely kitchen. This is perfect cycling terrain – for the experienced! You can also swim in the river, horse riding is six miles away, cookery lessons can be arranged, and Fabrizia's husband Nicola will give you archery lessons if you fancy something different.

Price	€65–€75. €280–€590 per week.
Rooms	4 apartments for 2-3.
Meals	Restaurants 12km.
Closed	Never.
Directions	SS E45 Orte-Cesena exit Montone-Pietralunga; SP201 to Pietralunga. At km12, Carpini (before Pietralunga); right at x-roads, signed.

	Fabrizia Gargano & Nicola Polchi loc. Monte Valentino, 06026 Pietralunga
Tel	+39 0759 462092
Fax	+39 0759 462092
Email	info@montevalentino.it
Web	www.montevalentino.it

Casale

Both house and setting are spectacular – and the garden is on its way. Tim and Austin, who have another Special Place in the Yorkshire Dales, have renovated beautifully. Behind the old Umbrian stones lie three cosy bedrooms, pristine bathrooms and a kitchen and living area worthy of a glossy interiors' magazine. The country dining table seats eight, there are sofas and an open fire, a stainless steel oven, masses of workspace and a sink with a view. Preparing your *tartufi neri* – Umbrian black truffles wrapped in pancetta – would be no hardship here. Nothing is busy or overdone, the views are amazing – there's a new 'look out' gazebo – and the saltwater pool, with terraces and wooden loungers, is impossible to resist. Visit Umbertide for provisions, hilltop Montone for narrow streets tumbling with geraniums, restaurants, bars and ancient-rampart views. At the end of a rough two-mile road this is remote – but Perugia, San Sepolcro, Cortona and Assissi are only an hour's drive. If you're more than eight, put your friends up at the agriturismo up the hill. *Minimum stay three nights.*

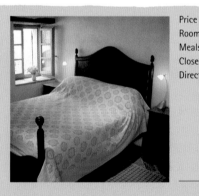

Price	£140 (£850-£1,800 per week).
Rooms	House for 6 + sofabed.
Meals	Restaurants 5km.
Closed	Rarely.
Directions	From Carpini signs for Monte Valentino, right at 3rd sign up to house.

Austin Lynch & Tim Culkin
loc. S. Faustino, Carpini,
06026 Pietralunga

Tel	+44 (0)1748 823571
Fax	+44 (0)1748 850701
Email	oztim@millgatehouse.demon.co.uk
Web	oztiminitaly.com

La Preghiera

Shady terraces, a sunken garden, a flower-filled loggia and a private chapel. So many tranquil spots in which to recharge batteries. This glorious 12th-century monastery, hidden in a wooded valley near Gubbio and Cortona, was a pilgrim's resting place. Now it is owned by the Tunstills (architect and interior designer) who have restored with English country-house flair and Italian attention to detail. The large sitting and dining rooms are elegantly scattered with sofas, paintings and antiques; there are a billiard room and a library of books and DVDs. Bedrooms combine original features – beamed and raftered ceilings, terracotta floors, wooden shutters, exposed stone – with sophisticated details. Bed linen is cotton and silk, furniture is hand-crafted, wardrobes have interior lights, bathrooms are marbled. Breakfast on the terrace, take afternoon tea by the pool, dine by candlelight on local boar and truffles. There are vintage bikes to borrow, horse riding and golf, medieval hilltop towns to visit, lovely staff to look after you. You can even book a massage by the pool. *Ask about half-price deals.*

Price	€150–€350.
Rooms	11 twins/doubles.
Meals	Dinner with wine, 4 courses, €50, by arrangement.
Closed	Rarely.
Directions	Exit E45 at Promano; for Città di Castello; left at r'bout; next r'bout right thro' Trestina; right to Calzolaro; before bridge left to Vecchio Granaio; road bears right, hotel on left.

Liliana & John Tunstill
via del Refari,
06018 Calzolaro

Tel	+39 075 9302428
Fax	+39 075 9302363
Email	info@lapreghiera.com
Web	www.lapreghiera.com

Casa Panfili

A steep, bumpy approach – but the welcome more than makes up for it. As for the position, overlooking the wooded hills and olive groves of the Niccone valley, it is glorious. The farmhouse, once used for drying and storing tobacco (spot the old ventilation bricks in the walls), has been rescued from ruin and is now immaculate. Typically Italian rooms – white-painted walls, arches, terracotta floors – have been given the English treatment with masses of books and rugs, old wooden chests and lacy cloths, prints and family photos. Beds have silky smooth sheets, spotless bathrooms are fragrant with fresh flowers, and Al and Betty, who were stationed in Naples for three years and decided they couldn't face returning to Whitehall, are generous, friendly hosts. They produce their own wine and olive oil and Betty offers Italian cookery classes in her kitchen. Meals are at a dining table gleaming with cut glass and silver, or outside under a vine-covered pergola. The gardens are tranquil and pretty, the olive trees screen the pool from the house and the nightingales serenade you at night. *Minimum stay two nights.*

Price	€120–€140.
Rooms	3: 2 doubles, 1 twin.
Meals	Lunch €10.
	Dinner with wine, €30; book ahead.
Closed	November-Easter.
Directions	Directions on booking.

Alastair & Betty Stuart
San Lorenzo di Bibbiano, 14,
06010 San Leo Bastia

Tel	+39 0758 504244
Mobile	+39 3483184033
Email	bettyalstuart@netemedia.net
Web	www.casapanfili.com

Villa Giulia

The gorgeous views from the house reappear as wall paintings in the beamed bedrooms – a hilltop castle, local scenes, the lake itself… Villa Giulia is at the foot of Mount Qualandro, surrounded by olive groves and looking out over the blue reaches of Lake Trasimeno. A small road runs in front of the house and the rose-filled garden has a delicious pool and – tucked discreetly away – a play area for children. Originally an 18th-century olive mill, the villa has been beautifully restored. In the main house, the ground floor is taken up by a farmhouse kitchen and a big uncluttered dining and living area. A sofabed here and another in the little reading room upstairs means there is scope to sleep an extra four. The two bedrooms on the first floor can also be reached by an outside staircase, and there are two more in the attic – one with a canopy bed and an antique writing desk. On each of the three floors is a bath/shower room, each a delight. The annexe is equally pleasing with simple, country-style interiors. Though the two are only let together during high season, they may be rented separately at other times of the year.

Price	€2,000–€3,500 per week.
Rooms	2 villas: 1 for 2, 1 for 8.
Meals	Pizzeria within walking distance.
Closed	Rarely.
Directions	From North motorway A1 exit Valdichiana Bettole; highway Siena-Perugia for Perugia, exit Tuoro sul Trasimeno. At X-roads left (not straight to Tuoro) dir Cortona. Signed.

Stefania Mezzetti
loc. Caselle 1, Borghetto di Tuoro,
06069 Tuoro sul Trasimeno

Tel	+39 0575 67451
Mobile	+39 335 8305853
Email	smezzet@tin.it
Web	www.villa-giulia.it

Casa San Martino

Perhaps this is the answer if you are finding it impossible to choose between Tuscany and Umbria – a 250-year-old farmhouse on the border. Sit with a glass of wine in your Umbrian garden, watch the sun set over the Tuscan hills. The lovely, rambling house is alive with Lois's personality and interests: she's a remarkable lady who has lived in Italy for years and is a fluent linguist. Her charming big kitchen is well-equipped; an arch at one end leads to a comfortable family room, a door at the other to a pretty veranda with a stone barbecue. Up the narrow staircase is a large light sitting room with flowery sofas, books and an open fireplace – perfect for roasting chestnuts. The whitewashed bedrooms and bathrooms are cosy and attractive. Lois lives next door, is there when you need her and offers guests an enticing number of courses to choose from (cookery, fresco-painting, hiking, the history of Italian gardens); she can even book you a chef. The big garden with its dreamy pool looks across the Niccone valley and there are two villages with shops close by. *Minimum stay three nights.*

Price	€140. Whole house €3,000 per week.
Rooms	4: 1 double, 1 twin/double; 2 twins/doubles sharing bath.
Meals	Dinner with wine, €30. Restaurants 3km.
Closed	B&B November-April. Self-catering May-October.
Directions	A1 exit Valdichiana. Then '75 bis' for Perugia, then for Tuoro & for Lisciano Niccone. At Lisciano Niccone, left to S.Martino. Follow signs to S.Martino. House on rhs near top of hill.

Lois Martin
San Martino 19,
06060 Lisciano Niccone
Tel +39 0758 44288
Fax +39 0758 44422
Email csm@tuscanyvacation.com
Web www.tuscanyvacation.com

Il Convento Mincione

Big Apple chic meets Italian tradition: an unexpected but elegant marriage in a 12th-century convent deep in Umbria. With that attention to detail that only a New Yorker can give, Joan has achieved a classy and minimalist mood. And she has created rooms you really want to spend time in. There are six apartments of varying sizes on the ground and first floors, each named after a lucky Tarot card, each with its own outdoor space. One, 'Dieci', has metre-thick walls and is thought to have been an old chapel. All have open-plan sitting, dining and kitchen areas, white or bare stone walls, fireplaces and rich old brick floors. Furnishings have been imaginatively thought through — sumptuous fabrics, comfortable sofas, tall wrought-iron candlesticks — and there's a refreshing absence of clutter. A large communal kitchen, used for cookery courses, is also available. The convent buildings are of creamy stone, clustered round a central courtyard (a real suntrap) with an old font set in the wall; all around are open pasture, rolling hills and old oak woodland. Fabulous. *Minimum stay three nights.*

Price	€700–€1,500 per week. Whole place available to one party.
Rooms	6 apartments: 2 for 2, 1 for 2-3, 3 for 2-4.
Meals	Restaurants 2-5km.
Closed	Rarely. Ask about Christmas group bookings.
Directions	E45 dir. Umbertide exit Pierantonio; left to Antognola & Pantano; right to Piano di Nese; Right at fork, signed Preggio; sharp right. Gates on left. Signed.

	Joan Halperin
	Val Racchiusole, Case Sparse 467, 06019 Umbertide
Tel	+39 0759 415169
Fax	+39 0759 415169
Email	joan_halperin@thisoldconvent.com
Web	www.thisoldconvent.com

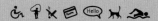

Casa San Gabriel

Enjoy David's wine on arrival, absorb the view of cultivated and wooded hills and unwind. Chrissie and David, warm, generous, thoughtful, bought the farmstead in a ruinous state and did it up all up in under a year. The little 'houses', private but close, each with its own terrace, are suitable for singles, couples or families so take your pick. For further space there's a living room in the main house with books and open fire. The restoration is sympathetic, unpretentious, delightful, the off-white décor and soft furnishings enhancing undulating beams and stone walls; the bathrooms are so lovely you could spend all day in them. Supplies are left for breakfast on your first morning and should last until you're ready to venture out. You may also pick produce from the vegetable gardens. David cooks on Tuesdays, Thursday is pizza night – your chance to use an original wood-fired oven. Bliss to have Perugia so near by – a 20-minute drive – and to return to a pool with views down the valley all the way to Assisi, a bottle of chilled Orvieto by your side. *B&B option Oct-April only.*

Price	B&B: €80.
	Self-catering: €400-€925 per week.
Rooms	3 apartments: 1 for 2, 1 for 2-4,
	1 for 4.
Meals	Dinner €25 (Tues); pizza €15 (Thurs).
	Wine from €6. Restaurant 5-minute
	drive.
Closed	Rarely.
Directions	E45, exit Pierantonio for Castle
	Antognolla; after 4.5km, left for Santa
	Caterina; 1.5km on white road.

Christina Todd & David Lang
CP No 29, V. Petrarca No 2,
06015 Pierantonio

Tel	+39 0759 414219
Mobile	+39 338 8916641
Email	chrissie@casasangabriel.com
Web	www.casasangabriel.com

Locanda del Gallo

A restful, almost spiritual calm emanates from this wonderful home. In a medieval hamlet, the *locanda* has all the beams and antique tiles you could wish for. Light, airy rooms with pale limewashed walls are a perfect foil for the exquisite reclaimed doors and carved hardwood furniture from Bali and Indonesia; your charming hosts have picked up some fabulous pieces from far-off places and have given the house a colonial feel. Each bedroom is different, one almond with Italian country furniture, another white, with wicker and Provençal prints; some have carved four-poster beds. Bathrooms are gorgeous, with deep baths and walk-in, glass-doored showers. A stunning veranda wraps itself around the house: doze off in a wicker armchair, sip a drink at dusk as the sun melts into the valley. The pool is spectacular, like a mirage clinging to the side of the hill; and there's a huge lime tree. Jimmy the cook conjures up food rich in genuine flavours, with aromatic herbs and vegetables from the garden; he and his wife are part of the extended family. Paola and Irish are interesting, cultural and warm.

Price	€112–€142. Suites €204–€224. Half-board €80–€90 p.p.
Rooms	9: 6 doubles, 3 suites for 4.
Meals	Dinner €28. Lunch €12.
Closed	December–Easter.
Directions	Exit E45 at Ponte Pattoli for Casa del Diavolo; for S Cristina 8km. 1st left 100m after La Dolce Vita restaurant, continue to Locanda.

Paola Moro & Irish Brewer
loc. Santa Cristina,
06020 Gubbio

Tel	+39 0759 229912
Fax	+39 0759 229912
Email	info@locandadelgallo.it
Web	www.locandadelgallo.it

Le Cinciallegre Agriturismo

This was once a tiny 13th-century hamlet on an ancient crossroads where local farmers met to buy and sell their produce. It's an incredibly peaceful spot, overlooking valley, meadows and woods, reached via a long, unmade road. Fabrizio used to be an architect and his conversion of these old houses is inspired: all feels authentic and delightful. In the cool, beamed living room, comfortable seats pull up around a 200-year-old wood-burning stove; there's lots of rustic furniture and a fine old dresser. The simple, comfortable bedrooms, named after birds, have their own terrace areas and immaculate bathrooms. You can cook in the outhouse but Cristina is a wonderful chef serving real country food and Umbrian wines so you're likely to leave her to it. Fabrizio and Cristina are warm, hospitable, interesting people, passionate about the environment, their natural garden, which is lovely, and the ten organic hectares of land full of wildlife. Fabrizio will be happy to tell you about the walking; indeed, he'll be disappointed if you don't have time to explore. *Quad bikes to hire.*

Price	€100.
Rooms	7: 3 doubles, 2 triples, 1 family, 1 single.
Meals	Half-board €75 p.p.
Closed	15 December–15 March.
Directions	A1 exit Val di Chiana for Perugia & follow E45 to Cesena. Exit Umbertide Gubbio. Follow 219 for Gubbio. Signposted from Mocaiana.

	Fabrizio & Cristina De Robertis
	fraz. Pisciano,
	06024 Gubbio
Tel	+39 0759 255957
Fax	+39 0759 272331
Email	cince@lecinciallegre.it
Web	www.lecinciallegre.it

Castello di Petroia

Brave the loops of the Gubbio-Assisi road and arrive at the castle at dusk. The front gate is locked, you ring to be let in; an eerie silence, and the gates creak open. Inside, dim lighting, stone walls, a splendid austerity. Come morning, you will appreciate the vast-fireplaced magnificence of the place, and the lovely terrace that catches the all-day sun. With a full house, dinner is a sociable affair, graciously presided over – in English and Italian – by the tweed-clad count. It takes place in one of two grand dining rooms and is rounded off by the house speciality, a fiery liqueur. Then up the stairs – some steep – to bedrooms with polished floors and shadowy corners, dark furniture and flowery beds. A feeling of feudalism remains – four staff serve 12 guests – and the landscape is similarly ancient. The castle is set on a hillock surrounded by pines in beautiful, unpopulated countryside and a marked footpath running through it. Walk to Assisi – it takes a day – then taxi back. Or take the bus into Gubbio and the funicular into the hills – the views are stupendous. And return to your 900-acre estate.

Price	€125-€150. Suites €160-€210.
Rooms	6: 2 doubles, 4 suites (1 in tower).
Meals	Dinner with wine, €30-€38.
Closed	January-March.
Directions	S298 from Gubbio south for Assisi & Perugia. After Scritto, just before Biscina & Fratticiola, take stony road signed to Castello.

Conte Carlo Sagrini
Scritto di Gubbio,
06020 Gubbio

Tel	+39 0759 20287
Fax	+39 0759 20108
Email	info@petroia.com
Web	www.petroia.com

I Mandorli Agriturismo

I Mandorli is aptly named: there's at least one almond tree outside each apartment. The blossom in February is stunning and, in summer, masses of greenery shades the old *casa padronale*. Once the centre of a 200-hectare estate, the shepherd's house and the olive mill in particular are fascinating reminders of days gone by. Mama Wanda is passionate about whole, lovely, rambling place and will show you around, embellishing everything you see with stories about its history. Widowed, she manages the remaining 47 hectares, apartments and rooms, *and* cooks, aided by her three charming daughters: home-grown produce and excellent gnocchi every Thursday. Bedrooms are sweet, simple affairs with new wrought-iron beds and pale patchwork quilts; small bathrooms are spotless. Children will love the wooden slide and seesaw, the old pathways and steps on this shallow hillside, the new pool – wonderful to return to after cultural outings to Assisi and Spoleto. This is olive oil country so make sure you go home with a few bottles of the best. *Laundry facilities small charge.*

Price	€40–€85 (€265–€650 per week). Apartments €65–€150 (€360–€700 per week).
Rooms	3 + 3: 1 twin/double, 2 triples. 3 apartments: 1 for 2, 2 for 4.
Meals	Breakfast €5 for self-caterers. Restaurants 500m.
Closed	Rarely.
Directions	SS3 exit Trevi-Montefalco for Bovara; signed from main road.

Famiglia di Zappelli Cardarelli
loc. Fondaccio 6,
06039 Bovara di Trevi

Tel	+39 0742 78669
Fax	+39 0742 78669
Email	info@agriturismoimandorli.com
Web	www.agriturismoimandorli.com

Hotel Palazzo Bocci

A beautiful townhouse in Spello's cobbled centre, whose pale yellow façade, dove-grey shutters and modest front door barely hint at the grandeur inside. Enter a tranquil courtyard with a tiny, trickling fountain; then through to a series of glorious reception rooms, most with painted friezes. The most impressive is the richly-decorated drawing room, the *sala degli affreschi*; and there's a reading room filled with old tomes and travel magazines. The whole building is multi-levelled and fascinating with its alcoves, nooks and crannies. Guest bedrooms are immaculate, with serene cream walls, polished chestnut beams, big comfortable beds, simple drapes. The suites have frescoed ceilings, the bathrooms are a delight. Delicious breakfasts are served on the herringbone-tiled terrace in warm weather; it overlooks Spello's ancient rooftops and makes a lovely spot for a sundowner. Step across the cobbled entrance to the restaurant, Il Molino – once the village olive mill – and dine under an ancient, brick-vaulted ceiling. A charming hotel in a charming town, run by delightful people.

Price	€130-€160. Singles €80-€100. Suites €180-€280.
Rooms	23: 15 doubles, 2 singles, 6 suites.
Meals	Lunch or dinner, €35. Wine from €13.
Closed	Never.
Directions	From Assisi for Foligno. After 10km, leave main road at Spello. Hotel opp. Church of Sant'Andrea in town centre. Private parking.

Signor Fabrizio Buono
via Cavour 17, 06038 Spello

Tel	+39 0742 301021
Fax	+39 0742 301464
Email	info@palazzobocci.com
Web	www.palazzobocci.com

Brigolante Guest Apartments

In the foothills of St Francis's beloved Mount Subasio the 16th-century stone farmhouse has been thoughtfully restored by Stefano and Rebecca. She is American and came to Italy to study, he is an architectural land surveyor – here was the perfect project. The apartments feel very private but you can always chat over an aperitif with the other guests in the garden. Rooms are light, airy and stylishly simple, combining Grandmother's furniture with Rebecca's kind touches: a rustic basket of delicacies from the farm (wine, eggs, cheese, honey, olive oil, homemade jam), handmade soap and sprigs of lavender by the bath. Pretty lace curtains flutter at the window, kitchens are well-equipped, and laundry facilities are available. This is a farm with animals, so ham, salami and sausages are produced as well as wine. Feel free to pluck whatever you like from the vegetable garden – red peppers, fat tomatoes, huge lettuces. Warm, lively, outgoing and with two young children of their own, your hosts set the tone: a charming place, and bliss for families and walkers. *Minimum stay one week in high season.*

Price	€275–€550 per week.
Rooms	3 apartments: 1 for 2, 2 for 2-4.
Meals	Restaurant 1km.
Closed	Rarely.
Directions	Assisi ring road to Porta Perlici, then towards Gualdo Tadino, 6km. Right, signed Brigolante. Over 1st bridge, right, over 2nd wooden bridge, up hill 500m, right at 1st gravel road.

Signora Rebecca Winke Bagnoli
via Costa di Trex 31,
06081 Assisi

Tel	+39 0758 02250
Fax	+39 0758 02250
Email	info@brigolante.com
Web	www.brigolante.com

Hotel e Agriturismo Le Silve

The setting, deep in the heart of the Umbrian hills, takes your breath away. It's as beauiful and as peaceful as Shangri-La – so remote you'd do well to fill up with petrol before leaving Spello or Assisi. The medieval buildings have been beautifully restored and the whole place breathes an air of tranquillity. Superb, generous-sized bedrooms have stone walls, exquisite terracotta floors, beautiful furniture, old mirrors and (a rarity, this!) proper reading lights. Bathrooms with walk-in showers are similarly rustic with terracotta floors and delicious pampering extras. The apartments are spread across three converted farm buildings. We loved the restaurant, too – intimate and inviting indoors and out. The produce is mostly organic, the bread is homemade, the cheeses, hams and salami are delectable. There are tennis and table tennis, a pool with a bar, a hydromassage and a sauna, and hectares of hills and woods in which to walk or ride or walk. A happy, friendly place, and popular – be sure to book well in advance. *Minimum stay two nights in apartments.*

Price	Half-board €240-€300 for 2. Apartments €300 for 2 nights.
Rooms	20 + 13: 20 doubles. 13 apartments for 2-4.
Meals	Dinner €40. Wine from €15.
Closed	November-April.
Directions	Milan A1 exit Valdichiana for Perugia, then Assisi. Signs for Gualdo Tadino then Armenzano, km12; signs for hotel, 2km.

	Signor Marco Sirignani loc. Armenzano, 06081 Assisi
Tel	+39 0758 019000
Fax	+39 0758 019005
Email	info@lesilve.it
Web	www.lesilve.it

Agriturismo Alla Madonna del Piatto

The road winds up through woods and off the isolated track to a simple, centuries-old farmhouse in a hidden corner of Umbria. The position is stupendous, the views stretching over olive groves and forested hills to Assisi and its basilica. The old farmhouse was abandoned for decades until these Italian-Dutch owners fell in love with the view, then restored the building with sympathy and style, then replanted the olive groves. Bedrooms are large, airy, uncluttered, their country antiques mixed with Moroccan bedspreads, pottery or decorative wall lights picked up on Letizia's travels. One room has a loo with a view. Breakfasts are served on white china at mosaic-topped tables in the sitting/dining room, a fresh, modern space of white and rose-coloured walls and a warm sofa by an open fire. Your hosts — approachable, hugely helpful — share their home gladly. If you can tear yourself away from the terrace and its panorama, there are walks, medieval hill towns and all of Umbria to explore. *Minimum stay two night; three nights May & Sept. Ask about cookery courses.*

Price	€80–€110.
Rooms	6: 5 twins/doubles, 1 family room for 3.
Meals	Restaurant 1km.
Closed	Mid-December to mid-March.
Directions	From Assisi SS147 for Perugia; after Ponte San Vittorino turn right, via San Fortunato; uphill 6.5km; right; via Petrata.

Letizia Mattiacci
via Petrata 37, Pieve San Nicolo,
06081 Assisi

Tel	+39 0758 199050
Mobile	+39 328 7025297
Email	letizia.mattiacci@libero.it
Web	www.incampagna.com

Castello dell'Oscano Agriturismo

At the turn of the century, Count Telfner visited England and was so taken by the opulent intimacy of its grand country houses that he returned to Italy and did up his own place. Hence Oscano: a glorious, lovable parody of England. There's a grand, balustraded central staircase, suitably creaky, huge oils on most of the walls, a grand piano in the drawing room and a proper library – for afternoon tea. The sitting room would not look out of place in Kent. Owner Maurizio has nurtured the house almost since its rebirth. He returned from Belgium with a trompe l'œil, commissioned ceramics from Deruta and stocked the cellars with the best Umbrian wines. Bedrooms have a faded baronial elegance in the National Trust spirit: floral wallpapers, period furnishings and large windows which look over the garden and park. Bathrooms are big and modern. The rooms in the Villa Ada next door, though less stylish, are best described as 'well-appointed' and are extremely comfortable. The whole experience is one of comfort, unpretentious refinement, and tranquillity. And the food is excellent.

Price	€150–€230. Suites €290–€310. Apartments €325–€775 per week.
Rooms	30 + 13: 20 doubles, 10 suites. 13 apartments for 2-5.
Meals	Dinner €38.
Closed	Rarely.
Directions	Exit E45 Madonna Alta; Follow signs for Cenerente and San Marco. At Cenerente turn right after church. Signed.

Maurizio & Luca Bussolati
strada della Forcella 37,
06070 Cenerente

Tel	+39 0755 84371
Fax	+39 0756 90666
Email	info@oscano.com
Web	www.oscano.it

Le Torri di Bagnara

Aided by a staff of 30, Signora Giunta runs her family empire with professionalism and pride. Hers is a huge and magnificent estate, 1,500 acres of pastoral perfection with vast views, a pristine pool (floodlit at night), a 12th-century tower, an 11th-century abbey, three castles and many terraces. It is a medieval framework for a modern, holiday enterprise and you feel you're on top of the world. Four rustic but elegant apartments fill the tower, each on a different floor. Some have barrow-vault ceilings and Romanesque windows, strokeable fabrics and fine old furniture, swish galley kitchens and wonderful views. On the ground floor is a dining and sitting area for the sociable; outside, figs, peaches, olives, herbs and a shared laundry. Bedrooms in the abbey feed off a delightful paved courtyard with small church and tower and are as luxurious as the rest. The restaurant serves fresh, seasonal dishes or try the local specialities only three miles away; the motorway is conveniently close. Cookery classes, wine tastings, free mountain bikes… Giunta has thought of everything. *Bus stop 500m. Minimum stay two nights.*

Price	€110-€205.
	Apts €380-€1,250 per week.
Rooms	8 + 4: 4 doubles, 3 suites.
	4 apts: 1 for 2, 2 for 4, 1 for 5.
Meals	Breakfast €10 for self-caterers.
	Dinner with wine, from €35.
	Restaurants 5km.
Closed	January-March.
Directions	E45 exit Resina; north for Pieve San Quirico Bagnara; 4km, signed on left.

Zenaide Giunta
strada della Bruna 8, Solfagnano,
06134 Perugia

Tel	+39 0755 792001
Fax	+39 0755 792001
Email	info@letorridibagnara.it
Web	www.letorridibagnara.it

Self-catering

Umbria

San Lorenzo della Rabatta Agriturismo

Near Perugia but in another world, this tiny medieval hamlet is guarded by densely wooded hills. The houses congregate around a central space, their walls covered with ivy, wisteria and roses. This is a good place to bring children – pleasant, practical – and they'll be entertained by the agricultural touches: the rickety farm stools, the cattle stall converted into a seat, the wine barrel acting as a side table. One bed has an old gate for a bedhead and there are some four-posters too (draped in white nylon). The living spaces are open-plan, with gingham much in evidence; most have a fireplace and a big rustic basket of wood. The kitchen areas and bathrooms are small and basic but clean and adequate. Outside, narrow steps bordered with miniature roses lead you down to the pool and lovely views to the hills. There's also table tennis and a small play area for children set amongst the olive trees. It's all wonderfully peaceful, but more apartments are planned. Teodora, who lives on site and has a lovely smile, will, given a day's notice, cook you a five-course meal. *Minimum stay two nights.*

Price	€70–€120.
Rooms	8 apartments for 2-8.
Meals	Dinner, 5 courses, €16 (served in your apartment).
Closed	January-February.
Directions	A1 south exit Valdichiana. From south exit Orte. E45 dir. Perugia exit Madonna Alta. Follow signs for Cenerente & S.Marco. At Cenerente turn right after church. Signed.

	Paola Cascini
	loc. Cenerente,
	06134 Perugia
Tel	+39 0756 90764
Mobile	+39 334 1351849
Email	info@sanlorenzodellarabatta.com
Web	www.sanlorenzodellarabatta.com

Villa Rosa

The beautifully restored farmhouse looks out over fields and farms to the villages of Solomeo and Corciano, with Perugia in the distance. Distant church bells, the hum of a tractor, the bray of a donkey... yet you are five kilometres from the superstrada. You couldn't find a better spot from which to discover Tuscany and Umbria. Megan, who is Australian, and Lino are a helpful and hospitable couple, and will help you enjoy every aspect of your stay: hunt for truffles (or cashmere, in Solomeo!), book in for a twice-weekly cookery class with a chef from Perugia, take advantage of a personalised tour. There are three apartments here. For a family, the two-storey *casetta* at the end of the garden is perfect – a delightful mix of recycled beams and terracotta tiles, with open fire, air con, jacuzzi and perfect views. The flat on the ground floor of the farmhouse is similarly good – new bunk beds in the living area, cool in summer, a great terrace. There's a saltwater pool to cool you down, and the views from two of the apartments are wonderful. *Minimum stay three nights in apartments.*

Price	Cottage €160–€180 (€600–€1,200 per week). Apts €95–€120; €425–€750 per week.
Rooms	1 cottage for 6. 2 apartments, 1 for 3, 1 for 4.
Meals	Restaurant 1km.
Closed	Rarely.
Directions	Exit Perugia-Bettolle at Corciano, for Castelvieto thro' village (via underpass & bridge) to shrine. Left & on to 2nd shrine; right uphill; house after couple of bends.

Megan & Lino Rialti
voc. Docciolano 9, Montemelino,
06060 Magione

Tel	+39 0758 41814
Fax	+39 0758 41814
Email	meglino@libero.it
Web	www.villarosaweb.com

Villa Aureli

Little has changed since the Villa was built in the 18th century and became the country house of the Serègo Alighieri family 100 years later. The ornamental plasterwork, floor tiles and decorative shutters reflect its noble past, it is known to all the locals and is full of precious and historic treasures (walled up by a perspicacious housekeeper during the Occupation) which inspire the interest, attention and care of Pietro, son and heir of Sperello. The house in fact has its origins in the 16th century, and the grounds are suitably formal – overgrown here, tamed there, with lemon trees in amazing 18th-century pots in the *limonaia* and a swimming pool created from an irrigation tank. The apartments are big and beautiful, the one on the second floor the largest and grandest, with balconies and views. Floors have mellow old tiles, ceilings are high and raftered, bedrooms are delightfully faded. You are a step away from the village, so can walk to the few shops and bar. A quietly impressive retreat, wonderfully peaceful – and special. *Minimum stay one week in high season; two nights in low season.*

Price	€700–€1,400 per week.
Rooms	4 apartments: 1 for 4, 1 for 4-8, 1 for 5, 1 for 6.
Meals	Occasional dinner with wine, €36. Restaurant 2km.
Closed	Never.
Directions	From A1, exit Valdichiana for Perugia, exit Madonna Alta towards Città della Pieve. At square, sign for Bagnaia; on left after 200m. Alternatively, go to centre of Castel del Piano and ask.

Sperello di Serègo Alighieri
via Luigi Cirenei 70,
06132 Castel del Piano

Mobile   +39 340 6459061
Fax   +39 0755 159408
Email   villa.aureli@libero.it
Web   www.villaaureli.it

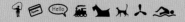

Entry 246 Map 12

The Country House Montali

An irresistible combination: a gorgeous place, and fine vegetarian cuisine. Alberto's expertise in restoring historic buildings and his desire to give vegetarians something more inspired than brown rice have resulted in the creation of Montali. Standing on a plateau surrounded by woodland, reached by a long, bumpy track, the gardens open to the hills and down to Lake Trasimeno; the walks are spectacular. The newly decorated guest rooms, in three single-storey buildings, have verandas, wide views and an attractively colonial air. White walls show off hand-carved teak furniture and oil paintings by Alberto's talented brother; terracotta floors are strewn with Indian rugs. As for the food – it's exquisite. Served with good local wines in the serene little restaurant, it's Mediterranean in essence, with touches of nouvelle and haute cuisine. Malu, Alberto's wife, is the head chef and Montali is fast making an international name for itself – they've even published a superb cookery book. He and she are delightful; keen musicians both, they occasionally hold concerts. Readers are full of praise. *Ask about cookery courses.*

Price	Half-board €160–€200 for 2.
Rooms	10 doubles.
Meals	Half-board only.
Closed	Rarely.
Directions	A1 from Rome, exit Fabro, follow signs for Citta della Pieve and Piegaro. 2km after Tavernelle, left for 'Colle San Paolo'. Up hill 7km, following signs. Left at top of hill, hotel 800m on left.

Alberto Musacchio
via Montali 23,
06068 Tavernelle di Panicale

Tel	+39 0758 350680
Fax	+39 0758 350144
Email	montali@montalionline.com
Web	www.montalionline.com

Villa di Monte Solare

A hushed, stylish, country retreat in a perfect Umbrian setting. This noble villa, encircled by a formal walled garden, has been transformed into a small hotel with uniformed staff, elegant rooms and fine restaurant. The grounds, which include the little chapel of Santa Lucia and a small maze, envelop the hotel in an atmosphere of calm. Bedrooms are spacious and lovingly tended, full of local fabric and craftmanship. The public rooms have kept their charm, their painted cornices and friezes, huge fireplaces, ancient terracotta floors. The restaurant, a gorgeous beamed room with a roaring fire in winter, seats bedroom capacity, so non-residents may only book if guests are dining out. Cappuccino from a bar machine at breakfast; at dinner, superb designer food and a choice 380 wines. The owners live for this place and eat with guests every night, the mood is refined and jackets are usually worn, though not insisted upon. In the old glass *limonaia* is a new beauty spa, for guests only. There are bikes to rent, pools to swim, even concerts and talks on Umbrian history. The view stretches out in every direction.

Price	€180-€250. Singles €115-€130. Suites & family rooms €250-€300.
Rooms	28: 21 doubles, 5 suites, 2 family.
Meals	Lunch €30-€40. Dinner with wine, €40-€65.
Closed	Never.
Directions	Exit A1 at Chiusi-Chianciano; right to Chiusi; right for Città della Pieve; signs for Perugia, wall on left; left for Perugia-Tavernelle (SS220); 1km after Tavernelle, left for Colle S. Paolo. 4km to Villa.

Rosemarie & Filippo Iannarone
via Montali 7, Colle San Paolo,
06068 Tavernelle di Panicale

Tel	+39 0758 32376
Fax	+39 0758 355462
Email	info@villamontesolare.it
Web	www.villamontesolare.it

Entry 248 Map 12

Villa Lemura

Live like an aristocrat but without the pomp or circumstance. This 18th-century building, once the country villa of Umbrian nobility, has an opulent but faded grandeur. Delightful Emma, Luca and family have made it their home: don't be surprised to find a bicycle propped against the gracious pillars of the entrance hall. Rooms will make you gasp – frescoed ceilings, richly tiled floors, Murano chandeliers – yet it all feels charmingly lived-in. Furniture is a comfortable mismatch of antiques and brocante finds. The high-ceilinged, elegant bedrooms might include an antique French bed, a chaise-longue or a painted ceramic stove. Most have frescoes, one has a private terrace. Sink into sofas in the ballroom-sized salon, browse a book in the library, breakfast on the terrace above the Italian garden. Dinner can be arranged – or you may rustle up your own in the delightful orangery. Lake Trasimeno, Perugia and Assisi wait to be discovered; or find a quiet spot in the villa's shady gardens, full of terraced pool, mossy statues, fountains, olive grove and views.

Price	€100–€150. Whole house on request.
Rooms	7: 3 doubles, 1 twin, 1 triple; 1 double, 1 twin sharing bathroom.
Meals	Dinner €30 (min. 8), on request. Wine from €10.
Closed	Occasionally.
Directions	From A1 exit Chiusi for Perugia; exit Perugia/Magione (not Panicale); signs to Panicale; thro' Macchie & Colgiordano (not up to Panicale); left to Lemura, Villa 1st on left.

Emma & Luca Mesenzio
via Le Mura 1,
06064 Panicale

Tel/Fax	+39 0758 37134
Mobile	+39 348 5852528
Email	villalemura@alice.it
Web	www.villalemura.com

Agriturismo Madonna delle Grazie

There are rabbits, dogs, horses, ducks and hens, and Renato will pluck a cicada from an olive tree and show you how it 'sings': children (and adults) who love animals will be in heaven. This is a real farm – not a hotel with a few animals wandering about – so don't expect luxury; it's agriturismo at its best and you eat what they produce. The simple guest bedrooms in the 18th-century farmhouse are engagingly old-fashioned; all have a terrace or balcony and the bathrooms are spotless. The farm is now fully organic and the food in the restaurant delicious, so make the most of Renato's own salami, chicken, fruit and vegetables, olive oil, grappa and wine. There's also a big playground for children, and table football in the house. The youngest offspring, free from the tyranny of taste, will love the Disney gnomes dotted around the picnic area. For the grown-ups there's riding, archery, a discount at the San Casciano Terme spa… and views that stretch to Tuscany in one direction, Umbria in the other. A great little place.

Price	€100–€130.
Rooms	6 doubles.
Meals	Dinner €20. Wine €8–€15.
Closed	Rarely.
Directions	From A1 North: exit Chiusi-Chianciano, rigth to Chiusi & Città della Pieve. From A1 South: exit Fabro, turn left; left after 1km to Città della Pieve.

Signor Renato Nannotti
Madonna delle Grazie 6,
06062 Città della Pieve

Tel	+39 0578 299822
Fax	+39 0578 297749
Email	info@madonnadellegrazie.it
Web	www.madonnadellegrazie.it

Hotel Vannucci

Slip behind wrought-iron gates, through quiet gardens and into a light and airy hall. The madding, medieval streets of Città della Pieve are only minutes away. This handsome Umbrian villa, by the city's walls, has a timeless elegance that enchants and soothes. Carefully restored by its American owner, it is more sleek and modern than rich and antique. There are pale parquet floors and Balinese tables, marble fireplaces and funky lighting, and the central, original staircase floats high above Empire chairs and bold modern art. The result is a quiet sophistication very easy on the eye. Bedrooms, some with balconies, are light uncluttered spaces, their carved bedheads and rich bedspreads adding warmth. Close to Tuscany this is perfect for Assisi, Perugia, Siena and the Umbrian hills. Then return to the garden, the small plunge pool or the library, for deep sofas and leather armchairs. With good wines and two restaurants in house – the coolly elegant Zafferano and the jolly Pizzeria Pievese with its garden terrace – you pretty much have everything. *Minimum stay three nights for half-board.*

Price	€95–€125. Half board extra €30 p.p.
Rooms	30: 14 doubles, 5 twins/doubles, 9 triples, 2 singles.
Meals	Dinner from €25.50. Wine €20.
Closed	Never.
Directions	A1 from Rome exit Fabbro, follow signs for Città della Pleve. Signed.

	Alison Deighton
	via I. Vanni 1,
	06062 Città della Pieve
Tel	+39 0578 298063
Fax	+39 0578 297954
Email	info@hotel-vannucci.com
Web	www.hotel-vannucci.com

Relais Il Canalicchio

Not only a pleasant detour between Perugia and Orvieto but a charming retreat. Once known as the Castello di Poggio, this pretty 13th-century hamlet high on an Umbrian hilltop is almost a principality in itself: 51 rooms, two pools, gym, tower, gardens with white roses, and ancient fortress walls. The decoration is a surprisingly international mix, a quirk reflected in the names of the bedrooms (Isabelle Rubens, Countess of Oxford); the décor is floral Italian chintz both on the walls and floors. Many rooms are tucked under white-painted rafters, others open onto little balconies or terraces and the bathrooms are a treat; those in the tower have views that sweep over an endless valley of olive groves, vineyards and woods. We liked the rooms in the new wing, with their sponged walls and hand-stencilled details. Downstairs, play a frame of billiards over a glass of grappa – having dined first at Il Pavone, where the views at sunset are breathtaking. Others may prefer to retreat to the Turkish bath or the quiet of the library. There's character here, masses of space, and a flurry of young and friendly staff.

Price	€160-€200. Singles €130-€160. Suites €230-€260.
Rooms	49: 35 doubles, 14 suites.
Meals	Lunch or dinner à la carte. Wine €18. Restaurants 15km.
Closed	Never.
Directions	Rome A1 for Firenze, exit Orte. E45 Perugia-Cesena, exit Ripabianca for Canalicchio.

Paolo Ferraro
via della Piazza 4,
06050 Canalicchio di Collazzone

Tel	+39 0758 707325
Fax	+39 0758 707296
Email	relais@relaisilcanalicchio.it
Web	www.relaisilcanalicchio.it

La Palazzetta del Vescovo Relais

Only the bells from a nearby convent or the hum of the tractor will disturb you. Paola and Stefano love to pamper their guests and there's a 'wellness' room in the cellar. Widely travelled and from the corporate world, they decided in 2000 to hang up their business suits and do something different. They bought this 18th-century hilltop palazzetta – once a summer residence for bishops, utterly abandoned in the 1960s – and restored it to its former glory. An informal elegance prevails. The four sitting rooms are cool, elegant and inviting; the bedrooms, each individual, each lovely, are composed in subtle, muted colours: pale walls, fine rugs, muslin'd four-posters, antique Neapolitan beds. What they have in common is a matchless view over steeply falling vineyards and the Tiber valley. On a clear day you can see as far as Perugia. The newly-planted gardens and the pool make the most of the outlook, too – as does the terrace, where you can enjoy an aperitif before Paola's Umbrian cuisine. She, like her house, is a delight – serene, smiling and friendly.
Minimum stay two nights.

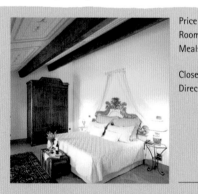

Price	€200-€250. Singles €140-€175.
Rooms	9 doubles.
Meals	Lunch €30. Dinner, 4 courses, €35. Wine €10.
Closed	15 January-15 February.
Directions	A1 Rome-Florence exit Perugia onto E45; exit Fratta Todina. On for 7km, left for Spineta, through Spineta; house on right after vineyard, up track behind gates.

Paola Maria & Stefano Zocchi
Clausura 17, Fraz. Spineta,
06054 Fratta Todina
Tel +39 0758 745183
Fax +39 0758 745042
Email info@lapalazzettadelvescovo.it
Web www.lapalazzettadelvescovo.com

Casale Campodoro

The interior of this restored 18th-century building has been embellished with style and a quirky humour: imagine an Indonesian hippo's head over a fireplace and a plastic goose as a lamp. Piero, a gentle, humorous and intelligent Italian, lives here with Carolina, four cats and three daft, friendly and boisterous dogs. In one shower room, a muscular plaster-cast juts out of the wall and serves as a towel rail; elsewhere, Scottish Grandmother's clothes – lace interwoven with scarab beetles – have been framed and hung. By the pool are plastic yellow Philippe Starck sofa and chairs; on the walls, religious icons. The garden sits on an Umbrian hillside and has little steps leading to hidden corners and a large aviary, whose birds escape and return at night. There are lovely views across to an old abbey, and other, more edible delights: breakfast brings warm, fresh, homemade bread and tasty jams. Once a week, guests get together for dinner with everyone contributing a national dish. Don't mind the animals or the odd bit of peeling paint – this is a joyously individual and eccentric place.

Price	€50-€60 (€360 per week). Apts €80-€130 (€480-€700 per week).
Rooms	3 + 3: 3 doubles. 3 apts for 3-5.
Meals	Restaurants nearby.
Closed	Rarely.
Directions	From Perugia-Cesena exit Massa Martana (316) to Foligno/Bastaro; left to San Terenziano; 1km; right to Viepri; 100m, track on left; 1st on right.

Carolina Bonanno
fraz. Viepri 106,
06056 Massa Martana

Tel	+39 0758 947347
Mobile	+39 333 3875740
Email	camporo@libero.it
Web	www.casalecampodoro.it

Tenuta di Canonica

The position is wonderful, on a green ridge with stunning views. The house was a ruin (17th century, with medieval remnants and Roman foundations) when Daniele and Maria bought it in 1998. Much creativity has gone into its resurrection. There's not a corridor in sight – instead, odd steps up and down, hidden doors, vaulted ceilings, enchanting corners. Cool, beautiful reception rooms are decorated in vibrant colours, then given a personal, individual and exotic touch: family portraits, photos, books; there's even a parrot. The bedrooms are vast, intriguingly shaped and alluring, with rugs on pale brick or wooden floors and gorgeous beds and fabrics. The dining room opens onto a covered terrace surrounded by roses and shrubs, a path sweeps down to the pool; there's good walking on the the 24-hectare estate. This is a house that reflects its owners' personalities. Daniele and Maria are vivid, interesting and well-travelled and, while they are away, Giovanna is on hand to welcome guests to the rich tapestry of rooms. *Minimum stay two nights.*

Price	€135–€220.
	Apartments €800–€950 per week.
Rooms	11 + 2: 11 doubles.
	2 apartments for 3-4.
Meals	Dinner €35. Wine €10–€40.
Closed	December-February.
Directions	Florence-Roma A1 exit Valdichiana; E45 Perugia-Terni exit Todi-Orvieto; SS448 for Prodo-Titignano; 3km, Bivio per Cordigliano; 1km, signed. Do not turn right to Canonica, continue until Cordigliano sign, then on left.

Daniele Fano
loc. Canonica m.75/76,
06059 Todi

Tel	+39 0758 947545
Fax	+39 0758 947581
Email	tenutadicanonica@tin.it
Web	www.tenutadicanonica.com

Le Logge di Silvignano

Wrought-iron gates swing open onto a courtyard... and there is the house, in all its unruffled, medieval beauty. Thought, care and talent have gone into its restoration. And the setting: the Spoleto hills with views to Assisi! Alberto's love of roses has been awoken in Diana and is wonderfully evident, while the recent planting preserves as many of the old inhabitants as possible: prune, Japanese persimmon and two ancient figs, source of breakfast jams. The graceful open gallery with octagonal stone pillars dates from the 15th century but the main building has its roots in the 12th. Guest suites, big and charming, have Amalfi-tiled bathrooms, pretty sitting rooms with open fireplaces, tiny kitchens for snacks and drinks; sumptuous fabrics woven in Montefalco look perfect against stone walls and massive beams. Diana and Alberto are delighted if you join them for a glass of wine in the newly restored 'club house' before you set off to dine, or even for a nightcap on your return. They're warm, interesting people, genuinely happy to share their corner of paradise. *Minimum stay two nights. Children over 12 welcome.*

Price	€180-€250.	
Rooms	5 suites. Kitchenette available for drinks for guests.	
Meals	Restaurants 1.5-4km.	
Closed	10 November-10 March; open New Year's Eve & upon request.	
Directions	A1 Florence-Bologna exit Bettolle-Sinalunga, then E45 for Perugia-Assisi-Foligno.SS3 Flaminia until Fonti del Clitunno then towards Campello-Pettino; 3km after Campello right for Silvignano, 1.5km.	

Alberto & Diana Araimo
fraz. Silvignano 14,
06049 Spoleto

Tel	+39 0743 274098
Mobile	+39 347 2221869
Email	mail@leloggedisilvignano.it
Web	www.leloggedisilvignano.it

Il Castello di Poreta

You approach via a steep and winding track through oak woods where truffles are found. The crumbling, ruined walls of the 14th-century village (which took a tumble after the 1703 earthquake) enclose the church and restored buildings that make up the Castello di Poreta. All was revived when a cooperative from the village won the right to transform the ancient stones and rafters into a country-house hotel – and a special one at that. Simple, comfortable bedrooms – the loftiest in the old priest's house, the rest in a new part off the terrace – reflect the pastel shades of the sun-bleached, olive-growing hills outside. There's a soothing and elegant sitting room and a light, airy restaurant with stunning views and interesting modern art. Donatella, the young chef, is enthusiastic and creative: the short menu changes often and is seasonally aware. There are small jazz concerts in the church in summer, young and cheerful service, wild boar safaris, birdsong and wild flowers. An unusual place to stay, well off the beaten track. *Minimum stay two nights at weekends.*

Price	€90–€115.
Rooms	8 twins/doubles.
Meals	Dinner €35 à la carte, with wine. Restaurant closed Monday evening.
Closed	Rarely.
Directions	Signposted on via Flaminia between Spoleto & Foligno.

Luca Saint Amour di Chanaz
loc. Poreta,
06049 Spoleto

Tel	+39 0743 275810
Fax	+39 0743 270175
Email	castellodiporeta@seeumbria.com
Web	www.ilcastellodiporeta.it

Le Marche • Abruzzo • Molise

Photo: istock.com

Locanda della Valle Nuova

In gentle. breeze-cooled hills, surrounded by ancient, protected oaks and on the road that leads to glorious Urbino, this 185-acre farm produces organic meat, vegetables and wine. It is an unusual, unexpectedly modern place whose owners have a special interest in horses and in the environment. Signora Savini and daughter Giulia – forces to be reckoned with! – make a professional team and cook delicious meals presented on white porcelain and terracotta. The breads, pastas and jams are homemade, the wines are local, the water is purified and de-chlorinated, the truffles are gathered from the woods nearby. The conversion has given La Locanda the feel of a discreet modern hotel, where perfectly turned sheets lie on perfect beds, and it's worth asking for one of the bigger rooms, preferably with a view. The riding school has a club house for horsey talk and showers; there are two outdoor arenas as well as lessons and hacks, and a fabulous pool. If you arrive at the airport after dark, Giulia kindly meets you to guide you back. *Minimum stay three nights; one week for apts.*

Their motto, that "one should tread lightly on the earth", colours every aspect of their lives; conservation and preservation are key concepts here. They use 100% renewable energy for heating and hot water, a low consumption wood stove heats the house and bed linen and towels are made from 100% natural fibres. The farm has been certified organic for nearly 25 years and 70% of the food that lands on your plate is home-produced; the rest is sourced from local organic producers. The Savini's fervent commitment to the environment is admirable; the installation of solar panels is next on the list.

Price	€104. Half-board €78 p.p. Apartments €680 per week.
Rooms	6 + 2: 5 doubles, 1 twin. 2 apartments for 2.
Meals	Dinner €30. Wine from €9.
Closed	Mid-November to May.
Directions	Exit Fano-Rome motorway at Acqualagna & Piobbico. Head towards Piobbico as far as Pole; right for Castellaro; signed. Bus from Pesaro or Fano to Fermignano, owners will pick up.

Giulia Savini
La Cappella 14, 61033
Sagrata di Fermignano,

Tel	+39 0722 330303
Fax	+39 0722 330303
Email	info@vallenuova.it
Web	www.vallenuova.it

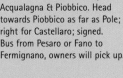

SPECIAL
GREEN ENTRY
see page 14

Map 9 Entry 258

Locanda Le Querce

Take a break from Tuscany and Umbria! The countryside in Le Marche is as captivating as
this house; behind soars the Monte Carpegna. The rooms of this delightful, mellow,
country-house B&B are in two buildings. White muslin flutters at the shuttered windows
of the barn where everything is well-crafted and has a light and airy feel. There's a cosy
sitting room with an open fire where you breakfast, and a kitchen where longer-staying
guests can make their own meals. Rooms in the Casa Vecchia are bigger, ideal for families
holidaying together: a two-room suite with homely kitchen on the first floor; above, three
bedrooms and a bathroom. The Blue Room, a sitting/music room with a fireplace dated
1580, is full of lovely things acquired by Federica. If organic dinner is as delicious as organic
breakfast, eat in. (Music and dancing may follow.) Alternatively, the local restaurant is a
short, winding drive. A great place for families: resident cats and children, summer
activities, a big open lawn and no fences to break the view… stroll out onto the footpath,
through the meadows, to Frontius for an idyllic half-hour walk.

Price	€65–€75. Apartments €130–€195.
Rooms	6 + 2: 6 doubles (with kitchen for groups).
	2 apartments: 1 for 4-5, 1 for 6-8.
Meals	Dinner €20–€30. Restaurant 4km.
Closed	Rarely.
Directions	From Rome-Umbria exit A14 at Orte, E17 to S. Giustino; for Bocca Trabaria to S. Angelo in Vado; for Piandimeleto. Thro' Piandimeleto; 10km; ignore left to Frontino; 3km on, then signed left.

Arch. Federica Crocetta
loc. Calmugnano,
61020 Frontino

Tel	+39 0722 71370
Mobile	+39 339 6897688
Email	lequerce32@hotmail.com
Web	www.locandalequerce.com

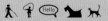

Villa Giulia

Pines, cypress oaks and roses surround the Napoleonic villa, wisteria billows over the lemon house wall. The gardens merge into the family olive farm and an ancient wood. No formality, no fuss, just an easy, calm and kind welcome from Anna, who moved here a year ago with her youngest son. The villa was named after an indomitable great-aunt (the first woman to climb Mont Blanc!) and the family furniture remains – large wooden mirrors, stunning antiques – along with a candle burn on the mantelpiece left by the Nazis. Bedrooms, the best and most baronial in the villa, have shuttered windows and old-fashioned metal beds; one noble bathroom has its own balcony, another is up a winding stair. The two suites in 'La Dependenza' have kitchenettes, while the apartments proper are divided between the Farmhouse and the 'Casa Piccola'. Sitting rooms are grand but easy, the dining room's chairs are gay with red checks and summer breakfasts are taken at pink-clothed tables on a terrace whose views reach to the Adriantic (the beach is a mile away). Atmospheric, historic, beautiful and good for all ages.

Price	€150–€300.
	Apartments €800–€1,800 per week.
Rooms	9 + 5: 3 doubles, 6 suites.
	5 apartments for 3–6.
Meals	Dinner €30–€50. Wine €10–€40.
	Restaurants nearby.
Closed	December–March.
Directions	SS16 from Fano for Pesaro, 3km north of Fano turn left; signed.

Anna Passi
via di Villa Giulia, loc. San Biagio, 40,
61032 Fano

Tel	+39 0721 823159
Fax	+39 0721 823159
Email	info@relaisvillagiulia.com
Web	www.relaisvillagiulia.com

Castello di Monterado

Orlando's great-great-grandfather bought the Castello, parts of which go back to 1100. The renovation continues, and is glorious! Orlando and Kira, quietly spoken, charming, expecting their first child, are deeply passionate about the family home whose exquisite revival has been achieved floor by floor. The Music Room, its terrace overlooking the Caseno valley and the distant sea, is a living museum, the Library combines vast armchairs with ancient tomes, there are frescoes on every wall and ceiling, antiques, art work, chandeliers – the sheer beauty will thrill you. A balcony opens for al fresco breakfasts in 2008; for now, you make do with the dining room (overseen by Bacchus and Arianna, of course). Bedrooms, all vast, all generously different, ooze splendour; cherubs chase each other across ceilings, beds are soberly but beautifully dressed, cupboards have been crafted from the cellar's barrels, one suite has its hydromassage bath positioned so you gaze on gardens as you soak. Very special; very good value.

Price	€190.
Rooms	4 suites.
Meals	Restaurants within walking distance.
Closed	Never.
Directions	A14 exit at Marotta, right for Pergola; after 7km left for Monterado. Signed.

Orlando & Kira Rodano
Piazza Roma, 18,
60010 Monterado

Tel	+39 0717 958395
Fax	+39 0717 959923
Email	info@castellodimonterado.it
Web	www.castellodimonterado.it

Castello di Monterado - Apartments

Cut off from western Italy by the Apennines is Le Marche; peaceful, charming and unsought-out. At the top of a steep wooded hill is Monterado, a small medieval town of cobbled streets and fabulous views. Beyond is the sea. On a small square in town, opposite the Castle of Monterado (see opposite), is a solid old stone building housing six apartments with a contemporary and luxurious feel. One is on the ground floor, two are on the first and two are on the second; 'Anemone', the largest, spreads itself over two levels. Lofty walls are plastered white, floors are polished parquet, styling is minimalist, classy and sleek. In the town are a handful of restaurants and shops, a swimming pool and tennis and, in May, a hog roast festival to which locals flock; the region is the home of *porchetta*. If you want beach resorts with a Sixties feel, then head west for the resorts of Le Marche. After a day's touring, return to the peaceful garden of the Castello, with its cedar trees and scented roses and, beyond, a landscaped woodland with winding paths.

Price	€315-€560. Breakfast included.
Rooms	6 apartments: 3 for 4, 2 for 5, 1 for 6.
Meals	Restaurants within walking distance.
Closed	Never.
Directions	A14 exit at Marotta, direction Pergola. After 7km left for Monterado. Signed.

Orlando & Kira Rodano
Piazza Roma, 18,
60010 Monterado

Tel	+39 0717 958395
Fax	+39 0717 959923
Email	info@castellodimonterado.it
Web	www.castellodimonterado.it

Locanda San Rocco Agriturismo

Decent, honest, without a whiff of pretension, the *locanda* is a summer-only agriturismo. Built in the late 1700s, the building has kept its purity of style: brick walls, exposed beams and expanses of quarry tiles remain delightfully intact. A lift (no stairs) transports you to five pleasing bedrooms (one, less good, downstairs); beds are of wrought iron or handsome wood, the furniture is properly old-fashioned and the walls rustically bare. Bathrooms have baths and are spotless. Heaps of space here: two country-characterful sitting rooms with billiards and piano, and a dining room with white-clothed tables. The 55-hectare estate supplies the guest house with fresh vegetables and fruit, wine, olive oil, cheese and poultry; throughout the summer, a Palestinian chef cooks superbly. Amazing views not from the house but nearby; the countryside is lusher than Tuscany's and the area less well-trodden. There are mountain bikes for exploring, riding nearby and great opera at Macerata in August and July. Delicious food, lively hosts, comfortable B&B. *Minimum stay two nights.*

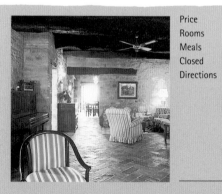

Price	€87. Apartment €550 per week.
Rooms	6 + 1: 6 doubles. Apartment for 2-4.
Meals	Dinner €26. Wine from €4.
Closed	Mid-September to June.
Directions	From SS361 left 1km after Castelraimondo for S. Severino Marche. In Gagliole signs for Collaiello & Locanda.

Signora Gisla Pirri
fraz. Collaiello 2,
62020 Gagliole

Tel	+39 0737 642324
Mobile	+39 338 8461123
Fax	+39 0737 636252
Email	locandasanrocco@libero.it

Self-catering

Le Marche

Caserma Carina Country House

Nothing is too much trouble for Lesley, whose easy-going vivacity makes this place a delight. Cots, toys, DVDs, a bottle of wine at the end of a journey, a welcoming smile – she and Dean provide it all. The apartments are immaculate, the gardens prettily landscaped, the pool has long views. A 15-minute walk down the hill from historic Mogliano (three restaurants, shops, banks and bars) is this magnificent 19th-century country house, its four new apartments spanning three floors. The unrestored part sits quietly, rustically alongside. Inside, all is new, inviting and spotlessly clean. Showers have cream tiles and white towels, kitchens are quietly luxurious, sofas gleam in brown leather, cushions add splashes of red, wooden furniture is stylish and new, indoor shutters cut out early morning light, and views are of rolling hills. You are in the heart of the lovely, unsung Le Marche, an easy drive from historic Macerata, and not much further from the Adriatic coast. Couples will love it and foodies will be happy: out of season cookery courses are planned. An all-year-round treat. *Shared laundry.*

Price	£350-€750 per week.
Rooms	4 apartments: 1 for 2, 2 for 2-4, 1 for 4.
Meals	Restaurant within walking distance.
Closed	Rarely.
Directions	Directions on booking.

Lesley McMorran
contrada da Mossa 16,
62010 Mogliano

Tel	+39 0733 557990
Mobile	+39 334 8260695
Email	info@caserma-carina.co.uk
Web	www.caserma-carina.co.uk

Torre Tenosa

Hard to believe this is the old watchtower – it's so peaceful now. The wooded hills and pastures of Sibillini National Park end in the snow-tipped southern Appenines; a gentle breeze ruffles the trees and grass. Drink in the stunning view (and a glass of local wine) from the terrace. Inside is open plan, with ruddy terracotta tiles underfoot and solid beams overhead. Downstairs you have a well-equipped kitchen area, a good-sized dining table and a jolly red sofabed. The bedroom is up on the wide open mezzanine. At night, sink into a red-striped, down-filled duvet; in the morning, peer out of a dear little stone-framed window from your bed. A smart, clean shower room and small utility room are up on a further level. Environmentally-sound behind-wall heating keeps everyone snug, the internet keeps you in touch. Karen, Frank and their young family live next door but you feel nicely private here, and have your own drive. Karen runs yoga retreats nearby, and the National Park is ten minutes – hike, bike, ski, or just tuck into delicious local food. Perfect for a couple, or close friends.

Price	€475-€550 per week.
Rooms	House for 2-4.
Meals	Restaurants within 5km.
Closed	Never.
Directions	From Camerino SE for Sfercia; left after 2km; right-hand bend signed 'Strada Condominiale'; phone Frank from there.

Frank Schmidt
loc. Santa Lucia 13,
62032 Camerino

Tel	+39 0737 633500
Mobile	+39 334 1846842
Email	frank@torretenosa.it
Web	www.torretenosa.it

Vento di Rose B&B

House, orchards, breakfasts, roses, people… in the foothills of Monterubbiano, ten minutes from the sea, is a place to relish, an unexpected treasure. Your gentle, happy, delightful hosts, with a little English between them, fill the house with artistic flourishes and love doing B&B. Emanuela's sunny personality infuses everything; on the first night Emidio will take you to a local restaurant to ensure you don't get lost. The kitchen/breakfast room, exquisitely Italian, is all blues and creams, its white lace tablecloth strewn with rose petals, then laden with garden cherries, peaches, pears, fresh frittata of artichokes, mulberry fruit tarts, warm bread from Moresco – a different treat every day. The garden's shady bowers are scented with roses, honeysuckle and jasmine; the views are long; the pillows carry sprigs of lavender at night. Bedrooms are bright and airy with pale colourwashed walls and embroidered linen, each with a sitting area; you are also welcome to share the lounge. A paradise of hospitality, tranquillity and blissful breakfasts.

Price	€80–€95.
Rooms	3: 2 doubles, 1 family room for 2-4.
Meals	Picnic available. Restaurants 4km.
Closed	January-February.
Directions	A14 exit Pedaso dir. Monterubbiano. After 200m, left at lights; on for 7km. After Bar Giardino on left, cont. 2km. On right, signed.

Emanuela Mazzoni & Emidio Di Ruscio
via Canniccio, 7,
63026 Monterubbiano

Tel	+39 0734 59226
Mobile	+39 348 7761166
Email	ventodirose@libero.it
Web	www.ventodirose.it

Agriturismo Contrada Durano

Spend a few days at this tranquil agriturismo and you'll never want to leave. The hillside farm, built in the late 18th century as a refuge for monks, has been lovingly restored by two generous, delightful and energetic owners: Englishman Jimmy and Italian Maria Concetta. No clutter, no fuss, just tiled floors, white walls, dark furniture. The bedrooms are simple and some are small, but the bar and sitting areas give you masses of space. And if you're after a room with a view – of olive groves, vineyards and perched villages – ask for rooms 1 or 2. There's dinner most evenings: food to make your heart sing – home-grown or local organic ingredients, prosciutto, pecorino, their own bread and wine. As you feast your eyes from all three dining rooms on distant mountains you may ask yourself, why eat elsewhere? In spring and summer, walk through wild flowers up to the village of Smerillo. And do visit the 'cantina' and stock up with Durano bounty: olives, preserved apricots and beetroot, wines from Le Marche and homemade passata – an Italian summer in a bottle. *Minimum stay two nights.*

Price	€85–€95. Singles €65.
Rooms	7 doubles.
Meals	Dinner with wine, €35–€45.
Closed	Rarely.
Directions	A14 Ancona-Bari exit Porto San Giorgio for Amandola, 38km. 10km after Servigliano, sign on left; house 2km off road.

Maria Concetta Furnari
Contrada Durano,
63020 Smerillo

Tel	+39 0734 786012
Fax	+39 0734 79359
Email	info@contradadurano.it
Web	www.contradadurano.it

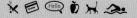

Borgo Storico Seghetti Panichi

Princess Giulia is passionate about her ancestral home, her garden and her red setters. Her country house started life as a medieval look-out tower and the façade was added in 1742; the magnificent, exotic gardens were planted in the 19th-century by a German botanist. The suites have rich colours, some oriental wallpapers, stone floors, metal bedsteads, family antiques. The apartments lie in a sensitively converted farmhouse next to the outdoor pool, their rooms smaller (though far from cramped), their décor more contemporary: muted colours and modern paintings. Breakfast and dinner in the restaurant are a treat, but, should you prefer, you may dine with your hostess. She is delightful and the food (much organic and home-grown) excellent. Some of the views are less than lovely and you can hear motorway hum but, on a clear day, the snow-capped Gran Sasso appears as a mirage; if you don't catch it, think about extending your stay! Shops, bus and train are all walkable – the village lies below – and you are a ten-minute drive from the medieval city of Ascoli Piceno. *Cookery & art lessons on request.*

Price	€50-€900.
Rooms	5 + 5: 4 suites for 2-3, 1 suite for 2-4.
	5 apartments for 2-4.
Meals	Dinner with wine, €40-€50.
Closed	Never.
Directions	From A14 exit San Benedetto del Tronto; superstrada for Ascoli Piceno; exit Castel di Lama.

	Giulia Panichi Pignatelli
	via San Pancrazio 1,
	63031 Castel di Lama
Tel	+39 0736 812552
Fax	+39 0736 814528
Email	info@seghettipanichi.it
Web	www.seghettipanichi.it

Casa Leone

In this stunning, glowing, hilltop village, along a narrow, arched street and up some steps, is the wool merchant's house, its 13th-century honeystone façade enlivened by red and pink geraniums dancing in the breeze. The owners have converted one wing into a self-catering set-up of simple cottage charm: little windows, white-washed walls, terracotta tiles, wooden floors. Bedrooms are spread across the three storeys, with one in the low-ceilinged attic; furniture is unfussy, curtains pretty and flowered and two good bathrooms ease queues. There's a cosy sitting room with cream and blue sofas, a supply of books, games and puzzles for rainy days, and a great view of the Medici tower (and a peep of the valley beyond). The kitchen is a convivial room with solid wood cupboards and a chunky table – you won't mind squishing up a bit if there are lots of you. It's well-stocked with crockery, utensils and appliances, and Anna will provide a welcome-pack of breakfast basics and fresh flowers. Glorious in summer – walks are plentiful; skiing a 40-minute drive. *Minimum stay three nights; fourth night complimentary.*

Price	€700–€1,400 per week.
Rooms	House for 8 (4 doubles).
Meals	Restaurants 3-minute walk.
Closed	Never.
Directions	From L'Aquila SS17 for Popoli/Pescara; 15km; left to S.Stefano; ask in village.

Wendy Sudbury
via degli Archi 24, 67020
S. Stefano di Sessanio

Tel	+44 (0)207 7231627
Fax	+44 (0)207 7237077
Email	wsudbury.camangroup@btinternet.com
Web	www.santo-stefano.org

Casa Torre del Cornone

Bon viveur Alessio is the inspiration behind this environmental project. Off a narrow street, hanging high on the walls of a lovely medieval village, the house's big wooden doors opened to guests in 2006. Come not for unbridled luxury but for wholesome simplicity and a sensational location. High up, overseeing the green valley and the wooded hills, the house has glorious views in fine weather and feels cosy when the winds whistle and the snows drift. The tower of this (in parts ramshackle) mid 17th-century house was one of many that controlled the valley; now the building has entered the 21st century with solar panels, cork-insulated walls and sustainable heating. In small, simple bedrooms, original floor bricks and oak ceiling timbers remain, while plaster walls have been rendered with a traditional calcium and earth mix. Bedsteads have been welded by local craftsmen and bedcovers woven in muted colours. There are cookery weeks and landscape courses to inspire you and bikes to keep you fit, and the walk to the bar for breakfast is spectacular. A special place with an offbeat style.

Price	€58–€63. Singles €42–€45.
Rooms	7: 5 twins; 2 twins sharing bathroom.
Meals	Breakfast not included. Restaurants nearby.
Closed	Never.
Directions	From Rome, A24 to l'Aquila Est; SS17 to Pescara/Popoli; exit at fork with SS261 for San Demetrio/Molina; Fontecchio 15km. Call mobile 30 mins before arrival: meet in Piazza del Popolo, in front of Bar La Fontana.

Alessio di Giulio
Cantone della Terra 22,
67020 Fontecchio

Tel	+39 0862 85441
Mobile	+39 328 0617948
Email	alessio.digiulio@ilexitaly.com
Web	www.torrecornone.com

Convento San Giorgio

Back at the start of the 17th century, the hill of San Giorgio was given to Franciscan monks by local landowners – as a deed 'good for the soul'. Stay in the monastery today and you'll soon find yourself leaving 21st-century materialism behind and focusing, instead, on "the things that matter". You won't be waited on here. High among forested hills overlooking the mountains life is basic and communal, but it is also wonderfully friendly and relaxed and you'll feel part of a working community. Whitewashed bedrooms are austere and clean, linen is only provided if requested, shower rooms are tiny and functional and a gong summons you to simple, mostly vegetarian, meals. Nanni is the presiding genius, unruffled, intelligent, well-travelled and devoted to sustainable living. Originally from San Remo, where he set up a group for sustainable tourism, he's attempting to make San Giorgio entirely self-sufficient. At its heart are the cool white cloisters, where visiting swallows swoop beneath the arches and sheep and goats graze close by.

Nanni's enthusiasm and determination for sustainability is infectious. And you may put yourself forward as a volunteer member of the Italian Greenpeace – Legambiente – as part of your stay. Help to keep bees, rebuild ancient paths, seek out fresh water springs or protect bears living in the Sirente Velino National Park. As a respected member of Legambiente, Nanni also runs the annual European Eco-Village Conference at the convent; later in the year he does the same for the Italians. We salute him for all of his hard work; be sure to enjoy all he has to offer you during your stay.

Price	Full-board €60 p.p. Half-board €45 p.p.
Rooms	22: 11 doubles, 6 twins, 5 bunk rooms for 3-6.
Meals	Half-board only. Restaurant 5-minute walk.
Closed	Mid-October to April.
Directions	A24 exit L'Aquila Est dir. Pescara. At 1st x-roads right to Fontecchio, thro' Fontecchio; 4km, right for Tione degli Abruzzi; signed on left 1km before Goriano Valli.

Leonardo (Nanni) Laurent
Goriano Valli Convento San Giorgio,
via Colle 1, 67020 Goriano Valli,

Tel	+39 0862 88368
Fax	+39 0862 88261
Email	info@conventosangiorgio.it
Web	www.conventosangiorgio.it

SPECIAL
GREEN ENTRY
see page 14

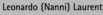 

Map 13 Entry 271

Bed & Breakfast Villa la Ruota

The floors are so beautifully polished they squeak. Elegant Adele, welcoming, unflappable, runs a super-organised B&B – a great place to stay on a walking holiday in the Abruzzo National Park. It's a balconied, shuttered, 60s-built chalet house, surrounded by a large garden and many pines. The sitting room is homely with an open fire and simply decorated bedrooms are comfortable. Doors have blue and red painted frames; basement rooms take an extra bed; two rooms share a balcony. There's a nice big dining room – and a garden terrace – for meals: warm rolls and packeted butters and jams at breakfast; straightforward regional dishes at dinner. Picnics can be arranged. In spite of the romance of early morning cow bells, you are only a mile outside Pescasseroli and far from isolated. You are in the oldest national park in Italy, there are maps in every room and you can book a mountain bike and a guide. Pescasseroli is well set up for skiers too, with a cable car and five lifts. *Easily accessible by bus and train; owner will pick up.*

Price	€60-€110.
Rooms	7: 2 triples, 3 twins/doubles; 2 doubles, sharing bathroom.
Meals	Restaurants 7km.
Closed	Never.
Directions	A24-A25 Rome-Pescara exit Pescina; SS83 for Pescasseroli. On central piazza, follow sign for skiing attractions; at r'bout, 3rd exit; signs for Villa.

Adele Gentile
Colle Massarello 3,
67032 Pescasseroli

Tel	+39 0815 446019
Fax	+39 0815 644911
Email	bnb@villalaruota.it
Web	www.villalaruota.it

Modus Vivendi

Walkers, birdwatchers, outdoorsy types will love it here. Views stretch over rolling hills dotted with towns while the mountains of the Majella National Park rise behind. Hospitable Emilia is a trained guide, keen on birds and flowers, and can suggest walks or even join you. Passionate about conservation, she's restored her creamy stone house using local artisans and friendly materials; there are ecological paints, wood-burning stoves, solar panels, recycled rainwater. Cool white and exposed stone walls, timbered ceilings and terracotta floors make rooms light and airy, while furnishings are traditional but uncluttered – wrought-iron or carved beds, richly coloured bedspreads, an antique armoire or a handsome chair. Bathrooms sparkle with chrome and pretty mosaics; all is fresh, new, pristine. The apartments have open-plan living areas with kitchens to one side, and terraces for dining. Or let Emilia cook, Abruzzese style. Everything is homemade, and the produce is local organic. In the summer, eat under the pergola and raise a glass of home-produced liqueur to those views.

Price	€60–€80.
Rooms	5 + 2: 5 doubles. 2 apartments for 4.
Meals	Lunch & dinner from €20. Restaurant 5-minute drive.
Closed	Rarely.
Directions	A25 Rome-Pescara exit Scafa. Follow signs for Abbateggio for 10km; signed.

Dario De Renzis
via Colle della Selva,
65020 Abbateggio

Tel/Fax	+39 0858 572136
Mobile	+39 393 7153584
Email	Info@ecoalbergomodusvivendi.it
Web	www.ecoalbergomodusvivendi.it

Dimora del Prete di Belmonte

The old palace hides among the cobbled streets of the medieval centre – a gem once you step inside. Venafro, a Roman town, lies in the lovely valley of Monte Santa Croce, ringed by mountains. The first thrill is the enchanting internal garden with its lush banana palms and citrus trees, where a miscellany of Roman artefacts and olive presses lie scattered among tables and chairs. Next, a frescoed interior in an astonishing state of preservation; painted birds, family crests and *grotteschi* adorn the walls of the state rooms and entrance hall. Bedrooms are furnished in simple good taste, one with a big fireplace and a sleigh bed, another with chestnut country furniture, most with views. Shower rooms are small – bar one, which has a bath. Dorothy is a wonderful hostess and has fantastic local knowledge; she and her son are a great team. They also run an organic farm with 1,000 olive trees (many of them over 400 years old), vines, walnut-trees and sheep. An area and a palace rich in content – and relaxed, delicious dinners do full justice to the setting. Breakfasts are as good. *Easy access by train.*

Price	€120. Suite €150. Apt €500 per week (€200 for weekend).
Rooms	5 + 1: 4 doubles, 1 suite. 1 apartment for 2-4.
Meals	Breakfast €10 for self-caterers. Lunch or dinner, with wine, €30.
Closed	Rarely.
Directions	Leave A1 Rome-Naples motorway at S. Vittore from the north, follow signs for Venafro, Isernia and Campobasso. The Palace is easy to find in the historical centre of Venafro.

	Dorothy Volpe via Cristo 49, 86079 Venafro
Tel/Fax	+39 0865 900159
Mobile	+39 333 9216370
Email	info@dimoradelprete.it
Web	www.dimoradelprete.it

Lazio

Photo: istock.com

Hotel Villa del Parco

The frenzy of Rome can wear down even the most enthusiastic of explorers, so here is a dignified place to which you can retreat: a 19th-century villa in a residential spot, surrounded by shrubs and trees. Inside the mood is relaxed, charming and friendly – the Bernardinis are quietly proud of the hotel that has been in the family for over 40 years. Good-sized bedrooms – the quietest at the back – are cosy and fresh and have wrought-iron beds, good lighting, crisp cotton, double glazing and carpets (not usual so far south). Shower rooms are tiled from top to toe – beautifully. The remnants of frescoes on the stairs are a comforting reminder of Italy's past, though the house is fin de siècle in spirit. A pretty terrace with wrought-iron tables and big parasols is shaded by tropical plants in big ceramic pots, just the the place for an early evening drink. The breakfast baskets are full of treats and the cappuccino delicious. There is a vaulted dining room and a pretty reading room, too. Delightful staff provide umbrellas for rainy days – and will help you negotiate the buses into town.

Price	€125–€200. Singles €95–€150. Triples €155–€240.
Rooms	29: 14 doubles, 10 singles, 5 triples.
Meals	Restaurants 200m. Snacks available.
Closed	Never.
Directions	From Termini station right into via XX Settembre; past Piazza di Porta Pia into via Nomentana. Bus: in square in front of station, no 36 or 84; 2nd stop after Villa Torlonia.

Signor Alessandro Bernardini
via Nomentana 110,
00161 Rome

Tel	+39 0644 237773
Fax	+39 0644 237572
Email	info@hotelvilladelparco.it
Web	www.hotelvilladelparco.it

Caesar House Residenze Romane

A calm, comfortable oasis above Roman din. The Forum can be glimpsed from one window, elegant cafés, shops and restaurants lie below, and the Colosseum is a five-minute stroll. Up the lift to the second floor of the ancient palazzo; grand reception doors open to a bright, welcoming space. Charming, stylish sisters, Giulia and Simona, run things together with the help of Grandma: a family affair. Bedrooms, named after celebrated *italiani*, have warm red ceramic floors, heavy curtains in maroon or blue, matching sofas and quilted covers, a choice of blankets or duvets, vestibules to keep luggage out of the way and every modern thing: air con, minibar, internet, safe, satellite TV. You breakfast in your room – it's big enough – or in the pretty dining room with its tables draped in cream linen, and modern art dotted here and there. There's even a gym for those who have surplus energy after a long day's sightseeing around the city's ancient ruins. The service here is exemplary – maps, guided tours, airport pick up, babysitting, theatre booking, bike hire. It's thoroughly professional, and personal too.

Price	€180–€230. Singles €150–€200. Extra bed €20.
Rooms	6: 4 doubles, 2 twins.
Meals	Restaurants nearby.
Closed	Never.
Directions	Metro: line B from Termini station to Cavour, then 5-minute walk or buses 74 or 40 down via Cavour.

Giulia & Simona Barela
via Cavour 310,
00184 Rome

Tel	+39 0667 92674
Fax	+39 0669 781120
Email	info@caesarhouse.com
Web	www.caesarhouse.com

Dépendance Valle delle Camene

Pick your way through the shady gravel garden – past weathered statues posing discreetly amongst ferns, palms and soaring magnolias – and up to the handsome 19th-century villa that sits, proudly, in this Roman garden. This is where Viviana lives; she and her daughter, Stefania, have breathed life into the guest annexe that lies to one end. It is small but beautifully formed, and you have the whole place to yourself. Blue and yellow tiles wash floors with colour, their vibrancy barely diminished after 200 years; there are chunky marble hand basins, their curves deliciously smooth from centuries of use, and walls and beamed ceilings that are refreshingly white. Modernity is cleverly concealed: the fabulously stylish jacuzzi bath hides behind a thick hessian curtain, the new bed lies under an embroidered quilt. Breakfast in your private little courtyard where the original Roman walls offer total seclusion. In the open-air sitting room at the front: plump cushions on wicker sofas encircled by young orange trees in portly ceramic urns – a blissful spot for a flop and a glass of something chilled after a day's amble round the city.

Price	€140–€160. Sofabed €20.
Rooms	1 double (+ sofabed).
Meals	Restaurants within walking distance.
Closed	Rarely.
Directions	Metro: Line B to Circo Massimo, then 5-minute walk.

	Stefania Agnello
	via di Valle delle Camene 3C,
	00184 Rome
Fax	+39 0670 493534
Email	info@valledellecamene.com
Web	www.valledellecamene.com

Casa Trevi I & II

A hop, skip and a jump from Italy's most famous fountain, the Casa Trevi is a treasure. Find yourself in an astonishingly peaceful courtyard, all olive trees, scented oranges and a fountain inhabited by small turtles. Though you're in Rome's most vibrant heart, not a sound penetrates from outside. The apartments are on the ground floor of one of the old buildings and open directly off the courtyard. Interiors are bright, soothing and minimalist in the most beautiful way: white walls and terracotta, glass shelving and concealed lighting, a mix of modern and brocante finds. There are no windows as such but the double glass-paned doors let in plenty of light. Hobs and fridges are provided in the airy, white kitchens, but serious cooking is not catered for (who wants to eat-in in Rome?). Shower rooms are gorgeous. On three sides are 17th-century buildings in yellows, ochres and reds; on the fourth, a modern monstrosity. Marta could not be sweeter, and the security – a big plus – is excellent, with a porter and security camera in the main entrance. Good value for central Rome. *Minimum stay four nights.*

Price	€140. €180 for 4.
Rooms	2 apartments: 1 for 2-3, 1 for 4.
Meals	Restaurants nearby.
Closed	Rarely.
Directions	Directions on booking; no parking in pedestrianised area. 10-minute taxi from Termini station. Metro: Piazza Barberini.

Signora Marta Nicolini
via in Arcione 98,
00187 Rome

Mobile	+39 335 6205768
Fax	+39 0669 787084
Email	info@casaintrastevere.it
Web	www.casatrevi.it

Casa Trevi III

This, too, is five minutes from the Trevi Fountain – most breathtaking by night – but in a separate street from Casas Trevi I and II. Marta – full of warmth, a busy bee – has waved her stylish wand again and created a deeply desirable place to stay. She employed one of the top restoration experts in Rome to make ceiling beams glow and terracotta floors gleam – and the result? Old Rome meets new. Up a tiny lift to the third floor and into an open-plan sitting, dining and kitchen area – black, white, grey, chic, with a polished wooden floor. A discarded shutter for a frame, an antique door for a bedhead, air con to keep you cool, double glazing to ensure quiet. The white-raftered twin and double rooms share a sparkling, 21st-century shower in beige marble. Modigliani prints beautify cream walls, mirrored doors reflect the light, silk cushions sprinkle the sofa and shutters are painted dove-grey. Never mind the tourists and the street vendors, Rome lies at your feet. And you have the unassuming Trattoria della Stampa, where the locals go, in the very same street. *Minimum stay four nights.*

Price	€140–€200.
Rooms	Apartment for 3-5.
Meals	Restaurants nearby.
Closed	Never.
Directions	No cars in pedestrianised area; 10-minute taxi from Termini station. Metro: Piazza Barberini. Directions on booking.

Signora Marta Nicolini
via dei Maroniti 7, 00187 Rome

Mobile	+39 335 6205768
Fax	+39 0669 787084
Email	info@casaintrastevere.it
Web	www.casatrevi.it

Hotel Fontana

Near chic shops, the Spanish Steps, Piazza di Spagna, Piazza Navona, the Pantheon, the Colosseum, and overlooking the most fabled fountain in the world. With the help of a small staff Elisabetta runs this romantic, quirky hotel with a smile. The 14th-century convent has an unassuming front door and the lovely large floor tiles remain. Simple windows are shuttered; in the day, when guests are out, it is a sweet retreat in a pulsating city. Updated bedrooms are cosy but simple, with pale wooden floors, whitewashed walls, cream linen drapes. More traditional rooms have classic colours, flowers in silver bowls, curtains falling to the floor. Bathrooms are tiny, bedrooms small; the quietest rooms, away from the fountain, are at the rear. (The latter have air con – a plus in summer.) On the fifth floor is the dining room – a special place for breakfast, cocktails and afternoon tea. Round tables are dressed in white and topped with flowers, cushioned bench seats grace one wall and you may have a table that overlooks the baroque glories below. Breakfast on the terrace is best – there everyone gets the view.

Price	€165–€280. Singles from €163.
Rooms	25: 19 doubles, 3 twins, 3 singles.
Meals	Restaurants nearby.
Closed	Never.
Directions	Metro: line A to Barbernini. Private parking 10-minute walk.

Signora Elena Daneo
Piazza di Trevi 96,
00187 Rome

Tel	+39 0667 86113
Fax	+39 0667 90024
Email	info@hotelfontana-trevi.com
Web	www.hotelfontana-trevi.com

Hotel Modigliani

There's a sense of anticipation the moment you enter the marble hall, with its deep, pale sofas and fresh flowers – Marco's wide smile and infectious enthusiasm reinforce the feeling. This is an unusual, delightful place, hidden down a side street just five minutes' walk from the Spanish Steps and Via Veneto. The house belonged to Marco's father, and Marco and Giulia (he a writer, she a musician) have turned it into the perfect small hotel. Marble floors and white walls are a dramatic setting for black-and-white photos taken by Marco, their starkness softened by luxuriant plants. The bread oven of the 1700s has become a dining room – all vaulted ceilings, whitewashed walls, cherrywood tables, fabulous photos. Bedrooms are fresh and elegant; some have balconies and wonderful views, all have small, perfect bathrooms. There's a lovely new sitting room for guests. The whole place has a sweet, stylish air, it's unusually quiet for the centre of the city and there's a patio scented with jasmine. Marco and Giulia will tell you about Rome's secret corners – or grab a copy of Marco's new guide and discover Rome for yourselves.

Price	€150-€195. Suite €208-€340. Family suite €330-€440. Apartments €200-€250.
Rooms	23 + 2: 20 twins/doubles, 2 suites, 1 family suite for 4-6. 2 apartments: 1 for 3, 1 for 6.
Meals	Breakfast included for all. Restaurants within walking distance.
Closed	Never.
Directions	Metro line A: 2nd stop Piazza Barberini. 5-minute walk from Spanish Steps.

Giulia & Marco di Tillo
via della Purificazione 42,
00187 Rome

Tel	+39 0642 815226
Fax	+39 0642 814791
Email	info@hotelmodigliani.com
Web	www.hotelmodigliani.com

Hotel Lord Byron

Down a peaceful cobbled street is an unexpected edifice of imposing proportions and immaculately dressed windows. The Lord Byron is shamelessly exclusive, extraordinarily hushed (is this Rome?) and not terribly Italian – but for luxuriousness it cannot be beat. The service is professional, generous, discreet, the sitting room is grand and inviting with huge sofas, big lilies and gilt-framed oils, and the basement dining room sparkles at night. Cocoon yourself in the Art Deco splendour of it all – the food is as good as it gets. Walls are strokeable, colours are bold, the Art Deco décor is in impeccably good taste. In your smallish but delightful double room, pad across a sumptuous wine-red carpet from cocoa velvet chair to cream marble bathroom to vast bed. If you want a view, book the suite on the top floor: it has the roof terrace. The hotel is far from bang in the centre, but there's a private daytime shuttle to the swish via Veneto six days a week and you are on the edge of the 'museum park' of Villa Borghese, Rome's most special green space. Be pampered big time! *Secure parking.*

Price	€300–€6,000. Suites €560–€975.
Rooms	32: 23 doubles, 9 suites.
Meals	Dinner, à la carte, from €50.
Closed	Never.
Directions	A1 for centre, exit via Saleria; right at Viale Liegi, follow tram tracks & left at end; after Residence Aldrovandi, right at lights onto via Mangili; cont. to Piazza Don Minzoni; via Giuseppe De Notaris; up hill, on left.

Amedeo Ottaviani
via G. de Notaris 5,
00917 Rome

Tel	+39 0632 20404
Fax	+39 0632 20405
Email	info@lordbyronhotel.com
Web	www.lordbyronhotel.com

Guest House Arco dei Tolomei

Up the graceful sweep of the dark wooden staircase and you enter a fascinating little B&B in the peaceful old Jewish quarter of Trastevere. The house has been in Marco's family for 200 years and those sedate gentlemen framed on the blue walls are just some of the past inhabitants. Marco and his wife Gianna are great travellers and have filled the family home with bits and pieces from their journeys abroad. Floor to ceiling shelves heave under the weight of books in the red drawing room, gorgeous pieces of art and sculpture beautify walls and tables, and floors are laid with exquisite parquet; there's plentiful dark wood and every square inch gleams. The long oval dining table awaits guests eager to sample Gianna's breakfasts. Bedrooms, reached through a guests' sitting room, have bold flowers – pinks, reds, yellows – or pinstripes on the walls, a backdrop to handsome bedsteads and great little bathrooms, while the best have miniature staircases up to private terraces with views that roll down over the terracotta patchwork of Trastevere's tiny terracotta roofs.

Price	€160-€220.
Rooms	5: 4 doubles, 1 triple.
Meals	Restaurants within walking distance.
Closed	Never.
Directions	From Ciampino airport to Trastevere train station; line H to Piazza Sonnino, then Via della Lungaretta to Piazza in Piscinula.

Marco Fè d'Ostiani
via dell'Arco dè Tolomei 27,
00153 Rome

Tel	+39 0658 320819
Fax	+ 39 0658 99703
Email	info@inrome.info
Web	www.inrome.info

Hotel Santa Maria

All around are cobbled streets, ancient houses and the bustle of cafés, bars and tiny shops that is Trastevere. Just behind the lovely Piazza de Santa Maria – whose church bells chime every 15 minutes – is a pair of green iron gates that open to sudden, sweet peace and the fragrance of honeysuckle. On the site of what was a 17th-century convent is this secluded single-storey hotel, its courtyards bright with orange trees. The layout is a tribute to all those earlier cloisters: rooms here open onto covered, brick-pillared terraces that surround a central, gravelled courtyard where you can sit out in summer. Authentic materials have been used – Peperino marble for the floors, walnut and chestnut for the ceilings – while the breakfast room has the original terracotta floor. Newly decorated bedrooms have soft yellow walls, high ceilings, big beds. There's no sitting room but a good bar, and the internet and bikes are free. Stefano runs a courteous staff and you are well looked after. He's also a qualified guide and has recently opened a sister hotel, Residenza Santa Maria, just around the corner.

Price	€170–€220. Triple €200–€280. Quadruple €230–€320. Suites €260–€480.
Rooms	18: 8 doubles, 4 triples, 1 quadruple, 5 suites (for 4, 5 or 6).
Meals	Restaurants 10m.
Closed	Never.
Directions	15-minute taxi from Termini station.

Paolo Vetere
vicolo del Piede 2,
00153 Rome

Tel	+39 0658 94626
Fax	+39 0658 94815
Email	info@hotelsantamaria.com
Web	www.htlsantamaria.com

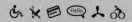

Casa in Trastevere

If you're independent souls, fortunate enough to be planning more than a fleeting trip to Rome, this apartment is a great base, a ten-minute walk from the old quarter of Trastevere. The area, though residential, has a great buzz at night and the shops, bars and restaurants are a treat to discover. Signora Nicolini, once a specialist restorer, has furnished this sunny first-floor flat as if it were her own home. She has kept the original 19th-century red and black terrazzo floor and has added contemporary touches: a cream sofa, an all-white kitchen (no mircrowave or oven, but you won't mind, with so many tempting restaurants on your doorstep), kilims and modern art. You have a large open-plan living/dining room with screened kitchen, a double and a twin bedroom, each with a white bathroom, and an extra sofabed. All is fresh and bright, and the big bedroom is very charming with its hand-quilted bedspread. Marta is a delight and does her best to ensure you go home with happy memories. Put your feet up after a long day, pour yourself a glass of wine... then set off to explore some more of this magical city. *Minimum stay four nights.*

Price	From €140 for 2; from €180 for 4; from €200 for 5-6.
Rooms	1 apartment for 2-6.
Meals	Restaurants nearby.
Closed	Rarely.
Directions	From Ponte Sisto cross Piazza Trilussa. Right into via della Lungara, left into via dei Riari, right into Vicolo della Penitenza. From Termini bus H. From Trastevere station bus 8.

Signora Marta Nicolini
vicolo della Penitenza 19,
00165 Rome
Mobile +39 335 6205768
Fax   +39 0669 787084
Email   info@casaintrastevere.it
Web   www.casaintrastevere.it

Hotel San Francesco

Trastevere – Rome's stylish and bohemian quarter – is at its best on a sleepy Sunday morning when the flea market unfurls and the smell of spicy *porchetta* infuses the air. But first, enjoy one of the most generous breakfasts Rome has to offer, served in a long, light room that overlooks a 15th-century cloister complete with friar, garden and hens... Built in 1926 as a training school for missionaries, this young hotel runs on well-oiled wheels. There's a black and white tiled sitting room with black leather armchairs, big white lilies and a piano, and a stylishly furnished roof garden with canvas parasols and views to the Vatican; gorgeous by day, ravishing by night. Marble stairs lead to carpeted corridors off which feed small, comfortable bedrooms – lined curtains at double-glazed windows, fabulous bathrooms, garden views at the back. Pop into the Santa Cecilia next door for a peep at Bellini's *Madonna*, stroll to the sights across the river, rent a bike. Not truly central – you'll be using the odd taxi – but a very pleasant launch pad for discovering the city.

Price	€135–€220.
Rooms	24 doubles.
Meals	Restaurants nearby.
Closed	Never.
Directions	From Termini station, bus 75, 44 or line H. Airport train to Travestere (35 mins).

	Daniele Frontoni
	via Jacopa de' Settesoli 7,
	00153 Rome
Tel	+39 0658 300051
Fax	+39 0658 333413
Email	info@hotelsanfrancesco.net
Web	www.hotelsanfrancesco.net

Hotel Villa San Pio

The Hotel San Pio is pristine. It was a residential villa, one of the many that gives the Aventine hill its air of serene calm and makes an evening stroll up here – past the Church of Santa Sabina to the orange gardens – such a joy. This large hotel congregates around a central space crammed with bougainvillea, camellias, roses and palms. An elegant, verdigris conservatory is where you breakfast, sometimes to the live accompaniment of a minuet or sonata; the new dining room is also conservatory-style, to pull the lovely leafiness in. Bedrooms have pretty painted furniture, brocade bedcovers and frescoed or stencilled walls – all gorgeous. There's much comfort, bathrooms are immaculate, the larger rooms have balconies filled with flowers and views and the family rooms are really special. The conveniences of the modern city hotel are all here – minibar, air conditioning, parking – and Signora Piroli rules the roost. A short walk to the metro whisks you into *centro storico* yet you wake to birdsong and the scent of orange blossom.

Price	€140-€240. Singles €98-€140. Family €170-€270.
Rooms	78: 61 doubles, 3 singles, 14 family rooms.
Meals	Dinner à la carte, €45.
Closed	Rarely.
Directions	5-minute walk from Metro Piramide.

Signora Roberta Piroli
via Santa Melania 19,
00153 Rome

Tel	+39 0657 50057
Fax	+39 0657 41112
Email	info@aventinohotels.com
Web	www.aventinohotels.com

B&B   Lazio

Villa Ann

Gentle, charming Lismay and John, so eager to ensure you go home with good memories, are reason enough to stay. She is a trained cook so dinners (Italian) and breakfasts (English) are delicious; John is a golfing enthusiast and will tell you where to play... Who would guess Italy's oldest golf course was so near? Indeed, the whole family is sports-mad which is why they chose this area: for sailors and windsurfers, hand-gliders, hikers and bikers it's a dream. The modern villa, named after John's mother, sits in its own olive grove and palm-filled gardens with a large pool in the orchard – yours for early morning or pre-dinner swims. There's a private entrance and a sitting room for guests; simple bedrooms have good comfy beds; bathrooms come with that Italian rarity – a bath! Best of all, your French windows open to a large and lovely balcony, full of morning sunshine and views to the hills. Wine tastings at Frascati are a short drive and the Rome express train gets you to the city in 20 minutes; your delightful hosts will drive you to and from the station. *30 minutes from Ciampino airport.*

Price	€40–€65.
Rooms	2 twins/doubles, sharing bathroom. Whole house available during holidays.
Meals	Dinner with wine, €20.
Closed	Rarely.
Directions	Directions on booking.

John & Lismay Garforth-Bles
via Mole del Giardino 4,
00049 Velletri

Tel/Fax	+39 0696 453398
Mobile	+39 328 7076157
Email	j.garforth@tiscali.it
Web	www.villa-ann.com

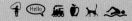

Entry 288 Map 12

Villa Monte Ripone

Slip through glass doors into a cool, welcoming space of fresh flowers, comfy sofas and richly tiled floors. This handsome country house, with its golden colours and olive green shutters, was Anna's family home. The open-plan, ground floor – all vaulted ceilings, polished tiles and beautiful antiques – includes an elegant dining room and comfortable sitting room. Upstairs is a maze of unexpected spaces, little steps up and steps down. Airy, boldly-coloured bedrooms are a mix of much-loved antiques and modern functional furnishings. Some are grander than others but all share dreamy views over fields and the family's olive groves and fruit trees. The views from the pool, hidden below the house, are equally enchanting. There are walks directly from the house and peaceful shady spots in the garden. Eat out in Nazzano (a five-minute drive) or here: it's regional cooking with organic veg from the garden. Anna, Renzo and their two children live next door and the atmosphere is family-friendly and easy. *Minimum stay three nights.*

Price	€80–€90. Family €120. Whole house, on request.
Rooms	5: 2 doubles, 1 twins/doubles, 1 family room for 4, 1 suite.
Meals	Dinner with wine €25, by arrangement.
Closed	November–March.
Directions	A1 Roma-Firenze exit Ponzano Sorrate for Nazzano; 2km after Ponzano Romano right fork for Rome; ignore turning to Nazzano; on left, supermarket, on right, via Civitellese; 200m on right, signed.

Anna Clarissa Benzoni
via Civitellese 2,
00060 Nazzano

Tel	+39 0765 332543
Mobile	+39 348 8829564
Email	monteripone@virgilio.it

Zampanò

Don't be put off by the fact that this property appears to be a bleak and abandoned ruin in the middle of nowhere. To the casual observer it is all those things and worse, but anybody with a bit of imagination will discover it is in fact a portal to a bizarre and abstract world. It is best to arrive when it is no longer day time but still not quite dark yet either. Once you slip off into that state of mind that hovers between sleep and wakefulness you will discover the delights of this extraordinary place. An interesting assortment of characters passes through on a regular basis so don't be surprised to find yourself in the company of paparazzi, frustrated film directors, retired dancers reliving their former glory, circus folk, libertines and the occasional free spirit. Views include a statue of the Madonna being airlifted by a helicopter and sea monsters washed up on the beach. The owner lives above the property – suspended mid-air with only a rope to keep him from floating away. Tugging on the rope usually brings him down to earth but it is, not surprisingly, a shame to do so. Enjoy.

Price	Providing a good song & dance routine usually suffices.
Rooms	8 half doubles.
Meals	An assortment of pig trotters.
Closed	Only if your mind is.
Directions	Follow the circus clowns.

Guido Anselmi
La Strada,
00000 Virtual Rome
Tel   00 000 000
Fax   00 000 000
Email   guido@zampano.unlikely
Web   www.zampano.unlikely

Azienda Agrituristica Sant'Ilario sul Farfa

Straightforward good value, and an hour from Rome by car. The approach, along a steep, unmade track, is marked by that typically Italian juxtaposition of the electric gates and an olive tree of staggering antiquity. This little farm sits on one of the steeply terraced hills above the river Farfa, with views from its terrace to the Sabine hills. Susanna Serafini is a chatty and creative hostess whose dinners – delivered on request, and using farm produce – are brilliant value. The aspect of the place is rather ranch-like, with bedrooms in two single-storey farm buildings, white with wooden shutters. Bedrooms are snug and wood-panelled with some fine antique bedheads, white walls and showers. The two apartments in the main house have small kitchens for simple meals: great for families. A pleasing tangle of trellises extends across the garden – more farmyard than formal. Take a dip in the pool or the river, spin off on a mountain bike, book onto an olive – or grape – harvesting weekend. There are painting classes for grown-ups, cookery and craft classes for children and little ones love it.

Price	€80. Half-board €55–€60. Apartment €600–€850 per week.
Rooms	6 + 3: 2 doubles, 4 family. 3 apartments: 1 for 3, 1 for 4, 1 for 5.
Meals	Dinner & Sunday lunch with wine, €20. Restaurants 2km.
Closed	January.
Directions	From SS4 Rome-Rieti exit to Osteria Nuova dir. Poggio Nativo. Just after Monte S. Maria sharp left onto track signed to Sant'Ilario sul Farfa.

Signora Susanna Serafini
loc. Colle,
02030 Poggio Nativo

Tel/Fax	+39 0765 872410
Mobile	+39 380 3572303
Email	info@santilariosulfarfa.it
Web	www.santilariosulfarfa.it

La Torretta

Casperia is a joyful, characterful, car-free maze of steepish streets in the stunning Sabine hills. La Torretta has the dreamiest views from its terrace, and interior spaces that have been beautifully designed by architect Roberto. A huge, ground-floor sitting room with beautiful frescoes around the cornice welcomes you with fireplace, modern sofas and chairs, books, paintings and piano. The upper room, where meals are taken, opens onto that terrace; it is a stunning, vaulted, contemporary space with open stainless-steel kitchen and views through skylights to the church tower and valley. Maureen, warm-hearted and hospitable, is passionate about the region and its food. She arranges cookery courses and will cook on request using whatever is in season – mushrooms, truffles, wild boar… and the finest olive oil. Whitewashed, high-ceilinged bedrooms are charming in their simplicity; beds are made and towels changed daily; bathrooms are a treat. The apartment is a five-minute walk from the house. Don't worry about having to leave your car in the square below the town: Roberto has a buggy for luggage.

Price	€90. Singles €75. Family room €150. Apartment €700 per week.
Rooms	7 + 1: 5 doubles, 1 single, 1 family room for 4. 1 apartment for 4.
Meals	Dinner with wine €35, by arrangement. Restaurant 50m.
Closed	Rarely.
Directions	From North, A1 exit Ponzano Soratte towards Poggio Mirteto. Continue on SS657 for 5km to T-junc. Left on SS313 to Cantalupo towards Casperia.

	Roberto & Maureen Scheda
	via G. Mazzini 7,
	02041 Casperia
Tel/Fax	+39 0765 63202
Mobile	+39 338 1451859
Email	latorretta@tiscalinet.it
Web	www.latorrettabandb.com

Entry 292 Map 12

Villa Sanguigni

The snow-capped Laga mountains, glimpsed from some windows and seen as full-blown panoramas from others, are a constant reminder of how close you are to some of Italy's most spectacular scenery. Yet, even though this tiny mountain village stands like Horatius at the gates of Umbria, Le Marche and Abruzzo, the temptation to stay indoors at Villa Sanguigni is strong. The delightful owners, the Orlandi Sanguigni, have restored their ancestral home with unusual sensitivity and care. The five good-sized double bedrooms are beautifully furnished with 18th and 19th-century bedheads, old washstands, chests, rugs and pictures, and the main rooms are even more delightful: the grand *sala* with huge fireplace, rafters and cream sofas; the elegant dining room, reminiscent of a banqueting hall, with long table and lovely pale stone walls. Best of all, perhaps, is the library, which guests are free to use: curl up with a book, or choose from Signor Sanguigni's vast collection of classical music CDs. *Minimum stay two nights.*

Price	€100. Singles €50.
Rooms	5 doubles.
Meals	Restaurants 3km.
Closed	Rarely.
Directions	From Rome, SS4 (via Salaria) for Ascoli Piceno to Bagnolo. At km129.400 before lake turn for Bagnolo. On right just inside village.

Anna Maria Orlandi Sanguigni
Bagnolo di Amatrice,
02012 Rieti

Tel/Fax	+39 0746 821075
Mobile	+39 360 806141
Email	sanguigni1@libero.it
Web	www.primitaly.it/bb/villasanguigni

L'Ombricolo- Country House Hospitality

Two decades years ago it was a ruin. Now it's a mellow stone house with a warmth and character all of its own. Dawne has employed local materials and craftspeople to restore the vaulted ceilings and flagged floors, then filled the interiors with her creativity. Where cattle once slept – their rub marks against the stone arches still remain – is now an inviting sitting room with a beautiful fireplace, cream sofas, music and books. The pretty bedrooms are equally individual, with steps here and there, odd corners and turns, and beamed, sloping ceilings. But the glorious heart of the house, created from an old, dismantled grocery store in Rome, is Dawne's kitchen. Here she will be, unhurriedly preparing a meal when you return from a day away, ready with a glass of wine and a smile. Settle down; unwind. She's a fascinating person to talk to, having lived in Italy for 40 years, worked in the film industry in Rome and travelled all over the world. Her garden is as relaxed and relaxing as her home; plants swoop over the veranda, there are shady trees for hot days and dogs and cats galore.

Price	€130.
Rooms	5 doubles.
Meals	Dinner €45.
Closed	Rarely.
Directions	From A1 to Orvieto, exit Baschi. Right for Castiglione in Teverina. After 2km left at fork for Bomarzo. Right in front of Battisti Cereali gates; house 1st on right.

Dawne Alstrom
01020 Civitella d'Agliano
Tel +39 0761 914735
Fax +39 0761 914735
Email dawne@lombricolo.com
Web www.lombricolo.com

Poggio Paradiso

The tower room, reached by a wrought-iron staircase, would be lovely for a writer – though the views would be undoubtedly distracting. Indeed, the views are irresistible from every window. The house stands on a hilltop in gardens of lawn, sage and rosemary and 18 hectares of land. The area, peppered with Etruscan caves and tombs, is protected: no hunting allowed. Giancarlo built the house in 1999, doing much of the work himself and going to great pains to use traditional methods and old materials. He has also taken a delight in filling it with objects collected from his travels: these dot the light, airy and plainly dressed bedrooms and the sitting room with its lovely arched window. Baskets of lavender, piles of cookery books... it is all deeply, authentically Italian, in particular the flagged, beamed and honey-coloured kitchen, whose double doors open to a columned loggia. There are decorative tiles, heaps of copper ladles, a dresser, a table that seats 12. Be prepared for a family-friendly feel – relaxed, nothing too kempt. Come for B&B – or take the whole place. *Minimum stay two nights; one week in apartment, June-August.*

Price	€70–€90.
	Whole house €1,340–€1,800 per week.
Rooms	5 + 1: 4 doubles, 1 twin.
	1 apartment for 8-10.
Meals	Dinner with wine, €25–€40.
Closed	November-March.
Directions	A1 exit Orte dir. Viterbo; exit Soriano & Chia dir. Soriano; follow signs to Vasanello. Call from Vasanello.

	Giancarlo Ibba
	loc. Poggio Paradiso,
	01030 Vasanello
Tel	+39 0761 409900
Mobile	+39 333 7640890
Email	sawday@poggioparadiso.eu
Web	www.poggioparadiso.eu

La Locanda della Chiocciola

Perhaps the name has something to do with the pace of life at 'The House of the Snail'. This is an unhurried place. Maria Cristina and Roberto have turned a 15th-century stone farmstead in the Tiber valley into an entrancing small hotel and restaurant. Gardens full of flowering shrubs and peaceful walkways are set in 25 hectares of woods, olive groves and orchards, and there's a wonderful pool. Be welcomed by mellow, gleaming floors and furniture, and the intoxicating smell of beeswax. A beautiful staircase sweeps up to the bedrooms, each of which has its name painted on the door: 'Mimosa', 'Coccinella', 'Ciclamine'... they are arresting rooms – big, uncluttered, individual – some with four-posters, one with a vast bath. Terracotta tiles contrast with pale walls and lovely fabrics, family antiques with elegant modern furniture or pieces that Maria Cristina and Roberto have collected on their travels. They're a charming and gentle young couple, proud of what they have created. The food is delicious and the new Turkish bath, sauna and jacuzzi are a treat.

Price	€110-€140.
Rooms	8: 3 doubles, 2 triples, 2 suites, 1 family room.
Meals	Half-board €80-€95 p.p.
Closed	Mid-December to mid-January.
Directions	Exit autostrada at Orte for Orte Town. After 3km, right for Amelia. Left for Penna in Teverina after 300m. After 2.5km, sign for La Chiocciola on left.

Roberto & Maria Cristina de Fonseca Pimentel
Seripola,
01028 Orte

Tel	+39 0761 402734
Fax	+39 0761 490254
Email	info@lachiocciola.net
Web	www.lachiocciola.net

Agriturismo Buonasera

Stefano is an ambassador for the region — endlessly enthusiastic and knowledgeable — and people love it here, surrounded by open meadows. The house, once a hunting lodge (antlers still hang above the stairs), has been attractively restored. Terracotta floors, beamed ceilings, stone and plaster walls give a warm, rustic simplicity; the bedrooms, not wildly exciting, are pleasant nonetheless, and spotless. There are also two ground-floor, open-plan, lofty apartments in the converted grain store — less characterful than the rooms in the house but immaculate and comfortable. This is a good place for families; the garden, surrounded by ten hectares of farmland, has swings and a slide, neat lawns, lavender and roses. The farm produces its own ricotta cheese, olive oil, honey and marmalade, and self-catering guests are welcome to help themselves from the vegetable garden. Regional dishes prepared from local produce are served under the arches of the restaurant, open to the public. This may not be prime tourist country but you are within easy reach of some real treasures. *Minimum stay one week in August.*

Price	€78-€88. Half-board extra €25 p.p. Apartments €600-€700 per week.
Rooms	5 + 2: 4 doubles, 1 double/triple. 2 apartments for 2-4.
Meals	Dinner, 5 courses, €25. Wine from €6.
Closed	Never.
Directions	A1 from Rome exit Orvieto, follow signs for Montefiascone. Signed from Bagnoregio.

	Stefano Augugliaro
	loc. Buonasera 18, 01022 Bagnoregio
Tel	+39 0761 792397
Fax	+39 0761 792397
Email	info@agribuonasera.com
Web	www.agribuonasera.com

Campania

Photo: istock.com

Masseria Giosole Agriturismo

A wonderful place for families. Sixty hectares of olives and fruit trees – help yourself! – a children's playground, a stunning pool, free bikes, tennis and a relaxed, no-rules atmosphere. Children scamper safely, parents flop around lazily... occasionally ambling off via the orchards to the river with just the birds for company. The di Maglianos, a handsome lively couple whose family have farmed here for three centuries, have created a place that reflects their gracious, easy-going nature. Rooms in the sprawling, peachy coloured *masseria* are large and airy with terracotta or wooden floors, high beamed ceilings and pale washed walls, and lightly sprinkled family antiques. Colourful textiles add dash. Bedrooms, some with a garden terrace, are uncluttered and restful, their bathrooms small but spotless. Nearby are ancient churches and palazzi in Capua, the Royal Palace at Caserta, and Naples and Pompeii are under an hour's drive. Come back to a delicious meal of local dishes – home-produced, naturally – dining around the fire in winter, in the garden in summer. *Minimum stay two nights.*

Price	€86-€98. Suite €110-€135. Apartments €90-€115.
Rooms	5 + 2: 3 doubles, 2 suites for 2-4. 1 apt for 2-4, 1 apt for 6-8.
Meals	Breakfast €8 for self-caterers. Dinner €25, by arrangement. Restaurants 2km.
Closed	Rarely.
Directions	A1 Rome-Naples exit Capua. Follow signs for Capua and Agriturismo Masseria Giosole for 7km. Pass San Giuseppe Church on right, after 500m turn right, on for 1.5km; signed.

Barone Alessandro e Baronessa Francesca
Pasca di Magliano
via Giardini 31, 81043 Capua

Tel	+39 0823 961108
Fax	+39 0823 627828
Email	info@masseriagiosole.com
Web	www.masseriagiosole.com

Azienda Agricola "Giravento" Agriturismo

Stay here and tread lightly on the planet. Sweet Serena is a passionate environmentalist
– but never sacrifices comfort. The new handsome pink farmhouse oozes character and
charm. Built to high environmental standards (local bricks, naturally treated wood
floors, old-fashioned terracotta tiles) on a site surrounded by olive groves and orchards
with views of the Taburno Camposauro regional park, the whole place is a paradise for
birds, wild flowers and animals. Bedrooms, with private entrances, are light, airy and
thoroughly natural: voile curtains, stripped floors, eco lighting, solid country furniture,
and jewel-like splashes from rugs and bed throws. Heaps of space and walk-in showers,
too. Flop around the pool or in the open-plan living area with those views across the
valley and a delicious wood-burner for winter. Share a meal around the table and
discover Serena's passion for cooking – and her delectable 'invention' *ciocannurca*, slices
of low-sugar apples dipped into bitter chocolate. Raise a glass and watch the magical
fireflies perform. *Minimum stay two nights.*

Price	€70.
Rooms	3: 2 doubles, 1 triple.
Meals	Brunch (summer only) €12.
	Dinner with wine €30, by arrangement.
Closed	Rarely.
Directions	Directions on booking.

Serena Bova
vicinale Castagneto 7,
82030 Melizzano

Mobile	+39 347 2708153
Email	info@giravento.it
Web	www.giravento.it

Azienda Mustilli Agriturismo

Since ancient times, Benevento and the surrounding area has been famous for its wines; here is a chance to stay on an estate steeped in the art of viticulture. The Mustilli Wine Company, run by Leonardo and Marilì Mustilli, is housed in a 16th-century palace, one wing of which has been restored and converted for guests' use. The azienda is right in the centre of a charming village, at the end of a maze of alleyways, on a piazza away from the restaurants and bars; you can easily explore the upper reaches of Campania from here. Traditional bedrooms up under the roof have tiled floors, antique beds, patterned wallpapers, perhaps a roof terrace; bathrooms are more modern. There's a wine bar in the cellar with music on Saturday nights, and the restaurant is huge and geared towards weddings. The dishes are Campanian, the wines are as good as you'd expect. If you're lucky you'll meet the family; naturally they know a lot about the history of the area and can arrange for you to take a tour of the vineyards – or of the historic town centre.

Price	€80. Half-board €65 p.p. Suite €140.
Rooms	5: 4 twins, 1 suite for 4.
Meals	Lunch & dinner (weekdays only) €25. Festive lunch €30.
Closed	Rarely.
Directions	Leave Rome-Napoli Autostrada at Caianello towards Beneveneto & S. Agata dei Goti. Azienda Mustilli signposted from *centro storico*.

Leonardo & Marilì Mustilli
Piazza Trento 4,
82019 S. Agata dei Goti

Tel	+39 0823 717433
Fax	+39 0823 717619
Email	info@mustilli.com
Web	www.mustilli.com

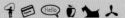

Il Cortile Agriturismo

Arriving here is a memorable moment. The black door in the suburban street opens onto a beautiful flagged courtyard rich in jasmine and oranges – ravishing in spring. The villa was built as a summer retreat for Arturo's forebears, and now includes two self-contained homes facing the courtyard with secluded entrances. Guests have their own sitting room/library filled with family antiques, comfortable sofas and pictures, and cool, spacious bedrooms, with pale washed walls, tiled floors and some good antiques; shower rooms are crisply white. Access to one bedroom is through the other, making this absolutely perfect for families with children. Dutch Sijtsken is charming and thoughtful, serves truly delicious food and brings you little vases of flowers from her and Arturo's lushly lovely garden. This *giardinello delle delizie* – a little garden of delights – is surprisingly large. Three tall date palms, two ancient magnolias, beds stuffed with calla lilies, hedges of glistening roses and camellia, paths that meander… choose a deckchair and dream. Special people, special place. *Minimum stay two nights.*

Price	€66-€70.
Rooms	2: 1 suite for 2-3, 1 suite for 4-5.
Meals	Dinner €25. Wine from €4.
Closed	Never.
Directions	From Rome or Naples: highway to Bari exit Nola. Follow signs to Cimitile & Cicciano. House 10-minute drive from highway.

Signori Arturo & Sijtsken Nucci
via Roma 43,
80033 Cicciano

Tel	+39 0818 248897
Mobile	+39 335 5614760
Fax	+39 0818 248897
Email	dupon@libero.it

Relais Castelcicala

Live like a prince in a country villa. This raspberry pink, 18th-century mansion was the neglected holiday home of the Princes of Castelcicala; now it has been restored, with care and passion, by Gherardo, architect son of the current Prince. In his family home – charming wife Barbara, three beautiful daughters – you will be swept up by a genuine warmth and a love of family history. Rooms are in the former stables, a comfortable mix of ancient and new: an antique washstand, a modern floor lamp, Indian bed throws and terracotta tiles, old beams and new exotica. Relaxed and inviting – expect Sicilian liqueurs, generous bathroom unguents – you could be staying as a family friend. Most rooms have sitting areas, one a private garden, and there's a salon – deep sofas, open fire – a sun terrace and a small curvy pool. Naples, Pompeii, Herculaneum are within 30 minutes; the lovely Amalfi coast is an easy day trip. Or soak up the villa's jasmine-scented gardens, orchards and olive groves. Dine at their lovely restaurant just up the hill – a locals' favourite. Perfect for pampering far from the crowds.

Price	€140–€170. Suites €175-€200.
Rooms	6: 2 doubles, 4 suites for 3-4.
Meals	Dinner €25. Wine €10.
Closed	Rarely.
Directions	A16 Napoli/Salerno exit Nola onto SS7bis dir. Avellino; then dir. Casamarciano, then to Nola. On for 2km, left after hospital into via Castelcicala; right after 200m; house on left.

Gherardo & Barbara Sallier de la Tour
via Cappuccini 1,
80035 Nola

Mobile	+39 348 6602787
Email	relais@castelcicala.com
Web	castelcicala.com

Megaron Rooms & Breakfast

In the fashionable-funky heart of Naples, a stylish, minimalist B&B. The crumbling frontage of the noble 1900 palazzo and sober internal-courtyard conceal a luxurious interior and the whole feel is one of silence, serenity and calm. A lift glides past the *piano nobile* up to the third floor where a smart 24-hour reception is revealed and large double doors open to large, light-filled bedrooms or suites – each a symphony in cream and black. Imagine muslin curtains at tall windows, big beds, deep sofas which convert into extra beds and antique tables and chairs. Bathrooms are exquisite in grey marble, with every little luxury. The suites have two bedrooms each and two bathrooms; one is on two levels linked by a fine walnut stairway. The breakfast room is similarly splendid. At your feet lies the enchantingly faded grandeur of one of Europe's liveliest cities; the bohemian Piazza Dante comes alive at night when the street musicians play and by day with its fantastic market. Find an outdoor table at the pizzeria of the same name and watch the literati drift by, drop into Cafe Mexico for the best coffee in town. Naples and the Megaron are a treat.

Price	€70–€150. Singles €70–€90.
Rooms	5: 4 twins/doubles, 1 suite.
Meals	Restaurants nearby.
Closed	Never.
Directions	A1 Rome-Naples; follow Tangenziale (ring road) exit Capo di Monte; follow 'centro' for Piazza Dante. On right after National Museum.

Adele Gentile
Piazza Dante 89,
80135 Naples

Tel	+39 0815 446109
Fax	+39 0815 644911
Email	bnb@megaron.na.it
Web	www.megaron.na.it

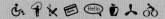

Parteno Bed & Breakfast

From the Neapolitan courtyard, steps lead to a glass and wrought-iron door and, with luck, Alessandro, who, with Italian charm, impeccable English, and a delightful English-speaking staff, settles you in with welcoming words and a cup of tea. The bedrooms, some with balcony, are named after flowers; from 'Petunia' to 'Orchid' they spell out 'Parteno'. The décor is charming: wrought-iron mirrors, tables, chairs, beds and chandeliers have been crafted by local artisan Mazzella, the gorgeous hand-painted bathroom tiles by an artist from Vietri sul Mare. The early 20th-century décor has been restored and the raftered ceilings will delight you: this feels more like a charming Italian home than a swish hotel. Modernity is revealed in air conditioning, small fridges and walk-in showers. The Parteno is in a lovely part of Naples, almost on the waterfront, near bustling cafés, restaurants and beautiful squares. Choose the room at the front: what a joy to eat breakfast looking out over the bay of Naples and the ferries heading for Sorrento, Capri and Ischia, or in the lovely breakfast room with equally delightful views.

Price	€125–€169. Singles €90–€110.
Rooms	6 + 6: 4 doubles, 2 triples. 6 apartments for 4.
Meals	Lunch or dinner from €20. Wine from €8.
Closed	Never.
Directions	A1 Rome-Naples; follow Tangenziale (ring road) exit Fuorigrotta for centre. Parteno 1st building right off Piazza Vittoria, across from sea.

Alex Ponzi
Lungomare Partenope 1,
80121 Naples

Tel	+39 0812 452095
Fax	+39 0812 471303
Email	bnb@parteno.it
Web	www.parteno.it

Palazzo San Teodoro - Riviera 281

Naples is vibrant and brimming with history; right at its heart, the luxurious Palazzo soothes and calms. Elegantly neoclassical yet warmly inviting – thanks to Elena and her team, who speak good English, are full of smiles – it has a peachy position in a smart residential area, five minutes from the palm tree-edged waterfront. Through an archway, a lift whisks you to the third floor and a vast apartment of parquet floors, white walls, sofas with silk cushions, huge windows, and rattan chairs on terraces with views to the waterfront and the rosy rooftops. Bedrooms, all with private terraces, are airy modernist spaces, a mix of antique and contemporary jazzed up with bold art and colourful fabrics. Bathrooms indulge in marble, glass and chrome. Breakfast on the terrace then plunge into the city's heady mix of museums, galleries, markets – most within walking distance. Elena, who lives below, is a joyful, generous Neapolitan, and will help with restaurants, theatres, sight-seeing. Return to a nightcap and the lights of Naples below you. Heaven to take the whole place.

Price	€140-€170.
	Whole apartment €3,150 per week.
Rooms	3: 2 doubles, 1 suite.
Meals	Restaurants nearby.
Closed	Rarely.
Directions	Directions on booking.

	Elena Basile
	via Riviera di Chiaia 281,
	80121 Naples
Tel/Fax	+39 0817 641427
Mobile	+39 337 566635
Email	info@riviera281.it
Web	www.riviera281.it

La Murena Bed & Breakfast

Views from your rooftop terrace stretch to chestnut forests and the Gulf of Naples below. Here, high on the slopes of Vesuvius, the peace is palpable and the air cool and pure. Giovanni and his son live on the ground floor of this modern house, while the guests have the option of self-catering or B&B: the three bedrooms and kitchen are upstairs, and you share Giovanni's living room (with a fascinating display of Giovanni's hand-carved jewellery) below. There's also a large outside area for children to romp in. Breakfast appears each evening in the fridge as if by magic: peaches, apricots and oranges from the garden, cheeses and homemade jams. The larger of the bedrooms has a fancy wrought-iron bed with a golden cover, writing desks are antique with marble tops and floor tiles are patterned blue. The kitchen, too, is prettily tiled, there's blue glassware in a sea-blue cupboard, a white-clothed table, no shortage of mod cons and a good sofa to curl up into. For lovers of archaeological sites the place is a dream: Herculaneum, Pompeii, Torre Annunziata, Boscoreale, Paestum. *Minimum stay three nights. Airport pickup.*

Price	B&B €80. Singles €60. Whole house (self-catering) €240 (€1,500 per week).
Rooms	3 doubles.
Meals	Restaurants nearby.
Closed	Rarely.
Directions	From autostrada Napoli-Pompei-Salerno exit Torre del Greco; follow signs for Il Vesuvio (via Osservatorio).

Signor Giovanni Scognamiglio
via Osservatorio 10,
80056 Herculaneum

Tel	+39 0817 79819
Mobile	+39 340 2352037
Fax	+39 0817 779819

Villa Giusso

This is where Napoleon's brother-in-law spent his last days before his exile from Naples; it has barely changed since. Once a monastery, the villa stands high on a promontory overlooking the Bay of Naples. There are several sitting rooms including a wonderful salon (wisely roped-off) full of collapsing 19th-century sofas and silk-covered chairs. Bedrooms have worn 17th-century furnishings and huge paintings; most overlook the ramshackle courtyard where friendly, well-behaved dogs roam; two, away from the main house, are in the old monks' quarters. You breakfast on figs (in season), fresh ricotta and homemade cakes in the vaulted kitchen, magnificent with fireplace and old Vetri tiles, at tables that seat at least 20. Giovanna has her hands full – she looks after the estate and two young children – but always finds time for guests, and gives fascinating tours of the property. Roam the garden or surrounding vineyards, drink in the views of the Sorrento coast. It's an adventure to be here and an adventure to arrive – bring a small car with plenty of ground clearance! *Minimum stay two nights.*

Price	€90-€130.
Rooms	7: 5 doubles, 1 suite for 4; 1 double with separate bathroom.
Meals	Dinner with wine €28. Restaurant closed Mondays.
Closed	November-Palm Sunday.
Directions	A3 Napoli-Salerno exit Castellammare di Stabia; signs for Sorrento. At Seiano, after Moon Valley Hotel, left for M. Faito; 4.6km, right after Arola sign, follow signs to Astapiana Villa Giusso.

Famiglia Giusso Rispoli
via Camaldoli 25, Astapiana, loc. Arola,
80069 Vico Equense

Tel	+39 0818 024392
Fax	+39 0818 790966
Email	astapiana@tin.it
Web	www.astapiana.com

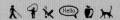

Agriturismo La Ginestra

There is a fresh, rustic feel to this farmhouse, and its position, 680m above sea level, is incredible. From the flower-rich terraces, sea views stretch in two directions: the Bay of Naples and the Bay of Salerno. The hills behind hold more delights, particularly for serious walkers: the 'Sentieri degli Dei' is a stone's throw away, and some of the paths, especially those down to Positano, are vertiginous and tough. The delightful owners do not speak English but will happily organise guided nature walks; they are also hugely proud of their organic farm status. Bedrooms and shower rooms are charming and mostly a good size, some with their own terrace. Some of the farm's produce – nuts, honey, vegetables, olive oil – is sold from a little cottage; it's also served in the stable restaurant, where delicious Sorrento dishes are served at check-clothed tables to contented Italians. Sunday lunch is a joyous affair. This is quite a tribute to La Ginestra as it is not the most easily accessible of places – but not so inaccessible that the local bus can't make it up the hill. Great value. *Minimum stay three nights.*

Price	Half-board €90. Triples €125. Family €165.
Rooms	8: 2 doubles, 3 triples, 3 family rooms.
Meals	Half-board or full-board only. Lunch or dinner €23. Wine €5.
Closed	Never.
Directions	A3 exit Castellammare di Stabia; SS145 coast road to Vico Equense; SS269 to Raffaele Bosco; at Moiano-Ticciano follow road to Santa Maria del Castello.

Mostardi
via Tessa 2, Santa Maria del Castello, 80060 Moiano di Vico Equense

Tel	+39 0818 023211
Fax	+39 0818 023211
Email	info@laginestra.org
Web	www.laginestra.org

Azienda Agricola Le Tore Agriturismo

Vittoria is a vibrant presence and knows almost every inch of this wonderful coastline – its paths, its hill-perched villages, its secret corners. She sells award-winning organic olive oil, vinegar, preserves, nuts and lemons on her terraced five hectares. The cocks crow at dawn, distant dogs bark in the early hours and fireflies glimmer at night in the lemon groves. It's rural, the sort of place where you want to get up while there's still dew on the vegetables. The names of the bedrooms reflect their conversion from old farm buildings – 'Stalla', 'Fienile', 'Balcone' – and are simply but solidly furnished. Excellent dinners are often served to guests together; breakfast is taken at your own table under the pergola, and may include raspberries, apple tart and fresh fruit juices. You must descend to coast level to buy your postcards, but this is a great spot from which to explore, and to walk – the CAI 'Alta via di Lattari' footpath is nearby. Le Tore is heaven to return to after a day's sightseeing, with views of the sea.

Price	€90.
	Apartment €700–€1,000 per week.
Rooms	6 + 1: 4 doubles, 1 twin, 1 family room for 4. 1 apartment for 5.
Meals	Dinner €20, by arrangement. Restaurant (serving Vittoria's organic produce) 5-min walk.
Closed	November–Palm Sunday.
Directions	A3 Naples-Palermo, exit Castellammare di Stabia for Positano. At x-roads for Positano, by restaurant Teresinella, sign for Sant'Agata; 7km, left on via Pontone; 1km.

Signora Vittoria Brancaccio
via Pontone 43, Sant'Agata sui due Golfi,
80064 Massa Lubrense

Tel	+39 0818 080637
Fax	+39 0815 330819
Email	info@letore.com
Web	www.letore.com

Villa Oriana Relais

Leave Sorrento's busy piazza below, enter through a pair of electronic gates, and breathe in the scent of jasmine, honeysuckle and lemons. This is a world away (yet a 15-minute walk) from Sorrento bustle. The sleek white villa – decked with terraces like a cruise ship – enfolds you in coolness and calm. And you are immediately drawn to the living room with its wide terrace and spectacular bay-of-Naples views; the main rooms – uncluttered spaces of white walls, terracotta floors, crisp furnishings – are above the bedrooms to make the most of them. Family warmth fills the place, thanks to Pasquale and his mother Maria – and what a way to start the day, breakfasting on Maria's homemade breads, jams, cakes and fruit juices. Bedrooms are equally cool and airy, furnished with a mixture of antique and modern; linen curtains and Murano chandeliers, a walnut writing table, a lacy bedcover. Marbled bathrooms are luxurious and pristine. Restaurants are an easy walk down, a steep climb up... reward yourself with a swirl in the rooftop jacuzzi-with-views on your return.

Price	€75–€210. Suite €90–€245.
Rooms	6: 4 twins/doubles, 1 suite for 2, 1 family room for 3-4.
Meals	Restaurants in Sorrento.
Closed	Never.
Directions	From Naples direction Sorrento; left before 1st Agip garage in via San Martino. Villa on right.

Famiglia d'Esposito
via Rubinacci 1,
80067 Sorrento

Tel	+39 0818 782468
Fax	+39 0815 324830
Email	info@villaoriana.it
Web	www.villaoriana.it

Albergo Punta Regina

Catch the sea breezes as you breakfast on the roof terrace, drink in the views. The superb, rocky coastline disappears into a distant, shimmering haze yet, just across the bay, you can pick out the enchanted islands of Li Galli. Beside you, flowers tumble over pergolas and out of pots. This typical, white-painted, late 19th-century building – just a short walk from the town centre and approached by steps – clings steeply to the hillside, with terraces and balconies on its upper three floors. Once a *pensione*, it has been transformed by a local family into a small hotel with big, lovely, spotless rooms and delightful staff. It is a quietly welcoming place, where guests can enjoy B&B, then go off to explore. Some rooms have pretty vaulted ceilings, others have beds set into arched recesses; marble shower rooms are attractive; many have glorious views. Immediately off the cool reception area are two big shower rooms, so guests who have checked out but spent the day on the beach below – 300 steps down! – can bathe before moving on. And if all those steps get to you, there's the trusty Positano shuttle.

Price	€195-€315. Singles €150-€240. Suite €345-€390.
Rooms	18: 16 doubles, 2 suites.
Meals	Restaurants nearby.
Closed	November-March.
Directions	Leave coast road 163, drive right down into Positano. Full directions on booking.

Benedetta Russo
via Pasitea 224,
84017 Positano

Tel	+39 0898 12020
Fax	+39 0898 123161
Email	info@puntaregina.com
Web	www.puntaregina.com

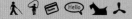

Casa Albertina

Positano is a honeycomb of houses clinging to the hillside between beach and high coast road – the famous 'Costiera Amalfitana'. Among the colourful façades you cannot miss the deep-red Casa Albertina. Mere minutes from the summer-thronged one-way road system, you climb to get here – or catch the bus to the top and walk down – leaving car and luggage in the able hands of the hotel staff. (There is a charge and you need to pre-book, or phone as you approach.) Here is the one-time refuge of the playwright Pirandello – a historic and unexpectedly peaceful *casa* with heavenly views. Air-conditioned bedrooms are comfortable and hotel-smart, many with terraces. No bar, no pool, but a wonderful roof deck and a stylish restaurant serving regional food, including the local *azzurro* (blue) fish. The wine list is pricey but long. Lorenzo, whose family owns the hotel, combines impeccable manners and relaxed charm with good English and his staff are delightful. A charming spot from which to visit Amalfi, Sorrento, Pompeii or Paestum. Or take the boat to popular Capri.

Price	€170–€230. Half-board €210–€290.
Rooms	20 twins/doubles.
Meals	Dinner €30–€45. Wine from €19.50.
Closed	Rarely.
Directions	From motorway, exit Castellammare di Stabia towards Sorrento & then Positano. Short walk from main street (call staff to pick up car & luggage).

Lorenzo Cinque
via della Tavolezza 3,
84017 Positano

Tel	+39 0898 75143
Fax	+39 0898 11540
Email	info@casalbertina.it
Web	www.casalbertina.it

Boccaccio B&B

No ordinary village house. Slip between the post office and the hardware store, climb the marble staircase, step into the bedrooms and your heart skips a beat. Spread 1,000 feet below, just across the road, is the dizzying curve of the Bay of Salerno. Vineyards, lemon groves, clusters of white houses, all cling to the steep valley sides in defiance of gravity; it's hard to pull yourself away from the window. Fortunately, all rooms share the view. This is a family affair and Bonaventura and his four children have refurbished the house (grandmother had these rooms; the family still live on the upper floor) in an understated modern style that has a welcoming simplicity: beech wood furniture, crisp bed linen, sleek lighting and sunny, hand-painted Vietri floor tiles. All have smart walk-in showers, one room has a private terrace. Two minutes from Ravello's picture-postcard piazza, and the Rufolo and Cimbrone gardens… what a position! Expect some tourist hubbub in season. Your host – who worked 35 years in the film industry – is warm, charming, easy-going. *Discounted parking: book ahead.*

Price	€75-€95.
Rooms	4 twins/doubles.
Meals	Restaurants nearby.
Closed	Rarely.
Directions	2-min walk from central pedestrian square of Ravello.

Signor Bonaventura Fraulo
G. Boccaccio 19,
84010 Ravello

Tel	+39 0898 57194
Fax	+39 0898 586279
Email	infoboccaccio@hotmail.com
Web	www.boccaccioravello.com

Villa en Rose

You really get a feel here of what life must have been like before roads and motorised transport came to these steep hillsides. The position is stunning, halfway between Minori and Ravello on a marked footpath which was once a mule trail. In fact, the only way to get here is on foot, with about 15 minutes' worth of steps down from the closest road. (Lugging your provisions up here could be a challenge in bad weather!). The open-plan apartment is modern-functional not aesthetic and the bedroom is in an alcove off the sitting room, but the views are wonderful and the house is set amid lemon groves. You are miles from the crowds clustering around the coast, and the pool means you don't have to venture down to the beach. The second, much smaller apartment is on the owner's floor above, and has no seating space as such. If you don't feel like cooking, the walk up to the main square in ravishing Ravello would certainly earn you a cappuccino and a brioche. And don't miss the glorious gardens of the Villas Rufolo and Cimbrone. *Minimum stay three nights. Air conditioning extra charge.*

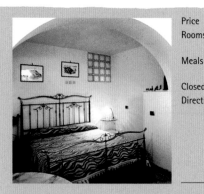

Price	From €104.
Rooms	2 apartments: 1 for 2-4 (+ sofabed), 1 for 2-3.
Meals	Breakfast €6. Restaurants in Ravello 1km.
Closed	Rarely.
Directions	Details on booking. Valeria will meet you in Ravello.

Signora Valeria Civale
via Torretta a Marmorata 22,
84010 Ravello

Tel   +39 0898 57661
Mobile   +39 333 8779628
Email   valeriacivale@yahoo.it

Hotel Villa San Michele

Stone steps tumble down – past lemon trees, palms, geraniums, bright bougainvillea, scented jasmine – to the rocks below, and a dip in the deep blue sea. It is a treat to stay in this small, intimate, family-run hotel, with its smiley staff and dreamy views. The gardens and bedrooms are terraced, and the dining room and reception are at the top – light, airy, cool. Almost everyone gets a balcony or terrace, everyone gets a view, and at night you are lulled to sleep by the lapping of the sea. Floors are cool and pale-tiled, some in classic Amalfi style, some white; beds have patterned bedspreads, colours are peaceful, shower rooms are clean. It is all charming and unpretentious, from the white plastic tables to the blue stripy deckchairs from which you can gaze on the sea and watch the ferries slip by, heading for Positano or Capri. Delectable aromas waft from a cheerful kitchen where Signora is chef; the menu is short, the dishes local Atrani and Amalfi are walkable, though traffic is heavy in summer; for the weary, a bus stops in front of the hotel. *Use of pool at Villa Scapariello.*

Price	€100-€190.
Rooms	12 doubles.
Meals	Dinner €28. Wine from €15. June-Sept half-board only.
Closed	7 November-25 December; 7 January-14 February.
Directions	A3 to Salerno exit Vietri sul Mare; follow signs to Amalfi; hotel 1km before Amalfi on left. Discuss parking on booking.

Nicola Dipino
SS 163 Costiera Amalfitana,
84010 Castiglione di Ravello
Tel +39 0898 72237
Fax +39 0898 72237
Email smichele@starnet.it
Web www.hotel-villasanmichele.it

Azienda Agrituristica Seliano

Just a mile from Seliano, the agriturismo has been in the family for 200 years and is now home to the warm-hearted, dog-loving Baroness Cecilia Baratta. She and her sons keep a 900-strong buffalo herd in the *masseria*, the milk from which makes fine butter and mozzarella. The four bedrooms in the old stone barn and pigeon loft are furnished in laid-back country style, and there are more rooms in the converted stables, cowshed and the tower. It gets pretty busy at times! You eat with other guests – authentically, generously – at a long table in the dining room or under the pergola in the scented gardens. There's also a sitting room to share, furnished with sofas and country pieces. When he has a spare moment, Ettore is happy to give farm tours; children love seeing the buffalo up to their necks in their pools of black mud. The beach is only a bike or horse ride away (experienced equestrians only), and there's a lovely pool at the main house; an easy retreat after a day's sightseeing at the Greek temples at nearby Paestum. *Minimum stay two nights.*

Price	€75–€120.
Rooms	15 doubles.
Meals	Dinner with wine, €20.
Closed	Mid-January to mid-February.
Directions	From A3 to Battipaglia, right onto SS18 to Cappacioscalo (20km). Signs to Seliano on right.

Baroness Cecilia Bellelli Baratta
via Seliano,
84063 Paestum

Tel	+39 0828 724544
Fax	+39 0828 723634
Email	seliano@agriturismoseliano.it
Web	www.agriturismoseliano.it

Villa Giacaranda

Listen to the gentle rustle of the jacaranda and olive trees as you relax in the vast terraced gardens. The trees were brought by Luisa from Africa and planted here. Having eaten lightly in the day, dine classically on the Franco-Italian cuisine at night. The adorable Luisa loves people as much as she loves food and every year visits Paris to brush up her gastronomic skills. Her 19th-century farmhouse is deeply traditional yet is in part being transformed. Four beautiful, contemporary bedrooms are being created, all grey slate floors, primary colours, internet connections and stunning showers. The existing bedrooms are traditional and more modest, but still have hand-embroidered sheets and their own terraces. The lovely light dining room is a fitting background for the food, and guests of different nationalities are encouraged to mingle – but only if they wish. The next day Luisa delights in showing you how you could recreate the previous evening's dishes. No rush? Wander down to the beach just a kilometre away – and return to Debussy and a deep cream sofa.

Price	€120.
Rooms	6 doubles.
Meals	Dinner, 5 courses, €40.
Closed	Rarely.
Directions	From St Marco di Castellabate follow signs for Hotel Hermitage. At hotel, left up hill; left track; Villa at end.

Luisa Cavaliere
Cenito,
84071 San Marco di Castellabate
Tel   +39 0974 966130
Fax   +39 0974 966800
Email   giaca@costacilento.it
Web   www.giacaranda.it

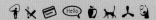

Campania

B&B

La Mola

You'll catch your breath at the views as you step onto your balcony. La Mola is perched high up in the old town, way above the tourists who congregate down the hill in Santa Maria. It is a grand old 17th-century palace and incorporates a 12th-century tower – an interesting building in its own right. The balconies are superb and wrap around the house; the terraced garden is lovely; the restaurant a joy. The huge round stone olive press found in the cellars during restoration gives the hotel its name; now it forms the base of a vast, glass-topped drinks table. The sea is everywhere – your room looks onto it, as do the communal sitting areas, and the terrace where you take summer meals. Furnishings are pristine, bedrooms have tiled floors, wrought-iron bedsteads with embroidered linen and the odd antique, bathrooms are charming. La Mola is the ancestral home of Signor Favilla, who spends every summer here with his wife, running the B&B with admirable and amiable efficiency. Away from the seafront resorts the countryside up here is lovely, and Paestum, Agropoli and Velia are a short drive away.

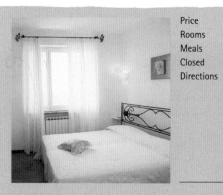

Price	€114–€124. Singles €80.
Rooms	5 doubles.
Meals	Dinner with wine, €40.
Closed	November-March.
Directions	From Naples A30 south to Battipaglia, then Agropoli-Castellabate. La Mola is in *centro storico*.

Francesco & Loredana Favilla
via Adolfo Cilento 2,
84048 Castellabate

Tel	+39 0974 967053
Fax	+39 0974 967714
Email	lamola@lamola-it.com
Web	www.lamola-it.com

Entry 318 Map 14

Calabria • Basilicata • Puglia

Photo: istock.com

La Bouganville

You could spend weeks here, there's so much to do – snorkelling, sailing, swimming in caves. And to see: the town of Praia, the grottos of Dino Island, the Tower of Fiuzzi, waterparks and beaches. Softly-spoken Giovanni will meet you and settle you in; he and his son live in Herculaneum (see La Murena Bed & Breakfast) and in August this is their holiday home. On its peaceful residential street you can barely see the house for the flowers and the trees; the garden was established 25 years ago when the house was built. The garden, enclosed and perfect for little ones, is full of scents and shade; a gardener comes several mornings a week and from the terrace is a fantastic view of tiny Dino Island. Inside, rooms are simple and comfortable: cheerful checked bedcovers on plain wooden beds, a gleaming white bathroom and a shower, a well-equipped kitchen and a brightly tiled sitting/dining room with a sofabed, a pine table and chairs and a hearth for winter. You can walk to the resort of Praia a Mare and the beaches are special, with crystal clear water and fine sands. Excellent for families. *Minimum stay one week.*

Price	€750-€850 per week. €450-€600 for 2 per week.
Rooms	1 apartment for 4-5.
Meals	Restaurants nearby.
Closed	August.
Directions	Autostrada Napoli-Salerno exit Lagonegro Nord; continue for Praia a Mare. Ask owner for precise directions.

Signor Giovanni Scognamiglio
Parco Bouganville,
87028 Praia a Mare

Tel   +39 0817 79819
Fax   +39 0817 779819

Il Giardino di Iti Agriturismo

The farm, peaceful, remote and five minutes from the Ionian sea, has been in the family for three centuries. A massive arched doorway leads to a courtyard and vast enclosed garden (rabbits for the children, pigs, goats and cats too). Meals are served here in summer; at night, the lemon and orange trees glow from little lights tucked into their branches. The large, cool bedrooms have been simply and prettily decorated. Ask for one that opens directly off the courtyard, its big old fireplace (lit in winter) and brick-paved floors intact. Each room has a wall painting of one of the farm's crops, and is correspondingly named: 'Lemon', 'Peach', 'Sunflower', 'Grape'. The bathrooms are old-fashioned but charming, the apartment kitchens basic. Courses are held here on regional cooking; weaving, too. If neither appeals, revel in the atmosphere and the gastronomic delights of the restaurant and atone for the calories later. There's a host of activities on offer in the area, and, of course, heaps of history. Signora is gentle and charming. You'll be sad to leave.

Price	Half-board €40-€55 p.p. Full-board €50-65 p.p.
Rooms	12 + 2: 10 family rooms; 2 doubles sharing bath. 2 apartments for 3-4.
Meals	Half-board or full-board only. Wine from €18. Limited self-catering in aparments.
Closed	Never.
Directions	A3 Salerno-Reggio Calabria exit Sibari. Rossano road (SS106) to contrada Amica, then towards Paludi.

Baronessa Francesca Cherubini
contrada Amica, 8
7068 Rossano

Tel/Fax	+39 0983 64508
Mobile	+39 360 237271
Email	info@giardinoiti.it
Web	www.giardinoiti.it

San Teodoro Nuovo Agriturismo

A haven in a green sea of citrus and olive groves. Bougainvillea disguises the lower half of the delightful Marchesa's old rose-tinted mansion; shutters peep from above. Rent an apartment furnished with family antiques in a wing of the house, or choose one of four beautifully converted ones a short stroll away – in the old stables where the restaurant is housed. All rooms are large and light, some with marvellous vaulted ceilings, and elegantly and charmingly furnished; they even have small parterre gardens. A whitewashed chapel alongside adds a Mexican feel, and there's a fine pool. You will appreciate the range of Basilicata cuisine here; breakfasts and dinners – candlelit, atmospheric – are excellent, the vegetarian choices are superb and you'll probably want to book into a cookery class after sampling the food. Follow the routes taken by 18th-century travellers, visit workshops devoted to reproducing classical antiques. You are five minutes from the Ionian Sea and white sands, golf courses are nearby, archaeological sites abound. *Minimum stay two nights. Ask about cookery courses.*

Price	€120–€140 (€840–€980 per week). Half-board €80–€90 p.p.
Rooms	9 apartments for 2, 4 or 6.
Meals	Dinner €25–€30, by arrangement.
Closed	Never.
Directions	Directions on booking.

Marchesa Maria Xenia D'Oria
loc. Marconia,
75020 Marconia di Pisticci

Tel/Fax	+39 0835 470042
Mobile	+39 338 5698116
Email	info@santeodoronuovo.com
Web	www.santeodoronuovo.com

Forestaria Illicini

Come for the views of the tiny islands of Matrela and Santojanni, the caves and rocky coves, the water lapping at the beach… This bewitching place could be a setting for *The Tempest*. Gugliemo's father bought the whole spectacular promontory and surrounding park of olive trees, holm oaks and myrtles 50 years ago. They spent every family holiday here. Now Gugliemo, a gentle architect, and his wife Diane have turned it into a deliciously unmanicured B&B. Foreigners have not discovered the area yet, so, outside the Italian holiday months, park, beach and pool are blissfully quiet. A buffet-style breakfast is served in a little breakfast room overlooking the sea, and at the height of the season there's a restaurant that serves local dishes. The bedrooms, two with terraces, are housed in little cottages just a few yards back from the shoreline, neatly and simply furnished, with comfortable beds and a faintly colonial air, and small spotless bathrooms bright and inviting. The sea views are, of course, extraordinary. Good value.

Price	€80–€130.
Rooms	11: 8 doubles, 2 family rooms for 3-4, 1 single.
Meals	Dinner €30 (July only). Wine from €11. Half-board €190 (August only)
Closed	Mid-October to mid-May.
Directions	Directions on booking.

Gugliemo & Diane Rivetti
loc. Illici,
85046 Maratea
Tel +39 0973 879028
Fax +39 0685 42914
Email staff@illicini.it
Web www.illicini.it

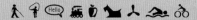

Villa Cheta Elite

Villa Cheta Elite is a godsend in an area with few really nice hotels. It's a gracious Art
Nouveau Villa a twisty drive up from the coast road, with a terraced garden of winding
paths, tropical trees, scented plants and views that keep you rooted to the spot. Relax in
the shade of the gardens, or cross the road and plunge down 165 steps for a swim in the
clear green waters below. (Then trek up again!). Bedrooms are classic Italian: antiques
and fine fabrics, marble floors, large windows and plenty of light, the loveliest with a
view of the sea. The public rooms, with ornate cornices and mouldings, are exquisitely
furnished with good paintings and a number of portraits of previous occupants. There's
also a small sitting room, and a library where you can bone up on the history of the
region. The restaurant is fabulous: delicious food served beneath Murano glass
chandeliers on embroidered linen. In summer you dine on the terrace with views of the
sea and the moon. It's an undeniably romantic spot; you may even hear nightingales sing.
Stefania and Piero are delightful hosts, their staff courteous and kind.

Price	€136-€280. Half-board €188-€364.
Rooms	20 doubles.
Meals	Lunch or dinner, €35-€45. Wine €18.
Closed	November-Palm Sunday.
Directions	From A3 exit Lagonegro-Maratea; 10km, SS104 right to Sapri. In Sapri left onto coast road for Maratea. Villa 9km along coast, above road on left.

Signora Stefania Aquadro
via Nazionale,
85041 Acquafredda di Maratea
Tel   +39 0973 878134
Fax   +39 0973 878135
Email info@villacheta.it
Web   www.villacheta.it

La Chiusa delle More

The Italians flock here in August. Out of season, the lovely beaches and fresh-fish restaurants are wonderfully uncrowded; on the seafront, you can watch the fishermen sort their catch. Foreign tourists have not yet discovered Peschici, so come out of season. Francesco and Antonella's 16th-century farmhouse is 500 metres from the sea: park under an ancient olive tree and climb up to the reception terrace from where you can drink in the views. Nearby, on another terrace, teak loungers flank a sparkling pool, and the air is scented with citrus. The B&B rooms, in a small block to one side, are light, cool and simply furnished, with small but good shower rooms. Francesco and Antonella, a delightful pair, vibrant and full of fun, have five hectares of olive groves and a big kitchen garden. The olive oil and vegetables supply their restaurant and the food is divine – hard not to love the typically Puglian dishes and the local wines. Breakfast on the terrace is a treat too, a wonderful start to a day discovering the splendours of the Gargano National Park.

Price	€160–€200.
Rooms	10: 8 doubles, 2 family rooms for 4.
Meals	Dinner €30. Wine €5–€50.
Closed	October–April.
Directions	1.5km from Peschici; signed from Peschici.

Francesco & Antonella Martucci
loc. Padula,
71010 Peschici

Mobile	+39 330 543766
Fax	+39 0884 964926
Email	lachiusadellemore@libero.it
Web	www.lachiusadellemore.it

Lama di luna - Biomasseria Agriturismo

The sister of Pietro's great-grandmother lived here until 1820; Pietro bought the farm in 1990, then discovered the family connection. It was "meant to be". Lama di Luna is the most integrated organic farm in Italy: 200 hectares of olives and wines, 40 solar panels for heat and hot water, beds facing north, feng shui-style. Petro, who lives here with his family, is young, lively, charming, passionate about the environment and this supremely serene place. The farm goes back 300 years and wraps its dazzling white self around a vast courtyard with a central bread oven, its 40 chimney pots "telling the story" of the many farm workers that once lived here. Each bedroom, complete with fireplace and small window, once housed an entire family. Pietro searched high and low for the beds, the natural latex mattresses, the reclaimed wood for the doors. There's a library for reading and a veranda for sunsets and stars, and views that reach over flat farmland as far as the eye can see. Breakfast here on homemade cakes and jams, orchard fruits, local cheeses. Remote, relaxing, memorable. *Pool planned for 2008.*

This is one of the 'greenest' places we have seen, presided over by the delightful Pietro Petroni. The three-year restoration was meticulous in its respect for history and natural materials: limewashed walls, stone floors, traditional tiles, linseed-stained wood, organic bed linen, naturally dyed hessian, olive soaps, no bleaches, no chemicals, not a hard edge in sight, just natural shapes and people living in harmony with nature. Rainwater is harvested in an eight metre-deep tank and the olives, cherries, almonds and vines are organically grown. It is a privilege to stay.

Price	€140-€200.
Rooms	10 twins/doubles.
Meals	Dinner with wine, €25. Restaurants 2km.
Closed	January-March.
Directions	A14 exit Canosa; Canosa-Andria, turn off for Montegrosso. After Montegorsso, 3.5km dir. Minervino. On left.

Pietro Petroni
loc. Montegrosso, 70031 Andria,

Tel	+39 0883 569505
Fax	+39 0883 569505
Email	info@lamadiluna.com
Web	www.lamadiluna.com

SPECIAL GREEN ENTRY
see page 14

Map 15 Entry 325

Masseria Serra dell'Isola

Spirits may fall as you lose your way down tiny lanes in a featureless landscape… no matter. Rita's smile as she scoops you up to guide you home brings instant cheer. Step over the threshold of the somewhat gaunt white *masseria* and you'll feel even better. The great hall with its uneven stone floor was once part of an olive mill (see where the presses used to stand) and, like the rest of the house, is filled with portraits and antiques with stories to tell. The light, gracious bedrooms are named after the women who once occupied them – Donnas Angelina, Ritella, Annina – and the elegant old beds bear new mattresses. The house has been in the family since 1726 and Rita is passionately proud of her heritage. You're welcome to browse through her impressive library of history books; she'll also gladly tell you about less well-known local places to visit. She organises courses, too, in art, antiques, restoration, cookery; dine by candlelight and you'll sample ancient family recipes and liqueurs from the time the Bourbons reigned in southern Italy. Unusual and authentic. *Minimum stay two nights.*

Price	€130. Whole house €3,300–€3,900 per week.
Rooms	6: 4 doubles, 2 twins/doubles.
Meals	Dinner, 3 courses, 35–€40. Wine €12–€18.
Closed	Rarely.
Directions	SS16 Bari-Brindisi exit Mola-Rutigliano, dir. Mola. When you reach bridge call Rita to come & guide you.

Rita Guastamacchia
S.P.165 Mola, Conversano n.35,
70042 Mola di Bari

Mobile	+39 349 5311256
Email	info@masseriaserradellisola.it
Web	www.masseriaserradellisola.it

B&B Masseria Piccola

Who could fail to be enchanted by the round walls, the conical roofs, the charming little rooms? These *trulli* were built a century ago by Nicola's great-grandfather; now they have been converted into one delightful, good value, B&B. You are on a quiet side street in Casalini di Cisternino, with a terrace in front of you and a patch of garden behind. A wicker sofa and chairs in the entrance hall invite you in. Snug, spotless bedrooms have pale walls and stone arches and are furnished with country antiques; beds are very comfortable, shower rooms are well-equipped and breakfast is at the big table in the kitchen or out under the flowers on the terrace. Nicola, shy, young, charming, looks after his guests well and you have a half-board option of a fixed-price dinner at a restaurant a ten-minute walk away... La Terrazza del Quadrifoglio has a great terrace, an authentic atmosphere and is popular with the locals (most of them Nicola's relatives!). The town is nothing special but Cisternino, with its lively weekly market, is well worth the visit.

Price	€80. Half-board extra €20 p.p. Wine from €8.
Rooms	4: 3 doubles, 1 single.
Meals	Half-board only. Restaurant 1km.
Closed	Rarely.
Directions	A14 Bari-Lecce exit Cisternino-Ostuni, then SP7 & SP9.

Nicola Fanelli
via Masseria Piccola 56,
72014 Casalini di Cisternino

Tel	+39 0804 449668
Mobile	+39 393 9796727
Email	info@masseriapiccola.it
Web	www.masseriapiccola.it

Villa Santoro

John and Gill fell for the views, the olive and almond trees, the figs, apricots, pomegranates and pears. The crumbling pile of stones they inherited were by the by – but all were reclaimed in the end. Limestone is from Fasano, the wood is Italian oak, the outdoor dining slab is Trani marble, the seating is the palest cream leather. The combination of an Austrian designer and a Milanese architect has ensured that the restoration of the Villa Santoro is, quite simply, exquisite. Local craftsmen have created chunky tables, stone benches, rustic arches; a bedroom in one *trullo* cone, a sunken bath in another, a fireplace opening onto both the sitting room and the kitchen... a design magazine's dream, yet the villa is a relaxing and much-loved family home. There's a lake-like pool for high summer and a steady gentle breeze, but this would be special all year round. Weekly markets in every ancient town, shops that range from the artisan to the chic, a modest supermarket on the way here and delightful Christine, the gardienne, who lives 15 minutes away. *Perfetto. Minimum stay one week. Cook available.*

Price	£1,950-£4,250 per week.
Rooms	House for 8-10 (1 double, 2 twins, sofabed; 1 independent double).
Meals	Self-catering. Restaurants 5-8km.
Closed	Rarely.
Directions	Directions on booking.

John Dabney
cd. Santoro 26,
72017 Ostuni

Tel	+44 (0)208 8065130
Mobile	+44 (0)7974 430586
Email	john@villapuglia.com
Web	www.villapuglia.com

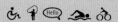

Masseria Il Frantoio Agriturismo

So many ravishing things! An old, white house clear-cut against a blue sky, mysterious gardens, the scent of jasmine and private beaches five kilometres away. Armando and Rosalba spent a year restoring this 17th-century house (built over a sixth-century oil press) after abandoning city life. Inside – sheer delight. A series of beautiful rooms, ranging from fairytale (a froth of lace and toile) to endearingly simple (madras bedcovers and old desks) to formal (antique armoires and doughty gilt frames)… a gloriously eclectic mix. Dinner is equally marvellous – put your name down. Rosalba specialises in Puglian dishes accompanied by good local wines; Armando rings the courtyard bell at 8.30 and the feast begins, either in the arched dining room or outside in the candlelit courtyard. It will stay in your memory – as will other details: an exterior white stone stairway climbing to a bedroom, an arched doorway swathed in wisteria. Armando is deeply passionate about his totally organic *masseria*, surrounded by olive groves and with a view of the sea; Silvana is on hand ensuring you bask in comfort. *Minimum stay two nights.*

Price	€176-€220. Child €54-€64. Apartment €319-€350.
Rooms	8 + 1: 3 doubles, 2 triples, 3 family rooms. Apartment for 2-4.
Meals	Dinner with wine, €55, by arrangement. Cold supper, €31.
Closed	Never.
Directions	From Bari airport superstrada E55 exit for Pezze di Greco towards Ostuni. On SS16, watch for Ostuni until km sign 874. Right into drive.

	Silvana Caramia
	SS 16km 874,
	72017 Ostuni
Tel	+39 0831 330276
Fax	+39 0831 330276
Email	prenota@masseriailfrantoio.it
Web	www.masseriailfrantoio.it

Palazzo Bacile di Castiglione

The palazzo's 16th-century walls dominate Spongano's Piazza Bacile; behind is a secret oasis. The charming *barone* and his English wife offer you a choice of apartments for couples or families, and B&B for groups; the history is interesting, the comforts seductive. On the first floor, a series of large terraces and four bedrooms open off a vaulted baronial hall – beige check sofas, an open fire (replete with home-grown cones and logs), a grand piano. Expect choice fabrics and new four-posters, pink, yellow or marble bathrooms, wardrobes dwarfed by lofty ceilings, kitchens for cooks. The outbuildings at the end of the long garden are similarly swish: olive wood tables, big lamps, framed engravings, books and CDs; kitchens reveal the owners' passion. (They are also keen greens, saving energy, going solar and composting madly.) The garden is lovely, all orange trees and wisteria, secluded walkways and corners, old pillars and impressive pool; at twilight, scops owls chime like bells. Beyond lie the baroque splendours of Lecce, Gallipoli and Otranto – and the coast. Borrow the bikes! *Minimum stay four nights.*

Price	€700–€2,464 per week.
Rooms	7 apartments: 2 for 2, 3 for 4, 1 for 6, 1 for 8.
Meals	Restaurant 500m.
Closed	Never.
Directions	From Lecce N16, exit Nociglia (after Maglie); to Surano, then Spongano; cross railway into centre; on Piazza Bacile, entrance to left of Farmacia. Please call Giuseppe +39 3476524477 if lost.

	Sarah & Alessandro Bacile di Castiglione 73038 Spongano
Tel	+39 0832 351131
Fax	+39 0836 940363
Email	albadica@hotmail.com
Web	www.palazzobacile.it

La Macchiola Agriturismo

The palazzo's courtyard walls drip with creepers and geraniums; in front, across a little road, is a verdant citrus grove worth resting in. This *azienda agricola*, dating from the 17th century, is devoted to the production of organic olive oil (massages available) and Anna's family turn out some of Puglia's finest. Through the massive gates the narrow and unremarkable streets of Spongano village are left behind and you enter, via a Moorish arched portico, a white-gravelled, white-walled courtyard dotted with elegant wrought-iron tables and chairs. Off the creeper-clad inner courtyard, ground-floor apartments have been carefully converted into a series of airy and beautifully furnished rooms. Walls are colourwashed warm yellow and soft blue, sleeping areas are separated by fabric screens, ceilings are lofty and stone vaulted. One apartment for two has a 'dining room' squeezed into an ancient fireplace, bathrooms have pretty mosaic mirrors and most of the kitchenettes are tiny. *Marmellata* and cakes for breakfast, a vast roof terrace, beaches a short drive. *Minimum stay three nights.*

Price	€70-€100. Apartments €570-€1,500 per week.	
Rooms	4 + 3: 2 doubles, 2 family rooms for 4. 3 apartments for 2, 4 or 6.	
Meals	Restaurants 300m.	
Closed	5 November-22 December; 9 January-16 March.	
Directions	Directions on booking.	

	Anna Addario-Chieco via Congregazione 53/57, 73038 Spongano
Tel	+39 0836 945023
Fax	+39 0832 246255
Email	lamacchiola@libero.it
Web	www.lamacchiola.it

Masseria Varano

Wines and olive oils from the estate, local breads, pasta and cheeses – the generous welcome sets the tone for your stay. Victoria and Giuseppe, an Anglo-Italian couple, combine the best of English and Italian hospitality – gentle, warm, easy – reflected in their handsome creamy stone and green-shuttered *masseria*. The apartments, each with private entrance and terrace, are in the main house and two cottages. Elegant and airy, with creamy tiled floors, white walls and handsome chestnut fittings, rooms are decorated with modern furniture and old family pieces. Dotted with family photographs, Victoria's paintings, pretty fabrics and objects collected from travels, there's a gentle country-house feel, a home from home; the best wows you with a fleet of French windows and a vast terrace. Kitchens are light and modern, equipped to please the serious cook. Masses to do: beaches, Gallipoli, the harbours of Tricase and Santa Maria di Leuca… or just make the most of the pretty walled gardens and the pool. The owners are happy to leave you alone or have a chat over a glass of wine.

Price	€350–€1,300 per week.
Rooms	4 apartments: 1 for 2, 3 for 2-4.
Meals	Restaurant 4km.
Closed	November-Easter.
Directions	M'way Brindisi-Lecce, take Tangenziale (ring road) west of Lecce, exit 13 dir. Gallipoli; exit Ugento-Taurisano. After 3km, left onto via Trappeto di Varano.

Giuseppe & Victoria
Lopez y Royo di Taurisano
contrada Varano, 73056 Taurisano

Tel/Fax	+39 0833 623216
Mobile	+39 348 5151391
Email	lopezyroyo@hotmail.com
Web	www.masseriainsalento.com

Sicily • Sardinia

Photo: istock.com

Hotel Quartara

You arrive by boat; waves glitter in the sun, white houses dazzle on the shore. The exterior of this beautiful hotel may be typically Aeolian but bedrooms are eclectic: Melanesian, Chinese and Indonesian hand-crafted furniture, Sicilian crocheted bedspreads and tiled floors. Four overlook the sea. Bathrooms have soft lighting and a generous supply of lotions and potions, and every room has a terrace. The solarium is a family-popular retreat, thanks to wide terraces equipped with teak loungers, cool shade, endless sea views and pool. Out of season will be quieter – though too quiet for some. Breakfast on figs, pears, honey, prosciutto, yogurt; dine on risotto with prawns and saffron. The restaurant has arched ceilings, crisp white linen decorated with special seashells, art on the walls. This is a laid-back family affair: Signor Capelli's garden supplies fragrant basil, lemons and glossy aubergines, attentive Maria and her sisters are usually around and the children stop by to say hello. The lovely isle of Panarea, a refuge for the rich and famous, has three villages and golf carts for cars. *Minimum stay two nights.*

Price	€180–€420.
Rooms	13: 10 doubles, 2 singles, 1 triple.
Meals	Dinner €30–€40. Wine from €18.
Closed	November–March.
Directions	Arrange pick-up from port of Panarea. By electric shuttle, or on foot; from port, right onto via S. Pietro. Hotel 200m up lane.

Maria Pia Cappelli
via San Pietro 15,
98050 Panarea, Aeolian Islands

Tel	+39 0909 83027
Fax	+39 0909 83621
Email	info@quartarahotel.com
Web	www.quartarahotel.com

Hotel Signum

Leave the car and Sicily behind. Salina may not be as famous as some of her glamorous Aeolian neighbours (though *Il Postino* was filmed here) but is all the more peaceful for that. The friendly, unassuming hotel sits so quietly at the end of a narrow lane you'd hardly guess it was there. Dine on a shaded terracotta terrace with chunky tile-topped tables, colourful iron and wicker chairs; gaze out over lemon trees to the glistening sea. Traditional dishes and local ingredients are the norm. Then wind along the labyrinth of paths, where plants flow and tumble, to a simple and striking bedroom: cool pale walls, pretty antiques, a wrought-iron bed, good linen; starched lace flutters at the windows. The island architecture is typically low and unobtrusive and Clara and Michele (Luca's parents) have let the hotel grow organically as they've bought and converted farm buildings. The result is a beautiful, relaxing space where, even at busy times, you feel as if you are one of a handful of guests. Snooze on a shady veranda, take a dip in the infinity pool – that view again – or clamber down the path to a quiet pebbly cove.

Price	€110–€340.
Rooms	30: 28 doubles, 2 singles.
Meals	Dinner à la carte, €30–€40. Wine from €15.
Closed	December-February.
Directions	By boat or hydrofoil from Naples, Palermo, Messina & Reggio Calabria. If you want to leave your car, there are garages in Milazzo.

Luca Caruso
via Scalo 15, Malfa,
98050 Salina, Aeolian Islands

Tel   +39 0909 844222
Fax   +39 0909 844102
Email   salina@hotelsignum.it
Web   www.hotelsignum.it

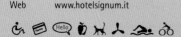

Entry 334 Map 18

Green Manors

Your hosts spotted the remote and dilapidated 1600s manor house years ago; it has been gloriously revived. Bedrooms, some with terraces, are rustic-refined: rich colours, tiled floors, heavy curtains, Sicilian patchwork, laced linen, family antiques, flowers… tapestries and paintings are illuminated by chandeliers, tapered candles stand in silver candelabra. Bathrooms come with huge baths or showers, delicately scented homemade soaps and waffle towels. Chris, Paolo and Pierangela have also been busy establishing their bio-dynamic orchard and you reap the rewards at breakfast, alongside silver cutlery, antique napkins and linen. The homemade jams are divine – cherry, apricot, ginger; the juices are freshly squeezed. Languid dinners are delicious and served outside behind a curtain of shimmering plants, or by the huge fireplace when the weather is cooler. There are two charming wooden cabins in the olive groves, with outside kitchens and bathrooms; a lush tropical park with peacocks and ponies; occasional summer concerts beneath the mulberry tree. Exceptional. *Minimum stay two nights.*

Price	€100–€180. Cabins €80–€120 (summer only).
Rooms	10 + 2: 5 doubles, 3 suites, 2 singles. 2 cabins for 2.
Meals	Dinner €35. Wine €10–€60. Restaurants 1km.
Closed	Rarely; Cabins available summer only.
Directions	Messina-Palermo, exit Barcellona dir. SS113 Palermo; immed. before Terme bridge, sharp left. Signed.

Pierangela & Paolo Janelli Verzera
& Chris Janelli Christiaens
Borgo Porticato, 98053 Castroreale

Tel	+39 0909 746515
Fax	+39 0909 746507
Email	info@greenmanors.it
Web	www.greenmanors.it

Hotel Villa Belvedere

It is perfectly named – stunning views sweep down over the botanical gardens to the azure sea below. Each front room has a balcony or bougainvillea-draped terrace; tantalizing glimpses of the sea can be caught from every angle. The five rooms on the first floor have beautiful big private terraces (no. 25 is particularly lovely, with arched windows and alcoves), those on the second have pretty little French balconies, and the bright-white 'attic' rooms on the top floor are delightful, with smaller terraces. The family rooms are at the back with views to the hills. The hotel has been in the family since 1902. Monsieur Pécaut, great-grandson of the founder, is French, his wife Italian, and they are a friendly, helpful and very hands-on. There is no restaurant but delicious light lunches of pasta, sandwiches and snacks can be taken by the pool, a cool oasis shaded by sub-tropical vegetation and dotted with waving, century-old palms. A short walk away is a cable car that takes you down to the sea; medieval, cliff-hung Taormina, where Lawrence wrote *Lady Chatterley's Lover*, is known as the St Tropez of Italy.

Price	€110-€228. Singles €80-€148. Family room €140-€280 for 3.
Rooms	52: 43 doubles, 9 family rooms.
Meals	Buffet lunch €10-€22. Wine from €15. Restaurant 100m.
Closed	25 November-February.
Directions	Signs to town centre, then ring-road. At Hotel Méditerranée, left into via Dionisio. At piazza S. Antonio, via Pietro Rizzo left of chapel, then via Roma. Right into Bagnoli Croci.

Signor Christian Pécaut
via Bagnoli Croci 79,
98039 Taormina

Tel	+39 0942 23791
Fax	+39 0942 625830
Email	info@villabelvedere.it
Web	www.villabelvedere.it

Entry 336 Map 18

Hotel Villa Schuler

Late in the 19th century, Signor Schuler's great-grandfather travelled by coach from Germany and built his house here, high above the Ionian Sea. He chose the site well – the views of the Bay of Naxos and Mount Etna are a joy – and he built on a grand scale. When he died in 1905, Great Grandmama decided to let out some rooms, and the villa has been a hotel ever since. Though restored and brought up to date, it still has an old, elegant charm and a relaxed, quiet atmosphere. Lavish breakfasts are served in the chandelier'd breakfast room or out on the terrace. Individual bedrooms vary: some have beautifully tiled floors, antique furniture and stone balconies, while the more modern top-floor suites have beamed ceilings and large terraces. All come with jacuzzi showers and look out to sea or over the garden – a delight: vast, sub-tropical, scented with jasmine and magically illuminated at night. Hidden away behind a stone arch is a delightful, very private little apartment. A path leads through the gardens and out into the town's pedestrianized Corso Umberto.

Gerhard's eco efforts are exemplary for such a large hotel. Here they go beyond the usual recycling, re-using and composting (although these practices are devoutly followed). Breakfasts are organic, as is all the linen; hot water for showers is heated by solar panels (installed 15 years ago); low energy appliances are used throughout; cleaning products are eco friendly. It's a challenge that Gerhard thrives on, and he and his staff are keen to share their philosophy with guests. Their dedicated environmental policy has won them recognition from various leading hotel and tourism agencies.

Price	€124–€192.
	Apartment €240–€370 for 2.
Rooms	26 + 1: 22 doubles, 4 triples.
	Apartment for 2-4.
Meals	Restaurants 100m
	(special prices for hotel guests).
Closed	Mid-November to February.
Directions	A18 exit Taormina; 3km; at 'Lumbi' car park into 'Monte Tauro' tunnel; around 'Porta Catania' car park to Piazza S. Antonio; right at P.O. into via Pietro Rizzo; right into via Roma. Directions on booking.

Christine Voss & Gerhard Schuler
Piazzetta Bastione, via Roma, 98039 Taormina,

Tel	+39 0942 23481
Fax	+39 0942 23522
Email	info@hotelvillaschuler.com
Web	www.hotelvillaschuler.com

SPECIAL GREEN ENTRY
see page 14

Map 18 Entry 337

Villa Carlotta

There's a pretty, peaceful village above (Castelmola), a private beach below (Lido Stockholm), and a roof terrace that catches the sea breezes. Breakfasts up here are a joy, with their views of Mount Etna. The setting is perfect, the hotel is comfortable, the staff are attentive and friendly: this must be one of the best-loved hotels in Sicily. The building is an aristocratic villa built at the end of the 19th century with 15th-century pretensions, renovated in modern style with theatrical flourishes. Breakfast chairs are dressed in pleated linen, dove-grey sofas front glassy tables that mirror the sea, bedrooms trumpet generous beds and swagged curtains, a square blue pool nestles in a lush garden, and shaded loungers line up on two sides. Here a barman serves stylish drinks on silver platters – magical at night. No lounge but an exotic bar in the Roman catacombs (there's a Roman road in the gardens, too: perfectly preserved); no restaurant but plenty in clifftop Taormina, a stroll away, or a hotel shuttle. It's a pretty place but gets busy when the cruise ships drop by. Better by far to be here.

Price	€150–€270. Suites €250–€440.
Rooms	23: 7 doubles, 16 suites.
Meals	Restaurants within walking distance.
Closed	May.
Directions	A18 exit Taormina. In town, left on via Pirandello.

Andrea & Rosaria Quartucci
via Pirandello 81,
98039 Taormina
Tel   +39 0942 626058
Fax   +39 0942 23732
Email info@villacarlotta.net
Web   www.villacarlotta.net

Hotel Villa Ducale

The ebullient Dottor Quartucci and his family have restored this fine old village house with panache, re-using lovely old terracotta tiles and mixing family antiques with local fabrics and painted wardrobes and chests. Taormina, with its fabulous bays and young clientele, is the chicest resort in Sicily, and rich in archaeological and architectural sites. From the terrace high on the hill, distance lends enchantment to the view. You can see the sweep of five bays and the looming presence of Mount Etna as you breakfast on delicious Sicilian specialities – linger as long as you like. Flowers are the keynote of this romantic little hotel: bunches in every room, pots placed like punctuation marks on the steps, terraces romping with geranium and bougainvillea. Bedrooms, not large, are full of subtle detail, each one with a terrace; shower rooms come with slippers and robes; five of the suites lie across the road. The style is antique-Sicilian; the extras – air conditioning, internet, satellite TV – entirely modern. The buses don't run very often into Taormina so the shuttle to the private beach is handy.

Price	€130-€250. Suites €250-€440.
Rooms	17: 11 doubles, 6 suites for 2-4.
Meals	Lunch or dinner, €20. Wine €18-€45.
Closed	10 January-10 February.
Directions	From Taormina centre towards Castelmola. Hotel signed.

Andrea & Rosaria Quartucci
via L. da Vinci 60,
98039 Taormina

Tel	+39 0942 28153
Fax	+39 0942 28710
Email	info@villaducale.com
Web	www.villaducale.com

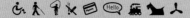

Palmento la Rosa Agriturismo

A chunky ten-metre beam dominates the vast living area: a reminder that Palmento la Rosa housed a wine press. Now it is a sophisticated wine estate ('palmento') and a charming place to stay, 700 metres above sea level (never too hot), surrounded by acres of Etna vines. Your stylish, lively, delightful hosts, Zora and Franz, have swapped Paris for this green haven at the foot of Europe's most celebrated volcano, sharing their passion for life, culture, sunshine and good food with guests. Served at one big granite table on the terrace in summer, meals are fresh and colourful Sicilian, desserts are magnificently baroque, wines are from Biondi and Benanti. There is true generosity of spirit here, visible in the large rooms with their sweeping chestnut floors, the sprawling sofas, the several fireplaces, the original art and the bedrooms flooded with light. Those on the ground floor open to palm trees and roses, those on the first have sea views. Trek in the National Park or climb the lower craters of Etna; cable cars can replace legs if need be! *Minimum stay two nights.*

Price	€95–€160.
Rooms	4: 3 doubles, 1 twin.
Meals	Lunch €20. Dinner €35.
Closed	February.
Directions	Directions on booking.

Franz & Zora Hochreutener
via Lorenzo Bolano 55,
75030 Pedara

Tel	+39 0957 896206
Fax	+39 0959 19945
Email	info@palmentolarosa.com
Web	www.palmentolarosa.com

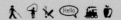

Borgopetra

The renovation is complete – an exquisite revival of a 400-year-old farmstead, an oasis of beauty and peace. Five years ago journalist Cristina left the high life in Milan to join Toto in the restoration of his family *borgo*. On the southern slopes of Mount Etna, self-contained yet unremote, your luxurious apartments wrap themselves around a square courtyard scented with jasmine. The attention to detail is second to none, from the ergonomic beds to the soaps hand-made in Catania, from the Mascalucia olive oil in the kitchens to the thyme-infused honeys at breakfast. In the guest quarters, stunning antique rubs shoulders with stylish modern: perhaps a chic red basin on an ancient terracotta floor, an old country wardrobe, a sleek chaise-longue. Among apricot and orange trees and the pergola of an ancient vine is a cool pool; in the old marionette theatre, a massage room, gym, bar, and shelves crammed with Cristina's crime mysteries and board games. Cristina and Toto are the warmest pair you're ever likely to meet. A fine beginning for them… one to watch! *Minimum stay two nights.*

Price	€100-€200.
Rooms	4 + 2: 1 double, 3 suites: 1 for 2-3, 2 for 3 (both with kitchenette). 2 apartments for 6.
Meals	Restaurant 300m.
Closed	20 November-20 December; 8 January-15 February.
Directions	15km from Catania; from m'way, exit Gravina-Etna. Detailed directions on booking.

	Cristina Pauly
	via Teatro 9,
	95030 Mascalucia
Tel	+39 0957 277184
Mobile	+39 333 8284930
Email	info@borgopetra.it
Web	www.borgopetra.it

Chez Jasmine

Down by the 27-centuries-old Phœnician port you are enveloped in the history of Palermo and some breathtakingly fine buildings. Jasmine stands in a 10th-century courtyard in the old Arab town, just reviving from centuries of neglect. Irish-turned-Sicilian (almost), the delightful Mary lives round the corner, leaves fresh breakfast in your super modern kitchen, is involved in conservation, and can keep you entertained for hours with her insights into local mores. Her vertical, newly renovated 'doll's house' is adorable. It starts on the first floor (and you can barbecue in the courtyard). Expect a pleasing little all-Italian shower room and a bedroom with its own wicker sofa and writing table; then up to an open-plan living area, well-lit and comfortably furnished, marrying northern minimalism and southern colour. Finally, an iron spiral leads to a pretty terrace shaded by bamboo blinds, decorated with eager creepers and plants. 'Kalsart', a feast of music, art and many talents, makes summer evenings in La Kalsa so very pleasurable. *Minimum stay three nights.*

Price	€110–€130.
Rooms	Chalet for 2-4.
Meals	Restaurants on doorstep.
Closed	Rarely.
Directions	From port road in Palermo go towards La Kalsa; at Piazza Kalsa, right; house to left of Chiesa della Pietà.

Mary Goggin
vicolò dei Nassaiuoli 15,
90133 Palermo

Tel	+39 0916 164268
Mobile	+39 338 6325192
Email	info@chezjasmine.biz
Web	www.chezjasmine.biz

Palazzo Cannata

The stone escutcheon over the door justifies the palatial name, the tenderly scruffy yard inside tells today's humbler tale. One of the most exuberantly hospitable men you could hope to meet, Carmelo inhabits the top of the former bishop's palace: you can see Palermo's domes from the terrace. All her treasures are within walking distance – and quite a bit of the traffic. The flat is as full of eclectic interest as Carmelo's captivating mixed-lingo conversation. He teaches mechanics, with deep commitment, and breathes a passion for dance and music. Everywhere are paintings and photographs, bits of furniture and cabinets of mementos, yet there's plenty of space for everything to make sense. One could explore the details for hours, including the madonnas in the high-bedded double room and the painted beds in the twin. A fount of insight into his home town, Carmelo will tell you all. After the pastry breakfast he has prepared before going to work, you will discover his fascinating city. You will also meet friends Argo, the superb bouncing dog, and Enzo, his sociable master from next door.

Price	€80–€90.
Rooms	2: 1 double, 1 triple, sharing bathroom.
Meals	Restaurants nearby.
Closed	Rarely.
Directions	In Palermo, from Palazzo dei Normanni, left down small street off via del Bastione.

Carmelo Sardegna
vicolo Cannata 5,
90134 Palermo
Tel   +39 0916 519269
Mobile   +39 333 7200529
Email   sardegnacarmelo@hotmail.com

Limoneto Agriturismo

Dogs doze in the deep shade of the veranda. In the lemon grove, ladders disappear into trees and occasionally shake as another full basket is lowered down. This is 'rustic simplicity' at its best. The main house is modern and white, with as many openings as it has walls, through which chairs, tables and plants burst out on all sides. Lemon and olive trees (you'll be served homemade *limoncello* after dinner) stop short of the terrace where meals are taken throughout the summer. The bedrooms are simple cabin-like affairs with unapologetically plain furniture. Spotless shower rooms, air conditioning, no TV. Those in the main house look out across the garden to a play area; three larger rooms in the pale pink *casa* across the courtyard sleep five, with twin beds on an upper mezzanine level. The lovely and engaging owners, Adelina and husband Alceste, believe in the traditions of the region and are full of ideas for you: visit Noto, Palazzolo and the soft sands of Siracusa. Homemade dinners are good value; tennis, golf and swimming are a short drive. *Child discounts.*

Price	€90–€120. Singles €70.
Rooms	10: 4 doubles, 3 triples, 3 family rooms.
Meals	Sunday lunch (except Jul & Aug) €22. Dinner €22. Wine from €8.
Closed	November.
Directions	From Catania towards Siracusa, when road becomes motorway, take exit for Palazzolo & follow signs for 'Limoneto'.

Signora Adelina Norcia
via del Platano 3,
96100 Siracusa

Tel	+39 0931 717352
Fax	+39 0931 717728
Email	limoneto@tin.it
Web	www.limoneto.it

Monteluce Country House

Hiding in deep country just four miles from gorgeous sleepy baroque Noto, Monteluce is a jewel of design and warm-heartedness. Architect-designers Claudio and Imelda have created a discreet wilderness bolthole from the grey urban north and genuinely welcome guests who bring news of the outside world. As carefully as these two houses lie respectfully low among the olive and citrus orchards, their sense of space and style will wrap you gently in colour, texture, excitement (Imelda's paintings, Claudio's gliding shots) and extreme Italian comfort. Brilliant, individually tiled bathrooms, some fun furniture, superb beds, fine detailing, nothing tacky, and each room with its own garden. If you are self-catering in one of the apartments, your kitchen will be another delight of colour and style, your beds may be on really generous mezzanines. A perfecly complementary couple, they share the caring: Claudio makes a wonderful breakfast (different cake every day) which is brought to your table, inside or out, and Imelda entertains with her fascinating talk of north and south, Sicilian life.

Price	€120–€160. Apartments €900–€1,400 per week.
Rooms	3 + 2: 1 double, 2 suites (with kitchenette). 2 apartments for 3.
Meals	Restaurant 7km.
Closed	Rarely.
Directions	From Noto take SP19 for Pachino; 5km, SP22 for Vaddeddi; 2km, head for Monteluce.

Imelda Rubiano
contrada Vaddeddi, Villa del Tellaro,
96017 Noto

Mobile	+39 335 6901871
Email	info@monteluce.com
Web	www.monteluce.com

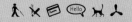

Entry 345 Map 18

Bed & Breakfast Villa Aurea

Once the family's summer house, Villa Aurea is now a gentle, friendly place to stay, thanks to the owner's son, Enrico, who has given up city hotels for this. His father shaped these surroundings, his architect's eye and his attention to detail ensuring the place feels calm, spacious and uncluttered; his mother bakes fabulous cakes and tarts and delivers a divine breakfast, enjoyed in the garden in summer. Cupboards blend discreetly into the walls, stylish shutters soften the Sicilian light and low round windows are designed to allow moonlight to play in the corridor. Bedrooms are minimalist with bright white walls and bold bedcovers. Upstairs rooms share a long terrace shaded by a huge carob tree; two rooms interconnect for families. Tiled bathrooms – some huge, with sea views – sparkle and use solar-heated water. A tree was planted to mark the birth of each of the three children and the garden is now luscious and filled with all kinds of tree: banana, orange, lemon, almond... you can idle in their shade, work up a steam on the tennis court, or cool off in the striped pool.

Price	€60–€110.
Rooms	7: 5 doubles; 2 doubles each with separate bathroom.
Meals	Restaurants 1.5 km.
Closed	Rarely.
Directions	From Siracusa to Ispica; SP46 Ispica-Pozzallo for Pozzallo, house 4km. Signed.

Francesco Caruso
contrada Senna,
97014 Ispica

Tel	+39 0932 956575
Fax	+39 0932 797552
Email	villa.aurea@gmail.com
Web	www.marenostrumpozzallo.it/villaaurea/index.htm

Cambiocavallo Unesco Area & Resort

The blinding white, cobalt blue and fiery terracotta of this ancient house suggest that they do things differently here. Step in to a high tech, high design look straight from an architectural magazine: sharp, stark and very zen. Windows and doors are stained black, walls are exposed stone or colourwashed, furniture is clean-limbed, lighting is funky. The effect is rich yet soothing. Bedrooms are clutter-free zones of crisp black or metallic pieces (with four-posters in the suites), polished black floors and chestnut beamed ceilings. Bold flowers and giant photographs add colour. Bathrooms are super-modern, unspeakably high tech! Relax on your private decking overlooking the olive and almond groves, or among the palms, cactus and orange trees of the newly created garden. In the summer, breakfast is served in the courtyard, a cool combination of white and blue walls, clipped box hedging and an ancient carob tree. After discovering the baroque towns (Unesco-protected), the fish restaurants and the local beaches, how wonderful to return to this clean, spare space and chill. *Pool planned for 2008.*

Price	€120–€220.
Rooms	8: 6 twins/doubles, 2 suites.
Meals	Restaurants nearby.
Closed	November.
Directions	E45 S from Catania; past Siracusa, to Ispica. Follow signs to Pozzallo, then to Modica; signed from here, on left.

Salvatore Tringali & Rosanna La Rosa
contrada Zimmardo Superiore,
97016 Modica

Tel	+39 0932 779118
Fax	+39 0932 779549
Email	info@cambiocavallo.it
Web	www.cambiocavallo.it

Hotel Locanda Don Serafino

The hotel lies in the heart of the stepped city, rich with baroque churches and mansions – a World Heritage Site. The sitting and breakfast room are cool all year round, their rock walls revealing that this part of the 19th-century building was hewn straight from the hillside – and most inviting with their cream couches and bright red rugs. Doubles are small, suites larger; your bathroom could be as narrow as a corridor or house a tub of Olympian proportions. But all bedrooms are delightfully simple, spotless with mod cons, their wooden furniture designed by a local architect, some with balconies, some with direct access from the street. And you'll sleep well: there are deeply comfortable mattresses and a choice of pillows, soft or firm. The staff here are wonderful, thanks to gentle, friendly Guiseppe. Homemade breads and hot chocolate are served for breakfast; for dinner, there's the family's restaurant, a ten-minute walk to the stables of an 18th-century mansion – elegant, intimate, very good. *Flexible breakfasts & check-out.*

Price	€100–€195.
Rooms	10: 4 doubles, 1 single, 5 suites.
Meals	Owner's restaurant 10-minute walk.
Closed	Never.
Directions	Ragusa-Ibla road. Down Corso S. Mazzini to Piazza della Repubblica; along via della Repubblica; 50m past Chiesa del Purgatorio; right into via XI Febbraio.

Famiglia La Rosa
via XI Febbraio 15,
97100 Ragusa Ibla

Tel	+39 0932 220065
Fax	+39 0932 663186
Email	info@locandadonserafino.it
Web	www.locandadonserafino.it

Agriturismo Gigliotto

The Savoca family are from Piazza Armerina, famous for its August Palio. They bought the ancient farmhouse 15 years ago – before their several children were born – and opened in 2000. They speak English hesitantly but they are easy hosts. Cypress trees border the property, vineyards and garden surround it, painted Sicilian carts lie in corners, farm labourers come and go. The estate produces, in order of rank: figs, grapes, artichokes, olives, aubergines, tomatoes, peppers, pears, peaches and cherries, many of which you'll taste. Breakfasts are basic but dinners are good: homemade pasta, barbecued roasts, Sicilian cheeses and hams, cakes, honey and homemade jams. The vaulted cellar restaurant caters for 300, much of the produce used is organically grown. The bedrooms, in the characterful old farmhouse or in the outbuildings, have the usual terracotta floors, local wooden furniture and attractive wrought-iron beds, perhaps an antique cot in the corner or a basket of magazines; shower room are small. From the pool is a spectacular view, reaching to Mount Etna on fine days.

Price	€80–€100.
Rooms	15 twins/doubles.
Meals	Lunch or dinner €25–€30. Wine €10.
Closed	Rarely.
Directions	From Piazza Armerina, SS117 to Gela exit Mirabella Imbaccari; 9km from town; 1st right, follow signs.

Elio & Laura Savoca
C. Da Gigliotto,
94015 Piazza Armerina
Tel   +39 0933 970898
Fax   +39 0933 979234
Email gigliotto@gigliotto.com
Web   www.gigliotto.com

Agriturismo Sillitti

Drive through rolling farmland, up past the almond and olive groves, until you can climb no further. This is it: stunning 360 degree views over the island and, on a clear day, Mount Etna in the distance. Silvia's family have farmed for generations. She's passionately organic – grows olives, almonds, wheat, vegetables – and loves to share both recipes and kitchen garden. The farmhouse is new, its apartments bright and simple, furnished in unfussy style with cream floor tiles, modern pine and colourful fabrics. Open-plan living areas include tiny kitchens for rustling up simple meals. Rooms won't win design prizes but are spotless and airy and have superlative views. Silvia and Bruno (a doctor in Palermo) are open and welcoming; you'll be won over by their warmth and her cooking! Breakfast on homemade bread, cakes and james; dinner is a feast of Sicilian dishes. A great spot from which to explore the island – castles, temples, Palermo, Taormina – or enjoy the views from the large but yet-young garden, with pool, terrace and shady pavilion. Space, peace, lovely people. *Minimum stay two nights.*

Price	€80. Apartment €460 for 2, €920 for 4 per week.
Rooms	5 + 3: 5 doubles. 3 apartments for 2-5.
Meals	Dinner, 4 courses with wine, €25, by arrangement.
Closed	Rarely.
Directions	A19 exit Caltanissetta. After SS640, dir. Agrigento; 50km then right for Serradifalco; 300m then left; phone for further directions.

Silvia Sillitti
via Gabrielli 7,
93100 Caltanissetta

Tel/Fax	+39 0934 930733
Mobile	+39 338 7634601
Email	info@sillitti.it
Web	www.sillitti.it

Fattoria Mosè Agriturismo

The town creeps ever up towards the Agnello olive groves but the imposing house still stands proudly on the hill, protecting its private chapel and a blissfully informal family interior. In the main house, high, cool rooms have superb original floor tiles, antiques and family mementos. The B&B room is plainer, has an old-fashioned idiosyncratic bathroom and olive-grove views. Breakfast is in a huge, shutter-shaded dining room or on the terrace, the dumb-waiter laden with homemade jams served on silver. Chiara's family used to come to escape Palermo's summer heat: a cooling breeze frequently blows. Your hostess, a quietly interesting ex-architect, has converted the stables into six airy modern apartments with high, pine-clad ceilings, contemporary fabrics and good little kitchens, plain white walls, paper lampshades, no pretensions. Most have their own terrace, all spill onto the lovely plant-packed courtyard (with barbecue), and there are Chiara's olive oils, almonds and fruits and vegetables to buy. The 'Valley of the Temples' is a short and hugely worthwhile drive. *Minimum stay two nights.*

Price	€88. Apts €434 for 2; €869 for 4; €1,092 for 6. Apt prices per week.
Rooms	1 + 6: 1 double. 6 apartments for 2, 4 or 6.
Meals	Breakfast for self-caterers €8. Restaurants 2km.
Closed	November-22 December; 7 January-March.
Directions	From Agrigento SS115 for Gela-Siracusa. At end of Villaggio Mosè road (past supermarkets, houses) left at sign for Fattoria Mosè; signed.

Chiara Agnello
via M. Pascal 4,
92100 Villaggio Mosè

Tel	+39 0922 606115
Fax	+39 0922 606115
Email	fattoriamose@libero.it
Web	www.fattoriamose.com

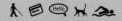

Villa Ravidà

The unremarkable town of Menfi conceals, behind the pale uniformity of its streets, a rare gem. Still under restoration (scaffolding intact), the four massive columns of its stone portico – approached across a courtyard of patterned paving – are built of that same rose-honey stone as the great neighbouring temples at Selinunte. There is an ethereal elegance to the state rooms with their heavenly frescoed ceilings and their 18th-century furniture; even the light bulbs are old. The stable block, at right angles to the villa and with its own little courtyard, has been converted to make a series of simply furnished bedrooms with high wooden ceilings. The charming and noble Ravidà family, whose summer residence this is, will give you a tour of the farm and provide excellent itineraries. Signora, a fine cook, runs courses throughout the summer in the historic kitchen, or outside, at a huge marble table: carpaccio of tuna, focaccia stuffed with figs, gorgonzola and prosciutto. The food is delicious, the olive oil the finest – the family is a celebrated producer.

Price	€130. Singles €117.
Rooms	3 twins/doubles.
Meals	Lunch or dinner with wine, €40, by arrangement.
Closed	5-20 August; December-March.
Directions	From Palermo A29 for Mazara del Vallo; exit Castelvetrano; take Agrigento road to Menfi.

Nicolo Ravidà
via Roma 173,
92013 Menfi

Tel	+39 0925 71109
Fax	+39 0925 71180
Email	ravida@ravida.it
Web	www.ravida.it

Villa Mimosa

Overlooking the sea, a short drive along the main road that passes quite close by, are the breathtakingly beautiful Greek temples of Selinunte. The villa was a ruin when Jackie found it crumbling among umbrella pines and olive groves; she has restored and rebuilt as traditionally as possible, collecting a few stray cats along the way. Three of the apartments (you can self-cater or go B&B) stretch along the back and open onto a long, pergola-shaded terrace and a garden of vines, olives and orange trees (and poppies in spring). The fourth apartment is on the first floor, and has a balcony. Each is open plan, with a shower room and a kitchenette. They are homely, cosy spaces, traditionally furnished with chunky, carved Sicilian armchairs, high antique beds, fine linen and pictures on the walls. If you dine with Jackie, you'll eat out on the terrace on her side of the house – or in her *salotto* if the weather isn't good. She's lived in Sicily for over 25 years and is very knowledgeable about the island. Wonderful beaches and nature reserves are close by.

Price	€70–€90. Apts €400–€550 per week.
Rooms	4 apartments: 3 studio apts for 2-3. 1 apt for 2-3.
Meals	Dinner 3 courses with wine, €35. Restaurants 6km.
Closed	Rarely.
Directions	From Agrigento SS115 to very end, exit Castelvetrano. At end of slip-road sharp right; 2nd entrance on left.

	Jackie Sirimanne
	La Rocchetta, Selinunte,
	91022 Castelvetrano
Tel	+39 0924 44583
Mobile	+39 338 1387388
Email	j.sirimanne@virgilio.it
Web	www.aboutsicily.net

Entry 353 Map 18

Zarbo di Mare

A simple stone-built house, slap on the sea, on a beautiful stretch of coast to the north-west tip of the island, designed to catch the sun. Sun worshippers can follow the progress of the rays by moving from terrace to terrace through the day; those who prefer the shade will be just as happy. A vine-clad courtyard behind the house is a lovely place to take breakfast; you might move to the large shady terrace with a barbecue at the side of the house for lunch, and take dinner on the front terrace looking out to sea. There are two bedrooms, each with two beds, and an open-plan sitting-room with a pine-and-white kitchen. Below the house are steps down to a private swimming platform, fine for the sprightly; the sea is deep here, and perfect for snorkelling. (Families with small children may prefer to swim from the beach nearby at San Vito, where the water is shallow.) There are some lovely things to see in this part of Sicily; visit the extraordinary Greek temple at Segesta, standing gravely and peacefully at the head of the valley. *Contact numbers are in Belgium.*

Price	€750–€800 per week. Ask about shorter stays.
Rooms	House for 2-4.
Meals	Restaurant 4km.
Closed	7 July–25 August.
Directions	Approx. 120km from Palermo airport. Motorway to Trapani, exit Castellammare del Golfo. Coast road SS187 to Trapani. San Vito clearly signed. House 5km after village.

Barbara Yates
contrada Zarbo di Mare 37,
91010 San Vito Lo Capo
Tel   +32 2512 4526
Email   barbara.yates@belgacom.net

Hotel Su Gologone

Lavender, myrtle and rosemary scent the valley. The dazzling white buildings of Hotel Su Gologone stand among ancient vineyards and olive groves at the foot of the towering Supramonte. The hotel takes its name from a nearby spring and began life in the 1960s as a simple restaurant serving simple Sardinian dishes – roast suckling pig, wild boar sausages, ice cream with thyme honey. Now the restaurant is known throughout Europe. Run by the founders' daughter, Giovanna, it employs only local chefs and has a terrace with views to the mountains. In this wilderness region of the island this is an elegant and magical place, only 30 minutes from the coast and wonderful beaches. Juniper-beamed bedrooms have intriguing arches and alcoves and make much of local craftwork and art: embroidered cushions, Sardinian fabrics, original paintings, ceramics and sculpture. Browse a book about the island from the library, curl up in one of many cosy corners. Hiking can be arranged, the pool is fed by cold spring water, and there's an outdoor jacuzzi. Marvellous. *Book in advance May-September.*

Price	Half-board €310-€510 for 2.
Rooms	69: 54 twins/doubles, 15 suites.
Meals	Half-board only. Wine from €10.
Closed	Rarely.
Directions	From Oliena towards Dorgali. Right at sign for Su Gologone; hotel on right.

Luigi Crisponi
loc. Su Gologone,
08025 Oliena

Tel	+39 0784 287512
Fax	+39 0784 287668
Email	gologone@tin.it
Web	www.sugologone.it

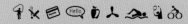

Hotel Villa Las Tronas

It could be the setting for an Agatha Christie whodunnit (Hercule Poirot perhaps?): a crenellated, late 19th-century hotel dramatically set on a rocky spit of land jutting into the sea. The outer walls, gate and entry phone give the requisite aloof feeling and the atmosphere within is hushed and formal. Originally owned by a Piemontese count, it was bought by the present owners in the 1950s and they take huge pride in the place. The big reception rooms and bedrooms — formal, ornate, immaculate — have a curiously muted, old-fashioned air, while the high-ceilinged bathrooms are new — vibrant with modern fittings and green and blue mosaic tiles. On all sides, windows look down at accusatory fingers of rock pointing into azure Sardinian waters. There's a little lawned garden, a swimming pool and restaurant area poised immediately above the rocks; delightful to hear the waves lapping below as you dine. Close by is the pretty, interesting old quarter of Alghero, and there are fabulous beaches and good restaurants up and down the coast. *Brand new Wellness Centre.*

Price	€170–€398. Suites €400–€580.
Rooms	25: 20 doubles, 5 suites.
Meals	Dinner €65.
Closed	Never.
Directions	Leave Alghero, signs for Bosa & Lungomare. Hotel on right.

Dott. Vito La Spina
Lungomare Valencia 1,
07041 Alghero

Tel	+39 0799 81818
Fax	+39 0799 81044
Email	info@hvlt.com
Web	www.hvlt.com

Li Licci

Not so long ago, this tranquil place was inaccessible. Deserted after the death of Gianmichele's grandfather, it was rescued by Jane and Gianmichele in 1985. Once they had moved in, the almost nightly entertaining of friends began. English-born Jane is an inspired cook of Sardinian food and the entertaining grew into the creation of a delightful restaurant (now with a Michelin mention) that is based on home-grown, organic produce: pecorino, ricotta, salamis, hams, preserves, liqueurs. And they have added four immaculate, simple, white-walled bedrooms, each with a shower. Jane looks after guests as she would like to be looked after herself, so staying here is like being in the home of a relaxed and hospitable friend. Li Licci has its own wells, producing the most delicious clear water, and a 2,000-year-old olive tree. Breakfast is outside in summer, overlooking the oak woods and hills of Gallura, or by the fire in the converted stables in winter: either way, a superb start to a day's walking, climbing or sailing... or lazing on the north coast beaches.
Minimum stay two nights.

Price	€100. Half-board €65-€75 p.p.
Rooms	4: 2 doubles, 1 twin, 1 family for 4.
Meals	Dinner with wine, €30-€40.
Closed	Epiphany-Easter.
Directions	Through S. Antonio to r'bout, then towards Olbia. After 3.5km, right at sign. From Olbia Airport dir. Palau exit S.Mariedda-Tempio. 2km after Priatu, left at sign.

Jane & Gianmichele Abeltino
loc. Valentino, Priatu,
07023 Calangianus

Tel	+39 0796 65114
Fax	+39 0796 65029
Email	info@lilicci.com
Web	www.lilicci.com

Entry 357 Map 19

Ca' La Somara Agriturismo

A short drive to the coast, a far cry from the fleshpots of Costa Smeralda, Ca' La Somara's white buildings stand out against the peaceful wooded hills and jutting limestone crags of Gallura. As you'd expect from the name, donkeys feature here – they're one of Laura's passions. She's an ex-architect who gave up city life and has converted the stables with charm and flair. Once used to shelter sheep, they are now ranch-rustic. You get a striking, galleried living/dining room, its stone walls decorated with harnesses and lanterns, farm implements, baskets and the odd amphora, and bedrooms small and simple, with whitewashed walls, carved beds and little shower rooms with hand-painted tiles. Don't miss the pretty village of San Pantaleo, an artists' community just up the hill. Return to cushioned benches in the garden or hessian hammocks in the paddock, with views of the valley and its windswept cork oaks. Dinner is fresh Mediterranean, served with Sardinian wines. It's all deliciously restful and undemanding – and there's a sparkling pool. *Vegetarian meals only in high season. Relaxation therapies available.*

Price	€58–€136.
Rooms	8 doubles.
Meals	Dinner €25.
Closed	Rarely.
Directions	From Olbia, S125 dir. Arzachena. Look out for track on right, for San Pantaleo; through village, dir. Porto Cervo. Signed at bottom of hill on right.

Alberto & Laura Lagattolla
loc. Sarra Balestra,
07021 Arzachena

Tel	+39 0789 98969
Fax	+39 0789 98969
Email	info@calasomara.it
Web	www.calasomara.it

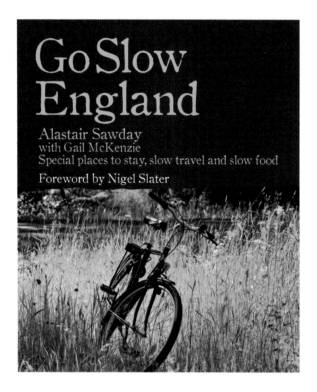

Special places to stay, slow travel and slow food

The Slow Food revolution is upon us and this guide celebrates the Slow philosophy of life with a terrific selection of the places, recipes and people who take their time to enjoy life at its most enriching. In this beautiful book that goes beyond the mere 'glossy', you will discover an unusual emphasis on the people who live in Special Slow Places and what they do. You will meet farmers, literary people, wine-makers and craftsmen – all with rich stories to tell. Go Slow England celebrates fascinating people, fine architecture, history, landscape and real food. A counter-balance to our culture of haste.

Written by Alastair Sawday, with a foreword by Nigel Slater.

RRP £20.00 To order at the Readers Discount price of £13.00 (plus p&tp) call 01275 395431 and quote 'Reader Discount IT'.

As Britain begins to re-embrace the idea of buying real food – seasonal, local and, as far as possible, organic – we might consider looking south for a bit of guidance. Such has been the Italian way for millennia, and real food continues to be fundamental to *la cucina italiana*. When it appeared to be threatened, in the 1980s, by the emergence of the fast food industry that had already gained a hold in Europe, the Italians hit back with a movement that epitomised Italian gastronomy: Slow Food.

Recycling, composting, rainwater harvesting and 'bikes to borrow'

"Are you 'green'?" we asked our Italian owners. And, from the northern alpine valleys to the southern shores of Sicily, tales of environmental heroism flooded in – of agriturismi dishing up 100% organic home-grown, home-reared produce fresh from the fields, of medieval homes running on solar energy, and of eco-sensitive restorations of rural farmsteads and 16th-century *palazzi*. Whittling down a selection bursting at the seams was no mean feat. In doing so, we had to put to one side a whole host of worthy owners waving their green flag, so here is a taster of places that didn't make the top six but who, we feel, most definitely deserve a mention.

Since then, agriturismi have been throwing open their doors to guests, giving us the chance to immerse ourselves in deep-rooted Italian rural culture. Within these pages lies a mouthwatering selection of agriturismi. Pluck your own breakfast fruits from the 350 trees surrounding Cascina Papa Mora (entry 14); sip homemade wines with an ancient heritage, lovingly nurtured from grape to bottle at Agriturismo La Faula (entry 79); marvel at the varieties of olive oil at Podere La Casellina (entry 167); go truffle-hunting at Fattoria Barbialla Nuova (entry 154); lose yourself in acres of vines and olive groves at Casa del Grivò (entry 80). And if it's a purely organic experience you're after, there are plenty of agriturismi to

Photo: Casa del Grivò Agriturismo, entry 80

pick from: Tenuta Le Sorgive (entry 39), Limoneto (entry 344) and La Ginestra (entry 308) to name just a few.

A quick flick through the guide will also bring you in to contact with many authentic restorations of crumbling houses – well-represented in every region. But some of our owners have gone that one step further to ensure that their home, and the running of it, has a minimal impact on the planet. Witness the eco-bio architecture of Casa Clelia (entry 31), the recycled wooden ceilings at Bio-Hotel Hermitage (entry 42), and the craftsmanship of local artisans at Modus Vivendi (entry 273), painstakingly carried out in line with a strict ecological ethos.

Organic home-grown, home-reared produce fresh from the fields

Many of our owners' green roots go deeper than mama's homemade tortellini, organically reared cattle and environmental restorations. Italians everywhere, it seems, are waking up to the notion of sustainable living. Solar energy is a favourite among those wishing to take advantage of the Italian sunshine. Guests at Casa Simonicchi (entry 185) and Agriturismo Madonna delle Grazie (entry 250), for example, can lather up in hot water powered by the sun's rays. Respectful use of natural resources is

Photo: Limoneto Agriturismo, entry 344

another: at Cà del Rocolo (entry 49) you may rest your ecological conscience in a bed made from sustainable wood, between sheets sourced from sustainable cotton. Recycling, composting, rainwater harvesting and 'bikes to borrow' cropped up on our questionnaires time and again; you might even spot the odd wind turbine hidden amongst these pages!

We have many more stories from our 'green' owners but we'll let you discover the rest – at first hand. Whether or not you understand what's being said, there is nothing more exciting than watching and listening to an Italian – eyes sparkling, arms flying – as they discourse on a subject they are passionate about.

All our owners are passionate about what they are doing, so I urge you now to do your bit – head out to Italy and find them.

Florence Oldfield

If you have any comments on entries in this guide, please tell us. If you have a favourite place or a new discovery, please let us know about it. You can return this form or visit www.sawdays.co.uk.

Existing entry

Property name: _____

Entry number: _____   Date of visit: _____

New recommendation

Property name: _____

Address: _____

_____

Tel/Email/Website: _____

Your comments

What did you like (or dislike) about this place? Were the people friendly? What was the location like? What sort of food did they serve?

_____

_____

_____

_____

_____

Your details

Name: _____

Address: _____

_____

_____   Postcode: _____

Tel: _____   Email: _____

Please send completed form to:
IT, Sawday's, The Old Farmyard, Yanley Lane, Long Ashton, Bristol BS41 9LR, UK

Quick reference indices

Quick reference indices

WiFi
Wireless internet access available for guests.

For the dream wedding
Want to tie the knot? You can here.

Cookery courses
Cookery courses on site.

Agriturismo
Produce grown and sold here.

Quick reference indices

Photo: www.istockphotos.com

① Lazio   Hotel ②

③④

Hotel Modigliani

There's a sense of anticipation the moment you enter the marble hall, with its deep, pale sofas and fresh flowers – Marco's wide smile and infectious enthusiasm reinforce the feeling. This is an unusual, delightful place, hidden down a side street just five minutes' walk from the Spanish Steps and Via Veneto. The house belonged to Marco's father, and Marco and Giulia (he a writer, she a musician) have turned it into the perfect small hotel. Marble floors and white walls are a dramatic setting for black-and-white photos taken by Marco, their starkness softened by luxuriant plants. The bread oven of the 1700s has become a dining room – all vaulted ceilings, whitewashed walls, cherrywood tables, fabulous photos. Bedrooms are fresh and elegant; some have balconies and wonderful views, all have small, perfect bathrooms. There's a lovely new sitting room for guests. The whole place has a sweet, stylish air, it's unusually quiet for the centre of the city and there's a patio scented with jasmine. Marco and Giulia will tell you about Rome's secret corners – or grab a copy of Marco's new guide and discover Rome for yourselves.

Price	€150–€195. Suite €208–€340. Family suite €330–€440. Apartments €200–€250.	⑤
Rooms	23 + 2: 20 twins/doubles, 2 suites, 1 family suite for 4–6. 2 apartments: 1 for 3, 1 for 6.	⑥
Meals	Breakfast included for all. Restaurants within walking distance.	⑦
Closed	Never.	⑧
Directions	Metro line A: 2nd stop Piazza Barberini. 5-minute walk from Spanish Steps.	⑨

Giulia & Marco di Tillo
via della Purificazione 42,
00187 Rome

Tel	+39 0642 815226
Fax	+39 0642 814791
Email	info@hotelmodigliani.com
Web	www.hotelmodigliani.com

⑪ Entry 281 Map 12   ⑩